THE POLITICAL LIFE
OF THE
AMERICAN STATES

*Copublished with the
Eagleton Institute of Politics
Rutgers University*

THE POLITICAL LIFE
OF THE
AMERICAN STATES

edited by
Alan Rosenthal
and
Maureen Moakley

American Political Parties and Elections

general editor:
Gerald M. Pomper

PRAEGER

PRAEGER SPECIAL STUDIES • PRAEGER SCIENTIFIC

New York • Philadelphia • Eastbourne, UK
Toronto • Hong Kong • Tokyo • Sydney

Library of Congress Cataloging in Publication Data
Main entry under title:

The Political life of the American states.

   (American political parties and elections)
   Includes index.
   1. State governments.   2. State governments—Case
studies. I. Rosenthal, Alan, 1932–   . II. Moakley,
Maureen. III. Series.
JK2408.P625 1984   320.973   83-17756
ISBN 0-03-060327-7
ISBN 0-03-060328-5 (pbk.)

Published in 1984 by Praeger Publishers
CBS Educational and Professional Publishing
a Division of CBS Inc.
521 Fifth Avenue, New York, NY 10175 USA

©1984 by Praeger Publishers

456789 052 987654321

Printed in the United States of America
on acid-free paper

Preface

This is a book about state politics, one of not very many books on that subject today. In the field of political science the study of state politics has been neglected, by and large. This book attempts to redress that neglect, at least in part. Such an attempt is particularly appropriate now, at a time when the states are becoming more active and more powerful actors in the American political system.

This work is intended to differ from others that also deal with politics in the states, or with selected aspects of politics in the states. The underlying assumption here is that, although the 50 states resemble each other in certain respects, they are fundamentally very different creatures. Thus, to appreciate the political life of the American states overall, it is necessary first to appreciate the peculiar qualities of some of the individual units. Our purpose, therefore, is to give readers a sense of what politics is about in some of the American states, 12 to be precise. In the regional ordering in which they are presented in the following chapters, the states are: California, Colorado, Iowa, Michigan, Texas, Florida, Georgia, Kentucky, New Jersey, New York, New Hampshire, and Vermont.

To figure out what politics is really about, one must discriminate between the more important and the less important. One needs an approach, a strategy, or a conceptual framework that helps to fasten on the more salient and enduring features of a state's political life. We have developed such a framework; one that specifies three principal dimensions of state politics and, within these dimensions, eight critical elements. The framework would appear to make conceptual sense, but the real test is in its application. It is applied here—rather effectively, we believe—by each of the authors in their analyses of the 12 states.

Including the editors, 14 political scientists are contributors to this volume. One of us, who is familiar with a number of the nation's states, developed the framework. His efforts benefitted from the helpful comments of the other contributors. And his explication of the framework in Chapter 1 makes use of materials from the individual state analyses to illustrate conceptual points. The framework, at the outset, has flesh as well as bones and demonstrates some of the results of its application.

It would not have been possible for each contributor to learn his state's politics from scratch for present purposes. It was necessary for each to start off with a thorough background and the ability to probe further. Thus, the political scientists who are contributors to this book have had considerable experience in the states about which they have written. In their states they are experts, and their expertise, we trust, is evidenced in the chapters that follow.

As co-editors, two of us have put the project together and have enjoyed doing it. We are grateful to our colleagues for making it all possible. We thought there was a need for a book like this one and we are fortunate that at least 12 other individuals thought so too. Our collaborative enterprise has been extremely interesting and we hope that readers, from their point of view, will find it worthwhile as well.

Gerald Pomper, a friend and colleague (who also happens to be the editor of the series in which this volume appears) promoted the endeavor from the very beginning. Edith Saks worked on it throughout—typing and proofreading, cutting and pasting—and prepared the manuscript for publication. Sandy Wetzel and Joanne Pfeiffer proofed the final pages, so if any errors remain it is their fault. Susan Fuhrman read through several drafts and provided some very useful information. The maps were furnished by the Cartography Lab of the Center for Coastal and Environmental Studies of Rutgers University. Finally, we wish to acknowledge the support of the Eagleton Institute of Politics at Rutgers. Eagleton deserves much of the credit for this book, just as it deserves credit for other endeavors that make the political life of the American states a bit more comprehensible to those who observe it as well as to those who live it.

Alan Rosenthal
Maureen Moakley

Contents

THE POLITICAL LIFE
OF THE
AMERICAN STATES

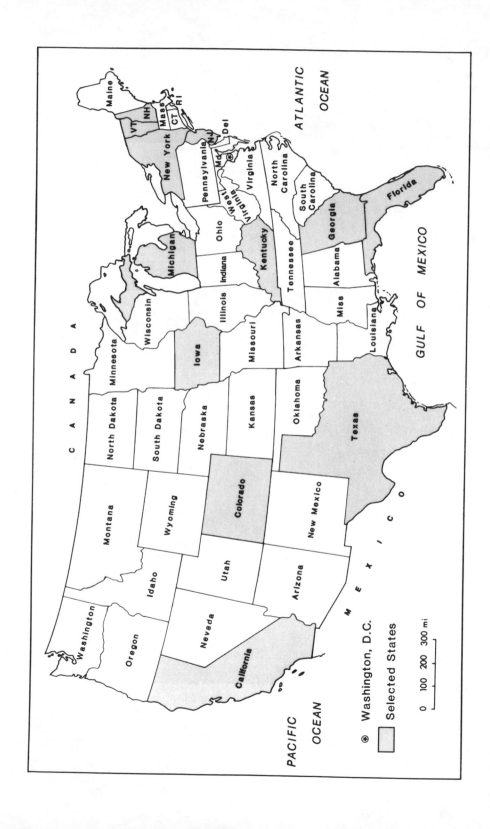

PACIFIC
OCEAN

ATLANTIC
OCEAN

GULF OF MEXICO

CANADA

MEXICO

Maine

NH

VT

Mass

CT

RI

New York

NJ

Del

Pennsylvania

Md

Ohio

West Virginia

Virginia

North Carolina

South Carolina

Georgia

Florida

Michigan

Indiana

Kentucky

Tennessee

Alabama

Miss

Wisconsin

Illinois

Missouri

Arkansas

Louisiana

Minnesota

Iowa

North Dakota

South Dakota

Nebraska

Kansas

Oklahoma

Texas

Montana

Wyoming

Colorado

New Mexico

Idaho

Utah

Arizona

Washington

Oregon

Nevada

California

⊕ Washington, D.C.

Selected States

0 100 200 300 mi

1
On Analyzing States
ALAN ROSENTHAL

Once upon a time, state governments were the principal actors on the American political stage. Through the 19th century, and into the first decade of the 20th, state capitals were where this nation's politics were largely practiced. The location of political power was at the state level.

Nationalizing forces—in commerce, industry, finance, and communications—began to shift the action from the states to Washington, D.C. The buildup of the federal establishment got underway with Franklin Roosevelt's New Deal. It continued through the Second World War and its aftermath. It burgeoned during the presidencies of John F. Kennedy and Lyndon B. Johnson. It survived the efforts of both Richard M. Nixon and Jimmy Carter to restore balance in the federal system. While the federal establishment was at its zenith in the 1960s and into the 1970s, the states reached a low ebb as far as the balance of power in the American system of federalism was concerned. By means of programs of entitlement and categorical grants, Washington exercised significant leverage over state policy and managed to dominate the scene.

Lately, however, power has been moving in the other direction—outward from Washington to the governments in the states. One reason for this is that, since the 1960s the states have undergone major change, enhancing their capacities and strengthening themselves. According to the Advisory Commission on Intergovernmental Relations: "The transformation of the states, occurring in a relatively short period of time, has no parallel in American history."[1] For some years the states had been gearing up for and starting to demand a larger role in the federal system and less regulation and control by Washington. Then, President Reagan turned the national spotlight on the issue of federalism. Block grants instead of narrow categoricals and sorting out of federal, state, and local responsibilities—these were the key elements in the Administration's New Federalism, enunciated by the President in his 1982 State of the Union address. The President's federalism initiatives have had a rocky road since then; nonetheless, the states have been coming into their own. The prospect ahead for the rest of the 1980s is for national and state political systems to be brought into more equal balance.

The pendulum of power swings back and forth in our federal system, at times favoring the national government and at other times favoring governments in the states. But even when the pendulum swings far in the direction of national power, the state role is still a substantial one. To resort to another metaphor, the piper may play a federal tune and the states may dance to it, but it is not the only tune that gets played in this nation of 50 states. There are many others as well.

WHY STUDY STATE POLITICS

Regardless of what is going on in Washington, the 50 states are important subjects of study. Each of them has functions to perform and powers to exercise. The Tenth Amendment guarantees that powers not delegated by the U.S. Constitution to the federal government, nor prohibited by it to the states, are reserved to the states. Although the interpretation of that amendment has been bent to suit our nationalistic mood, it remains one reason why each state is a significant political entity in its own right—no matter what the current state-federal balance of power happens to be.

Each state impacts significantly on individuals who live there. Each bears ultimate responsibility for promoting the public welfare of its citizens. This requires the establishment of policy and the provision of services on the one hand, and the imposition of taxes to pay for them on the other. If expenditures are an indicator, then the federal government has come to pay the major share of costs and to have the principal say in public welfare, in housing and urban renewal, and in social insurance programs. But even in these areas the states pay a share and have a voice. In other areas, by contrast, it is the states (together with localities) that pay the major share and have the principal say. This is the case in education, health and hospitals, highways and transportation, justice, and natural resources. By means of the federal income tax and social security contributions, Washington raises about 60 percent of all governmental revenues. Yet, the role of the states in taxation is critical. Recently, it has become more so, in part because of school finance reforms, popular demands for local property tax relief, and revenue and expenditure limitations imposed by constitutional amendments or statutes. Furthermore, many of the federal programs enacted during the past 20 years rely on the states for policy and regulatory inputs as well as for administration. Programs promoting the quality of the environment—such as air and water—are good examples of federal initiatives where the states are also playing a vital role.

In the domains of health, education, welfare, and elsewhere, the states have broad scope. They can choose to be relatively liberal or relatively conservative in their policies, to spend more or less of their monies, to innovate or follow along in their programs, to provide for predominantly centralized or predominantly decentralized control in different ways.

Each state is ultimately responsible for the structure of its government and politics. That includes the maintenance of the machinery by which people are selected for public leadership and by which public policy is made and implemented. The legislature, the executive, and the judiciary have elements in common from state to state. The legislature in California, however, is quite different from the one in Vermont, the administrative apparatus of New York contrasts with that of Iowa, and the courts of Kentucky are not like the courts of New Jersey. Electoral arrangements vary, as do political-party systems and interest-group configurations. Of course, national influences and organizations make themselves felt in the political life of the states, especially as they are mediated by mass communications. Watergate and Abscam, inflation and interest rates and unemployment, and the pressures of powerful associations and groups, all impact on the states. Yet, just how they impact depends on the peculiar nature of the states as individual entities.

The states, then, are critical because of the governmental structures each of them commands, the political machinery each of them operates, and the policy functions each of them performs. They are also critical because collectively they help shape the politics of the nation. Although, thanks primarily to the overwhelming impact of television, the political arena is a national one today, presidential and congressional elections are still fought out in the states. Candidates begin wooing people state by state very early on, and presidential primaries are essentially state affairs. After candidates are nominated, the battle for 535 electoral votes to win the presidency keeps the action in the states. Congressmen, it is true, relate mainly to their own districts, but their states are by no means irrelevant to their lives. Delegations of congressmen from the same state (often including members of each party) maintain a united front whenever they can. Undoubtedly, the most salient interest members have in common is reelection. Every ten years, when state legislatures or special commissions reapportion congressional districts, congressmen are remarkably attentive to what is going on in the capitols of their states.

The states have become of increasing concern to the national political parties. Both the Democrats and the Republicans believe that it is necessary for them to build from the bottom up. That means taking an active interest in state legislative elections and trying to gain political control whenever possible. The Republican party began a serious effort along these lines in 1977 and has had considerable success; the Democratic party began to get underway several years later. Now, both parties are paying greater attention and devoting more resources to state elections than they have ever done before.

The states are where much of the action has been and continues to be in the current era of revived federalism. Beyond all this, however, the states are fascinating entities. They provide wonderful targets for inquiry; moreover, they provide manageable targets. It is possible to get some sense of politics in a state, and particularly of the politics of the state in which one lives. Although a state political system can be large and complex, it is still easier to fathom than the political system at the national level. California and New York, admittedly, are tough to comprehend, but most other states are not too difficult to get a handle on. Thus, by exploring the political life of the states, we can enrich our appreciation of government and politics in general. We can learn a great deal, if not effortlessly, then with a high ratio of benefits to costs.

THE STUDY OF STATE POLITICS

Over the years the study of state politics has been held in less than high repute. As early as 1966, Coleman Ransone referred to the study of state government as "Dullsville, U.S.A."[2] As recently as 1982, Malcolm E. Jewell referred to the study of state politics as a "neglected world."[3] Although we can agree with Jewell that this field has received "too low priority and too few resources," political scientists have been conducting research on state politics and state government for a long time. They have produced some valuable material; and, as befits practitioners of any scholarly discipline, they have approached their enterprise in different ways. Indeed, what defines the study of state politics as much as anything else is the focus of inquiry chosen by the scholars involved.

Some scholars, like V.O. Key, Jr.[4] and Malcolm E. Jewell and David M. Olson,[5] concentrate on state political parties and elections. Others, such as Harmon Zeigler and Michael Baer,[6] deal mainly with interest groups and their agents. Many concern themselves with the major institutions of state government, governors in the case of Larry Sabato[7] and legislatures in the case of Alan Rosenthal.[8] A few, like Wayne L. Francis,[9] analyze issues, but more scrutinize specific policy domains, as do Nicholas A. Masters and his associates.[10] These are only some of the areas and some of the concerns of students of state politics; there are many more.

As with other fields, the examination of state politics has been specialized, confined to one particular aspect or another—elections, legislatures, parties, policies, etc. Relatively few studies encompass a number of elements or a broader range of politics within the states. But some do, and they deserve special mention here.

Of those that cast a wider net, there are studies of both individual states and of regional groupings of states. Single-state studies, many of which are written for textbook adoption, are common to California and Texas. For instance, six California texts were published between 1979 and 1981, including three in their first edition and one in its tenth. These six and others were competing for a market of about 25,000 undergraduates seeking to satisfy a state requirement that they take a course on the government of California.[11] Otherwise, there are scattered volumes covering the overall politics of a specific state,[12] and there are other, more elusive materials as well.[13] Studies of states within a region used to be in fashion, but are less evident today. V.O. Key's *Southern Politics*[14] set the style and Duane

Lockard followed with a book on the New England states,[15] John Fenton with books on the Border and Midwestern states,[16] and Frank Jonas on the Western states.[17] Each of these volumes was limited in what was examined, again with the major focus on parties and elections. In recent years relatively little work has been done along these lines. Southern politics has been taken on by Jack Bass and Walter DeVries,[18] rural politics (in Montana, Mississippi, and Vermont) by Frank Bryan,[19] and New England politics by more than a dozen scholars in one of the latest ventures along these lines.[20]

The most ambitious contemporary study of state politics was not by a political scientist, but by a journalist, Neal R. Peirce. Emulating John Gunther, another journalist, who almost 25 years earlier visited all the states of the nation and published *Inside U.S.A.*,[21] Peirce spent one and one-half years traveling through the 50 states. The products of his journalistic inquiries were published in seven volumes from 1971 to 1976.[22] Among other things, Peirce inquired in each of the states: What is the state's essential character? Who holds the power? How did the politics evolve to where they are today, and what is the outlook for the future? The results of his efforts were invaluable background materials—bits and pieces and larger chunks on the political, economic, and social characteristics of the American states. Although the studies were not systematic by disciplinary standards, much of what Peirce reported held up over the decade of the 1970s. But, as happens in the case of journalism and of political science too, many observations have become outdated with rapid change taking place. Therefore, a decade after his extraordinary effort began, Peirce and a colleague updated and abridged in a single large book their seven earlier volumes on all of the states.[23]

Among the studies of state government and politics, there are finally the textbooks (which usually cover local government as well) written by political scientists. They contrast sharply with the state-by-state journalistic de-scriptions of Peirce and with the state studies of political scientists them-selves. A text has more and different ground to cover, and its purposes are pedagogical rather than scholarly or reportorial. There are perhaps a half dozen leading texts currently on the market, and by and large they take on state politics in one of several ways.

The first approach is a topical one, illustrated in books by James McGregor Burns, J.W. Peltason, and Thomas E. Cronin,[24] by Daniel R. Grant and H.D. Nixon,[25] and by Duane Lockard.[26] In texts taking a topical approach, there are sure to be chapters on federalism, state constitutions, the legislature, the governor, and the courts, and probably chapters on voters and voting, parties and elections, interest groups, and the bureaucracy. A variation of the topical approach has a particular perspective or theme, such as Sarah McCally Morehouse's special concern with the political party and party government.[27] While books such as these cite examples from particular states, emphasis is on structures, processes, issues, and problems at a general level, and not on the fabric of politics in one or several states.

The second approach is a comparative one, which is of later vintage and is best exemplified in a book edited by Virginia Gray, Herbert Jacob, and Kenneth N. Vines[28] and another written by Thomas R. Dye.[29] The former, one of the leading sellers in the field for a decade or so, is critical of the topical approach and purposely takes a different path. In the preface to the first edition, the editors maintain that too often in the literature one or another state has been selected to illustrate a point, allowing for colorful description but introducing biases. Instead, they claim, their work brings contemporary political science concepts and techniques to bear, examines the states comparatively and empirically, and in quantitative terms tries to account for all the states and the variation among them. A tall order, and one that does not permit any individual state to be given much attention or for the distinctive sense and flavor of individual states to be communicated to the reader.

Although the literature on state politics offers a great deal, some important ingredients are necessarily lacking. The scholarly studies usually are limited in coverage. Single-state inquiries focus on one case only; multiple-state studies are few and far between. The few fasten on one theme or another or tend to be of transitory nature. The textbooks, of course, cover a lot of territory. Either they describe in general terms the significant topics of organization, structure, procedure, and behavior, or they diligently make comparisons and strive wherever possible to explain variations among the 50 states. With all that is available, however, what is not available is an illuminating analysis of the central stuff of politics—the *principal dimensions and elements of the political systems* in the states.

THE STATES

Our purpose in this volume is to supplement the currently existing literature and related materials with analysis of the principal dimensions and elements of politics in twelve of the 50 American states.

Our concern is primarily with the warp and woof of politics within states, rather than with a range of topics and issues that cut across states or systematic comparisons among states. Others have attended to topical and comparative concerns, but few have tried to specify, describe, and bring to life the essential fabric of politics in a number of individual states. This is our major objective, and in pursuing it we hope first to educate and interest the reader, and second to add to the body of literature on state politics.

The 12 states selected for analysis are neither representative nor typical of all 50. Nor could they be. There are obviously similarities among the 12, whether in terms of aspects of their economics, their politics, or their cultures. But the closer we come to examining the actual political life of a state, the more unique each place seems. As a long-time practitioner of state governmental relations observed, "From state to state we dress differently, we talk differently, and our humor is different."[30] They are all different, and selecting fewer than all 50 states leaves something to be desired; however, there is no way in a volume such as this one (the aim of which is to serve as a supplementary text) to cover them all or more than a dozen or so. So, a dozen it is.

Those we have selected for scrutiny are: California; Colorado; Florida; Georgia; Iowa; Kentucky; Michigan; New Hampshire; New Jersey; New York; Texas; and Vermont. In our selection we purposely overrepresent the major states, the "megastates" in Neal Peirce's terminology. Of Peirce's original ten megastates,[31] six are included here—California, Florida, Michigan, New Jersey, New York, and Texas. We have tried to give the nation geographical coverage, with one state from the Far West, one from the Rocky Mountains, two from the Midwest, one from the Southwest, two from the South, two from the Middle Atlantic, one from the Border States, and two from New England. As for the latter region, New Hampshire and Vermont were both selected because, although they are popularly considered to be quite similar, actually they are different in major political respects.

We have also chosen to scrutinize states that represent a range of demographic characteristics—population, income, urbanization, and industrialization. As Table 1.1 shows, these twelve states run the gamut. While six are among the largest in terms of population, four others are at the medium level and two are small. They range in per capita income, with six above the national average and six below it. They show similar dispersion on measures of urbanization and industrialization, thus exhibiting the variation that exists among the 50 states. We have also tried to select states that cover a broad spectrum politically. An indication, in terms of control of the executive and legislative branches of government from 1960 through 1983, is shown in Table 1.2. Four states—Florida, Georgia, Kentucky, and Texas—are entirely Democratic as far as control of state government is concerned, although a Republican has been elected governor in three of them. California and New Jersey are primarily Democratic. Michigan has split, while Colorado, New York, and New Hampshire have leaned toward the Republicans. Two other states—Iowa and Vermont—are mainly, although not completely, Republican.

ELEMENTS AND DIMENSIONS

It has been said—and on more than one occasion—that the field of state politics is not highly developed from a theoretical point of view. Jewell posed the question recently: "Can we develop a theoretical perspective that will help us to identify the forces that distinguish one state from another . . . ?"[32] In part, at least, that is what we shall attempt to do in this introductory chapter. Our major purpose here is to establish a conceptual framework for the analysis of 12 states. Using the framework, succeeding chapters will examine the states one by one in order to give the reader an appreciation of the principal dimensions and elements of politics in each of them.

TABLE 1.1
Demographic Characteristics of Selected States, 1980

State	Population[a]	Rank	*Per Capita Income[b]	Rank	Urbanization[c]	Rank	Industrialization[d]	Rank
California	23,668,562	1	$10,938	3	91.3	1	0.11	26
Colorado	2,888,834	28	10,025	14	80.6	13	-0.71	40
Florida	9,739,992	7	8,996	29	84.3	8	-0.11	31
Georgia	5,464,265	13	8,073	36	62.4	34	0.48	18
Iowa	2,913,387	27	9,358	24	58.6	37	-0.41	35
Kentucky	3,661,433	23	7,613	46	50.9	43	0.29	20
Michigan	9,258,344	8	9,950	16	70.7	19	1.31	5
New Hampshire	920,610	42	9,131	27	52.2	41	0.79	13
New Jersey	7,364,158	9	10,924	4	89.0	2	1.67	1
New York	17,557,288	2	10,260	11	84.6	6	1.08	9
Texas	14,228,383	3	9,545	18	79.6	14	0.05	29
Vermont	511,456	48	7,828	40	33.8	50	-0.54	37
	226,504,825		9,521		66.9			
	(U.S. Total)		(U.S. Average)		(U.S. Average)			

*Series was computed with preliminary revised population estimates prepared by the Census Bureau.
[a] Source: U.S. Bureau of Census, *1980 Census on Population and Housing, Advance Reports* (Washington, D.C., U.S. Government Printing Office).
[b] Source: Bureau of Economic Analysis, *Survey of Current Business*, Vol. 61, July 1981 (Washington, D.C., U.S. Department of Commerce).
[c] Source: U.S. Bureau of Census, 1980, *Characteristics of the Population*, U.S. Department of Commerce.
[d] Source: Sarah McCally Morehouse, *State Politics, Parties and Policy* (New York: Holt, Rinehart and Winston, 1980), pp. 513–514. State rankings were computed from individual state factor scores presented in Morehouse on industrialization which were derived from fifteen standard socio-economic indicators.

TABLE 1.2.
Political Characteristics of Selected States, 1960–1982

State	Party Control of Governor and Legislature (number of years)					
	Democratic Governor and Democratic Legislature	Democratic Governor and Mixed Legislature	Democratic Governor and Republican Legislature	Republican Governor and Democratic Legislature	Republican Governor and Mixed Legislature	Republican Governor and Republican Legislature
California	15	—	—	5	2*	2
Colorado	3	2	7	4	2	10
Florida	20	—	—	4	—	—
Georgia	24	—	—	—	—	—
Iowa	2	1	4	5	1	11
Kentucky	20	1*	2	4	—	—
Michigan	—	2*	—	11	6*	4
New Hampshire	—	6	4	—	4*	10
New Jersey	10	8	1	2	—	2
New York	—	—	8	2	2	11
Texas	20	—	—	4	—	—
Vermont	—	—	10	—	2	12

*Includes years when neither party held a majority.

Sources: *The Book of the States* (Lexington, KY: The Council of State Governments), Volumes 1960–1961 through 1980–1982; 1983 figures, *Congressional Quarterly Weekly Report*, Vol. 40, No. 46, 11/13/82.

It is possible, of course, to write a book on each one of the states that is dealt with in this volume. There is so much to say, not only about California and New York but about Kentucky and Iowa as well. But it is not our mission to write books about individual states. Therefore, we are severely constrained by space in what we can say. Not everything can be taken into account in a rather brief analysis of a state. The problem is, determining what gets included and what has to be omitted. We want to cover those things that are most important. We want to focus on what is most significant. Thus, we choose to deal with those features or aspects that constitute the *salient* and *enduring* elements of a state's politics. That leaves us to figure out just what is salient and what is enduring, and what is not.

Take the matter of saliency. Not all elements of politics are salient. Not every one is prominent or striking. Nor does every element have meaning for the manner in which the political system operates. Many items can be excluded, because they are essentially peripheral or transitory. When dealing with the salient, there is no need to become preoccupied with organizational arrangements in the executive branch, staffing patterns or committee practices in the legislature, electoral procedures in party primaries, and the like. They are not at the core of politics in the state and they tend usually to be products of the elements that we will be considering here.

Take the matter of endurance. Not all elements of politics are enduring. Not every one is durable or lasting. Some, such as those related to the outcomes of specific elections and the disposition of particular policy issues, are passing. They come and they go. To be enduring, an element should have import over a period of time, at least over the decade of the 1970s and perhaps the 1960s too. This does not mean that no change whatsoever takes place, but rather that the element persists in one form or another and is not merely ephemeral. The professionalization of government in New York, the relative strength of political parties in New Jersey and their relative weakness in California, and the potency of economic elites in Texas are examples of elements that exhibit a lasting quality. They have been around, and in roughly similar form, for a while. Thus, even though we deal here with features of contemporary politics in the states, our perspective is longer range and our treatment of the present includes in it some recognition of the past.

These salient and enduring elements, it should be noted, are not precisely the same in each of the states. Frequently, comparative analysis impels us to compare each and every characteristic across the range of cases. There is certainly justification in doing so, but not here. Some elements may be significant in some places, but relatively insignificant in others. Therefore, although it is necessary in the state analyses to concentrate on particular elements where they count, it is not necessary to attend closely to them where they count much less.

Although elements that are salient and enduring may vary somewhat from state to state, the principal dimensions in which they fit conceptually and can most usefully be organized are the same. The several elements we have in mind can be located conceptually within the dimensions of *political culture, political style,* and *political interaction.*

This conceptualization is not an unfamiliar one, because its intellectual antecedents are in the mainstream of political science. Indeed, in his major work on American federalism, Daniel Elazar comes close to the present formulation, when he identifies three aspects of politics most influential in shaping political life in the states.[33] First is a set of perceptions of what politics is and what can be expected from government. This generally corresponds with our notion of *political culture.* Second is the kinds of people who become active in government and politics, as holders of elective offices and in the bureaucracy. This is part of what we have in mind with respect to *political style.* Third is the actual way in which the art of government is practiced by citizens, politicians, and public officials in light of their perceptions. This corresponds to the dimension of *political interaction.*

POLITICAL CULTURE

One of the most appealing concepts in contemporary political science is that of political culture, which is "a somewhat open-ended, multi-faceted, sensitizing concept."[34] It is useful, in part, because it is inclusive and imprecise—and sensitizing.

There are times, however, when even political culture is stretched beyond legitimate bounds. Then, it serves to include whatever does not fit conveniently elsewhere; it functions as a residual category, a depository for data and findings that cannot be covered by other labels. Take Gerald Stollman's study of Michigan's state legislature, for example.[35] Here, a chapter devoted to political culture deals with the background or setting in which legislators work, ethnic characteristics, voting patterns, demography and geography, issues, interest groups, and more. Stretching the concept that far is not very helpful.

If we wish to make better use of the concept, greater discrimination is called for. That entails distinguishing among the *sources*, the *manifestations*, and the *effects* of political culture, as Elazar tries to do.[36] Race, ethnicity, life experiences, and environmental variables can be considered sources, and not actual manifestations of political culture. Malcolm Jewell and David Olson make a similar distinction in their book on parties and elections in the states. They point out that the first step in understanding the political culture of a state is to identify the kinds of persons living in the state as well as economic and social development. "In other words," they write, "the political culture of a state today is a product of its entire history."[37] At the other end of the spectrum are effects—actions, institutions, and policies. Political culture presumably has bearing on how people participate in political activities and the interactions among individuals and institutions.

If Elazar and Jewell and Olson are correct in their approach, it makes sense to focus in the 12 studies in this book on manifestations of political culture rather than on sources or effects. For present purposes, at any rate, it is most appropriate to try to figure out what a state's political culture is. We will deal relatively little with its sources, although we will deal somewhat more with its likely effects when we examine political interaction.

As far as manifestations are concerned, political culture can be conceived of primarily as *orientations*. Over 25 years ago, a leading comparativist, Gabriel Almond, pointed out that a political system is embedded in a particular pattern of orientations to political action, and that these orientations include symbolic, evaluative, and cognitive responses to authority, the constitutional order, and the political community.[38] Another comparativist and a collaborator of Almond, Sidney Verba, reiterated the definition: "The political culture of a society consists of a system of empirical beliefs, expressive symbols, and values which defines the situation in which political action takes place."[39] In line with this tradition, reference here is to a system of general beliefs, and not to specific attitudes or to formal or informal structures of political interaction.

Over the years students of state politics have adhered, at least roughly, to the specifications laid down by Almond and Verba. Sometimes they have gone further, including what we term political style as part of political culture. Patterson, for example, considers political culture to be a belief system, and in applying the concept refers to basic attitudes, political identifications, participant-subject orientations, and also political styles.[40] Jewell and Olson specify the major elements along similar lines as: attitudes toward the role of government in society; attitudes toward public participation in the political process and the degree of deference toward political authority; willingness to change society or preferences for the status quo; attitudes toward the party system and identification with and loyalty to political parties; and, sense of state identity and pride. But they also include styles of political activity and, beyond this, attitudes on major social questions—a departure from the narrower interpretation of Almond and Verba.[41]

Elazar has done the most in applying the concept empirically to the states,[42] and his imaginative and provocative efforts have had a marked effect on the field. Elazar's types of state political cultures—the Individualistic, the Moralistic, and the Traditionalistic—have found their way into many textual treatments of state politics and by now are part of popular usage. They are worth specifying here, not only because of their prominence but also because they are referred to in several chapters in this book.

The Individualistic political culture characterizes states where politics is a matter for professionals rather than for citizens and the role of government is strictly limited. The Moralistic culture prevails in states where politics is the concern of everyone and government is expected to be interventionist, promoting the public good and advancing the public welfare. The Traditionalistic culture is found in states where primary concern is with the preservation of tradition and the existing social order, and where public participation is limited and government is by an established elite. According to Elazar's categorization, the states included in this volume are as follows:[43]

Moralistic	Colorado, Michigan, Vermont
Moralistic Individualistic	California, Iowa, New Hampshire
Individualistic Moralistic	New York
Individualistic	New Jersey
Traditionalistic Individualistic	Florida, Kentucky, Texas
Traditionalistic	Georgia

Of great heuristic value and a source of constant reference, Elazar's scheme has also been used in the conduct of a number of studies within one or a few individual states as well as for comparisons among all 50.[44]

What is of principal interest here are not the types themselves, but their basis—conceptions, orientations, and beliefs with regard to the role of government, the character of political participation, and the nature of political activity and politics. Our specification of the elements of political culture follow from and are also in accord with the early definitions of Almond and Verba. For present purposes, it is useful to regard political culture as the *orientations of rank-and-file citizens,* in terms of their *identifications*, their *expectations*, and their *support.* This is a restricted definition, that distinguishes manifestations from sources and effects and orientations from behavior or activity. In practice, allowances have to be made, for it is much simpler to delineate a concept abstractly than to apply it empirically.

Identifications—one of the principal elements of political culture—are orientations toward the state as a political entity. How do people feel about the state in which they reside? Is the culture of the state well integrated or is the state divided by dissimilar regions, by rival cities, by competitive groups, or by contentious philosophies?

Although no state is perfectly integrated, in some cases identification is unambiguous and intense. The southern states appear to fit this pattern most closely.

Texas is probably prototypical in this respect. Texans take great pride in their state, with children raised on stories of heroes of the Alamo and the leadership of Sam Houston, and adults exhibiting as much chauvinism as any other group in the nation. Kentucky may be an even more interesting case. Although somewhat defensive of the backwardness of their state in certain areas, Kentuckians identify intensely because of the pride they take in a number of home-grown institutions. The *Louisville-Courier Journal* is among the best newspapers in the country. The University of Kentucky is an excellent educational institution, and its basketball team, the Wildcats, seldom misses the NCAA finals or semi-finals. Finally, there is the Bluegrass, both as a place and a state of mind. Fed by myth and fact, an outpouring of romance for Kentucky binds the citizenry together.

Georgia follows suit, at least up to a certain point. Georgians take pride in their state's institutions, such as the University of Georgia, its football team, and also its law school and agricultural extension division. Jimmy Carter's election to the highest national office was another source of pride. So is Georgia's history, which is continuously honored. Georgia is one of the few places where practically every school child visits the state capitol. Yet, for all the loyalty and pride Georgia does not have a completely integrated state personality. There are too many schisms—black versus white, native versus immigrant, Appalachian north versus center, coastal plain, black belt. Most important, perhaps, are people's strong identification with their home counties and the separate status of Atlanta.

California is another place where schisms conflict with statewide identification. Citizens of the Golden State would rather be Californians than anything else, and public opinion polls have indicated that virtually all of them find California "one of the best places to live." Yet, there is a strong sense of regionalism within the state, north opposing south with the Tehachapi Mountains as the dividing line. In addition to region, the state is divided by issues of liberalism versus conservatism, the economics of water, life style, and political power.

Probably more than any other factor, geography is the one that takes a toll on identification with the state as a whole. Colorado's geography divides the state into an urbanized corridor along the Front Range of the Rocky Mountains, the mountains and the plateaus in the western area, and the eastern plains. Despite disintegrative forces, stemming from geography and migration as well, identifications with the state persist. The tourism motto of "Colorado—above all" is a slogan in which most residents truly believe.

Several other states also divide along generally geographical lines, although state identifications recently have been getting stronger. New Jersey, for instance, has been at one end of the continuum in terms of fragmentation. People in the Garden State are drawn either toward New York City in the north or toward Philadelphia in the south. At the same time, their loyalties are to their local communities and they regard "home rule" almost as a religion. Things are changing now, but forging a statewide identity in New Jersey is a very slow process indeed.[45]

New York is less localistic than its neighbor, but it also suffers from fragmented identification. On the one hand there is New York City and on the other upstate, with the City's suburbs and upstate's urban, suburban, and rural areas further dividing loyalties. But with economic hard times and with intense campaigns to promote economic development, overall identifications appear to be increasing. Still, friction and distrust exist among the various parts of the Empire State.

Nothing is perfectly stable, in political culture or anything else. Vermont provides an excellent illustration of how identifications change over time.

Here, the tradition of localism dominated for many years. It was reinforced by the apportionment of the lower house of the legislature, with one representative for each of the state's towns and cities. But after the U.S. Supreme Court's decision in *Baker v. Carr* in 1962 and the radical shift in the reapportionment of the legislature, dramatic change took place. Progressive-liberal orientations emerged, state government came to play a larger role, and statewide identification began to increase. Vermont is very different today than it was a decade or two ago.

Identification is not a clear-cut matter. People may identify with some aspects of their state, but not with others. Iowa illustrates the point. Generally, Iowans are positive about their state, but they exhibit ambivalence. They take pride in Iowa's land, in its physical beauty, and in its productivity. At the same time, they have a tendency to deprecate their state's politics. Pride outweighs deprecation; but pride does not extend to government and politics, which citizens find satisfactory but which they also take for granted. They expect a lot, and are not especially grateful or allegiant because they are well served.

Overall, the element of identification discriminates nicely among the states. In four of them—Kentucky, Texas, Colorado, and Georgia— identification is stronger; in the other eight—Iowa, New Hampshire, Michigan, California, Florida, New Jersey, New York, and Vermont—it is weaker. Even in those places where identification is stronger, however, it is only concentrated in Kentucky and Texas while it is more diffuse (because of geographical and/or social diversity), for example, in Colorado and Georgia.

Expectations, which encompass elements previously employed by Elazar, relate to the role politics and government should play and the manner in which that role should be pursued. What should the size and scope of government be? On the one hand, government might be positive, active, or innovative. On the other, it might be negative, passive, or conservative.

At one extreme is New York, where citizens insist that their elected officials produce results and that, not only vital services, but a wide array of services be delivered. New York is big government.

Less is expected of government in Kentucky and Iowa. The public wants of Kentuckians are limited. Traditionally the single objective of citizens has been roads; now they are into other forms of public works, such as community colleges. For Kentuckians that is what state government is primarily about. For Iowans government is just about the same. They do not expect too much of Des Moines; because for them the role of government should be minimal, with individual volunteerism always preferable to governmental action. People in Colorado are similar in not expecting terribly much from state government. With economic health, mountains, and general contentment, Coloradans mainly want to preserve a pleasant status quo. They just want to be left alone.

At the other extreme from New York are Georgia and Texas. Although recently their orientations have become somewhat more activist in social, economic, and environmental matters, Georgians still want government to play a relatively minor role. The historical bourbon tradition of limited governmental involvement hangs on, with people expecting little from government and not expecting to pay much for what little they do get. Texas is even more so. Here Social Darwinism is the prevailing economic ideology. What Texans want from government is for it to let individualism and the free-enterprise system work their will.

How should government and politics be conducted? Are government and politics expected to be open or closed, honest or corrupt, or what? Expectations differ, but within limits. Citizens in some places are suspicious of the activities of politicians and governmental officials and are leery of politics. Suspicion is commonplace in New York, where people assume politics is likely to be corrupt, particularly in the City. Still, politics is important to New Yorkers, and it is believed that hanky-panky can be kept within bounds if citizens maintain a vigilence. Kentuckians, too, expect corruption—but mainly at the local level and not at the state capital. They tolerate some grease and some graft, but do not want scandals to touch their governors, whom they insist on holding in esteem.

Elsewhere, public officials are expected—and generally thought—to be honest, or at least as honest as citizens themselves. Georgians, for instance, may not be overly concerned about conflict of interests and minor peccadillos, but they do not tolerate outright corruption. In California people are used to even more, in terms of how government, and politics are conducted. Thanks to the lasting influence of progressivism and the reforms of the early 20th century, Californians assume government will be honest, and efficient and responsive as well.

As for expectations in general, the major distinction is between those places where people believe that government should play a larger and more general role and those where they believe it should play a smaller and more limited one. In the first category are California, Michigan, New Jersey, and New York. Here, state government and state politicians are expected to produce results, provide services, and deliver goods. In the second category are Colorado and New Hampshire (where people want to be left alone), Kentucky (where people rely on government for public works, but not much more), Georgia (where little government has been becoming slightly bigger, but not too big), Iowa and Vermont (where the role of government should be minimal), and Texas (where people most want law and order and not too much else out of government).

Support has been given a good deal of attention in the literature, although not necessarily in connection with political culture. This element is not unlike the idea of participant-subject orientations. What is important are citizen orientations toward authority, and how positive or negative they are. More specifically, are citizens deferential, allegiant, respectful, or cynical when it comes to the authority of the state, its political institutions, and public officials?

As an element of state politics, support is difficult to discern. Support can encompass a variety of orientations and objects, and so the picture is never clear-cut. In Texas, perhaps there is relatively little support, since government is viewed as a necessary evil that must be kept small and unable to interfere with free enterprise. Basic support exists in California; nevertheless, confidence in government is declining. This is evidenced by the growth in the number of initiative measures that furnish citizens an opportunity to express their dissatisfaction with the workings of regular governmental institutions.

Elsewhere, too, the picture is mixed. Georgians have respect for their governmental institutions and for their public officials, but there is still an undercurrent of distrust among citizens. In New York, while authority is regarded as legitimate, it is not accorded deference. Essentially, there is confidence and trust in government, although less on the part of people in New York City than on the part of people in other areas of the state.

Support has been high in Iowa. Recent governors—Harold Hughes and Robert Ray—have had no problem in building support for themselves and for executive institutions generally. Similarly, there has been strong underlying support for the legislature as a constitutional and historic entity and as a mechanism for lawmaking. Yet, despite these positive orientations, a strain of cynicism and a general lack of deference toward political authority characterize Iowan politics—reflecting the existentialism and egalitarianism a rural way of life breeds.

In none of the states examined here does support seem to be given without doubt or without reservation. No states belong at the allegiant end of the continuum. New Hampshire, New Jersey, and Texas, however, belong to the other end, in a distrustful or cynical grouping. The rest are mixed cases, evidencing support for programs and governmental officials, but skepticism about, or little confidence in, government or in particular institutions.

POLITICAL STYLE

While *political culture* has received at least some attention from political scientists, political style is an undeveloped dimension of state analysis. All of us have an intuitive notion of what "style" means, particularly when it has reference to the behavior of individuals. We think of the styles of individual politicians. "Leadership style" and "presidential style," for example, are often dealt with, although seldom systematically. As a pattern variable or aggregate behavior, however, style is virtually ignored in the literature on state politics.

When style is referred to in characterizing states, commentary is brief and usage loose. Patterson, for instance, notes that where political cultures differ, political styles are likely to differ as well. Even where cultures are alike, styles may vary. On the basis of his own experience and of various studies of state politics, Patterson characterizes states stylistically as follows: Iowa as pragmatic, non-programmatic, and cautious; Virginia as distinctive in its sense of honor and gentility; Louisiana and Mississippi as dominated by the demogogic-horatory style; and Massachusetts, Pennsylvania, and California as primarily ideological in style.[46] Rosenthal also attends, albeit briefly, to such matters, pointing out that anyone who spends time in a number of states is aware of stylistic differences among them. A strong disposition of compromise pervades Oregon; hard work and a general conservatism are obvious features of Kansas; Indiana is intensely partisan, Wyoming mainly individualistic, and Ohio fundamentally conservative; and ethnicity—the dominance of the Japanese in Hawaii, the influence of the Irish in Massachusetts, and the Mormon ascendancy in Utah—shapes the style in other states.[47]

There is little doubt that an understanding of state politics requires that style be taken into account. In order to do so, further clarification of this dimension is necessary. Verba made a start, when he noted that political style lies on the border between political culture and political interaction (just where we position it) and involves, according to him, "those informal norms of political interaction that regulate the way in which fundamental political beliefs are applied in politics."[48] For Patterson, however, these norms are "an important *part of* political culture."[49] As a general rule, when style has been dealt with in the literature, it has been subsumed under culture.

Like Verba, we regard political style in conceptual terms as a separate dimension, albeit with a recognition that it may be difficult empirically to distinguish from political culture on the one hand and political interaction on the other. Style, for us, refers to the ways in which orientations are applied in politics, and thus it pertains most appropriately to behavior or activity—to the consequences of orientations and not to orientations themselves. Moreover, while culture relates to the orientations of many, of rank-and-file citizens, style relates to the behavior of a relative few, of political elites. Style, then, mainly has to do with *by whom and how government and politics are practiced*. Thus, it is useful to conceive of style as encompassing two principal elements—one relating primarily to *personnel* and the other relating primarily to *process*.

Personnel style refers to the kinds of people who have leadership roles in politics and government. Are they—or how are they—different from the rest of the people in the state? Are their characteristics distinctive in terms of age, sex, education, religion, ethnicity, or occupational background? Is leadership in a state relatively homogeneous or heterogeneous? How do these relative few approach politics in their individual roles as candidates and as officeholders?

Several states evidence substantial homogeneity, as far as style is concerned. Vermont is a good example. Here reliance is on a personalized, amateur-citizen approach to politics and public service. Because the stakes are not large, government can be essentially a part-time enterprise. The Vermont political ethos stresses political involvement as a civic duty; social barriers to political involvement are virtually nonexistent. Still, the middle and upper classes participate to the greatest degree and they run Vermont's government, insofar as it is run. Iowa's style of politics is referred to as "bland," and it is conducted mainly by small town lawyers, businessmen, and professionals. Although ethnic groups have a presence in the state, ethnicity plays only a minor role in Iowa.

Kentucky, too, has a coherent political class, mainly insiders and the courthouse crowd, with outsider and "fresh-face" types surfacing here and there and from time to time. Texas politics has had a narrower political base, with power in the hands of relatively few. What has been, and continues to be, important in the Lone Star State is the business-political alliance, known as the "Establishment." For the most part, Texans like their political leaders to be rich, but sometimes they take them poor—as in the cases of Sam Rayburn, Lyndon Johnson (when he started out), and Jim Hightower (a Progressive-Populist who won statewide election for commissioner of agriculture in 1982).

By contrast to these states, New York is characterized by a much more inclusive politics. Everybody can wade in. Because of the ethnic and cultural diversity of the Empire State, a "balanced ticket" has been the historical pattern. It continues to be important today, but with more groups included in the balance than in the historical past.

In addition to such characteristics, motivations and other qualities have to be taken into account. What are the principal motives of people who seek and win elective office—profit, patronage, or public service? What personal qualities normally come into play? How do elite participants behave themselves in running for office and in running government? Different stylistic features emerge from an examination of the states under scrutiny here. In Iowa political leaders are people with a sense of public service. In Vermont high value is placed on independence of mind and personal integrity. Assertiveness, even stridency, result from the intense competitiveness in New York. Because of the increasing significance of the media, energy, articulateness and knowledgeability are also standard qualities among New York's political leaders. In California, elected executives generally have exhibited pragmatic, non-ideological, and managerial styles, while legislators have become increasingly professional since the mid-1960s.

Florida and Texas have undergone a change in the style of leaders recently. It used to be fashionable to be a character in Texas politics, but clowning is no longer necessary for success. It used to be that Florida politics was dominated by the so-called "Porkchoppers," with their down-home, good-ole-boy style. No longer; now there is a greater diversity of types in Sunshine State politics.

Georgia illustrates the heterogeneity of style in a state that strives for stability as it adapts to change. The Empire State of the South, as Georgia is called, values in its public leaders: rugged individualism, combined with social conformity; material success, along with moral restraint; and informed intellect, guided by practical experience. Officials here have to appear more successful than the voters, but not too much so. They have to be conservative and take a "common-people" approach, even though fewer of them today are "good-ole-boy" politicians and many more exhibit a new "middle-management" style.

In summarizing personnel style, the amateur nature of political people in Colorado and Vermont and the professional nature of political people in California and New York (at least at the state level) are worth note. Moreover, there is an interesting contrast between those states—like Georgia, Iowa, Kentucky, and Texas—that appear to be more homogeneous in terms of political personnel and those—like Colorado and New York—that are rather heterogeneous.

Process style refers to the ways in which people in leadership roles engage in the practice of politics. This element reminds us of rank-and-file expectations of how government and politics should be conducted. But the two elements are not the same and belong to different dimensions. There are various possibilities along these lines. Verba pointed out the contrast between ideological and pragmatic styles, the former with an expressive emphasis and the latter with an instrumental one.[50] Others make the distinction between innovative politics and policy, as in California and New York, as opposed to conservative politics and policy, as in Texas. In any case, process style is a complex matter, with different features salient in different places.

What comes across in New York is the tough, professional character of politics. There is energetic discussion, frenetic activity, and continual maneuvering. The New York City or downstate style is loud and aggressive; and while the upstate style is less "pushy," it is just as calculating. Not everything is pure and sweet in New York, but thanks to a strong reform tradition the processes are open and politics is visible. Backrooms are by no means obsolete, but they are not used as frequently as in earlier years.

California, Colorado, and Iowa are somewhat different than New York. California's process is open, bureaucratic, and professional, and largely nonpartisan. The state's moralistic culture has had considerable influence on its political style, so much so that even the most "hardball" politics is rationalized in moralistic terms. Moralism permeates Colorado politics as well. There is virtually no political patronage here; and a constitutional amendment in 1976 that would have allowed for about 100 exempt positions at the middle-management level was defeated in referendum by a three-to-one margin. Political corruption in Colorado is rare. Iowa is about the same in these respects. Hawkeye politics is marked by honesty, fair play, honorable intentions, and good, solid government. The system is extremely open and, although there is political conflict, it is civil and high minded.

Georgia, Kentucky, and Vermont are different still. But these states seem to have one thing in common—politics is essentially personal. People in Georgia, for example, do their business on a first-name basis; the social relations maintained outside of politics and government assume importance inside politics and government. In Kentucky everyone who is politically active knows just about everyone else who is politically active. Politics and government are small, even familial, and quite manageable. Vermonters also are accustomed to a very personalized style of politics, "where local officials, state legislators, and even the governor are approached in village stores and in post offices to hear citizen complaints and to receive advice on pending public issues." In states such as these people deal with people one-on-one, and not through indirect or bureaucratic processes.

With respect to process style, a number of features serve to summarize distinctions among the states. First is whether the process is personal, as in Florida, Kentucky, Georgia, New Jersey, and Vermont, or impersonal (and bureaucratic), as in California and New York. Second is whether the process is marked more by accommodation (with an emphasis on consensus politics), as in Georgia, Iowa, and New Jersey, or by confrontation (with an emphasis on moralism, ideology, or hard-ball competition), as in California, Colorado, and New York. Third is whether the process is open, as in California and Colorado, or somewhat closed (although more open now than earlier), as in Kentucky and New Jersey.

POLITICAL INTERACTION

By *political interaction* we have in mind the traditional stuff of state politics—participation, interest groups, political parties, governmental institutions, and intergovernmental relations. This dimension is taken for granted in the literature; although it has received little or no conceptual attention, it has undergone considerable empirical scrutiny. Thus, while political style is generally ignored and political culture is treated theoretically but seldom empirically, it is within the dimension of political interaction that almost all of the research and writing in the field of state politics is done.

The challenge here is not primarily one of conceptualization. It is rather that of specifying elements generally and then figuring out which ones are most salient and enduring. We would suggest concentrating on three elements, each of which is general in nature and familiar to students of politics: participation, organization, and power. Within the parameters of each of these elements, what specifically is most important in portraying the politics of a particular state?

Participation has to do with the scope, nature, and channels by which people get involved in politics. Of most direct relevance in this regard is voting turnout in elections. Other types of involvement are pertinent, too— voting on initiatives and referendums, membership and activity in interest groups, and so forth. Is participation high or low, broadly or narrowly based?

In some places, such as California, participation is high, wide, and (some might say) handsome. Even though voting in presidential and state elections has been diminishing of late, there are always the initiative and referendum to encourage other forms of participation in California. The initiative and referendum are also features of Colorado's participatory process, but here—unlike in California—the two parties offer significant opportunities for rank-and-file participation through precinct caucuses and then county, congressional district, and state preprimary conventions.

In other places participation is more limited. Iowa, for instance, has high turnout in presidential elections but lower turnout in gubernatorial elections. Despite its caucus systems, the level of participation is uneven, mainly because of Iowa's low-key, nonideological, middle-of-the-road qualities of discourse and its "good government" ethos. Participation is less broadly based in Texas and in Georgia. Politics is the preserve of a small establishment in Texas, and indigenous groups that maintain grass-roots contact with voters are lacking. In Georgia, too, voting participation is low compared to elsewhere, with an attitude of not-getting-involved typical, especially in rural areas.

Organization is the largest category of elements in our scheme. This category applies to how political life is organized and how political organizations function. Included here are political parties and party factions and interest groups of all sorts and persuasions. Much, of course, has been written about these subjects; but the issue at hand involves what features of party and group life are most important in particular places, and whether parties and groups are relatively strong or relatively weak.

Parties deserve consideration just about everywhere, although they vary in strength and in how they are organized from place to place. The Democratic and Republican parties in New York have been weakened by reform, by the emergence of third parties, and by the growing independence of political candidates. Nonetheless, the two major parties remain relatively strong in the Empire State. Colorado's parties are strong, too. Partisanship in the Centennial State is considerable, ideological differences are pronounced, and conflict is frequent. In Iowa the parties are equally significant, and are at the center of state politics. Each party has a state headquarters, staff, and county and precinct organizations.

Parties matter less elsewhere. Although partisanship in California has increased since the 1960s, it influences only a handful of issues. The volunteer party organizations, that were active but not really strong, have declined as well. What counts more in California's politics, and particularly in electoral politics, are the personal organizations of incumbents that dissolve when they leave office. And even organization is not that important anymore, having been replaced by money and media that put a premium on personalities and fresh faces. In terms of parties, Georgia is perhaps typical of most of the southern states. There is little party organization, but instead factionalism that recurs on scattered issues. The Republicans here are still without a solid base of support, although they have shown some signs of grass-roots organization in the 1980s.

Interest groups exist everywhere, but may be worthy of special treatment only if they are quite strong, or dominate the politics of a state, or simply are more imposing than anything else on the scene. New York and California can be considered interest-group states, with every possible group organized and at least several strong lobbies. In New York the public service employee unions play a particularly important role, but other groups have their say too. Interest groups in California are checked only by massive publicity or by competing groups. No single group dominates, but many are strong and often exert decisive influence because they are the only voices heard on an issue.

The influence of interest groups is somewhat more limited elsewhere. In Florida the groups that stand out are business, agriculture, gambling, and tourism, with senior citizens having great potential but less actual power as of now. In Texas labor is weak, while business groups are entrenched and share an alliance with the dominant political community. Business groups are also most influential in Georgia, where the so-called "corporate lobbies" (Southern Bell, Georgia Power, Coca Cola, Chamber of Commerce, etc.) are among the principal actors in the political system. Interest group influence overall is rather weak in Iowa. While groups, such as the Iowa Farm Bureau, still have a role, they have been replaced by the political parties as the main actors.

It should be noted that the press can also function as a major interest group in a state. There is no doubt that in New Hampshire the one statewide newspaper, the *Manchester Union Leader*, for years has been the most potent force on the political scene. Although not as powerful as in the past, it continues to play a substantial role. In New Jersey the *Star-Ledger* is a statewide newspaper with which public officials must reckon. Elsewhere, although newspapers matter, they are by no means as strong nor as politically involved. Take California, for example. The state's major newspapers used to set the policy agenda, define alternatives, and advance positions. No longer; the press now lacks cohesion, it is fragmented, and newspapers have lost their former leadership role because of the entry of television on the statewide scene.

In summary, the strength or weakness of political parties and interest groups is a most important characteristic of the element of organization. In Colorado, Michigan, and New York parties and interest groups are both strong; in Georgia and Vermont they are both weak. California, Florida, Kentucky, and Texas have stronger groups and weaker parties; Iowa and New Jersey have weaker groups and stronger parties.

Power has to do with the distribution of authority and influence within a state, primarily among governmental institutions and levels of government, but also between the public and private sectors. Most attention with respect to power has been devoted to the nature of executive and legislative institutions and the balance between the governor on the one hand and the legislature on the other.

In some states the governor is strong and the legislature relatively weak. Kentucky is an example, although the power of the legislature has been increasing of late. Georgia is another example. By dint of his personality, political acumen, and control of the budget, the governor of Georgia maintains power. Until the mid-1960s his domination of the legislature was almost complete. He named the speaker, the majority leader, and the chairmen of major committees in the house and exercised considerable influence in the senate. This has changed in the past decade, but the governor in Georgia still has a substantial advantage.

In some states the legislature is strong and the governor is weak by comparison. Colorado and Florida are examples. The Colorado legislature dominates, even over a popular governor. Here, although the executive prepares one state budget, the legislative joint budget committee drafts its own version. It is the latter budget that is acted on. Florida's legislature gained power in the late 1960s, and it continues to hold it today; meanwhile, the governor is constrained by elected members of a cabinet provided by the constitution.

There are cases where power is pretty well balanced between the governor and the legislature. Iowa is one. Here, Governor Robert Ray's administrative leadership and long tenure overcame the executive's formal weakness. Now there is more of a balance and greater tension between the two branches of Iowa's government. In New York and California a balance also exists, with the two branches rather strong. It used to be that the governor dominated in both states, but not any longer. New York's governor has had to become accustomed to dealing with an aggressive legislature, led by powerful senate and assembly leaders. California's governor still has the predominant political position, but the legislature has the ability—behind the leadership of the speaker in the assembly and, more recently, the president pro tem in the senate—to exercise countervailing power.

Despite the strength of the governor and/or the legislature, power is not usually centralized at the state governmental level. In most places there is some dispersion. Iowa's public power is widely diffused, with much exercised by counties and local communities. New Jersey's situation is not dissimilar. Georgia's 159 counties are also important; they no longer have the "unit vote" of the past, but the influence of county courthouses is still felt by state government. Before the 1970s, California's public power was fairly well balanced between state and local levels, but the balance has shifted lately. As a result of the state supreme court's school finance decision in 1971 and Proposition 13 in 1978, the state has come to have more control over funding for counties, local schools, and special districts.

In some states there is an overlapping—even a symbiosis—of public and private power. Take Georgia, for instance. Here, public and private officials strive for consensus, mainly in order to protect economic prosperity. Their objectives are to maximize cooperation among interest groups on policies and programs, to bring everyone in, to keep things non-ideological, and to avoid moral or ethical issues that might be divisive. Given Georgia's conservative state government, its localism, the many interest groups, and the norm of consensus politics, it is little wonder that political power is spread "widely and thinly." Or take Texas, which as much as any other state mingles public and private power. Although the governor, the lieutenant governor, and the speaker of the house dominate Texas politics, there also exist independent baronies run by elected officials such as the attorney general, the land commissioner, the agriculture commissioner, and the railroad commissioners. Then there are the business interests, the influence of which is pervasive. Perhaps business domination has been eroding gradually in recent years, but control by the monied establishment in Texas still exists. It is clearly expressed and popularly accepted.

In summary, power as an element brings to light the balance between the governor and the legislature on the one hand, and the concentration or dispersion of governmental control in the state on the other. In several states the distribution of power is out of balance. The legislature dominates in Colorado and Florida and the governor dominates in Vermont, Georgia, Kentucky, and New Jersey (although change is currently underway in the latter three states). In other states the distribution is in balance, with both the governor and the legislature relatively strong in California, Michigan, and New York. The two are coequal, but of lesser strength, in Iowa and Texas.

In none of the states under scrutiny does power seem to be centralized, but in a number of them decentralization is apparent. Power in California is divided among state and local authorities and between the public and private sectors. In Georgia it is spread out; in Iowa it is diffused among the state and its counties and localities; in Michigan labor and the dominant economic interests have a piece of action; and in Texas, although the governor, the lieutenant governor, and the speaker of the house are most important, a number of elected public officials and, in particular, the business establishment share in the exercise of public power.

SIMILARITIES AND DIFFERENCES

The 12 state analyses presented here rest on three principal assumptions. First, states are important entities in the federal system. Second, states differ from one another, not in every respect, but in many. Third, certain dimensions of state politics are universally significant, and within these dimensions certain elements are also significant, if not everywhere then in most places.

Each of the following chapters analyzes one particular state. The 12 analyses taken together enable us to look at the states from a more comparative perspective. We have done so in the previous pages of this introductory chapter, discussing identifications, expectations, support, personnel style, process style, participation, organization, and power, and seeing how they applied in each of the states. In terms of these elements, and perhaps more important, in terms of the three major dimensions, the states appear to be of differing types.

As far as political culture is concerned, the states range in terms of the orientations people hold. At one extreme is Texas, a state with which people identify strongly but whose attitudes are anti-governmental. At the other extreme are California, Florida, Michigan, and New York where identifications are weaker and more diffuse, but where government and its work are positively regarded. In other cases orientations toward government are moderate or ambivalent, while identifications tend to be stronger, as in Colorado, Georgia, and Kentucky, or they tend to be weaker, as in Iowa, New Hampshire, and New Jersey.

It is difficult to generalize about political style on the basis of the states analyzed here. What appears to be stylistically most salient in one or two places does not appear so elsewhere. Still, a few interesting contrasts emerge. On the one hand are those places where the political style—people and process alike—is essentially "small-town." Georgia, Iowa, Kentucky, Vermont, and probably New Jersey are in this category. On the other hand are those where the political style is "big-time." California and New York are such places, and Florida is on its way. Colorado seems to belong somewhere in between, with some features in common with the small-town states and others in common with the big-time states.

Political interaction encompasses so many diverse features that there is no satisfactory way to cumulate information on participation, organization, and power and come up with some encompassing characterization. What deserves mention, however, is the general distribution of power within the states—among branches and levels of government and between the public and private sectors. There are places where the private sector is powerful, but power therein is still dispersed, as in Florida, Georgia, and Vermont. In Texas, the private sector is as powerful, but its power is more concentrated. By contrast, there are places where the public sector is the principal one, but public power is dispersed, as in California, Iowa, Michigan, and New York. Among the states explored here, there are no examples of ones in which public power clearly outweighs private power and is also centralized in a few hands at the state level.

Similarities inevitably emerge as we compare the elements and the dimensions of political life in these states. The states do have a number of features in common. Still, each of the twelve is a distinctive political unit in a nation of diverse states. Each can be characterized, for the most part, in terms different from the other.

- California is quite unlike anywhere else, it is a nation within a nation.
- Colorado is well endowed, self confident, energetic, and independent.
- Iowa is a case of middleness, of typicality, of manageability.
- Michigan is progressive and big, and is fighting decline now.
- Texas has its Establishment, which dwarfs just about everything else.
- Florida is marked by growth and by change.
- Georgia has relatively little government, but much more politics.

- Kentucky has a deep sense of political community.
- New Jersey is only lately developing as a collective, statewide political entity.
- New York is big, professional, and highly politicized.
- New Hampshire is enduringly conservative, despite liberal strains.
- Vermont has been shifting from a bastion of conservatism to a more liberal state.

The most prominent feature of each state would seem to be peculiar to that state alone. The American states have been—and continue to be—very different places.

The conceptual framework outlined here focuses on the salient and enduring characteristics of the political life of 12 American states. As employed in the analyses that follow, it should enable the reader to spot similarities and differences among the states and, most particularly, begin to understand what is distinctive and most interesting within each of them. That, at least, is the major purpose the contributors to this volume had in mind.

NOTES

1. Advisory Commission on Intergovernmental Relations, *In Brief: State and Local Roles in the Federal System* (Washington, D.C.: The Commission, November 1981), p. 3.

2. Coleman Ransone, "Scholarly Revolt in Dullsville: New Approaches to the Study of State Government," *Public Administration Review*, 26 (December 1977):344–352.

3. Malcolm E. Jewell, "The Neglected World of State Politics," *Journal of Politics*, 44 (August 1982):638–657. Also see Samuel K. Gove, "State Government Research: Getting into the Mainstream?" *National Civic Review*, 71 (September 1982):407–414, 424.

4. V.O. Key, Jr., *American State Politics: An Introduction* (New York: Knopf, 1956).

5. Malcolm E. Jewell and David Olson, *American State Political Parties and Elections* (Homewood, Ill.: Dorsey, 1978).

6. Harmon Zeigler and Michael Baer, *Lobbying: Interaction and Influence in American State Legislatures* (Belmont: Calif.: Wadsworth, 1969).

7. Larry Sabato, *Goodby to Good-Time Charlie* (Lexington, Mass.: Lexington Books, 1978).

8. Alan Rosenthal, *Legislative Life: People, Process, and Performance in the States* (New York: Harper and Row, 1981).

9. Wayne L. Francis, *Legislative Issues in the Fifty States* (Chicago: Rand McNally, 1967).

10. Nicholas A. Masters, Robert H. Salisbury, and Thomas H. Eliot, *State Politics and the Public Schools* (New York: Knopf, 1964).

11. See Alvin D. Sokolow, "Facts and Analysis for the Golden State: A Review of California Government Textbooks," *Western Political Quarterly*, 35 (June 1982):274–281.

12. A good example is Joseph F. Zimmerman, *The Government and Politics of New York State* (New York: New York University Press, 1981).

13. Recently the American Political Science Association has begun publishing, in its *News for Teachers of Political Science*, bibliographic essays on source materials for the study of individual state governments. Thus far, the following bibliographies have appeared: Michigan (by Charles Press), Summer, 1980; Arkansas (by Diane Kincaid Blair), Fall, 1980; Illinois (by

Samuel K. Gove), Winter, 1982; New Jersey (by Richard Lehne), Pennsylvania (by Benjamin R. Schuster), and Texas (by Robert D. Thomas), Spring, 1982; and Florida (by E. Lester Levine and Douglas St. Angelo), California (by Irving Schiffman), and Maine (by Kenneth T. Palmer), Summer, 1982.

14. V.O. Key, Jr., *Southern Politics* (New York: Knopf, 1949).

15. Duane Lockard, *New England State Politics* (Princeton: Princeton University Press, 1959).

16. John Fenton, *Politics in the Border States* (New Orleans: Hauser Press, 1956), and *Midwest Politics* (New York: Holt, Rinehart and Winston, 1966).

17. Frank Jonas, *Western Politics* (Salt Lake City: University of Utah Press, 1961).

18. Jack Bass and Walter DeVries, *The Transformation of Southern Politics* (New York: Basic Books, 1976).

19. Frank Bryan, *Politics in the Rural States* (Boulder, Colo.: Western Press, 1981).

20. Josephine F. Milburn and Victoria Schuck, eds., *New England Politics* (Cambridge, Mass.: Schenkman, 1981).

21. John Gunther, *Inside U.S.A.* (New York: Harper and Row, 1959).

22. See Neal R. Peirce, *The Mid Atlantic States* (New York: Norton, 1972); *The Pacific States of America* (New York: Norton, 1972); *The Mountain States of America* (New York: Norton, 1972); *The Great Plains States of America* (New York: Norton, 1973); *The Deep South States of America* (New York: Norton, 1974); *The Border South States of America* (New York: Norton, 1975); and *The New England States* (New York: Norton, 1976).

23. Neal R. Peirce and Jerry Hagstrom, *The Book of America* (New York: Norton, 1983).

24. James McGregor Burns, J.W. Peltason, and Thomas E. Cronin, *State and Local Politics: Government by the People*, 3rd ed. (Englewood Cliffs, N.J.: Prentice-Hall, 1981).

25. Daniel R. Grant and H.D. Nixon, *State and Local Governments in America*, 3rd ed. (Boston: Allyn and Bacon, 1975).

26. Duane Lockard, *The Politics of State and Local Government*, 3rd ed. (New York: Macmillan, 1983).

27. Sarah McCally Morehouse, *State Politics, Parties and Policy* (New York: Holt, Rinehart and Winston, 1981).

28. Virginia Gray, Herbert Jacob, and Kenneth N. Vines, eds., *Politics in the American States: A Comparative Analysis*, 4th ed. (Boston: Little, Brown, 1983). Earlier editions were edited by Jacob and Vines without the collaboration of Gray.

29. Thomas R. Dye, *Politics in States and Communities*, 4th ed. (Englewood Cliffs, N.J.: Prentice-Hall, 1981).

30. Martin Ryan Haley, at a meeting of the Public Affairs Council, Washington, D.C., 7 January 1983.

31. See Neal Peirce, *The Megastates of America* (New York: Norton, 1972).

32. Jewell, "The Neglected World of State Politics," p. 653.

33. Daniel Elazar, *American Federalism: A View from the States*, 2nd ed. (New York: Crowell, 1972), p. 90.

34. Samuel Patterson, "The Political Cultures of the American States," *Journal of Politics*, 30 (February 1968):188–191.

35. Gerald Stollman, *Michigan: State Legislators and Their Work* (Washington, D.C.: University Press of America, 1978).

36. "Introduction," in *The Ecology of American Political Culture: Readings*, eds. Daniel J. Elazar and Joseph Zikmund II (New York: Crowell, 1975), pp. 5–6.

37. Jewell and Olson, *American State Political Parties and Elections*, pp. 5–7.

38. Gabriel Almond, "Comparative Political Systems," *Journal of Politics*, 18 (August 1956):391–409.

39. Sidney Verba, "Comparative Political Culture," in *Political Culture and Political Development*, eds. Lucian W. Pye and Sidney Verba (Princeton: Princeton University Press, 1965), pp. 513–518.

40. Patterson, "The Political Cultures of the American States," p. 191.

41. Jewell and Olson, *American State Political Parties and Elections*, pp. 7–8.

42. Elazar, *American Federalism: A View from the States*, pp. 84–126.

43. *Ibid.*, p. 117.

44. For analyses within individual states, see, for example, Arthur R. Stevens, "State Boundaries and Political Culture: An Exploration in the Tri-State Area of Michigan, Indiana and Ohio," *Publius*, 4 (Winter 1974):111–125; Alan D. Monroe, "Operationalizing Political Culture: The Illinois Case," *Publius*, 7 (Winter 1977):107–120; and Robert L. Savage and Richard J. Gallagher, "Politicoculture Regions in a Southern State: An Empirical Typology of Arkansas Counties," *Publius*, 7 (Winter 1977):92–105. For comparative analyses of the 50 states, see, for example, Ira Sharkansky, "The Utility of Elazar's Political Culture: A Research Note," *Polity*, 2 (Fall 1969):66–83; and Charles A. Johnson, "Political Culture in American States: Elazar's Formulation Examined," *American Journal of Political Science*, 20 (August 1976):491–509.

45. Illustrative of New Jersey's identity problems are the comments by Virginia Gray in her introductory chapter to the fourth edition of *Politics in the American States*. She writes about her strong identification with her own state, but the low interest of citizens of New Jersey in their state. " . . . I am often surprised when asking someone where he or she is from to get the answer, 'I'm from New York.' 'Oh, what part?' I ask. 'New Jersey.' " Gray continues: "We hope this book will demonstrate, even to students living in New Jersey, that state politics is important to their daily lives." p. 24.

46. Patterson, "The Political Cultures of the American States," pp. 202–203.

47. Rosenthal, *Legislative Life*, pp. 112–113.

48. Verba, "Comparative Political Culture," p. 545.

49. Patterson, "The Political Cultures of the American States," p. 191.

50. Verba, "Comparative Political Culture," p. 547.

2

California

CHARLES G. BELL

Politics in California is rooted in an amazingly rich and varied social, geographic, economic and cultural complex. Cross-cutting and often obscuring these factors is the almost unique California mystique; it is a land of metaphor and myth, of exaggerations and image. Whatever has been said about the Golden State is at least partially true—and almost everything has been said about it.

Essentially, however, much of California's image and reputation exists simply because it has been a focus of national and international attention ever since the gold rush. Journalists focus on the unusual and bizarre; the state has had enough of the unusual and bizarre to fill the columnist's needs. As a popular folk singer observed about life, "The truth is hard to come by."* Even in exaggeration, much is still left unsaid or understated about California.

Neal Peirce, in his massive *Megastates*, asserts that more has been written about California than any of the other 49 states.[1] Typical of the fun and games had with the Golden State might be Mike Royko:

> ... California's major export to the rest of the country has not been its fruits and vegetables; it has been craziness. It comes in many forms—bad TV shows, bad architecture, junk foods, auto worship and creepy lifestyles ... from the doped-up flower children to the souped-up motorcycle gangs ....You name it: if it babbles and its eyeballs are glazed, it probably comes from California.[2]

A more balanced observation can be found in *The Real Majority* by political writers, Scammon and Wattenberg:

> California ... is not really, atypical, screwballs notwithstanding ... California is ... a barometric state. Among large states, Illinois and

---

*From John Denver's song: "Some Days are Diamonds (Some Days are Stones)."

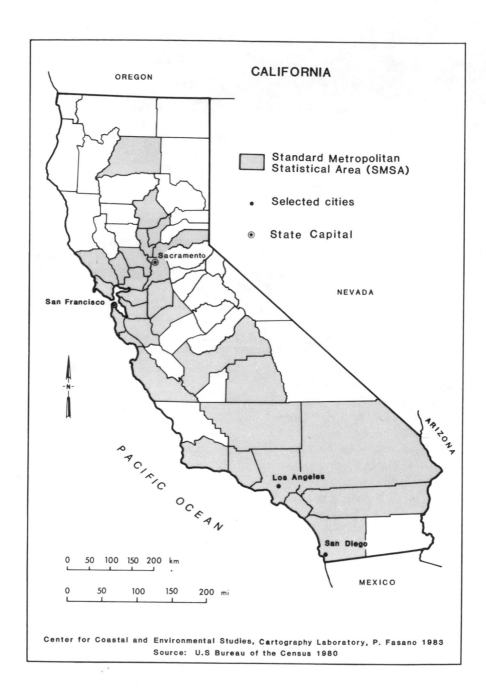

CALIFORNIA

OREGON

Standard Metropolitan
Statistical Area (SMSA)

• Selected cities

⊛ State Capital

Sacramento

NEVADA

San Francisco

-N-

PACIFIC OCEAN

ARIZONA

Los Angeles

San Diego

0 50 100 150 200 km

0   50   100   150   200 mi

MEXICO

Center for Coastal and Environmental Studies, Cartography Laboratory, P. Fasano 1983
Source: U.S Bureau of the Census 1980

California are the two that vote most consistently like America as a whole.[3]

Some observers have described the state as having no basic dimensions, as having a "putty culture." But that misses one of the most essential dimensions of the state's history and culture—change. As Gladwin Hill observed:

> The endless tide of immigration, peculiarities of geography, and the forced-draft growth of California's economy have made it a kaleidoscopic succession of states, changing from year to year, almost from day to day.[4]

California is not completely formed, it is consistently changing, innovative, perhaps even ahistorical. But there are constants—a firm core of factors and forces—which explain much more about California, the wunderkind of the American family of states.

Neil Morgan probably first coined the phrase, "A Nation Within A Nation."[5] California's capacity to function independently (geographically, economically, socially) from the rest of the nation, within the larger family of nations, has been well understood for some time. James Bryce observed in *The American Commonwealth* that of all the states subsequent to the original 13, only California had a genuine natural border. John Gunther later commented that California was the one state, above all others, that could exist alone. The point is, simply, that the state's large population, mixed economy, wealth of natural resources, and geographic situation make it a viable "nation." It should come as no surprise, then, that the state's politics resemble those of a nation's (for example the United States) more than most of the other 49 states.

POLITICAL CULTURE: A NATION WITHIN A NATION

Political culture is the glue that holds together a society and its political system. In California, which is often viewed as more disorganized than any of the other 49 states, political culture is quite complex. At the same time, it is more like that of the nation's as a whole because California has drawn migrants from all of the other states and with them their specific and different cultures. Add to that rich mixture the fact that California has more foreign born residents than any other state in the Union, and the state presents a truly complex and fascinating political culture.

California's people are a yeasty mix reflecting the constant tide of migrants from other states and other nations. Born in a gold rush, nurtured in hope and sustained by myth, California is more than a state; it is a state of mind. The year 1849 is probably one of the most widely known dates of American history. The original gold seekers came to California with every intention of making their fortune and returning east with their new found wealth. But, while few found golden wealth, many stayed because they found something else—golden opportunity. Hundreds of thousands, then millions came in the following decades seeking a new life, a dream come true. There is a California dream, and most who live in the Golden State are not only aware of it, but feel an obligation to live up to it—it is a dream not just of material success, but of happiness and of fulfillment.

It would be a mistake, however, to ignore the drive toward material success. As one highly insightful analysis of California suggests, the gold rush opportunities and migrant mentality have combined into a latter-day entrepreneurial-free-lance business set of values that rejects New Deal notions of helping the needy and, in a twist of nostalgia, yearns for the Old West where every economic gambler has a fighting chance to strike it rich.[6] Thus, California identifies with its western neighbors, rejects the dead hand of the eastern past, and looks to the Pacific Rim for its future.

Certainly, the migrant played, and plays, a key role in California's state of mind. Twenty years ago, about 75 percent of the state's adult population were migrants. Today, about 60 percent of the state's adults are from one of the other 49 states. In addition, Hispanics, blacks, Asians, native Americans, Pacific Islanders, and other miscellaneous "non-white" groups make up 43 percent of the state's total population—not counting illegal Mexican immigrants. Clearly, given current population growth trends, California is well on its way to becoming the first U.S. mainland "third world" state.

Recent patterns suggest that California's frantic growth rate may have finally slowed. According to one recent study, high unemployment and high housing costs may have erected quite a substantial and long-lasting barrier to future immigration.[7] Since about half of California's population growth is directly attributable to migration, the decline in migrants removes a traditional factor from the state's future economic and political dynamics.

Living in California appears to hold universal appeal. A major statewide survey found that seven out of ten residents described California as "one of the best places to live."[8] When asked what they specifically liked about their state, respondents most frequently said the "weather" (59 percent), followed by "beautiful scenery" (28 percent), "friendly people" (24 percent), and "job opportunities" (22 percent). Such responses by state residents are not unusual. But, when an earlier Gallup Poll asked a *national* sample where they'd most like to live, San Francisco "won" by a two-to-one margin over its closest rival, Los Angeles! Two studies by the Midwest Research Institute, scoring each of the nation's 65 major urban areas by some 120 criteria (economic, political, environmental, health, education, and so forth), rated California first overall. Individually, four of the Golden State's cities ranked in the top ten—Sacramento (2nd); San Jose (4th); San Francisco (9th); and San Diego (10th).

There are a few interesting differences in opinion about California by age, education, and home ownership. Younger people (those under 30), those with less education, and renters are less enthusiastic about life in California than are their counterparts. But, these differences may very well be rooted in general life-views, having nothing to do with the state at all. Overall, there are only a few differences between natives and migrants. Since some 60 percent of the adult population are migrants, the lack of any meaningful differences is important.

For all this general enthusiasm about living in California, it is probably true that some identify more with their local community or region than with the state as a whole. There are too many migrants and too much residential mobility within the state for any broad sense of place-history-tradition to develop. There are, however, some significant regional identifications. People who live in San Francisco feel a very strong sense of identification with their city and the Bay Area as a whole. Similarly, those who live in the northern coastal towns, the central valley, and rural communities also feel a strong sense of identification for their "place."

As a general rule of thumb, the further south one travels in the state, the less one is likely to find a strong sense of community or identification. The rapidly growing suburbs of Los Angeles, Orange County, and San Diego County, as well as the western edges of San Bernardino and Riverside Counties are simply a place to live in, a place to leave from for work, and a place to return to after work. Most of all, one's residence is a place that one plans on moving from soon. However, in the last few years, population growth has increased in northern California. As a result, that region may soon experience a decline in identification as well.

While the sense of identification in southern California may be weaker than that in the north, there is at least one obvious sense of regionalism within the state—north versus south*—that has a long and significant history. Much of that regional conflict is rooted in the failure of San Francisco and the northern areas to keep pace with southern growth.

As the first major gateway to California and center of the state's commerce, culture, and politics, following the gold rush era, San Francisco dominated the state until the early 1920s. Not until the reapportionment of 1921 was it clear that southern California had grown larger than the north. The ensuing political fight over apportionment of the state's legislature dragged on for five years until a compromise constitutional amendment in 1926 converted apportionment of the state senate from population to counties. Since the north had 44 counties to the south's 7, this guaranteed the less populated north control of one legislative house. The reapportionment conflict greatly increased a sense of regional identification in the north.

The north, particularly San Francisco, never recovered from the psychic jolt of being in second place. Old World cultured, the "Paris" of the West with a strong sense of the past, San Francisco and its northern satellites view

---

*"North" and "south" have various definitions. But certainly, the most commonly used division falls along the Tehachapi Mountains, which run east and west separating the southern seven counties from the rest of the state. The southern counties are: Imperial, Los Angeles, Orange, Riverside, San Bernardino, San Diego, and Ventura. They contain 57 percent of the state's population.

the south and southern growth with both fear and distaste. New World growing, young with an eye to the future, Los Angeles and southern California have an equally jaundiced view of San Francisco's decadence.

Court ordered reapportionment of the state senate in 1965 destroyed the north's lawmaking veto, weakening the region politically and heightening its apprehensions. The north has good reason for fear because there are significant differences between the two regions. In the 1920s and 1930s Prohibition divided the state with the south supporting Prohibition while the north opposing it. The differences are commonly attributed to the larger Catholic population in the north, and the fundamentalist Protestants in the south.[9]

Ironically, for the past 30 years, the allocation of the state's water resources has also divided the state along "wet" and "dry" lines. About 70 percent of the state's population lives south of Sacramento, while about 70 percent of its water is north of it. The south, which wants to bring some of that water to its thirsty cities and farms, prevailed in 1960 with approval by voters of a $1.75 billion water project. However, in June 1982, the south lost out when voters rejected a subsequent water project. In both cases the vote divided along regional lines.

Sometimes the issues are less serious. A 1981 Field Survey showed that opinion about the proposed move of the Oakland Raiders football team to Los Angeles had a distinct regional flavor.[10] Northerners wanted the Raiders to stay in Oakland, southerners wanted them to move south.

The north-south split goes beyond questions of political power in the legislature, the economics of water, or matters of regional pride in the Oakland Raiders. On many ballot measures and in a number of elections, the north has shown itself to have a more liberal style and political philosophy than has the south.

There are frequently north-south differences in presidential, gubernatorial and even minor statewide executive elections. One of the most famous north-south splits occurred in the 1964 GOP presidential primary when Arizona's Senator Barry Goldwater defeated New York's Governor Nelson Rockefeller. The south went for Goldwater, the north for Rockefeller. Goldwater went on to win his party's nomination at the Cow Palace (ironically) in San Francisco. Probably the most interesting ideological regional conflict within the Democratic party occurred in 1972 when U.S. Senator George McGovern and Vice-President Hubert Humphrey split the state north and south with Humphrey cast as the "conservative" candidate.

Several philosophical-ideological differences between north and south have emerged in response to ballot measures such as allowing the death penalty, permitting homosexuals to be teachers, state budget limits, a cut in the state's income tax, fair housing, loyalty oaths, school busing, obscenity controls, marijuana controls, and "right to work" laws.

The fundamental causes for these north-south differences are not clear. Sometimes it appears that the difference is more in life style than in political ideology. Several recent public opinion polls show no statistically significant regional differences in political ideology. Moreover, a systematic examination of the standard demographic, social, and economic variables revealed no significant differences by region.[11] The findings did suggest, as have others, that the south's more conservative politics might in part be due to: the region's conservative press; the historically weaker position of organized labor; the larger Catholic (European) population in the north; and perhaps some selective migration of fundamental Protestants in the south. Finally, they suggested that the larger proportion of migrants in the south may contribute to the region's conservatism.

One political correlate of the north-south split in California, however, is clear: the Republican party appears to be becoming a southern regional party. While 56 percent of the state's current assembly seats are in the south, 65 percent of the GOP assembly members are from the south. Conversely, Democratic assemblymen are disproportionately from the north.

Political expectations in California are complex and diverse within the state, flowing from regional-community identification, social and economic characteristics, and supposedly from the various political cultures. These expectations operate within the pervasive influence of reforms instituted between 1911 and 1913 by a group of progressive Republicans who were part of a national reform movement of that era.[12]

Following completion of the transcontinental railroad in 1869, the Southern Pacific Railroad and its corporate allies gained increasing power over California's economy and government. By the turn of the century, the railroad controlled the state—corrupting officials, wresting lucrative concessions from the government, and charging "what the traffic would bear." Perhaps the most succinct description was provided by Fremont Older, a leading newspaper reporter of the time.

> In those days there was only one kind of politics and that was corrupt politics. It didn't matter whether a man was a Republican or a Democrat. The Southern Pacific controlled both parties, and he either had to stay out of the game altogether or play it with the railroad.[13]

Indeed, descriptions of corruption and abuse rival those often associated with traditional eastern big-city machines.

Against this, arose a politically moderate, virulently reform-minded group of progressive Republicans who were able to take advantage of a spectacular criminal trial involving political corruption in San Francisco, and a major tactical error by the railroad in the 1910 elections. Following their upset victory, progressives lashed out in several directions at once to destroy the vehicles of corruption and place in voter's hands direct instruments of control. Thus, they eliminated partisan local elections, established cross-filing in partisan primary elections, established home rule, extended civil service, instituted the direct primary, and restructured statutory party organizations. In addition, they instituted the holy trilogy of direct democracy—the initiative, referendum, and recall. All of this badly weakened the state's party organizations.

Progressives continued to hold power until the early 1920s when the drama of reform spent itself and the state returned to quieter politics. Most of the reforms, however, remain in effect and wield substantial influence today, 70 years later. These progressive reforms significantly altered political expectations. Broadly speaking, Californians expect government to be honest, efficient, responsive, and not very partisan or ideological. On the whole, they get it.

The fact that the progressive reforms of 1911–1913 survived over time, in spite of the massive in-migrations from other states and other divergent political cultures, is amazing. Certainly, the literature about California is replete with examples of different and even conflicting cultures. One of the most insightful and potentially useful descriptions of those different cultures can be found in Daniel Elazar's *American Federalism*, in which he develops and examines three American political subcultures—Moralist, Individualist, and Traditionalist.[14] According to Elazar, all three of these subcultures can be found in California within various geographic areas. Elazar's sub-state data shows that California is an amalgam of Moralist and Individualist political cultures with a strong pocket of Traditionalist in the south, particularly in San Diego, and the southern part of the central valley.

Californians have traditionally been supportive of government. In part, at least, this support flows from the highly visible and successful progressive political reform movement of the early 1900s. While the successes and failures of the progressive reforms are open to debate, a very positive image of those reforms lives on today in the press and in the school texts.

However, as a general proposition, confidence in government is lower today than it was ten years ago. In 1981, a random sample of the state's adult population was asked, how much confidence they had in 34 public and private institutions.[15] Compared to similar surveys starting in 1973, levels of confidence in those institutions examined have dropped across the board with the exception of the U.S. Supreme Court. But the mercurial nature of Golden State politics may obscure the extent and nature of this erosion in public support. New issues, personalities, and protest movements come and go, seemingly overnight. The great California tax revolt is a case in point.

Proposition 13, the 1978 property tax-cut initiative, was hailed across the nation as the beginning of a mighty new political movement. However, in 1980, just two years later, California's voters rejected another initiative measure that would have cut the state's income tax in half. On the other hand, in 1982, voters approved a ballot measure abolishing the state's inheritance tax, while at the same time approving several bond issues. Lipset and Schneider suggest that the tax revolt was not an attack on the welfare state or part of any conservative resurgence; rather, they assert, it was rooted in perceptions of government waste, the behavior of government officials, and the ravages of inflation.[16] Their analysis suggests that people still want all of the governmental services they have become accustomed to. In short, they argue, the tax revolt was specific to an issue and not general to government as a whole.

Lipset and Schneider notwithstanding, there are some broad trends that clearly indicate the dimensions and perseverence of declining confidence in government. For example, in times of distress the number of initiative measures seems to increase. During the 1930s, after the Depression hit, 66 initiative measures qualified for titling and circulation, although only a few got enough signatures to actually get on the ballot. No other decade, previously or subsequently, had such a high number of initiatives circulating until the 1970s. In that decade, Watergate, Viet Nam, taxes, crime, inflation, school busing, and a whole host of controversies and problems generated high levels of public discontent. During that time, 140 initiative measures were titled and circulated—a record number. According to a recent press release from the state's attorney general, 65 initiatives qualified for titling and circulation in 1980 and 1981. At that rate, the 1980s will see another record number of over 300 initiative measures being circulated for signatures.

It is important, however, to distinguish between support levels for specific government programs or attitudes about specific taxes, and generalized expressions of confidence in government in the abstract. A recent statewide survey found substantial support for all standard state government programs, with very little negative opinion about any of them.[17] Moreover, a subsequent poll indicated that Californians are ready to spend more money in most public and human service areas and cut back in only a few, such as environmental protection programs and business regulations.[18] Thus, not only do the state's citizens voice support for most state programs, but in most cases they are also willing to spend more money on these programs. It is not surprising then that neither political party nor ideology is very much associated with such positions.

As suggested above, specific program support does not translate into general confidence in state and local government. In comparing current confidence levels in specific public and private institutions, the federal government clearly evoked more confidence than did state and local government.[19] Also, private institutions such as TV and newspapers and "action groups," such as consumer protection, scored slightly higher than did most state and local government institutions. More telling, perhaps, are the rankings achieved by most of the state and local institutions. With the exception of "local police," which evoked very high levels of confidence, and "local government," which essentially broke even in terms of positive and negative responses, all other state and local institutions generally evoked negative appraisals.* Thus, while Californians appear to have little confidence in most state and local institutions, they also feel most government programs are important and should be funded. These findings support the argument that the widely touted tax revolt may have been more a comment

---

*As one might reasonably expect, there are differences in the levels of confidence between whites, blacks, and Hispanics. For example, whites have substantial confidence in the president, but blacks do not. Interestingly, Hispanics have a confidence level in police similar to that of whites. Overall, of the six state and local governmental institutions surveyed, whites are mildly negative, blacks are substantially negative, but Hispanics are mildly positive in their confidence levels.

on citizens' feelings about the ability of state and local government to use revenues wisely and efficiently than an ideological rejection of government sponsored activities.

POLITICAL STYLE: REFORMERS AND PROFESSIONALS

Given the wide cultural variations within California, it would be surprising if there were not wide variations in political style, and there are. The style of leaders and activists is open, moderate, and at the local level, usually amateur.* Most elected officials serve part-time. Of some 24,000 elected officials in the state, no more than a few hundred occupy full-time positions. Of these few hundred, however, the dominant style is increasingly professional. In a state that is so heavily dominated by the media and where Hollywood is more than just a place, political style, in some cases, often becomes substance.

Modifying fundamental style patterns are specific political situations. Clearly, California's major political executives such as the governor, many statewide officials, and the large-city mayors, exhibit a different political style than does the lawmaker in the state legislature or on the city council, the bureaucrat, the judge, or the lobbyist. Moreover, while most local officials are "parochial" in scope, state officials tend to take a more "global" view of their activities. This is clearly the case for elected executives, with the governor's interests reaching out far beyond the state's borders.

Elected executives in California tend to be personable and, if not charismatic, highly articulate. This may be a function of political Darwinism, since most of these executives rely heavily on media campaigns to achieve office. These officeholders almost uniformly exhibit pragmatic, nonideological, managerial, and usually nonpartisan styles. In addition, the presidential potential of the governor and U.S. senators tends to enhance this "professional" dimension. Moreover, the state's professional campaign managers, public-relations firms, and media managers exhibit a hardball rigidly professional style—which is what their clients seek.

Legislators are not quite as often personable or articulate. "Service" is a theme often heard at the state level, while "duty" is more the local style. More "trustee" than "delegate" and most often "politico," state legislators increasingly exhibit a highly pragmatic, nonpartisan style.[20] Until the mid-1960s, state legislators were clearly "amateur." But following a major constitutional amendment leading to a full-time, highly paid legislature,

---

*"Amateur" style does not necessarily mean amateur abilities. Many local governments are blessed with a large number of people who devote considerable time, energy, and skills to them. While they are part-time and paid little or nothing, they provide a broad range of interpersonal skills and technical abilities to their cities, schools, counties, and other local governments.

legislators have assumed a somewhat more professional style. Most legislators now view their job in a statewide framework.[21] This professional style is further enhanced by the essentially trustee-politico representational role most legislators have assumed in recent years. Given the very large size of California's legislative districts, being a delegate is difficult to impossible.

In contrast, local lawmakers, city council members, county supervisors, and school and special district board members exhibit the amateur style more in keeping with their usually part-time situation. With no independently elected executive (except in a handful of cities), and operating within a nonpartisan, unicameral setting, compromise rather than conflict becomes the norm, and notions of civic duty as well as localism dominate.[22] According to a study of 82 San Francisco Bay Area city councils, a benevolent governing style is most frequently the norm.[23] This style is, essentially, the "City Father" orientation within the basic California local nonpartisan system. It is not so very different from the classic "trustee" legislative orientation except that in most California cities, council members are part-time officials who have previously been involved in several other aspects of city life and governance. Most have served on one or more commissions or boards such as traffic, planning, parks and recreation, and many have worked with community volunteer groups such as homeowners, rotary, and parent-teachers associations.

Judicial styles are nonpartisan and largely apolitical. Recently, an unprecedented number of election challenges to judges has caused substantial discussion and some consternation over the "politicization" of California's judiciary. California judges are subject to a form of "referendum" election at the end of their terms, but few have been challenged and even fewer rejected; reelection has become, traditionally, pro forma. In keeping with a modern judiciary, there is a strong professional and even specialist style among most judges combined with a technical and traditional orientation.

In partisan terms, there is considerably more variation in style among Democrats than Republicans. This is because the GOP is fairly homogeneous, being largely white, middle-class, urban Protestant, well-educated, and middle-aged or elderly. Republican style is usually analogous to Republican politics—conservative, dull, technically precise, and managerial. Now and then, a dynamic personality like Ronald Reagan, or a maverick such as S.I. Hayakawa emerges, but not very often.

Democratic style is considerably more variable. Flamboyant ethnic; blue-collar solid; hilltop liberal-ideological; radical-guild student; pragmatic technocrat; fundamentalist Protestant; urban Jew; Irish Catholic and more recently Mexican Catholic—the variations are almost endless. Perhaps equally significant, Democrats appear to enjoy politics more than do Republicans. In 1981, Assemblywoman Jean Moorhead crossed the political aisle, abandoning the GOP and re-registering as a Democrat. While attending her first Democratic party caucus she was called upon for a brief speech. Afterward, she reported: "What I said was that for two years I had listened to [the Democrats] on the other side of the wall, and it sounded like they had more fun."[24]

One clear-cut indication of the substantial assimilation of migrants into the state's social and political system is the large number of elected officials who were born out-of-state. Twenty of California's 43 congressmen (47 percent) were born in another state.* Similarly, 62 percent of the state's assembly members in 1975 were from out of state. It is not uncommon for several members of the assembly to be foreign born; Hungary, New Zealand, Iraq, England, and the Netherlands have all been recently "represented" in the legislature. Legislators from northern California are more likely to be natives than are those from southern California.

Cross-cutting most styles in California is a strong reform dimension. Rooted in the moralist political culture and reenforced by the prevailing political mores, reform is more than a theme or condition, it has become an essential ingredient in style. Concomitantly, the "eastern" style of up-front, *quid pro quo* hardball politics, for naked advantage, seldom appears. California's politics has become "hardball," particularly at the state level, but it is usually masked in moralistic terms and often conducted in a manner somewhat reminiscent of international diplomacy.

In keeping with the state's moralist political culture and reform tradition, the style of California's political process is basically open, bureaucratic, and innovative at both the state and local levels. However, while state government tends to be "professional" and "high-pressure," local government tends to be "amateur" and "low-pressure."

The open process was well illustrated and enhanced by passage of the state's Fair Political Practices Act of 1974. That act, among other things, requires detailed quarterly reports by capitol lobbyists about their legislative and administrative agency contacts, as well as reports of campaign contributions and expenditures. These requirements, combined with very substantial press coverage, have served to sensitize public officials and citizens about conflict of interest problems, campaign finance, and lobbying practices.

State legislative committee votes are recorded. This procedure provides considerable knowledge about lawmakers' positions on legislation and is particularly important since about 90 percent of the legislation that is approved in committee goes on the consent calendar. Again, intensive press coverage plus lobbyists' reports to interest group clients serve to inform at least the interested public of the political activities of the legislature.

Local government receives considerably less attention from the major urban press, but there are over 100 local community newspapers that specialize in local news. There are usually a number of local groups that keep a critical eye on the city council, county board of supervisors, and school

---

*In 1981 the state gained two more congressional districts as a result of the 1980 census, bringing the total delegation to 45 in 1982.

board. Some of these are the traditional citizen groups such as the chamber of commerce, homeowners, downtown businessmen, and parent-teacher associations. Since these groups are major recruitment sources of local elected officials, they do not often tend to be broadly critical. However, in some communities, frequently campus towns such as Berkeley, Santa Monica, Davis, Chico, or Santa Cruz, highly mobilized leftist groups (often a part of Tom Hayden's Campaign for Economic Democracy) have considerable clout. The average number of local recalls on the ballot each year (about 44) suggests a fairly high level of political attention and information on the part of some citizens.

At the state level, the process is clearly professional. Particularly since the progressive reforms of 1911–1913, the state's bureaucracy has converted to a merit system, and since the professionalization of the state's legislature in 1966, lawmakers are on a par with the state's elected executives as full-time professionals. The larger local governments have followed suit, and as a result, government in California has a substantial professional and technical tone. Professional managers or chief administrative officers give most local governments a strong bureaucratic "nonpolitical" flavor. As a result of the state's size, multiple constituencies, and professional bureaucracy, government has become less accessible to its citizens in recent years.

Innovation appears to be another major component of California's political process style. Comparative studies consistently show the state's government to be one of the most innovative.[25] California has become an "early distant warning system" and, for some, a model of the future.[26] Indeed, California's reputation as a reform leader has become so great that it is sometimes credited with leading the way when, in fact, it has not. Thus, the state's 1978 Proposition 13 tax initiative was widely hailed as the opening gun in a national tax revolt. In fact, several other states had previously instituted similar reforms but their actions did not attract much attention. Similarly, quite a few writers have cited California's Fair Political Practices Act (Proposition 9, 1974) as the first of its kind. In fact, California's initiative was based on an earlier Washington plan. When reform happens in most states, it usually is not news, but when it happens in California, it usually is news.

Finally, nonpartisanship, even at the state level, is a significant component of the California process style. No more striking recent example could be found than the appointment by Democrat Jerry Brown of a Republican, B.T. Collins, as his executive secretary. Earlier, Collins had served as the governor's legislative affairs secretary. Interestingly, Republican Collins had considerably better relations with the Democratic controlled legislature than did the governor. This is not to say that party is never important. The governor's appointments often have a partisan dimension and those selected must not only be competent but of the correct party and/or philosophical persuasion. In the legislature, such issues as reapportionment, the budget and taxes, welfare, and labor evoke party conflict, particularly in the lower house.

At the local level, with few exceptions, partisanship is not relevant. Recruitment into the city council is most frequently a result of civic activities.[27] In only a handful of large cities does party become relevant. Once in a while some local party group or leader tries to achieve partisan advantage in local government. Sometimes a member of the legislature will try to build a more powerful political base by supporting candidates for city council, county supervisor, or the school board on a partisan basis. But generally party has little influence in local politics.

POLITICAL INTERACTION: COMPETING FOR HIGH STAKES

Political organization in California appears to be about the same as in the other 49 states. There are the three traditional branches of government, and also political parties, interest groups, lobbyists, and the media. Each of these can be considered a vital part of any state's political organization. In addition, California has some relatively unusual political components in the way of direct democracy, campaign management firms, and some interesting variants of volunteer political groups. How these usual and unusual components are combined, their interaction and effects, tell a lot about politics and government in the Golden State.

Political participation in California can be measured in several ways: the proportion of eligible citizens who register; turnout at elections; the extent to which voters mark a complete ballot; the extent to which "average" citizens are a source of campaign funds; the extent to which citizens participate in volunteer groups; or the extent to which citizens access the system through a third party or nonpartisan avenues. In California all these patterns consistently point to declining levels of citizen participation.

Political participation, as measured by voter turnout, exhibits two distinct patterns.[28] In presidential election years, the percentage of registered voters going to the polls showed a slow but steady increase from 1928 through 1960, rising from 79 percent to 88 percent. After 1960, participation steadily declined, reaching 77 percent of registered voters, which was just over 50 percent of the state's eligible voters in 1980. On the other hand, during that same period, participation in state elections fluctuated widely, moving sharply upward during the Depression decade to 75 percent and then dropping down to a low point of 59 percent during World War II. From 1942 to 1958, the trend was upward again, reaching 79 percent. After 1958, participation levels slowly dropped, bottoming out at 65 percent in 1974 and then turning slightly upward.

A close examination of turnout levels over the last twenty years suggests that Watergate, lowering the voting age to 18, and a general increase in citizen disaffection have been at work, as is shown in Figure 2.1. Indeed, the rather precipitous slump in 1974 is due in large part to the combined effects of Watergate and the 18-year-old vote. Without these two events, the 1958

FIGURE 2.1. Voter Participation 1958–1982

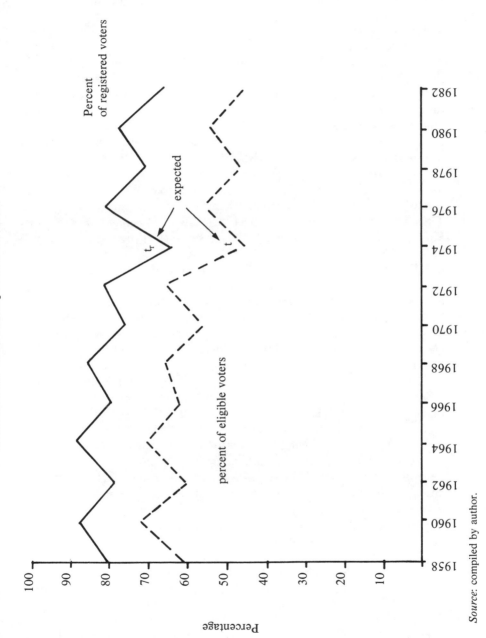

Source: compiled by author.

to 1970 trend line would have predicted a participation level some nine points higher, as is shown by the "expected" turnout in Fig. 2.1. Thus, the recent upturn in participation may be no more than a short term phenomenon that represents a restoration from the doubly depressing impact of Watergate and the lowering of the voting age.

Parallel with the steady decline in recent California voter participation has been a steady increase in minor party and independent voter registrations. Earlier in California's history, when the state was strongly one-party Republican, some 15 percent of the registered voters were affiliated with third parties or classified as Independents. That proportion of voters declined quickly between 1928 and 1936 when it bottomed-out at 4 percent. Then, during the 1960s and 1970s, the trend began a slow increase. By 1980, minor party and Independent registration reached 12 percent.

Voter participation in California is also influenced by some aspects of the state's election code. Local elections are frequently conducted independently of state and presidential elections and they are all nonpartisan. Thus, while statewide voter turnout in 1962 was 78 percent, turnout in the San Francisco Bay Area local elections in 1961–62 ranged typically between 23 and 67 percent with some elections attracting as few as 1 percent to 3 percent of registered voters.[29] These low turnouts tend to occur in special districts holding elections at odd times with no other question on the ballot except selection of two or three members to the district's governing board. Since few people are even aware of the district's existence, let alone what it does, not many go to the polls. On the other hand, county government elections are consolidated with the statewide elections and elicit a relatively high level of turnout.

One other significant component of the decline in political participation is surely the increase in minority population that has been growing at a more rapid rate than the white population. A recent analysis of the 1980 elections reported that while 60 percent of adult whites went to the polls, only 35 percent of adult blacks and 25 percent of adult Hispanics voted.[30]

Another facet of citizen participation is the Progressives' legacy of direct democracy, the initiative, petition referendum and recall. California is one of a half dozen states where continuous and substantial use of both the initiative and recall is a political fact of life. However, while the recall is typically a grass-roots device, the initiative is most often the tool of militant organizations or of the larger or more wealthy interest groups.

In recent years, initiative use has grown rapidly, but numbers tell only part of the story; the subjects offered to the voters via initiative tell another part. Political reform; tax reform; obscenity control; decriminalizing marijuana; "right to work"; environmental protection; nuclear energy restrictions; school busing/segregation; death penalty; rent control; and restrictions on homosexual teachers, guns, and smokers are only some of the moral and economic reform issues appearing on the California ballot in recent years.

Typically, about 70 percent of initiatives fail because they are not well thought out, have major policy faults, offend a militant minority, are confusing, complex, or badly worded. Moreover, of those approved by the voters, most are struck down by the courts on constitutional grounds. Often they fall victim to sophisticated and expensive media attacks. Initiative campaigns are essentially 30-second spot, short-slogan media campaigns. Since initiatives have neither personality nor party, media campaigns are the only way to reach the voter and very large amounts of money have been spent on some of them. For example, in 1978 tobacco companies poured over $6 million into their successful effort to defeat a smoking regulation ballot measure.

There has never been a successful statewide recall, but it is a device that has been frequently used with considerable success at the local level. Half of those recalls that qualify lead to success in removing the challenged local officeholder. The pain of voter rejection has been experienced about equally by county, city, and school officials. In the 1970s there was an average of 44 local recall elections per year in California. At almost any given moment, somewhere in the state, some beleagured elected official is fighting a recall action.

Traditionally, political party is considered to be the core of political articulation in Western democratic systems. In California, as elsewhere, the concept and implementation of "party" is highly complex and includes: statutory organization; volunteer groups; candidate and citizen identification; voter registration and preference; and the structure within and between formal governmental organizations.

The statutory political party in California is essentially meaningless. County central committees are elected by assembly or county supervisoral districts in what often resembles a lottery. They have neither money nor a grass-roots membership and are denied by law from making pre-primary election endorsements. The state central committees are similarly ineffective. Membership is controlled by the party's nominees, which are usually the incumbents. These committees are typically debating societies, though now and then they may be used to funnel a few dollars to deserving party candidates. Law also prevents the state central committees from making pre-primary endorsements and these committees have no effective articulation with the county committees.

In order to at least partially fill the organization void, both Republicans and Democrats developed volunteer groups that could make pre-primary endorsements, raise some campaign money, and field a few precinct workers. In particular, the California Republican Assembly, organized in the 1930s, became a political power in the 1940s and 1950s. Democrats developed a similar organization in 1952–53, the California Democratic Council (CDC). However, the CDC never developed much political muscle. When Democrats captured control of the state in 1958 (due largely to factors other than the CDC), party incumbents soon discovered the liberal volunteer group was often an election embarrassment. The volunteers, in turn, were not happy with their party's incumbents' tendency to compromise on issues. In

Congress, in the early 1960s, the Republican assembly was caught up in a conservative-moderate power struggle within the GOP that soon rendered it ineffective. Neither volunteer group, nor others like them, are meaningful in contemporary California politics, except in a few local areas.

The one clear-cut exception to this generalization has been the Campaign for Economic Democracy (CED), organized by Tom Hayden after the 1976 U.S. Senate elections. A relatively small group of about 12,000, CED members are usually highly-motivated liberal Democrats or members of a minor left-wing party. To date, they have restricted their activities to local politics and issues, such as rent control and toxic waste dumps. As a result, they have enjoyed significant if limited success in a half dozen elections and have about 50 members or close allies holding elective office around the state. Reminiscent of some earlier ideologically motivated volunteer groups, the CED has attracted both young and old to political activity.[31] In 1982, Hayden successfully ran as a Democrat for the state assembly from a west Los Angeles district. But the compromises required to be an effective state lawmaker may blunt the CED's ideological fervor in the near future.

As in other states, political party is a major factor in structuring elections. A serious candidate runs as either a Democrat or a Republican. While third party and independent candidates often run for both legislative and statewide office, they do not win and seldom amass many votes. That is about as far as party goes in candidate strategy. Incumbents typically build personal organizations that last only as long as they stay in office. Party factions coalesce around elected officials. Whichever party is out of power (does not hold the governor's office), tends to be split by competing factions. More and more, regardless of power or ideology, elections are being decided by money and media, not by organization. This places a premium on personality and the "fresh face."

In the legislature, there has been a clear, though fluctuating trend toward increasing partisanship. As noted above, key policy issues engender partisan vote splits. In addition, the selection of legislative leadership is increasingly partisan and key committee chairs are usually members of the majority party. Perhaps most significant is the central partisan campaign role played by both assembly and senate leadership. Party caucuses, unknown 25 years ago, now play an important role in legislative politics.

"Party" is also important to many of California's voters. The overwhelming majority of voters are registered with one of the two major parties and about one-third of them believe that it makes a "great deal of difference" which party is in power.[32] In California, about a third of the electorate identify "strongly" with one of the two major parties. About 40 percent are "weak" identifiers, while the remainder call themselves Independents, assert "no preference," or identify with a third party. Thus, party can be important in elections when no other voting clues are available. Nevertheless, personality and issues easily cross cut party lines, particularly in statewide elections where the electronic media play a substantial campaign role.

This helps explain why Republicans can, and do, win statewide office more easily than they win legislative offices. A personable GOP candidate, utilizing mass media, can overcome the Republican party's minority status. Thus, even in the most disastrous of party years, Republicans have won at least one major statewide election every two years since 1960. Yet only once during this period did they win a majority in either legislative house; in the 1969–70 session, they controlled the state assembly.

While party organizations are essentially weak, the state's interest groups are concomitantly powerful. According to some comparative analyses, California is considered a moderately strong interest group state.[33] In the eyes of others, the state's interest groups are quite strong and persuasive. Bell and Price observe that for much of California's history, lobbyists have exerted substantial power in the legislature and the rest of state government.[34] Absent any countervailing power, such as might be provided by strong political parties or alternative sources of campaign funding like public financing, interest group strength is checked only by massive publicity, elected officials, or by some balance of power among competing groups. Since few legislative or governmental decisions are of broad interest, the media seldom discuss most of them. Hence, the media seldom exert comprehensive pressure on lobbyists. Also, when elected officials are beholden to interest groups for campaign contributions, there is some limit on the amount of the countervailing power or restraint placed on lobbyists by legislators or executives.

Most elected officials, however, are not in any real position of individual power to deliver for any particular interest group. Perhaps most important, few interest groups make such substantial contributions that they can reasonably expect to have unwarranted influence with any elected official. Given the vast amounts of money collected for a campaign, no one group contributes a large part of it. Probably, in the long run, interest groups exert influence simply because they are the only voice heard and, frequently, the legislator or administrator is predisposed toward the lobbyist's position anyway.

There are literally hundreds of lobbyists at the state capital; over 600 registered in 1981 under the requirement of state law. Lobbying is a full-time job and big business in Sacramento. Even if the legislature were part-time, the other governmental agencies would continue to operate year-round. In 1980, over $31 million was spent by lobbyists to influence government policy. The largest share, over $14 million, was spent by business, insurance, and financial interests, which is not surprising, since half of the interest groups registered in 1981 were from business, finance, and insurance.

In the pre-reform era before 1974, one ex-legislator-turned-lobbyist John Quimby recalled: Thursday was "Moose Milk", a lavish marvelous luncheon with lots of food, open bar, and good cigars; Tuesday was the "Derby Club" for lunch and drinks; and Wednesday the "Clam and Corral" at the Senator Hotel.[35]

The amount now spent on entertaining is relatively small. In 1980 the total was $116,581, an average of less than $25 a month per "key" legislative personnel; this includes 120 lawmakers and about 280 staff. Indeed, compared to the "good old days" entertainment has largely disappeared. The traditional watering holes around the capitol are relatively deserted now compared to the three-to-four deep crowds at the bars before reforms.

Recently, lobbying has become a corporate enterprise, with 39 such lobbying firms registered in 1981. These corporate firms employ 6 to 7 lobbyists and may have 20 to 30 clients. Lobby firms tend to be like law firms in that they will take on any client absent a conflict of interest. They tend to stress "access" and often hire as lobbyists people with previous government experience. These firms often employ legislative staff and former lobbyists from other state agencies, but contrary to popular belief, there are very few ex-legislators (fewer than 20 out of 600) in the lobbyist ranks.

The individual lobbyist, however, is still the mode in Sacramento. Four out of five represent a single client and they usually have a substantial expertise in their clients' interests. Many achieve great influence simply because they know more about a given subject than almost anyone else. In addition, several lobbies have very sophisticated statewide communication networks and are well-situated in most community power networks. They also make substantial campaign contributions. Some lobbyists make good money, and a few are reputed to make over $100,000 a year. Annual billings for the top ten lobbying organizations in 1980 were over $200,000 each, while the top firm billed $625,000.

Regardless of the lobbyist's style, background, or clientele, lobbying has become a highly complex and demanding profession in the Golden State. Symptomatic of this is the existence of two firms that provide daily computerized information on all pending bills. Lobbyists may subscribe to a wide range of information, the tracking of a specific bill, of all bills assigned to a specific committee, or of all bills of a particular kind. Lobbyists may even set up their own computer terminals and plug into a firm's data bank. Interestingly, the lobbyists utilized this information source before the legislature went "on line" in 1982. With approximately 7000 bills introduced in each two-year session, the computer makes sense.

One of the key arguments for the 1966 legislative reorganization was that a full-time, professional, well-staffed legislature would be less subject to lobbyist domination. Nevertheless, lawmakers still have very close relationships with lobbyists. These people continue to provide information about the substance of proposed legislation, the position of their clients on legislation, and frequently their own view of the political consequences of legislation. The 1966 reformers ignored the fact that lobbyists are a prime source of draft legislation. A recent and only partially completed study of the 1981–1982 legislative session found that about one-third of all bills introduced were prepared by a special-interest group. Lobbyists also perform much of the legislative leg-work for harried lawmakers, including meeting with other lobbyists to iron out differences and resolve conflicts. In point of fact,

California's lawmakers generally view interest groups as both necessary and legitimate and only a few lawmakers develop negative attitudes toward lobbyists after serving in the legislature.[36]

More recently, the increasing amounts of money spent on campaigns has made the lobbyist/interest group component a central part of a legislator's reelection plans. Even eight years after the approval of a major political reform initiative, Proposition 9, which was designed to curb lobbyists' power, interest groups wield as much—or perhaps more—power than before in Sacramento.

The press represents another kind of interest group. For some years the media have played a vital role in California's political process. Media have replaced the traditional precinct worker; TV, radio, newspapers, and computerized letters now carry the message in California.

Before radio and TV, print media was the dominant force in California politics. In particular, the Republican triumvirate of the *Los Angeles Times*, the Oakland *Tribune*, and the San Francisco *Examiner-Chronicle*, were powerful not only because of their circulation, but also because they were located in the state's major population areas and often spoke for (and dictated to) the state's Republican party. With a monopoly on public information, the state's major newspapers set the policy agenda, defined the alternatives, and trumpeted their position with unabashed fervor.[37]

Many would agree that it was Kyle Plamer, political editor/manager for the *Times*, who made Richard Nixon's early career. Much of the press' Republican power came from the fundamental organizational weakness of the GOP, the Democratic party's inability to successfully compete, and the obscuring effects of cross-filing. However, times have changed. Today, the press is fragmented and highly competitive. The size of the state, with substantial distances between major urban areas, means that newspaper, radio, and TV are limited in circulation to a minority of the state's population. Only the *Los Angeles Times*, Sacramento *Bee*, and the former Oakland *Tribune*, recently renamed *East Bay Today*, have significant circulation outside their home counties. In most urban areas there is more than one daily newspaper and more than one major TV and radio network station. Only three newspapers, the San Diego *Union*, the San Francisco *Examiner-Chronicle*, and the San Jose *Mercury*, dominate their home counties. Thus, competition is fierce and while TV has been blamed for the demise of afternoon newspapers, it should also be credited with stimulating competition and spurring newspapers to do what they can do best—in-depth coverage and analysis. TV has also forced newspapers to tone down blatant favoritism.

Making it all go in California—lobbying, ballot measures, campaign management firms, and the press—is money. "The mother's milk of politics", according to the politically astute Jess Unruh; money is the key ingredient linking the major components of political success.

The source, essentially, of all campaign money, is interest groups. In

1980, campaign contributions to the state's legislative candidates totaled near $36 million, which was up from $22 million in 1978. When combined with the approximately $30 million spent for lobbying in 1980, the amount spent by interest groups equals two-thirds of the state legislature's annual budget of $90 million, which is funded by the tax payers. Politics in California is expensive.

Incumbent assemblymen in 1980 spent, on the average, $85,000 for reelection. Those incumbents who were under heavy pressure from a strong challenger averaged $166,000, which is also about the average cost of a race for an "open" seat. Private individual contributions accounted for less than 5 percent of the total money spent.[38] Between 1975 and 1980, 20 groups gave a total of $10 million. When combined with the lobbying costs for the five-year period, the total amount becomes truly staggering and indicates just how important government is for many interests in California.

Given the central role of legislative committees, interest group campaign contributions tend to be concentrated on legislators who are members of relevant committees. Membership on a "juice committee," such as assembly finance, assembly insurance and commerce, senate banking and commerce, and senate insurance and indemnity, is greatly desired. The first three are obvious; banks, savings and loans, and insurance companies are particularly vulnerable to governmental regulations. Government organization committees in both houses are also well known for their campaign contribution potential. The lure of "governmental organization" lies in the fact that these committees hear legislation concerned with horse racing and alcoholic beverages.

A major and uniquely California source of campaign money is Hollywood.[39] The political punch of the star has become well known nationwide, but nowhere is it so powerful or pervasive as in California. The effect is particularly pronounced in a candidate's race for national office. Individuals are limited by national law to contributions of no more than $1000. That's not much for a Robert Redford, Jane Fonda, Warren Beatty, Pat Boone, Jimmy Stewart, and so forth. But by starring in, or even by making a cameo appearance at a concert, Tinseltown luminaries can bring in tens of thousands of dollars. The Hayden-Fonda CED is substantially funded by Jane Fonda and her Hollywood connections. (Jane Fonda holds the California record for individual political contributions, having given $840,000 in gifts and loans to her husband's successful 1982 state assembly race.) Hollywood personalities are often found speaking for or against a candidate or ballot measure. A classic example was the televised debate between Charleton Heston and Paul Newman on the 1982 nuclear freeze initiative (only in California would nuclear policy be debated by Moses and Butch Cassidy). Of course, Ronald Reagan is the prime example of Hollywood clout where name, fame, money, and connections are combined.

Traditional governmental institutions in the Golden State look and behave about the same as in other states. There are, however, some differences associated with California's unusual or unique situations and conditions. Nonpartisan primary elections stifle political parties in local politics and make them essentially meaningless. Since the passage of Proposition 13 in 1978, local governments and particularly school districts and counties, have become heavily dependent upon the state for revenues. The ability of cities to raise revenue, combined with local population growth and the effects of Propostion 13 on county services, appear to have encouraged municipal incorporation and annexation. Local quasi-governmental and advisory structures have also recently emerged to fulfill some of the traditional city functions.[40]

At the state level, the governor maintains a clearly predominant political position that depends in part on his legal power and in part on circumstances, personality, and ability. In particular, the budget and item-veto make California's governor one of the more powerful in the 50 states. That power is substantially augmented by the sheer size of the state. Mounting a campaign against an incumbent governor in California is a formidable task. During the period from 1946 to 1982, incumbent governors have been defeated only once in the last seven elections in which they were challenged.

The major disadvantage facing a challenger, aside from reaching the massive electorate, is establishing a power base. In order to mount a successful campaign, a challenger must have a statewide power base of "name" and political contacts. Thus, incumbent attorney generals and other statewide officeholders are the usual gubernatorial candidates. No legislator has won the governorship since 1938 and no mayor has been elected to that office since 1930.

Even today, being mayor of Los Angeles, the state's largest city, means a political base of only 13 percent of the state's voters and a media base of 40 percent of the state's population. Based on that broader media base, many political observers believed that Los Angeles' Mayor Tom Bradley might break the mayor's "jinx" in 1982 and also become the first black elected governor of a state. However, in a last minute come-from-behind finish, Attorney General George Deukmejian won by 7 percent of the vote. Thus, holding statewide office appears to have become a prerequisite to winning the governor's office. Ronald Reagan is the only exception to that since 1938, and his household name, even in 1966, illustrates the "rule"—NAME is the game in California, and media make the NAME.

Further enhancing the governor's power is the fact that incumbent California governors are almost automatically potential presidential candidates. Three of the last five governors were presidential contenders and one made it. California's governors have learned to use television, giving them an advantage after the nominating convention. In addition, most national domestic issues are also California issues and the governor can reasonably assert and show experience in dealing with these issues when most other governors cannot. Indeed, few U.S. senators can match the domestic issue experience of California's governors.

The presidential quest, however, can also be a burden to the governor.

Jerry Brown's protracted attack of White House fever took him out of the state so often that his executive secretary, Gray Davis, was in fact very often the acting governor. Legislators naturally resented this and it hurt Brown's relations with them. His frequent absences became the subject of numerous derisive comments. As the *California Journal* described him, " . . . the governor has become King of the Road, a wandering non-nuke, pro-swami minstrel he."[41]

Being powerful and popular helps in dealing with California's legislature, which is rated as one of the nation's most professional. Being full-time and more than adequately staffed, the legislature has the ability to exercise substantial countervailing power against the governor. Further enhancing that ability is the centralized power structure within the assembly. Recent speakers, when they firmly controlled the majority party in the assembly, could meet, confer, and negotiate with the governor on an almost equal basis.

The budget always plays a central role in legislative-executive relations. It is a particularly powerful tool for fiscally conservative governors. Since the budget needs a two-thirds vote in both houses, and since neither party very often has had that two-thirds, philosophical and partisan compromises must be made. In addition, given the governor's item veto, the budget process tends to produce compromise with a conservative bias. Veto overrides are extremely rare.

District size is also an important factor protecting incumbent legislators from challenge. Assembly districts average about 300,000 in population; state senate districts are twice as large. Compared to other states' legislative districts, California's are monstrously large. On the average, less than 10 percent of challenged incumbents are defeated. Incumbency, in turn, gives legislators considerable leverage in dealing with lobbyists. The commonly heard line in Sacramento is: "I'll be here next year voting on your legislation." Lobbyists know that it is true and try to maintain good working relations with the legislators.

Power in the Golden State is divided and fragmented. Public power was, before the 1970s, fairly well balanced between local and state, with the edge often going to the locals. However, a 1971 state supreme court ruling in *Serrano* v. *Priest*, on use of the property tax as a source of funding for public education, required the state to provide $1 billion more to fund local education. In 1978, the state's voters, via Proposition 13, cut local property tax revenues by 57 percent. As a result, the state has become the prime source of funding for local schools, counties, and many special districts. Concomitantly, "local policy" is formed or at least significantly influenced in the state capital.

At the state level, there has been a significant change in power relationships. Before professionalization of California's legislature in 1966, the governor was clearly the dominant figure. However, in the early 1960s, the governor was increasingly challenged by the Assembly Speaker Jess

Unruh, who was becoming the center of power within the lower house. By the mid-1970s, the "imperial speaker" was second only to the governor in power. Recently, with increased partisanship in the state senate, the president pro tem has begun to centralize power in the upper house to some degree and has been able to successfully challenge both the assembly speaker and the governor. Outside the state capitol, however, in matters of media and style, personality and pervasive influence, the governor is still the central power.

At the local level, with over 400 cities, 58 counties, and thousands of special districts, public and private power is fragmented and divided beyond imagination. Political power is held by those who learn to lead, as San Jose's Mayor Janet Hayes recently observed.[42] The powers of office establish potential and limits but the abilities of the occupant determine the extent of power effectively utilized. Since most of California's major urban areas have experienced substantial and prolonged population growth and change, power tends to shift over time and become more diffused.

Even more than the public sector, the private power structure is fragmented and diverse. There are, of course, some "natural" informal coalitions among similar businesses, among labor unions, religious groups, and the like. However, as often as not, current issues will divide these allies. Similarly, "natural" enemies such as business and labor find themselves working together in opposition to "over zealous" environmentalists, for example. But given the diverse culture and economy of the state, a fragmented private power structure would be expected. Even so, there have been some recent attempts within the business community to form some stable coalitions. Two notable examples are the Roundtable and United for California. Roundtable is an association of presidents, chairmen, and chief executives of the state's most powerful corporations. About 75 corporate heads form the Roundtable, a veritable "Who's Who" of California business.[43] The group looks at public policy from a broad perspective, opposing Proposition 13, for example, because it felt that the tax cut might damage long-range economic growth in the state. United for California, on the other hand, is a more traditional multiple-industry pack directly involved in making campaign contributions to candidates supportive of free enterprise.

There are, of course, a large number of regional and statewide organizations—professional, occupational, production, retail, ethnic, fraternal, charitable, religious, and issue-oriented organizations—that operate as more than simple interest groups. These organizations tie together the many levels and segments of California's private power structure, frequently linking it to the public power structure, and in a weak party, nonpartisan governmental system often providing the direction and definition of public policy.

California's position within the nation and, indeed, the world, tells us much about the state. Its population, size, economic vitality and high political visibility suggests that it has greater than proportional strength at the national level. For example, California has become a "presidential state" in the last three decades with at least one contender from the Golden State in almost every election since 1960. In 1964, the state's GOP primary gave Arizona's Barry Goldwater the Republican presidential nomination. Richard Nixon was only a heartbeat away from the presidency between 1953 and 1960, before being elected to the office in 1968. Earl Warren was another serious contender for the GOP nomination in 1948. Ronald Reagan's near miss for the 1976 GOP presidential nomination and eventual 1980 win highlights the trend.

In several significant ways, California has not lived-up to its presidential potential. In recent presidential elections, the California vote has not been crucial. In 1980, both Ronald Reagan and Jimmy Carter virtually ignored the state. Reagan could take it (as well as the entire West) for granted; Carter wrote it off. In both 1960 and 1976 the state went for the loser; in 1952, 1956, 1964, 1968, and 1972 it went with the winner who did not need California votes for victory.

As one of the nation's last and largest presidential primary states, California has a reputation as a "must" state.[44] Indeed, those who lose in California seldom win their party's nomination, but the same could be said for several other large states too. Democrats have weakened California's presidential convention clout with their proportional delegate rule. On the other hand, the state's GOP delegation is strong, thanks to the continued use by Republicans of the "winner-take-all" rule. The Reagan presidency, too, has further strengthened the state's GOP delegation.

California's congressional delegation was, until the late 1970s, regarded as highly influential on Capitol Hill. Several of the delegations' members held key committee positions by virtue of seniority. On several key state issues, such as water and defense spending, the state's large delegation acted as a single unit. However, rapid turnover in the 1978 elections, due to defeat, death, and retirement, wiped out most of the delegation's seniority. The 1980 elections completed the process, engendering some sharp conflicts within the delegation. In particular, the power struggle between the late Phil Burton and Anthony Beilison exacerbated the split contributing to the loss of choice committee assignments on rules, appropriations, commerce, banking, and foreign affairs. However, both Democratic and Republican congressmen are frequently in positions of party leadership (which do not depend on seniority), particularly in the U.S. Senate.

As one of the nation's electronic media centers, California plays a key role in national and western-Pacific communications. Relatively isolated until after World War II, the state's national and international influence has recently grown quite rapidly, parallel with the growth of air transport and electronic communications.

Today, however, California's own concerns are increasingly centered on the western United States and the vast Pacific Basin areas. It is not by chance that the state's capitol faces west, toward San Francisco Bay and beyond to the Pacific. While California has not turned its back on the nation, it is substantially involved with the economics of Japan, the Phillippines, China, Indonesia, Southeast Asia, Australia, New Zealand, and the Latin American west coast nations.

California is the major gateway between the world's largest economy and the world's fastest growing region. Richard Nixon's recognition of China is better understood within the Pacific Basin context. Repeated suggestions by both President Reagan and Governor Jerry Brown for some form of Canada-U.S.A.-Mexico common market makes good sense from the "western-perspective." California banks, which have steadfastly resisted attempts by eastern financial institutions to enter the state's economy, have welcomed with open arms foreign banking institutions, particularly the Japanese.

In 1980, foreign trade accounted for 15 percent of the state's gross product and 10 percent of its employment. About one-third of California's $40 billion annual foreign trade is with Japan. In 1980, 835 Japanese firms had their U.S. headquarters in California, including 16 Japanese banks. The future of California lies not in the east but in the west. Foreign trade with the Pacific Basin promises more than does Europe.

Two fundamental forces have driven the California dream—massive migration and an abundance of natural resources. The first has been sharply altered; the second has become limited. Migration from the other states has dropped sharply, replaced by Asian and illegal Hispanic immigration. Some population estimates indicate that the state's white population will be a minority by 1990. The extent to which the new migrants will be integrated and socialized into the state's economy and political culture remains an open question.

Two key resources, energy and water, present real problems of supply and cost. California must now import expensive energy. Thus, the state's fabled car culture and romance with the freeways may be at an end. Sharply altered transportation patterns combined with high interest rates may also replace the state's low-density suburbs with high-density condominiums. The condo has already become the "starter home" of the young in California. In another generation, the young-old generation conflict may well be exacerbated not only by the faltering social security system but also by a renter-owner division.

High interest rates and energy costs will also have a direct impact on the availability of water. In the 1982 June elections, southern California voters rejected an addition to the state's basic water system that would have supplied them with additional water because it would have cost "too much." Governmental costs have also led to restrictions of federal dollars. Aside from the continued subsidy of defense expenditures, California will not receive as much federal money as in the past.

Parallel with increasing population, water, and energy problems, California's voters have ironically restricted state and local government fiscal resources. While an increasingly independent and conservative electorate may drive elected officials to seek some "quick fix", such solutions are likely to create additional difficulties in the longer run.

Regardless, California, the state of mind, the place of dreams, home of the unexpected, where progress is taken for granted and change is the status quo, will probably surprise us all in the future—as in the past.

NOTES

1. Neal Peirce, *The Megastates of America* (New York: Norton, 1972). In this massive work, Peirce devotes 130 pages to California, as compared to 117 pages for New York and 69 for Texas.

2. Mike Royko, "Should America Fence Off California?" *Los Angeles Times*, 1 April 1979.

3. Richard Scammon and Ben Wattenberg. *The Real Majority* (New York: Capricorn, 1971), p. 137.

4. Gladwin Hill, *Dancing Bear* (New York: Putnam, 1968), p. 10.

5. Neil Morgan, "The Nation Within a Nation," *Saturday Review*, 23 September 1967.

6. Joel Kotkin and Paul Grabowicz, *California Inc.* (New York: Rawson, Wage, 1982).

7. Larry J. Kimbell and David Sculman, "Growth in California," *Public Affairs Report* 21 (Berkeley: Institute of Governmental Studies, October 1980).

8. Mervin D. Field, "Living in California," *California Opinion Index* (San Francisco: Field Institute, July 1981).

9. Michael P. Rogin and John L. Shover, *Political Change in California* (Westport, Conn.: Greenwood, 1969), pp. 114, 156–57.

10. Mervin D. Field, data from a statewide survey by *California Poll*, 2–11 April 1981.

11. Raymond E. Wolfinger and Fred I. Greenstein, "Comparing Political Regions: The Case of California," *American Political Science Review* 63 (March 1969):74–85.

12. George Mowry, *The California Progressives* (Berkeley and Los Angeles: University of California Press, 1951).

13. Fremont Older, *My Own Story* (New York: Macmillan, 1926), pp. 176–77.

14. Daniel J. Elazar, *American Federalism* (New York: Crowell, 1966), pp. 73–78.

15. Mervin D. Field, "Confidence in Institutions," *California Opinion Index* (San Francisco: Field Institute, October 1981).

16. Seymour Martin Lipset and William Schneider, "Is the Tax Revolt Over?" *Taxing and Spending*, 3 (Summer 1980):73–78.

17. Mervin D. Field, data from a statewide survey by the *California Poll*, 2–8 April 1980.

18. Mervin D. Field, *California Poll*, 2–11 April 1981.

19. Mervin D. Field, "Confidence in Institutions," *California Opinion Index* (San Francisco: Field Institute, October 1981).

20. Charles G. Bell and Charles M. Price, *First Term* (Beverly Hills: Sage Publication Co., 1975), p. 54.

21. *Ibid.*, pp. 94–95, 127–31.

22. Ritchie P. Lowry, *Who's Running This Town?* (New York: Harper & Row, 1962).

23. Heinz Eulau and Kenneth Prewitt, *Labyrinths of Democracy* (Indianapolis, Ind.: Bobbs-Merrill, 1973), pp. 119–21.

24. Claudia Luther, "Do Democrats Have More Fun—or Just Less Unity?" *Los Angeles Times*, 22 March 1981, p. 3, part I.

25. See, for example, Jack Walker, "The Diffusion of Innovation Among The American States," *American Political Science Review* 63 (September 1969):880–99; Virginia Gray,

"Innovation in the States: A Diffusion Study," *American Political Science Review* 65 (December 1973):1174–85; and Fred W. Grupp, Jr. and Alan R. Richards, "Variations in Elite Perceptions of American States as Referents for Public Policy Making," *American Political Science Review,* 69 (September 1975):850–58.

26. See, for example, Kenneth Lamott, *Anti-California: Report From Our First Parafascist State* (Boston: Little Brown, 1971); and Ted K. Bradshaw, "New Issues for California, The World's Most Advanced Industrial Society," *Public Affairs Report* 17 (Berkeley: Institute of Governmental Studies, August 1976).

27. Kenneth Prewitt, *The Recruitment of Political Leaders* (Indianapolis, Ind.: Bobbs-Merrill, 1970).

28. Data from: Eugene C. Lee, *California Votes, 1928–1960* (Berkeley: Institute of Governmental Studies, 1963); Eugene C. Lee and Bruce E. Keith, *California Votes, 1960–1972* (Berkeley: Institute of Governmental Studies, 1974); and subsequent reports by the Secretary of State, *Statement of Vote,* for the years 1974 through 1982.

29. Don Koep, "Elections and Voting: Nonpartisan Patterns," *Public Affairs Report* 3 (Berkeley: Institute of Governmental Studies, August 1962).

30. Mervin D. Field, "Ethnicity and the Political Process," *California Opinion Index* (San Francisco: Field Institute, March 1982).

31. Tom Bourne, "The Prop. 13 Boost to the Hayden-Fonda Team," *California Journal* 10 (August 1979): 269–70.

32. Mervin D. Field, data from a statewide survey by the *California Poll*, 15–18 October 1980.

33. Sarah McCally Morehouse, *State Politics, Parties and Policy* (New York: Holt, Rinehart & Winston, 1981); and Wayne L. Francis, *Legislative Issues in the Fifty States* (Chicago: Rand McNally & Co., 1967).

34. Charles G. Bell and Charles M. Price, *California Politics Today* (Homewood, Ill.: Dorsey, 1980).

35. Kerry Drager, "The New Breed of Sacramento Lobbyist," *California Journal* 11 (October 1980):393–96.

36. Bell and Price, *First Term*, pp. 94–99.

37. Robert Gottlieb and Irene Wolt, *Thinking Big* (New York: Putnam, 1977).

38. Common Cause, *Twenty Who Gave $10 Million* (Los Angeles: Common Cause, 1981).

39. Michele Willens, "The Hollywood-Washington Connection," *California Journal* 10 (August 1979):265–68.

40. Alvin D. Sokolow, et al., *Choices for the Unincorporated Community* (Davis, Calif.: Institute of Governmental Affairs, 1981).

41. Herb Michelson, "Governor Gray," *California Journal* 11 (February 1980):54–56.

42. Philip Trounstine and Terry Christense, *Movers and Shakers* (New York: St. Martin's Press, 1982).

43. Tony Quinn, "The California Roundtable," *California Journal,* 10 (December 1979):427–29.

44. William J. Crotty, *Political Reform and the American Experiment* (New York: Crowell, 1977).

3
Colorado
THOMAS H. SIMMONS

To the rest of the nation, Colorado evokes images of spectacular mountains, abundant recreational opportunities, and a generally enviable quality of life. Visiting the state in 1901, Theodore Roosevelt commented that "the scenery bankrupts the English language."[1] While Coloradans prize such aspects of their state, everyday life for the majority of the state's inhabitants occurs in an urban setting. Most residents are thus well acquainted with automobile-related air pollution, rising crime rates, uncontrolled urban development, and water shortages. In the early 1970s the Colorado Land Use Commission warned that existing trends in development could result in "long-term economic deterioration" and a major decline in "the quality of life of the majority of Colorado citizens."[2] It is the tension between rapid development and preservation of the natural environment that forms the context of Colorado politics.

POLITICAL CULTURE: COLORADO—ABOVE ALL

There is little in the physical boundaries of Colorado that would seem to foster a sense of unique state identity. Journalist Joel Garreau labels "Colorado" a misleading idea, arguing that:

> . . . back when there were few people to speak of in the territory and it didn't make much difference, "Colorado" was boxed off into a neat, perfect rectangle, and now the idea it represents has been around long enough to become self-perpetuating. People speak and think of Colorado as one identifiable place, despite abundant evidence to the contrary and for little better reason than that their fathers did it that way. That does not, however, make the idea useful.[3]

Such "artificial" political entities are useful for analysis precisely because

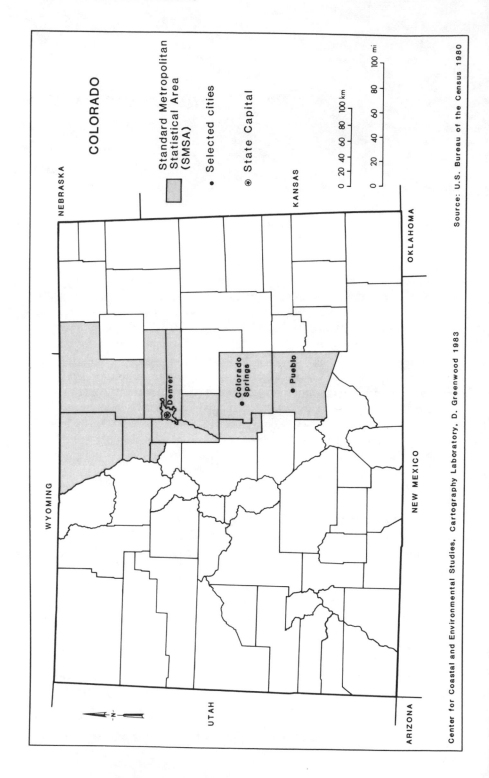

Source: U.S. Bureau of the Census 1980

Center for Coastal and Environmental Studies, Cartography Laboratory, D. Greenwood 1983

they have enduring meaning for people. Most Coloradans have a strong, positive identification with their state.

The settlement patterns of Colorado and adjacent mountain and plains states contributed to the development of individual state political identities. Daniel Elazar notes that the most intense settlement has occurred within the interior of such states, thus distancing the bulk of each state's population from that of its neighbors and "thereby reinforcing the political-cultural patterns that have developed in each."[4]

Internally, centrifugal forces exist that potentially conflict with the development of a unified state identity. Colorado's geography gives rise to a natural separation of the state into three principal divisions: the urbanized corridor along the Front Range of the Rocky Mountains, the mountains and plateaus forming the western two-thirds of the state, and the eastern plains.

The Front Range region stretches 165 miles along Interstate 25 from Fort Collins and Greeley in the north through the Denver metropolitan area to Colorado Springs and Pueblo in the south. This narrow band of land, that contains 80.5 percent of the state's inhabitants, experienced substantial subdivision development and loss of agricultural land over the past two decades. Previously separated cities have grown together and some observers foresee the emergence of a continuous strip city—a miniature Bos-Wash by the Rockies. The Denver metropolitan area, whose climate once attracted persons suffering from tuberculosis and other respiratory ailments, now has a serious air pollution problem. Automobile-related pollution, the basis of the region's problem, is aggravated by urban sprawl, an inadequate mass transportation system, and the area's high altitude.

The mountainous Western Slope was the fastest growing part of the state during the 1970s. From its earliest days the region has experienced a "boom and bust" history. The site of previous booms in gold, silver, and uranium, the region's current growth has been spurred by exploration and development of vast deposits of coal, oil, and oil shale. Many of the area's municipalities doubled or tripled their populations during the 1970s. While local boosters heralded the potential of oil shale as long ago as World War I, the industry still has not lived up to expectations. Exxon Corporation's decision in 1982 to withdraw from the multi-million dollar Colony Oil Shale Project near Rifle profoundly shook northwestern Colorado. The shutdown of the operation, coupled with a lack of federal support for such endeavors, was viewed as the beginning of another "bust" period.[5] The Western Slope, however, is not totally dependent on the energy industry; skiing, summer tourism, and agriculture remain important sectors of the area's economy.

The eastern plains, that rise gently from the Kansas border, are the state's most sparsely settled region, holding just over 5 percent of Colorado's people. More than half of the plains counties lost population during the past decade. Cattle ranching and wheat farming are dominant pursuits in the semi-arid, agriculturally oriented area. Southeastern Colorado was the birthplace of the protest-oriented American Agriculture Movement.

Socially, a north-south division also exists within the state. Pueblo and the other southern counties of the state are poorer, contain more Hispanics, and consistently vote Democratic in elections. On more than one occasion it has been suggested that all concerned would be happier if the area were detached from Colorado and joined with New Mexico. Pueblo, due to its orientation toward heavy industry, a concomitant air pollution problem, and melting-pot ethnicity, has been especially targetted for derisive comments. The attitude lingers despite recent progress in pollution-control efforts at the local steel mill and attempts to diversify the city's economic base.[6]

Issues, reflecting diversity of geography and lifestyle, have also divided the state. For the first half of the 20th century, the heavily populated areas of the state were underrepresented in the legislature and in the Congress. In the early 1960s it was possible for 29.8 percent of the population to control a majority of seats in the state senate; the minimum percentage for controlling the house was 32.1 percent. This apportionment lodged legislative control in the rural portion of the state. Both houses were redistricted on an equal population basis following the one person-one vote court decisions of the middle 1960s.

Water, too, has been a point of contention between the regions of the state. Exploring the eastern foothills and plains of Colorado in 1820, Major Stephen Long labelled the area the Great American Desert, concluding that the land was "wholly unfit for cultivation, and of course, uninhabitable by a people depending on agriculture for their subsistence."[7] Today, the Front Range possesses most of the state's population, while most of the state's water resources remain on the Western Slope. Front Range cities have defied Long's prediction by engaging in large scale transmountain appropriation of water. Without such diversions, the development of Denver, Colorado Springs, and other areas would have been impossible and further growth of this region will probably require more diversions.[8] In recent years, Denver and other metropolitan cities, faced with a shortage of treatment capacity, have imposed restrictions on lawn watering during summer months.

The dominant reality for Colorado since World War II has been tremendous population growth. In 1940 the state's population totaled just 1,123,296. Over the next 40 years, Colorado posted population increases that outpaced the national average: 1940s, 18.0 percent increase; 1950s, 32.4 percent; 1960s, 26.0 percent; and 1970s, 30.8 percent. During the last decade, Colorado was the eighth fastest growing state in the country, reporting a 1980 population of just under 2.9 million.

The principal component of Colorado's growth has been migration from other parts of the nation. Most newcomers settled in the Front Range section of the state, particularly in the ring of suburbs around Denver. By 1980 less than half of the state's residents were native-born Coloradans, compared to a national average native population of over two-thirds. The decisions of private corporations to locate major facilities or headquarters offices in the state stimulated migration. A number of high technology, energy, and defense firms, for example, settled in the Denver metropolitan area. In addition, Denver emerged in the post-World War II era as a major regional center for federal government agencies; currently, over 50,000 federal civilian and military personnel work in the Denver area.

While some conflict and resentment exist between long-term residents and recent arrivals (especially in energy boomtowns), migrants generally shed old loyalties and quickly seek assimilation. When some ambitious entrepeneur recently began selling "NATIVE" bumperstickers, demand soon developed for "SEMI-NATIVE" ones. As Elazar observed, "Most of the new Coloradans have been anxious to adapt to the Colorado way of life and, the longer they live in the state, the more like their predecessors they become."[9]

Despite the presence of such disintegrative factors as growth, geography, and divisive issues, the state's inhabitants possess a strong identification as Coloradans. The basis for this pride perhaps lies in the great physical beauty of the state and in the belief that a better quality of life is possible here. The state's new tourist motto, "Colorado—above all," is a slogan with implications beyond the elevations of the state's mountains.

Whether newcomer or native, most Coloradans seem relatively content with their state. A survey of Colorado registered voters found that 93 percent of respondents felt that the state was a "good" or "very good" place in which to live. Furthermore, over two-thirds of the sample believed that the direction of the state was improving or staying the same.[10] A separate poll of the electorate by a private polling firm revealed similar attitudes; 72 percent said that "things in Colorado are generally going in the right direction."[11]

The positive feelings most residents share stem in part from the relative strength of the Colorado economy. The unemployment rate is usually less than half that of the nation, while the median family income in Colorado exceeds the national average. One observer describes the state as "so thoroughly middle-class in income and lifestyle that most people consider the poor and minorities as problems that only other states have."[12] If not recession-proof, the state's economy appears to be at least recession-resistant.

Since Colorado represents the realization of the "good life" for most of its residents, substantial incentive exists for preserving the status quo. In assessing the 1976 election (which saw many of the Democratic gains of the 1974 Watergate election erased), the political editor of the *Denver Post* succinctly set forth the expectations of the state's voters: "Colorado, with its economic health, mountain splendor and general contentment, just wants to be left alone."[13]

Present-day Coloradans do not seem to expect a great deal from government. The majority is unwilling to embark on grandiose projects or to approve large increases in expenditures. Since recent migrants to Colorado have found a better quality of life here, they are reluctant to tamper with the existing approach to government. In addition, the personal characteristics of many newcomers to the state do not dispose them toward governmental activism.

There have been periods in Colorado's history when the electorate displayed greater willingness to experiment. In the late 19th century, the state embraced Populism, electing a Populist governor and supporting James B. Weaver for president in 1892. Colorado was the fourth state in the nation to approve women's suffrage in 1893. The Progressive movement was strong in the state from the turn of the century through World War I. Numbered among the fruits of the Progressive harvest were adoption of the initiative, referendum, and recall, passage of a primary election law, and support for various pieces of labor-related legislation.

More recent political innovations have included a fair employment law and a fair housing law in the 1950s; a liberalized abortion statute and a comprehensive reorganization and streamlining of state government in the 1960s; a state equal rights amendment, an open meetings and financial disclosure law, the creation of a commission to perform legislative redistricting and, a sunset bill to eliminate unnecessary or obsolete boards and commissions in the 1970s; and state energy tax credits for weatherization and use of alternative energy sources in the 1980s.

There is a tendency on the part of some national observers to view Colorado politics as a harbinger of national trends. A more realistic appraisal portrays the state's electorate as "at least moderately conservative despite occasional aberrations."[14] Democratic Governor Richard D. Lamm characterizes Colorado as "a progressive state in the 'human' area but conservative in the fiscal area." U.S. Representative Timothy Wirth, a moderate liberal Democrat, views the state as "a combination of pragmatism and conservatism."[15] Historically, the state has not embraced hidebound conservatism; rather, the attitude has been one of caution tempered by sufficient flexibility to adapt to changing conditions.

It would seem likely that a majority of Coloradans could be mobilized into support for greater governmental experimentation, if they could be convinced that inaction endangered the continuation of the status quo. Governor Lamm has argued for a decade that strong state efforts to control growth are necessary in order to preserve the existing quality of life. However, Lamm has had little success in building support for this position in the state legislature. The quality of life may have to further deteriorate before the public comes to support governmental action and the effectiveness of state action at that point may be greatly diminished.

Over two decades ago, William P. Irwin concluded that Coloradans were "wary" of politicians, noting that "not since William Jennings Bryan has the spark of hero worship been struck, and few political bosses worthy of the name have boasted any success."[16] Bryan received the 1908 Democratic nomination at the only major national party convention ever held in Denver and carried the state in each of his three campaigns for the presidency.

While Centennial State voters may harbor a general cynicism toward government and politics, they show moderately high levels of support for specific institutions and officeholders. A majority of registered voters rate the quality of state government as "fair" in public opinion surveys. Those describing the government as "good" or "very good," however, outnumber those giving "poor" or "very poor" evaluations by a two-to-one margin.[17]

Both the Democratic governor and GOP-dominated General Assembly receive strong approval ratings in polls. Fifty-eight percent of the state's voters approve of the conservative legislature's job performance, while an identical proportion feel the moderate-liberal governor as doing a good to excellent job.[18] The fact that the legislature and governor often vigorously disagree over appropriate state policies is not necessarily an indication that the electorate is indecisive. Some commentators on Colorado politics have suggested that voters deliberately elect a governor and legislature of opposing parties as an added check and balance on government.

State government draws more support and respect from Coloradans than does the national government. While 60 percent of residents told pollsters that they believed that state government was "efficient, responsive, or engaged in worthwhile activity," only 32 percent described the federal government in such terms. In contrast to the support state government generally received, Western Slope residents were more likely to give negative ratings.[19]

POLITICAL STYLE: AMATEUR IDEOLOGUES

Politics is not viewed as a profession in Colorado. Long service and apprenticeship in the party are not prerequisities to elective office. The process is open, but the political parties, due to the legal structure of the nominating system, have substantial influence over entry into politics. Since the parties are ideologically differentiated, Democrats generally nominate liberal candidates and Republicans choose conservatives.

There is no cadre of professional officeholders in Colorado. The General Assembly remains a citizen-legislature; most lawmakers view legislative service as a sideline to their principal livelihood. The base legislative salary is only $14,000 annually, less than two-thirds of the state median family income. While better compensated than legislators in neighboring states, Colorado lawmakers are relatively underpaid in terms of the growing length of legislative sessions. Before 1965, the long session of the legislative biennium averaged 90 days in length; in the subsequent period, sessions have averaged 160 days.[20] There has been some speculation in recent years that a year-round, professional legislature will eventually evolve.[21]

Birth outside the state does not bar one from winning office in Colorado. Only three members of the state's congressional delegation are natives; Governor Lamm was born in Wisconsin. The state chairman of the

Republican party is Howard "Bo" Callaway, who was a congressman from Georgia in the middle 1960s. Callaway came within a fraction of a percent of winning his party's nomination for U.S. senator in 1980. In a state where a minority of residents are natives, charges of carpetbagging are generally ineffective.

Many appointed positions in the executive department are also filled by nonnatives. GOP gubernatorial challenger Ted Strickland tried to make incumbent Lamm's appointment of out-of-staters to key administration posts a campaign issue in 1978. Lamm argued that through these appointments he hoped to generate new ideas and efficient techniques by bringing in outside advice.[22] Lamm's explanation probably struck a responsive chord with many voters who had been recruited from other states by companies located within Colorado.

As elsewhere, political officeholders in Colorado are usually better-educated professionals from the middle-class segments of the population. Hjelm and Pisciotte described the typical Colorado legislator of the late 1950s and early 1960s as white, Protestant, male, 35 to 55 years old, college educated, and a lawyer or businessman.[23] While some changes have occurred, this profile is essentially correct today.

Eight of ten Colorado governors serving since 1942 came from professional or business backgrounds; six were attorneys. The legislature has also been dominated by people from such backgrounds. Half to two-thirds of the lawmakers from 1970 to 1980 were professionals or businessmen; however, the number of lawyers serving in the General Assembly has declined in recent years. Although comprising a quarter to a third of total membership during the 1950s and 1960s, in 1980 there were only 3 attorneys in the senate and 11 in the house. The 1970s saw a sharp increase in the proportion of legislators who held no outside jobs; by the end of the decade, 14 percent of senators and more than a fourth of state representatives were full-time legislators.[24]

Due to malapportionment, rural interests for decades were considerably overrepresented in the General Assembly. During the 1950s and early 1960s, farmers and ranchers constituted a fifth of the legislative membership. Following the reapportionment revolution of the middle 1960s, legislators from agricultural backgrounds dropped to about 10 percent of all lawmakers. The impact of reapportionment has been somewhat diluted since the lower turnover and greater seniority of rural lawmakers has resulted in their holding a disproportionate number of top leadership positions.[25] For example, the speaker of the house in the 1981–82 and 1983–84 sessions was Carl B. Bledsoe, who hailed from Hugo, a community of less than 800 population on the eastern plains.

Male, white, Anglos still comprise the great majority of officeholders in the state. George L. Brown, a veteran black state senator, served as lieutenant governor from 1975 to 1979, but no Hispanic has ever been elected to major statewide office. In the General Assembly, blacks have won 3 percent of total legislative seats for the past several elections, closely reflecting their 3.5 percent share of the state's inhabitants. Hispanics, who comprised 11.7 percent of the state's population in 1980, have historically been underrepresented in the General Assembly. While steadily gaining numbers in the legislature over the past ten years, Hispanic lawmakers now total just seven percent of total membership. Though more numerous than blacks, Colorado Hispanics, hindered by the language barrier and internal divisions, have made less economic and political progress. The most dramatic political gain for Hispanics has been the 1983 election of former state representative Federico Peña as a mayor of Denver, where Hispanics comprise 19 percent of the population. A record 71 percent of registered voters cast ballots in the June municipal election, giving Peña 51 percent of the vote over former District Attorney Dale Tooley.[26]

All except one of the black and Hispanic legislators who have served in the General Assembly in the past decade were Democrats. This pattern of legislative representation reflects the voting preferences of Colorado minorities, who heavily support the Democratic party. Republicans have few minorities within their ranks from which to recruit candidates and little electoral incentive to actively pursue minority voters.

Colorado women are much better off in legislative representation than women in most other states; Colorado has one of the highest proportions of women legislators in the nation. Since the early 1970s, women have made substantial gains in the General Assembly, where they now constitute 25 percent of the total membership. Females are well-represented in both political parties.

It has been hypothesized that women might be more common in legislatures where the seat is either not a status position or where competition for the seat is not very intense. This theory, which seems to explain the presence of high percentages of women in the large, poorly paid legislatures of New England, does not seem to explain the success of women in Colorado. Legislators in the state receive $14,000 yearly and compete for a small number of seats in relation to the total state population.

Given Colorado's large number of female lawmakers, it has also been argued that women are more apt to succeed where women have held elected office frequently in the past. Colorado is a state that has been relatively advanced in terms of female equality. One of the earliest states to grant women suffrage, by 1921 it had four women in the legislature—second only to Connecticut.[27]

The tradition has continued. Colorado was one of the first states to ratify the Equal Rights Amendment (ERA) to the U.S. Constitution. A state ERA was adopted by a wide majority in 1972 and voters overwhelmingly rejected an attempt to repeal it in 1976. Moreover, Colorado women have enjoyed considerable success in seeking higher office. Patricia Schroeder, an outspoken and nationally prominent proponent of equal rights, is now the senior member of Colorado's U.S. House delegation, and the lieutenant governor and secretary of state are women.

While the congressional delegation and statewide offices have undergone considerable change, in recent years membership turnover in the General Assembly has been even greater. When the legislature convened after each election during the 1970s, sizeable proportions of each chamber were likely to be new members. On average, over a fifth of the senate and more than a third of the house were first-term members. The cause of high turnover does not stem from voters "throwing the rascals out" every two years; rather, the major component of legislative change consists of members retiring to private life or seeking other office.

The political process in the state is open, aided by reforms enacted during the 1970s. At the beginning of that decade, voters approved a "sunshine law," requiring public officials to disclose their financial interests, regulating lobbyists, and mandating that meetings of governmental bodies be open to the public. The law, initiated by Colorado Common Cause, provides that "all meetings at which either public business is discussed or formal action is adopted" must be open to the public. "Full and timely" notice must be given before such meetings are held. The Republican-controlled legislature has never liked the requirements of the sunshine law and would probably have repealed it but for fear of possible political repercussions. Compliance with the law has been somewhat grudging. The League of Women Voters and Common Cause issued a critique of GOP legislative leaders in May 1982, complaining that the "helter-skelter" scheduling that prevails in the General Assembly essentially violated the timely notice requirement of the law.[28] The vigilance of such interest groups serves as a constant prod toward openness in government. Moreover, the presence of two, strong, competing newspapers, the *Denver Post* and the *Rocky Mountain News*, in the capital has also been a positive factor in subjecting governmental actions to public scrutiny.

Colorado law also requires political candidates and political committees to periodically file contribution and expenditure reports, although no limits are placed on how much a candidate may receive in contributions. Attempts to provide for public financing of campaigns have been defeated in the legislature on party line votes, with Republicans opposing the concept.

Political corruption is rare in Colorado. Peirce describes the state's political character as "clean,"[29] Elazar agrees, noting that:

> ... the honest economic self-improvement of political figures is accepted, though Coloradans are clearly unwilling to tolerate the kinds of pecuniary gain available to politicians as a matter of course in Illinois.
> ... Pueblo County, which is considered to be "machine-ridden" in the rest of the state ..., is barely organized by Illinois standards and its political leadership would be considered incorruptible in the latter state.[30]

Political misbehavior that does take place seems limited to isolated instances of individual wrongdoing at the local level. A recent *cause celebre* at the state level involved a representative who used a letter opener to jam his electronic voting device in the "no" position while he was absent from the legislative chamber. The incident caused a minor uproar. The legislator escaped a resolution expressing bipartisan "displeasure" at his actions only after he publicly apologized to the house.

Political patronage at the state level is virtually nonexistent, with most state workers hired under a merit system. Governor Richard Lamm has often complained that, "I have 54,000 employees and outside of the governor's office I can hire and fire 15 of them."[31] A constitutional amendment placed before the electorate in 1976 would have permitted the legislature to exempt middle managers (for example, division and institution heads) from the state personnel system. The approximately 110 positions affected would have been filled by department heads appointed by the governor. It was argued that such a change would allow the governor to develop his own managerial team by extending his control over key positions at the middle as well as top-management level.[32] Apparently unwilling to accept even a modest increase in "patronage," voters rejected the proposal by a three-to-one margin.

POLITICAL INTERACTION: ACTIVIST, INDEPENDENT, AND COMPETITIVE

Colorado is one of the more electorally competitive states in the nation, but the degree of competition depends on what offices are involved. Presidential and legislative elections are not very competitive, while statewide offices and congressional races are quite competitive. Generally, one can endorse the assessment of Martin and Gomez who categorize Colorado as a strong two-party state during recent decades, but with increased GOP strength after 1962.[33]

Since World War II, Colorado has clearly been in the Republican column in balloting for president. In only two of the past nine presidential elections have Coloradans supported the Democratic candidate. Excluding Lyndon Johnson's 1964 victory as merely the reflection of a national landslide, over 30 years have passed since the Democrats last carried the state—for Harry Truman in 1948. Even in the 1976 election, which was relatively close nationally, Gerald Ford easily defeated Jimmy Carter in Colorado by 124,014 votes.

The failure of Democratic presidential candidates to appeal to Colorado voters stands in sharp contrast to the success enjoyed by Democrats in state and congressional elections. Democrats have consistently done well in elections to the U.S. House of Representatives and have been as successful as Republicans in winning the governorship. Following the 1982 elections, one U.S. senator, three of six U.S. representatives, the governor, lieutenant governor, and treasurer were Democrats; the attorney general, secretary of state, and the rest of the congressional delegation were Republicans.

Democrats have been less successful in the General Assembly elections, controlling both houses simultaneously for just six years since 1948. The Democratic party last controlled the legislature during the 1961–1962 session. Democrats have not won the senate since then but have controlled the house following the 1964 and 1974 elections.

The caucus structure of the Colorado political system demands more of its citizens than that expected in pure primary states. Access to the primary ballot is not automatic. The state uses a preprimary assembly process that serves as a filtering mechanism for nominations, giving the political parties substantial influence over whom ultimate nominees will be.

Precinct caucuses are the first step in the process of gaining access to the primary ballot. Caucuses—neighborhood meetings of Democrats and Republicans—are held in May of even-numbered years. Participation in caucuses is limited to persons who are registered voters of their party. Attendance is generally light, averaging only 6 to 7 percent of those eligible. The caucus procedure demands more time and effort from participants than the relatively simple act of voting in an election.

Caucus attendees choose delegates to the county convention; the county convention, in turn, selects delegates to the congressional district and state conventions. A candidate must receive the votes of at least 20 percent of delegates at the appropriate assembly in order for his name to appear on the primary ballot. A candidate for governor, for example must receive 20 percent of delegate votes at the state convention. Candidates' names are listed on the primary ballot in descending order of assembly votes. The favorite of party regulars, therefore, receives top-line designation.[34] Although it is possible for one to petition onto the primary ballot, this procedure is seldom used since such signature gathering is time consuming, complex, and subject to legal challenge.

The primary election in Colorado occurs fairly late in the electoral season, taking place on the second Tuesday of September in even-numbered years. Crossover voting is not allowed; Democrats may only vote for Democrats and Republicans for Republicans. Unaffiliated voters are permitted to vote in the primary if they declare an affiliation for one of the major parties on the day of the election. Generally, few unaffiliates exercise this option.

Since 1972, turnout in primary elections for governor has averaged 47.4 percent; U.S. Senate primaries have drawn an average of 46.5 percent of registered voters to the polls. The closest and most widely publicized U.S. Senate primary of the past decade—a four-way GOP contest in 1980—produced a turnout of 55.7 percent. Voting participation in the general election is considerably higher, averaging 79.6 percent of registered voters in presidential election years and 64.2 percent in off years. The state switched to a four-year term for major state officers in 1958. The election of a governor in nonpresidential years may provide some insulation of state elections from national tides, although 1974 provides a counter example to such a theory. Coloradans vote at rates considerably higher than that of the nation as a whole. The turnout for the 1980 presidential election was 82.6 percent of registered voters. The competitive nature of the state's political climate, the higher educational level of the electorate, and a higher average median income level are factors contributing to higher rates of participation in the state.

The initiative, referendum, and recall devices provide additional outlets for participation. Citizens may initiate laws or constitutional amendments by securing signatures of a small percentage of registered voters on petitions. The proposition then appears on the general election ballot for voter approval or disapproval. Frequent use has been made of the initiative since its adoption in 1910; many important issues—such as reapportionment, equal rights, the environment, and taxation—have been addressed by past propositions. The 1972 initiative campaign, that prohibited use of state funds for hosting the 1976 Winter Olympics in Colorado, was led by state Representative Richard Lamm; the name recognition and political organization thus established helped propel Lamm to the governorship in 1974.

Political parties are strong and relatively well-organized in Colorado. Both parties maintain year-round state headquarters, but Republicans seem to be better organized and better financed, and seem to have a more professional organization. Democrats, for example, still rely primarily on volunteer headquarters help, while the GOP has several full-time, paid staff members. Activists of both political parties regard the state Republican party as the more effective political organization.

In Colorado, political parties, rather than interest groups and other nonparty organizations, dominate the recruitment process for public office. Neither party seems to have difficulty in filling its slate; since 1972 every race for Congress or major statewide office was contested. In legislative elections, both parties ran candidates in three-quarters of senate races and 80 percent of house races; opposition candidates were not contested in hopelessly one-party districts.

The vigor of political parties in Colorado is enhanced by the nature of the preprimary caucus system. The process by which party activists designate candidates for the primary ballot usually guarantees that the candidate preferred by party activists will win the nomination. The results of contested primaries from 1972–1980 for congressional and major statewide offices shows that 72 percent of the top-line candidates on the primary ballot won their party's nomination. An even higher proportion of top-line designees in legislative races won. The influence the parties have over nominations makes it unlikely that someone grossly out of step with a party's philosophy will be nominated.

The power of political parties in Colorado is somewhat diminished by the great independence of the Colorado electorate. While in Colorado, as elsewhere, the two major parties dominate, neither Democrats nor Republicans have been able to hold overwhelming or sustained control of the state. William P. Irwin argues that Colorado politics has been typified by "balance—a two-party balance, but in the midst of political experiment and diversity."[35]

Citizens who refuse to identify with either political party have averaged 37 percent of Colorado's registered voters since 1972. This is an usually high proportion of unaffiliates. In 1976, of those states having statewide, partisan voter registration, only nine had more than 25 percent of their electorate registered as unaffiliated; only two states had higher percentages of unaffiliates than Colorado: Alaska at 56 percent and Massachusetts at 42 percent.[36]

The existence of such a large block of independent voters, coupled with the traditional independence of the Colorado electorate, lends an air of unpredictability to election outcomes. Ticket-splitting is commonplace and a large "floating vote" exists. In 1972, for example, voters gave Richard Nixon landslide support in the presidential race, while unseating a conservative, Republican U.S. senator and approving a ballot proposition against using public funds to stage the 1976 Olympics in the state. The election of 1978 provided an even more dramatic example of ticket-splitting: Richard D. Lamm, a moderate-liberal Democrat, was reelected as governor with 60 percent of the vote, while William L. Armstrong, a conservative Republican, was chosen as U.S. senator with the same percentage of the vote.

The political parties in Colorado are ideologically differentiated, with Democrats generally liberal and Republicans conservative. On key issues, particularly the ones affecting state revenue and expenditures, there are significant differences between the two major parties. Moreover, partisan members of the legislature attempt to enact these differences into law when they control the legislature. When asked to classify themselves ideologically, one-sixth of Colorado state senators in 1976 described their political philosophy as liberal, almost half listed moderate, and over one-third chose conservative. Democratic senators were considerably more likely than Republicans to describe themselves as liberal.[37]

Partisan differences are also reflected in the ratings given members of the General Assembly by various interest groups. In most cases, one party receives a support rating from a group that is far above average, while the other earns a rating far below average. For example, in 1979–1980 senate Democrats received an average rating of 89 percent from the AFL-CIO Committee on Political Education, whereas senate Republicans recorded 11 percent. On the other hand, house Republicans tallied a 78 percent support level from the Colorado Conservative Union, while house Democrats received a 30 percent average. Democrats in both chambers received higher ratings than GOP members for the 1975–1980 period from such groups as labor, environmentalists, senior citizens, teachers, and a committee concerned with human services and consumer issues. Republicans were given high ratings by two conservative ideological groups—the Colorado Conservative Union (the state chapter of the American Conservative Union) and the Colorado Eagle Forum (the local chapter of the national group headed by Phyllis Schlafly).

Similar differences in interest-group rankings are found for the state's congressional delegation. In 1980, the average rating given by the liberal Americans for Democratic Action was 72 percent for the Democrats in the delegation, compared to 23 percent for Republicans. GOP members were rated much higher than Democrats by the American Conservative Union; 94 percent versus 8 percent.[38]

The ideological schism between the two parties is also manifested in the views of each party's activists, who have great influence over which candidates appear on the primary ballot and receive their party's nomination.[39] A comparison of the ideological self-classification of state convention delegates surveyed in 1980 revealed that 66 percent of Democratic activists regarded themselves as somewhat to very liberal. By contrast, 90 percent of GOP delegates classified themselves as somewhat to very conservative. Inter-party disagreements existed on ten of sixteen issues that were included on the survey questionnaire. For example, Democratic delegates (in sharp contrast to their GOP counterparts) heavily favored the Equal Rights Amendment, national health insurance, and strong state efforts to control growth.

Over the past decade, Colorado politics has been characterized by extreme partisanship and gloves-off confrontation. The ideological differences between the parties result in high intra-party cohesion in legislative voting. A comprehensive study of nonunanimous roll calls in the Colorado General Assembly between 1961 and 1970 found that both parties showed a strong orientation toward standing united against the opposition on roll-call votes. The research concluded that a legislator's party was a more important determinant of his voting behavior than the type of region he represented and that the parties vote on opposing sides of legislative issues more frequently than blocs differentiated along urban-rural lines.[40]

The Republican party's practice of adopting binding caucus positions on some issues accentuates the differences between the parties. For certain bills, such as appropriation measures, majority GOP legislators adopt positions that commit all party members in the chamber to vote as the majority of the caucus has directed. Informal sanctions, such as awarding or withholding committee chairmanships and committee assignments and killing bills sponsored by maverick legislators, are available to the leadership to keep members in line. Minority Democrats have argued that they have been excluded from decision making, since issues are often decided in the Republican caucus rather than in the legislative chamber.

Interest groups are not as critical as parties, but they are still important in Colorado politics, with business groups more successful in influencing state policy than labor or environmental organizations. In the early years of statehood, the mining industry and the Colorado Cattlemen's Association were the preeminent interest groups. Since then, other pressure groups, such as realtors and homebuilders, have become important.

One of the most prominent of the business groups is the Colorado

Association of Commerce and Industry (CACI), whose political-action committee receives major support from such large corporations as Public Service Company of Colorado, AMAX Incorporated, Colorado Interstate Gas Company, Ideal Basic Industries, and Adolph Coors Company. The executive secretary of CACI asserts that his organization strives "for business orientation in the Legislature . . . we want a good business climate to keep the economy pumping."[41]

Labor unions are not as important a factor in Colorado as they are in eastern industrial states. Much of the growth in the state's labor force has occurred in high-technology and white-collar industries, where unions have experienced difficulties recruiting members. The percentage of workers in labor unions has dropped from 23 percent in 1961 to about 13 percent in 1978. The state's 128,000 member AFL-CIO is active in elections through its Committee on Political Education. The Colorado Education Association, that represents most public school teachers, also plays a major role in political campaigns.

The Colorado Open Space Council (COSC) is an umbrella organization for many of the state's environmental groups. COSC monitors governmental activities, lobbies the state legislature, and publishes ratings of lawmakers. The 1982 election saw efforts by Colorado environmental groups to mobilize the "green vote" by supplying volunteers and funds to targetted races.

In 1980, an estimated 110 political-action committees were active in Colorado. Patterns of campaign contributions reveal that each type of interest group tends to support candidates of one of the major political parties and oppose those of the other. Labor unions, educational organizations, and environmental groups generally support Democrats, while business and professional associations back Republicans.

Within state government the General Assembly is the most powerful branch, while the office of governor is relatively weak. Although the public may expect the governor to solve pressing state problems, it is difficult if not impossible for the governor to take unilateral action on such matters. Democratic Governor Richard D. Lamm has echoed the views of previous chief executives in asserting that "The governor of Colorado has the responsibility but not the authority to run the state government."[42]

In terms of formal authority, the Colorado governorship appears powerful. Schlesinger's index for assessing the formal powers of state governors results in a fairly high overall ranking for Colorado.[43] The Colorado governor serves a four-year term and can succeed himself as many times as the voters choose to reelect him. He possesses the regular veto and also the item veto over specific items in appropriations bills. He appoints, subject to senate confirmation, the heads of 15 of the 20 principal state departments. The governor also prepares a state budget and submits it to the legislature. However, when one probes below the formal powers, one appreciates Lamm's view that Colorado has a weak-governor concept written into the constitution. He notes that:

> The Grange helped form our constitution. They came riding out of Kansas vowing to raise less wheat and more hell and they essentially wanted to make sure that nobody had the power to act as governor.[44]

The veto is essentially a negative tool and is a poor weapon with which to exercise leadership. The great bulk of state employees are part of a merit personnel system beyond the governor's power to appoint or remove. In addition, the heads of the department of state, law, and treasury are independently elected, while the directors of education and higher education are appointed by state boards. Although the governor does prepare an executive budget, it is generally ignored by the legislature, whose powerful, well-staffed joint budget committee drafts the state budget. The power of the governor to specify what subjects the legislature may consider during short sessions (for example, those in even-numbered years) was removed by a constitutional amendment approved by voters in 1982.

Structurally, the legislative branch of Colorado government consists of a 35-member senate and a 65-member house of representatives. Legislators are selected from single-member districts in partisan elections occurring in November of even-numbered years, with half of the senate and the entire house standing for election every two years.

The legislature is extremely jealous of its prerogatives and has vigorously resisted attempts by the governor to make policy. The situation has been aggravated by partisan differences between a Democratic governor and a Republican legislature. In analyzing the 1979–1980 legislative session, the *Denver Post* concluded that each branch of government felt that it possessed a mandate from the voters to set public policy and run the state.[45]

The effect of growth on Colorado's quality of life has long been a major point of contention between Lamm and the legislature. Urban sprawl, manifested in five-acre ranchette subdivisions along the Front Range, was one factor in leading Lamm to ask the department of local affairs and the legislature to develop strategies for guiding growth. After three years of consultation with local officials, the department developed a set of human settlement policies. When the legislature failed to act on these recommendations, Lamm adopted them by executive order in 1979. The policies, in the form of instructions to state agencies, were intended to deny public assistance to development plans that were either overly expensive or endangered the natural resources of the state.

Lamm's unilateral promulgation of such policies set off a firestorm of legislative reaction. One Republican senator, who subsequently served as majority leader, denounced the policies asserting that Lamm was trying to usurp the policymaking authority of the General Assembly. Late in 1980, Lamm announced that he would rescind the human settlement policies as an "olive branch" to the legislature. While arguing that policies to handle growth were essential, the governor had concluded that the continuation of the present policies was not worth the acrimony that they had produced in the legislature.

Given a powerful, vigilant, and aggressive General Assembly, there is little room for significant policy making by the governor. Indeed, at times Lamm has opted to take a "low profile," declining to publicly back particular policies for fear that his blessing would doom them in the legislature. Asserts Lamm:

> ... If I want A, all of a sudden you find an amazing amount of support for Z. ... We've worked out a few small things with the Republicans, very few big things. The problem is that cooperation is looked upon by some Republicans as consorting with the enemy. That's the terrible state that Colorado politics has fallen into.[46]

Governor Lamm has been unable to persuade the Republican General Assembly that the state should have primary responsibility for controlling growth. The 1979 conclusion of the Conservation Foundation remains valid today: "There is no political mechanism with authority to control or manage growth on a regional or comprehensive basis, no centralized body, no state agency, no metropolitan government that can effectively implement plans and policies relating to growth."[47] The limited role of government in this and other areas is not surprising given the populace's preference against governmental activism. State government's ability to deal with such matters is hampered by the legislature's self-imposed 7 percent limit on increases in state expenditures, especially when one considers the impact of inflation and population increases.

The private sector has substantial power over the density of the state. Decisions on locations for new housing developments, industrial plant sites, and commercial centers are largely beyond the control of state government. For example, one small community recently authorized construction of a major regional shopping center at an interchange on the freeway linking Denver and Boulder. Such a development would greatly increase traffic and serve as a stimulus to further growth in the open land between the two cities. Despite opposition from Governor Lamm and Boulder County officials, the state had no legal means to prevent the project.[48]

The influence of large corporations has long been a powerful force in Colorado. Indeed, Lamm and historian Michael McCarthy argue that much of the state's history involved "eastern capitalists" who moved into the West, exploiting its resources and its wealth. Such interests succeeded in building a controlling power that far surpassed the influence of the federal government.[49] For example, vast quantities of gold and silver were extracted from the state, yet Colorado did not levy a severance tax on metallic minerals until 1977.

The presence of extensive federal landholdings gives the national government substantial control over Colorado's future. National forests, national parks, Bureau of Land Management holdings, and military installations cover over 37 percent of the state's land. How the federal government manages its holdings and what development it permits profoundly affect the state's quality of life.

The "sagebrush rebellion" is an effort to turn over the bulk of federal lands back to the western states. In 1981, the Colorado legislature approved a bill, subsequently vetoed by Governor Lamm, calling for such a transfer. Although reflecting western concern for local self-determination, the Sagebrush movement is also supported by large cattle, energy, and logging interests who, according to Lamm, seek "control of the public domain to their own ends."[50] The struggle is the latest chapter in the unfinished story of the dialectic between development and the quality of Colorado life.

NOTES

1. *Colorado Heritage News*, April 1982, p. 7.

2. Quoted in G. Michael McCarthy, *Hour of Trial: The Conservation Conflict in Colorado and the West, 1891–1907* (Norman, Okla.: University of Oklahoma Press, 1977), p. 252.

3. Joel Garreau, *The Nine Nations of North America* (Boston: Houghton-Mifflin, 1981), p. 3.

4. Daniel J. Elazar, "Political Culture on the Plains," *Western Historical Quarterly* 11 (July 1980):265.

5. See, Tucker Hart Adams, "Boom-Bust Cycle Still Plaguing Colorado Oil Shale Industry?" *Denver Post*, 7 March 1982, p. 4D.

6. Writing in the early 1970s, Daniel J. Elazar concluded that most Puebloans felt "that the rest of the state looks down upon their community." *Cities of the Prairie: The Metropolitan Frontier and American Politics* (New York: Basic Books, 1970), p. 349.

7. Quoted in Lyle W. Dorsett, *The Queen City: A History of Denver* (Boulder, Colo.: Pruett, 1977), p. xi.

8. See Conrad L. McBride, Rudolph Gomez, and Eleanore Bushnell, "Colorado," in *Impact of Reapportionment on the Thirteen Western States*, ed. Eleanore Bushnell (Salt Lake City, Utah: University of Utah Press, 1970), p. 94.

9. Elazar, *Cities of the Prarie*, p. 344.

10. Helen Ingram, Nancy K. Laney, and John R. McCain, *A Policy Approach to Political Representation: Lessons from the Four Corners States* (Baltimore: Johns Hopkins University Press, 1980), pp. 190–1. The survey was conducted in 1976.

11. "A Summary of Findings in Teeter's Colorado Survey . . . ," *Colorado Statesman*, 3 October 1981, p. 5.

12. Kenneth T. Walsh, "Colorado Voters Seem Content with the Status Quo," *Denver Post*, 12 December 1976, p. 24.

13. *Ibid.* p. 24.

14. Jack W. Germond and Jules Witcover, "Colorado Democrats Are Offering Voters a Choice," *Rocky Mountain News*, 6 October 1978, p. 65.

15. Quoted in Kenneth T. Walsh, "Conservative Current Running in State," *Denver Post*, 13 November 1977, pp. 1 and 16.

16. William P. Irwin, "Colorado: A Matter of Balance," in *The Politics of Reapportionment*, ed. Malcolm E. Jewell (New York: Atherton 1962), p. 64.

17. Ingram, Laney, and McCain, *A Policy Approach to Political Representation,* p. 192.

18. See, "A Summary of Findings in Teeter's Colorado Survey . . . ," p. 5; and Sharon Sherman, "Lamm Enjoys Bipartisan Support," *Denver Post*, 31 January 1982, p. 1F. The former poll was conducted statewide, while the latter was taken in five Denver metropolitan area counties.

19. Two-thirds of Western Slope respondents felt state government was not "efficient,

responsive, or engaged in worthwhile activity." Sharon Sherman, "60% Rate State Government OK in Colorado Poll," *Denver Post*, 28 March 1982, p. 1F.

20. Timothy Noah, "Rocky Mountain Breakdown," *The New Republic* 186 (12 May 1982):19. See, Alan Rosenthal, *Legislative Life* (New York: Harper and Row, 1981), p. 41, for a comparison with other states.

21. See, Noah, *ibid.*, for a discussion of the possible impact of the new federalism on citizen legislatures.

22. "State Personnel Director Livingston Quits," *Rocky Mountain News*, 7 July 1977, p. 8.

23. Victor S. Hjelm and Joseph P. Pisciotte, "Profiles and Careers of Colorado State Legislators," *Western Political Quarterly* 21 (December 1968):722.

24. Calculated from Colorado Public Expenditure Council, *The Colorado General Assembly 1955 to 1977* (Denver, Colo.: Colorado Public Expenditure Council, 10 October 1977) and Thomas H. Simmons, *Colorado General Assembly Senators and Representatives: An Informational Guide* (Boulder, Colo.: Bureau of Governmental Research and Service, 1979 and 1981).

25. See, Lee Olson, "'Rural Bosy' in Saddle," *Denver Post*, 25 September 1980, p. 22; and Cindy Parmenter, "Rural Lawmakers Have a Lasso on Legislature," *Denver Post*, 7 March 1982, p. 22A.

26. Gary Delsohn, "It's Peña Over Tooley," *Denver Post*, 22 June 1983, p. 1.

27. Irene Diamond, *Sex Roles in the State House* (New Haven, Conn.: Yale University Press, 1977), pp. 3–29.

28. The League of Women Voters and Common Cause, "It's Hard to See the Sunshine at the Gold Dome," *Colorado Statesmen*, 14 May 1982, p. 7.

29. Neil R. Peirce, *The Mountain States of American: People, Politics, and Power in the Eight Rocky Mountain States* (New York: Norton, 1972), p. 58.

30. Elazar, *Cities of the Prarie*, p. 348.

31. Richard D. Lamm, "I Have the Responsibility but Not the Authority to Run the State," *Colorado Statesman*, 29 March 1980, p. 22.

32. Colorado Legislative Council, *An Analysis of 1976 Ballot Proposals*, Research Publication no. 217 (Denver, Colo.: Legislative Council, 1976), p. 14.

33. Curtis Martin and Rudolph Gomez, *Colorado Government and Politics* 3rd ed. (Boulder, Colo.: Pruett, 1972), p. 158.

34. Top line designees won an average of 90 percent of primary contests in the state senate and 75 percent of the races in the house. Computed from Colorado, Secretary of State, *Abstract of Votes Cast* (Denver, Colo.: Department of State, 1972 through 1980). Candidate lists for the primary election were also used in calculating these numbers.

35. Irwin, "Colorado: A Matter of Balance," p. 64.

36. Malcolm E. Jewell and David M. Olson, *American State Political Parties and Elections* (Homewood, Ill.: Dorsey, 1978), p. 46.

37. Ingram, Laney, and McCain, *A Policy Approach to Political Representation*, pp. 93 and 95.

38. Calculated from data in Michael Barone and Grant Ujifusa, *The Almanac of American Politics, 1982* (Washington, D.C.: Barone, 1981), pp. 170–78.

39. Thomas H. Simmons, *Colorado Political Party Activists: Survey Results of the 1980 Democratic and Republican State Conventions* (Boulder, Colo.: Colorado Center for Public Policy Research of the Bureau of Governmental Research and Service, November 1980), pp. 19–20.

40. Susan W. Furniss, "The Response of the Colorado General Assembly to Proposals for Metropolitan Reform," *Western Political Quarterly* 26 (December 1973):758.

41. Jody Strogoff, "CPAC Invests in Pro-business Legislators," *Colorado Statesman*, 5 April 1980, p. 10.

42. Lamm, "I Have the Responsibility but Not the Authority to Run the State," p. 23. Lamm was quoting former Republican Governor John Love.

43. See, Joseph A. Schlesinger, "The Politics of the Executive," in *Politics in the*

American States: A Comparative Analysis, ed. Herbert Jacob and Kenneth H. Vines (Boston: Little, Brown, 1965).

44. Lamm, "I Have the Responsibility but Not the Authority to Run the State," p. 22.

45. "Governor vs. Legislature," editorial, *Denver Post*, 17 February 1980, p. 27.

46. Lamm, "I Have the Responsibility but Not the Authority to Run the State," p. 23.

47. "Colorado Seems Helpless in Face of Growth," *Denver Post*, 27 May 1979, p. 21.

48. Economic considerations, rather than state action, delayed construction and finally resulted in the cancellation of the shopping center project.

49. Richard D. Lamm and Michael McCarthy, "Outside Interests Continue to Milk the West," *Denver Post*, 28 March 1982, p. 3B.

50. Richard D. Lamm and Michael McCarthy, *The Angry West: A Vulnerable Land and Its Future* (Boston: Houghton Mifflin, 1982), p. 285.

4

Iowa

SAMUEL C. PATTERSON

Politically, Iowa is best known for the role its precinct caucuses have come to play in the early stages of the presidential nominating process. Former-President Jimmy Carter's nomination in 1976 owed a great deal to his successes in the Iowa caucuses. By the same token, Vice-President George Bush established a standing among Republicans in 1980 partly because of his initial support in Iowa. Iowa's importance in the quadrennial presidential nominating contests derives more from its timing than from its clout in national convention voting on nominees. These January Iowa caucuses provide the first polls and straw votes gauging the standings of presidential contenders in the two national political parties. Iowa's preeminence in the early days of presidential politics would not transpire if nominations were not contested, and its role would be much smaller even then if the outcomes of its caucus fissions were not made to be national media events. Yet, it could be argued that Iowa is not a bad early test of the appeal of national candidates. Iowa represents a certain "middleness," a kind of typicality and manageability, that may acquit it well as a litmus test of early presidential campaign potential.

POLITICAL CULTURE: MIDWESTERN MIDDLENESS

Iowa's middleness is reflected in a variety of ways. To some extent, it is merely geographical. Iowa is right in the middle of the county, "a Mesopotamia lying between the two great rivers that drain the continent."[1] Iowa literally is in the middle of the road—crossed by the Sioux tribes moving west, by the Mormons trekking to Utah, by the transcontinental railroad to San Francisco, and by Interstate 80. Those people who came to Iowa to live were mostly Yankees and northern Europeans, Germans being the most numerous immigrants, but with a substantial representation of Scandinavians, Dutch, Irish, and English settlers. Iowa's population remains

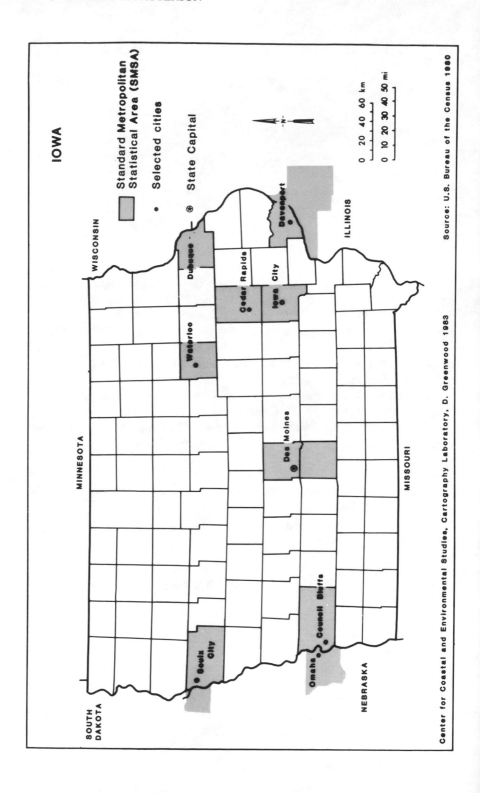

highly homogeneous, with an important but nevertheless small contingent of blacks and Hispanics (about 1 percent each).

Iowans exhibit a certain amount of ambivalence about their state. On the one hand, Iowans express firm pride in the land, the physical beauty, and the horticultural productivity of their state.[2] The Iowa Poll, conducted for the *Des Moines Register*, periodically asks a sample of Iowans how they like their state. In September 1978, the Poll for the first time asked how people would rate Iowa as a place to live, and whether or not they would prefer to live in another state. Fifty-nine percent rated Iowa as "one of the best" (63 percent of the native Iowans gave this rating compared to 55 percent of those who moved into Iowa from another state), and 65 percent said they would not move to another state even if they could do so. Similar questions produced similar results in a May 1982 poll, when 69 percent of the sample indicated a preference for living in Iowa; 29 percent preferred another state.

On the other hand, Iowans have a tendency to be rather deprecating of their state. In the 1978 ratings of the Iowa Poll, a full 40 percent rated Iowa "nice, but not outstanding" and "about average," although only 1 percent said their state was poor. Many Iowans do, in fact, migrate to other states; there are well-developed colonies in southern California (John Gunther once said: "Los Angeles is Iowa with palms."), Arizona, and Florida. The 1980 census showed that Iowa's population of 2.9 million had grown by only 3 percent in the 1970s, dropping the state from 25th to 27th largest in the country.

A few years ago, it was proposed in the state legislature that the phrase "beautiful land," sometimes the translation of the Indian word "iowa," be imprinted on the state's automobile license plates. The proposal was not adopted; many legislators felt it was pretentious, that Iowa was not that beautiful. Deprecating remarks about Iowa's farmers, weather, politicians, governing processes, and status among surrounding states are often made or repeated by Iowans. The state's development commission, seeking to foster economic development and tourism, adopted a slogan for Iowa—"Iowa, a Place to Grow." Some suggested "Iowa, a Place to Grope," or proposed that a better state slogan would be "Iowa, Gateway to Nebraska!"

Iowa pride certainly outweighs deprecation. Iowans are especially proud of the land and of the bounty of their production of corn, soybeans, and livestock, and well they might be: the productivity of Iowa agriculture is remarkable. Iowa contains some of the richest agricultural land in the world; however, rarely does state pride take a political direction. Although Iowans occasionally will express a grudging respect for the quality of their governing institutions, seldom do they express pride in their government and politics. Most Iowans assume that politics is supposed to be effective, efficient, and free of corruption; when this is the way politics and government are, no special pride in them is warranted. When the Iowa legislature was rated sixth in the nation several years ago by a national organization devoted to improving state legislatures, this news was received by many Iowans with some skepticism. The feeling was widely expressed that the other state legislatures must really be bad if Iowa was sixth!

The orientations of Iowans toward the role of the government and how politics should be conducted can best be described as both individualistic and moralistic.[3] Iowans' orientations to politics are individualistic in the sense that they have a tendency to view the government's role as that of fostering private initiative and success, feeling that beyond stimulating business and agriculture the state government should stay out of people's affairs. Iowans expect their government to be run in a businesslike way, yet they expect to be treated in a personal nonbureaucratic manner by the state agencies. Iowans' political orientations are moralistic in their emphasis upon public spiritedness, good government, public trust, and public service. Although many subscribe to the belief that the role of government should be minimal, and that individual volunteerism should always be preferred to governmental action, moderate growth in the government sector in Iowa has been widely acceptable. However, governmental growth has been relatively smaller in Iowa than in most states.

Notable ambivalence toward governmental action is characteristic of Iowans, particularly of farmers. Iowa farmers, although highly subsidized through federal government farm programs, are frequently quite vociferous in their anti-governmental individualism. In the spring of 1979, the Iowa Poll reflected this kind of ambivalence. When asked, "Which system better serves the farmer's interest—a free market or governmental price supports and loans?", a full three-fourths of Iowa farmers answered, "a free market." In the same survey, 55 percent of farmers indicated that the president should not be able to invoke grain embargoes as a foreign policy weapon, 75 percent said the government should not allow the importing of foreign meat, and 71 percent favored raising price supports on corn. In general, Iowa's farmers seemed to want a free market in principle, and increased corn subsidies in practice.

To the outside eye view, Iowans are often thought to be politically rustic and conservative; they are widely believed to represent American Gothic incarnate in politics. But the view that Iowans are ultra-conservative about the role of government in their lives is easy to exaggerate. For nearly 20 years, Iowans have elected politically progressive governors—Democrat Harold Hughes and Republican Robert Ray. For other offices, Iowans have elected liberals about as often as conservatives; in recent years the state has been served by two of the most liberal, and then two of the most conservative, U.S. senators (first Democrats Dick Clark and John Culver, then Republicans Charles Grassley and Roger Jepsen).

In truth, fewer Iowans consider themselves to be "liberal" or "conservative" in regard to the government's role than do Americans generally. Compared to their fellow Americans, Iowans are far more likely to regard themselves as moderates politically. In April 1979, both the Iowa Poll and the national Gallup Poll asked respondents questions enabling them to be classified as "liberals," "middle-of-the-road," or "conservative." Just over a fifth of Iowans were classified as liberal, compared to about a third of all Americans; 38 percent of Iowans and 44 percent of all Americans were classified as conservative; about 30 percent of Iowans, compared to only 10 percent of all Americans, were classified as middle-of-the-road politically.[4] Iowans are individualistic in regard to government; they certainly think state government should be limited and run on a businesslike basis. Beyond that, an especially large proportion of Iowans occupy the political middle ground.

Above all, Iowans and their politicians are moralistic about their politics. Iowa politics is blatantly characterized by honesty, fair play, honorable intentions, and good government. Iowans' expectations about how government and politics should be conducted are based upon such high standards, and generally speaking they are fulfilled so well, that Iowa politics is often not very interesting. There is very little corruption in Iowa politics, and thus, very few of those fascinating politicians who, in less pristine locales, make politics interesting for their chicanery. Pecadillos in politicking or administration bring down the wrath of the state's major newspaper, the *Des Moines Register*. Iowa is rather unusual in that a single newspaper blankets the state. The *Register* refers to itself on its masthead, as "the newspaper Iowa depends upon" and regards itself as something of the keeper of Iowa's political morality, among other things.

In recent memory, the state's principal political leader, the governor, has epitomized Iowans' altruistic standards of political virtue. Both Democratic Governor Harold E. Hughes (1963–1969) and Republican Governor Robert D. Ray (1969–1982) enjoyed exceptionally high personal popularity and respect. Governor Ray's popularity was particularly long-lasting, remarkably so by the usual standards of politicians' perishability. Any post-World War II president would be overjoyed to have the lasting popularity of Governors Hughes and Ray. After three years in office, Hughes retained a popularity rating of 73 percent approval.[5] Robert Ray has also been a persistently popular leader. First elected in 1968, Ray served three two-year terms. In 1972, the Iowa constitution was amended by popular vote lengthening the governor's term to four years. Ray was reelected in 1974 and in 1978 to four-year terms, making him one of the longest tenured governors in American history. Long service has not brought about the erosion of support for the Iowa governor, as it has done for postwar presidents.

Although Ray's popularity declined early in his governorship, it rose steadily during his second term. Between 1973 and 1981, Ray's approval rating never dropped below 71 percent; it reached a high of 82 percent in 1974. In 1978, after ten years as governor, 78 percent approved of his performance and by 1981, 73 percent approved.[6] In general, the popularity of Governors Hughes and Ray has been bipartisan (the 1980 ratings of Ray showed, for instance, that 78 percent of Republicans, 70 percent of Independents, and 66 percent of Democrats approved of his performance). That Iowans' support for their governor is highly personal is indicated by the fact that neither Hughes nor Ray was very successful in transferring their enormous popularity to other candidates of their own political party. The personal character of Hughes and Ray support is also illustrated by the fact both were odds-on favorites in an August 1980 poll that asked which individuals, on a list of well-known Iowans, people would like to have as a weekend guest in their homes.

Iowans' support for the state legislature is, relatively speaking, high. For reasons that are not easy to fathom, Iowans approve of the job their legislature is doing. While levels of approval have fluctuated, they generally have increased since the early 1960s.[7] This increased support may derive from the improvements in the legislature's organization for business, and from steadier confidence in the legislature's capacity to reapportion itself in a nonpartisan way. At least some of the readings of the Iowa Poll indicate that Iowans support their state legislature more than they support the U.S. Congress. Like Americans elsewhere, Iowans are more approving of their individual legislator than of the collective legislature. A revealing 1978 Iowa poll illustrates these trends:

	Percent Who	
	Approve	Disapprove
U.S. Congress	34	45
Congressmen	56	16
Iowa Legislature	45	30
State Representative	49	14

Although approval or disapproval of the performance of the state legislature can vary, and inexplicably so, over time, changing levels of support do not seem to have a significant effect upon the capacity of the legislative institution to function. Indeed, Iowans' underlying support for the legislature as a constitutional and historic entity, and as a mechanism for lawmaking, undoubtedly is very high.[8]

In recent years, much has been said in popular print and in academic analyses about changes in citizens' confidence in institutions of government and politics. In general, declines in trust and confidence in national political institutions have been noted, and bemoaned. The Iowa Poll does take readings of the public pulse, but the existing evidence does not indicate unmistakable deterioration in confidence in government in Iowa. It would be fair to think of Iowans' feelings of confidence in government as guarded. Such attitudes exhibit very distinctly what songwriter and playright Meredith Willson, a Mason City, Iowa native, referred to as "Iowa Stubborn." Willson had the townspeople in "The Music Man" sing:

Oh, there's nothing halfway about the Iowa
way to treat you. . . . There's an Iowa kind of

special chip-on-the-shoulder attitude. We've
never been without. That we recall. We can be
cold as our falling thermometers in December.
If you ask about our weather in July. And we're
so by God stubborn we can stand touchin' noses.
For a week at a time and never see eye-to-eye. . . . [9]

The rich data of the Iowa Poll certainly show differences in Iowans'
confidence in the variety of aspects of Iowa government. Interestingly
enough, support for the Iowa State Highway Patrol is very high among
Iowans. Probably the patrol is the state governmental entity Iowans have the
most confidence in (in 1977 the patrol was trusted more than the President of
the United States, but by 1981 the President slightly eclipsed the patrol).

Institutions and agencies of local government get high marks for public
confidence in Iowa, indicative of the long-standing localistic tendencies of
the state.[10] Consistently, the political confidence ratings in Iowa give local
government, judges and courts, and the state legislature standings higher than
that of the U.S. Congress or some federal administrative agencies (notably
the department of agriculture), and higher, indeed, than the state government
regulatory agencies. Beyond their uneven levels, generalizations about
Iowans' support for governmental institutions and authorities are difficult to
draw. Lack of comparable research in other states makes it hard to know
whether support is especially high in Iowa, or not. It does seem fair to
conclude that Iowans trust their state governing institutions at moderately
high levels, about all that "Iowa stubborn" will allow. There is an underlying
strain of cynicism among Iowans and a general lack of deference to political
authorities that seem to reflect the existentialism and egalitarianism a rural
way of life breeds.

POLITICAL STYLE: CIVILITY AND OPENNESS

If the style of Iowa politics had to be distilled into a single term, it would
be bland. Iowa's political leaders—its governor and constitutional officers,
administrative leaders, legislators, and judges—generally are people of high
quality who carry a sense of public service to their political or governmental
roles. Political conflict in Iowa is remarkably civil and high-minded.
Ideological extremes are not popular in Iowa in the way that such extremes
can be sustained in Minnesota or Wisconsin, or perhaps Illinois (to draw
comparisons with nearby states). To be sure, there is a strain of agrarian
radicalism in Iowa's past, but the emergence of agribusiness has largely
removed any traces of this tradition.[11]

Left-wing radicalism is almost unknown in placid Iowa. Iowa's tilt in a
conservative direction might suggest spore for right-wing radicalism; however, this has not been the case. When right-wing leadership made headway

elsewhere, it did not succeed here; in the 1950s, McCarthyism did not find fertile ground in Iowa, and since then rightist groups like the John Birch Society have not been especially popular in the state.[12]

The blandness of Iowa politics stems partly from the homogeneity of its people and, in turn, of its leadership. Iowa politicians tend to be small town lawyers, businessmen, and other professionals, regardless of party affiliation. Although the organized labor movement is important, growing, and mainly committed to supporting Democrats, it is not very large. Unlike the politics of many states, there is no metropolitan-versus-outstate cleavage in Iowa because there is no substantial metropolis—Iowans tend to live in small towns and small cities pretty widely scattered over the terrain. Des Moines, the state capital and largest city, is less than a half million people in size, and not at all politically dominant.

Moreover, although Iowa is not ethnically homogeneous, ethnicity plays no important statewide role in politics. Iowa is more ethnically diverse than is often thought, of course. The largest ethnic group—Germans—retains some communal identification in settlements like the Amana colonies. In addition, there are the Czechs in Cedar Rapids, the Dutch of Pella and Orange City, and the Norwegians of Decorah. National associations of both Bohemian and Norwegian descendants have headquarters in Iowa. Along with Germans and Scandinavians, Englishmen and Irishmen immigrated to Iowa in abundance. Iowa retains considerable ethnic identity and variety, but these interesting, colorful, ethnic remnants are not very relevant politically. By and large, Iowa's ethnic groups have not divided politically along ethnic lines.[13] For example, no Iowa governor has had a German name; ethnic ticket-balancing is never practiced; and ethnic appeals are not made in political campaigns.

If Iowa politics is on the bland side, it would also be right to say that the practice of politics is very open. The state is, for example, very much open in the legal sense. The Iowa legislature enacted legislation—a public documents law and an open meetings law—insuring that government at all levels would be conducted, as they say, in the "sunshine." For a number of years, sessions of the legislature were televised by the state's public television network, and also broadcast on public radio. But the practice of wide coverage gave way to selective reporting when it was concluded that much of the deliberation was not interesting enough to capture a significant television or radio audience.

In addition, Iowa politics is open in the participatory sense. Political parties cling to organizational practices that endeavor to foster face-to-face involvement in party affairs by rank-and-file party adherents. This kind of openness is best illustrated by the caucus system. Every election year, Iowa Democrats and Republicans hold caucuses in the state's 2591 precincts. These party meetings involve the selection of delegates to county party conventions, registration of candidate preferences, selection of precinct party officers, and deliberation on policy or party platform questions. Held in January, these caucuses have taken on special importance in presidential election years because they provide the first test of candidates' popularity. Participation in party caucuses has been relatively large, compared to other states with caucus systems. The 1980 caucuses drew about 100,000 participants in each party, which is approximately 20 percent of those registered as Democrats or Republicans (about half a million Iowans are registered as Democrats, and half a million as Republicans). Iowa politicians believe the precinct caucus system used by their parties is a measure of Iowa's political openness—an indication, they think, of the grass-roots permeability of Republican and Democratic party organizations.

POLITICAL INTERACTION: COMPETITIVE PARTY POLITICS

Iowa ranks fairly high in the extent to which its citizens vote in elections. Given the fact that the average Iowan is pretty well-educated, and moderately affluent, political participation should be high. That their pattern of participation is rather mixed makes Iowans something of a puzzle as political creatures.

Turnout in presidential elections traditionally has been high in Iowa, about 10 percentage points higher than the national average. Presidential election turnout has declined in Iowa at the same rate at which national turnout has fallen. In 1980, 63 percent of the voting age population of Iowa turned out to vote for president. Three-fourths of Iowans are registered to vote, a requirement for primary and general election participation throughout the state since 1975. About 84 percent of the registered voters went to the polls in 1980.

In state contests, on the other hand, participation has not been very impressive. Only 20 percent of Iowans registered to vote bothered to cast ballots in the senatorial primaries in 1980, and only 17 percent voted in the gubernatorial primaries in 1978. The 1982 primaries drew 21 percent of registered voters to the polls, a somewhat larger than usual turnout resulting mainly from the vigorous contest for the Democratic gubernatorial nomination. In this primary, Roxanne Conlin, a former U.S. attorney from Des Moines, won the Democratic party nomination for governor handily against both the former Iowa house majority leader, Jerome Fitzgerald of Ft. Dodge, and the former state party chairman, Edward Campbell of Des Moines. Fitzgerald had been the Demoratic candidate in 1978, but had lost in a Ray landslide; Campbell had the backing of former Governor Hughes, who served as his campaign manager. Roxanne Conlin was the first woman to have won a major party nomination for governor in Iowa. Moreover, the 1982 gubernatorial election involved an element of competitiveness not present in such races for many years, as both Governors Hughes and Ray won election by wide margins. As a result, turnout for governor was higher in the general election (half of the voting age population went to the polls) than it had been for some time. Conlin was defeated by Republican Lieutenant Governor Terry Branstad, who won 53 percent of the vote.

Explaining the often unimpressive turnout of Iowans in state elections is not easy. Low primary turnout may occur because of the closed-primary system and the comparatively large proportion of Iowans who are registered as Independents rather than as Democrats or Republicans. The closed-primary system means that voters must be registered as Democrats or Republicans; Independents cannot partake. Although party registration can be effected at the polls, so no person wishing to vote in the primaries need be deterred, the requirement of a declaration of party affinity probably attenuates turnout. Moreover, a full third of registered voters in Iowa are signed up as Independents, a proportion of political skittishness greater than in most other states requiring party registration.

The four-year term for governor, with the gubernatorial election occurring in the nonpresidential even-numbered year has provoked low turnout in contests for governor. Governor Ray's popularity in the polls was not translated into a flood of voters to the polls in 1978—only 41 percent of the eligible voters turned out, which was 54 percent of those registered. In post-World War II elections, turnout in gubernatorial primaries has been lower in Iowa than in most nonsouthern states.[14] It is not at all clear why turnout in these elections is so low.

Another area of puzzlingly low participation in Iowa concerns financing of elections. Iowa law provides for the public financing of elections (in part) by providing public funds to the political parties. Public funds for this purpose are derived from an income tax checkoff. On the income tax form the taxpayer can designate one dollar to the Republican or Democratic party, or check a box designating 50 cents to each party, for him or herself and spouse. It is made clear on the tax form that the one or two dollar contributions do not come out of the taxpayer's pocket, but rather, are deducted from the taxes he or she would pay anyway. Nevertheless, taxpayer participation rates in Iowa have not been impressive, and average well below the participation rates of taxpayers in other states with similar public funding arrangements.[15] In the 1970s, the checkoff participation rate averaged only 15 percent (compared to an average of 17 percent in Kentucky, 26 percent in Michigan, 24 percent in Montana, and 19 percent in Minnesota).

Uneven participation in politics in Iowa probably stems partly, and perhaps fundamentally, from the low-key, nonideological, middle-of-the-road qualities of political discourse, and the widely shared "good government" ethos that downplays conflict and struggle in favor of accomodation, honesty, decency, and standing pat. Consensual politics is highly valued, but this blandness in Iowa politics does not help much to stimulate grass-roots interest.

That political party competition could have emerged in such a homogeneous and consensual milieu is perhaps most remarkable. Nevertheless, Iowa has been quite politically competitive since the 1960s. This political competitiveness has been indicated in the distribution of party identification in the Iowa electorate. The Iowa Poll regularly asks whether respondents in its samples think of themselves as Republicans, Democrats, or Independents. Since 1965, the numbers of Democratic and Republican adherents have been nearly equal in size, but the proportion of Iowans declaring their political independence has almost monotonically increased. The escalation in the percentage of Iowans refusing to take on a political party label peaked in 1979, when 40 percent of those who were polled said they adhered to no political party; in late 1980, the proportion of Independents had dropped to 35 percent, with 33 percent declaring themselves Republicans and 30 percent identifying themselves as Democrats.

Similar patterns of partisan attachment and competitiveness are indicated by voter registration data. Since 1975, Iowans have been required to register in order to vote (before that year, only adults residing in urban areas were required to register). Prior to the 1982 gubernatorial and congressional elections, there occurred a small decline in the percentage of Iowans registered as Independents, and a small increase in Democratic party registration. In percentage terms, the score was: Democrats, 34.5 percent; Republicans, 32 percent; Independents, 33.5 percent. The shift in registrations to the Democrats foreshadowed the widespread Democratic party successes in the 1982 election, although the Democratic candidate for governor was unsuccessful.

Both polling and registration data suggest that there is a substantial sector of the Iowa adult population—perhaps as much as two-thirds—that is politicized and in which the two political parties are competitive as to the numbers of their loyalists. Then, there is a sector of Independents, constituting 30 to 40 percent of the adult population, who are not much involved in politics beyond voting, in some measure, in presidential elections. This group does not participate at all in the caucus-convention participatory structure, or in the closed party primary elections.

In some states, political competitiveness is confined to small pockets, limited to a few urban counties. The periphery is the land of the unwashed, stagnating, unipartisanship of habit and tradition. In others, there is a seemingly immutable regionalism in which the northern counties are Republican and the southern counties (the "little dixie") are Democratic. In Iowa, political competitiveness is pretty evenly spread over the landscape. The topography of political competitiveness is such that counties in which the Democratic and Republican parties vie more or less equally for the loyalties of voters are widely scattered about the state. There is an interrupted vein of Democratic support down the center of the state, from Palo Alto and Kossuth counties in the north to Wapello and Davis counties in the south, and centering on heavily Democratic Carroll and Polk counties.[16] This vein of Democratic strength is flanked on the east by Republican counties stretching from Hancock and Mitchell counties in the north to Van Buran, Henry, and Louisa counties in the southeast.

Democratic strength in eastern Iowa centers on heavily Catholic Dubuque County; Republican strength in western Iowa clusters in the northwestern and southwestern counties.

Iowa's political competitiveness is indicated by the outcomes of elections in recent years. Although Governor Ray did not face a serious challenge after he was first elected in 1968, his long governorship did not represent Republican domination by any means. For the past decade, at least half of Iowa's congressional delegation has been made up of Democrats; and Iowa has been represented in the U.S. Senate by Democratic Senators Harold E. Hughes (1969–1975), Richard C. Clark (1973–1979), and John C. Culver (1975–1981), and by Republican Senators Roger Jepsen (1979–   ) and Charles E. Grassley (1981–   ). Although the Republicans have had a majority of the membership in the state legislature most of the time over the last twenty years, Democrats have constituted a significant competitive threat. In the last two decades, Democrats have held a majority of the lower house for a third of the sessions; they won decisive majorities of both houses in 1982.

Iowa's political parties are quite well organized by the standards of American state political parties. The Democratic and Republican organizations are, comparatively speaking, among the better established parties among the states. The Republican party in Iowa has a very long tradition, having been established in 1856 and having been the dominant party in the state for many years.[17] Buttressed by the dominant forces in the interest group infrastructure—first the Grand Army of the Republic, then the Iowa Farm Bureau Federation—the Republican party was able to contain intrastate political conflict for three-quarters of a century. The Iowa Democratic party, although it was the majority party in Iowa's pre-Civil War history, has had an effective statewide political organization for a much shorter time. Support for the Democratic party has grown among farmers and urban dwellers since the New Deal, as "the Depression relaxed the party allegiances of many Iowa voters who were formerly wedded to the Republican legacy inspired by the Civil War."[18]

Democratic party organization strength was profoundly stimulated by the election of Harold Hughes as Governor in 1962, and by his two subsequent reelections. Stimulated by increased urbanization and bolstered by the political expertise provided by the state's emerging labor movement (especially the United Automobile Workers), Democratic party organization grew stronger through the 1970s.[19] Organizational strength in both parties was enhanced by the passage of the Campaign Finance Disclosure Act in 1973, which among other things provided for public funding of the parties. The Democratic party has, in particular, found public funds helpful in maintaining party organizational activities between elections.

Today, the county and precinct organization of Iowa parties is moderately well-developed. Although a recent assessment of the performance of local party campaign activities and organizational functions indicates that the Iowa parties rank near the middle among the 50 states in local party organizational strength,[20] it is quite likely that this assessment underestimates their actual strength. The precinct caucus role in selecting delegates and handling political issues in county, congressional district, state, and national party conventions helps to stimulate local party activists and leaders. Traditionally, party leaders have played a part in selecting candidates for elective offices, and in financing local campaigns.[21] Moreover, at the state level both Democratic and Republican parties have established party headquarters and permanent staffs, so that these party organizations are very much going concerns on a year-round basis and not, as before, merely ephemeral manifestations of the season of electioneering.

Political parties are at the center of politics in Iowa. They have not gone away. Nor have they declined, as so many commentators of parties have noted in other parts of the country. Since the 1960s, Iowa political parties have become much stronger—both Democrats and Republicans are organizationally more effective, programmatically more cohesive, and much more competitive. Iowa has quite a healthy party system.

The establishment of a competitive two-party system in Iowa has meant the erosion of power in other sectors, notably in the political interest group sector. More specifically, interest-group influence has declined in Iowa in the last quarter century; the dominant interest group for many decades, the Iowa Farm Bureau, collapsed as a potent force when it lost out in the legislative reapportionment struggles of the 1960s.[22]

Iowa politics is not primarily a politics of interest-group power. The collapse of the once-powerful farm bureau did not destroy interest groups. Today organized teachers, trucking companies, farmers, and various segments of agribusiness have political influence. Iowans would not want their state government, or any outside government, to do anything inimical to agriculture. But Iowa is not a farm state the way it used to be. Urbanization and industrial development have eroded the once overweening influence of agricultural interests. While the political role of the Democratic and Republican parties has grown, the role of interest groups has greatly diminished. The influence attempts of private groups is something to be regulated and controlled—the legislature makes their representatives register publicly, disclose their activities, and wear special identifying badges. So, while interest groups do have a certain role in Iowa politics, they are not the main actors.

Political power is, in fact, widely diffused in Iowa. Much of it is used up in the communities and counties of the state. Iowa has a very long tradition of strong and effective local government, a tradition brought to the state by its many Yankee settlers, a tradition of first informal and then constitutionally-sanctioned home rule for cities. Iowa counties (there are 99, many jewelled by lovingly preserved Victorian-era courthouses) are vibrant and modern units of government in many cases. Much of the governing that goes on in Iowa emanates from its cities and counties. Iowa, a land of small towns and small cities, is manageably governable. From the point of view of exercising political power, Iowa is, as has been said in other contexts, "a piece of cake." It is manageable, its problems are resolvable, and its people can, by and large, govern themselves through their local governments.

Iowa's central government has grown a great deal since the mid-1960s and the days of the Great Society, but as noted earlier, the growth of Iowa's governing apparatus has been less marked than in most other states. Moreover, Iowa's state bureaucracy remains relatively small, staffed by about 30,000 bureaucrats. The machinery of the state's executive branch is something of a melange, with some 70 separate offices, departments, commissions, bureaus, and boards. Even so, considerable reorganization and consolidation of state agencies has been undertaken in the last two decades, and Iowa's bureaucracy is, comparatively speaking, quite efficient.

The main attraction in Iowa government is in the relationship between the governor and the legislature. Since 1969, the Iowa legislature has met annually; its 100 house members elected from single-member districts that, when paired, form the 50 senate districts. The 16 house and 15 senate committees provide a very effective committee system that was substantially streamlined in the mid-1960s. The legislature is well-organized by the two political parties, each of which has a full panoply of party caucuses and floor leaders. The party caucuses meet frequently, and play a central role in legislative policymaking. The legislature also has a small, but a demonstrably able staff.[23]

Historically, Iowa had a weak governor system. Governors were elected for only two years, and a firm two-term tradition had developed that produced high gubernatorial turnover. The governor had a veto power, but the item veto was not provided in Iowa until the reforms of the late 1960s. Other state constitutional officers (secretary of state, auditor, treasurer, secretary of agriculture, and attorney general) are elected independently of the governor. But Governor Ray's administrative leadership and long tenure in the governorship have attenuated the formal weakness of the office in Iowa. By the end of his long gubernatorial service, Governor Ray had appointed all of the key administrative personnel in state government, and was in full control of the major departments that constitute the heart of state administration.

Governor Ray's relations with the bureaucracy had evolved so that he was effectively in charge; his relations with the legislature were significantly less satisfactory. Republican-controlled sessions of the legislature have always been eager to show their independence from the Republican governor, and Governor Ray sometimes seemed to get along better with legislatures under Democratic control. Until 1979, a progressive Republican, Arthur Neu, served as lieutenant governor and presided over the senate. His replacement, Terry E. Branstad, represented the conservative wing of the state's Republican party. Accordingly, in the last few years of his gubernatorial tenure Governor Ray did not have a strong friend in the senate leadership. As a result, the tension between the governor and the legislature, always the mainspring of Iowa politics, has grown. Despite the fact that

Governor Ray and Lieutenant Governor Branstad represented different wings of the Iowa Republican party, Ray was a fairly vigorous supporter of Branstad's successful gubernatorial race in 1982.

Iowa remains an attractive place to govern, and to be governed. The resources available to the state government are more or less commensurate with the demands made on government. Iowa can govern itself; it is probably more independent than most states (along with neighbors like Minnesota and Wisconsin). Its main-street politicians and its statehouse public officials have a sense that they are in charge, that the state is governable, that Iowa is a little republic responding rather effectively to its citizens' needs and demands.

Iowa gets its top politicians mainly from the main streets of its towns, though some still come from the farm. Overwhelmingly, these politicians are well-educated, quite cosmopolitan people. The Democrats and Republicans who fill the large ideological center of Iowa politics themselves exhibit, and rather firmly insist upon, an even-handedness, a fairness, an openness, and a balance that makes Iowa politics very much a politics of the "middle." As a consequence, these politicians rarely have much color; they are bland, and they make Iowa politics tempered, moderate, and occasionally dull. Yet, Iowa politics has become competitive, mainly because of changes in the social and economic configuration of the state, but partly because a competitive politics is an integral part of what many Iowans believe to be "good government." So, middleness, blandness, and competitiveness are leitmotifs for politics in Iowa. Iowa novelist Ruth Suckow once said that Iowa "combines the qualities of half a dozen states, and perhaps that is the reason why it so often seems, and more to its own people than to others, the most undistinguished place in the world."[24]

NOTES

1. Joseph F. Wall, *Iowa: A History* (New York: Norton, 1978), p. xvii.

2. Samuel C. Patterson, Ronald D. Hedlund, and G. Robert Boynton, *Representatives and Represented* (New York: Wiley Interscience, 1975), p. 162.

3. Daniel J. Elazar, *American Federalism: A View from the States*, 2nd ed. (New York: Crowell, 1972), pp. 90–120.

4. See the *Des Moines Register and Tribune Iowa Poll*, 29 April 1979. The poll release used national results that were drawn from the Gallup Poll.

5. Ronald D. Hedlund and Charles W. Wiggins, "Legislative Politics in Iowa," in *Midwest Legislative Politics*, ed. Samuel C. Patterson (Iowa City, Iowa: Institute of Public Affairs, University of Iowa, 1967), pp. 7–36.

6. Larry Sabato, "Public Opinion and Gubernatorial Power," *State Government*, 55 (Fall 1982):77.

7. Samuel C. Patterson, "American State Legislatures and Public Policy," in *Politics in the American States: A Comparative Analysis*, eds. Herbert Jacob and Kenneth N. Vines, 3rd ed. (Boston: Little, Brown, 1976), p. 164.

8. Patterson et al., *Representatives and Represented*.

9. See Meredith Willson, *The Music Man* (New York: Pyramid Books, 1962), p. 148.

10. Elazar, *American Federalism*, pp. 198–203.

11. Leland L. Sage, *A History of Iowa* (Ames, Iowa: Iowa State University Press, 1974), pp. 186–215.

12. See, for instance, Arnold A. Rogow, "The Loyalty Oath Issue in Iowa, 1951," *American Political Science Review*, 55 (December 1961):861–869.

13. For example, see Stephen H. Rye, "Danish American Political Behavior: The Case of Iowa, 1887–1936," *The Bridge: Journal of the Danish American Heritage Society*, 2 (January 1979):31–44.

14. Malcolm E. Jewell and David Olson, *American State Political Parties and Elections* (Homewood, Ill.: Dorsey, 1978), p. 143.

15. Ruth S. Jones, "State Public Campaign Finance: Implications for Partisan Politics," *American Journal of Political Science*, 25 (May 1981):342–361.

16. Charles Wiggins, a long-time student of Iowa's politics, has argued that the traditional vein of Democratic party support in the state runs diagonally across the state from northwest to southeast, roughly following the Des Moines River valley. He observes, in support of this interpretation, that the first Iowa settlers were southern Democrats who settled in the river valleys where timber was available for building cabins and for burning in winter. Moreover, most of the coal mining activity in Iowa was in river valleys, and the early miners were East European and German Catholics who supported the Democratic party. See Charles Wiggins, *Interest Group Power Within State Legislative Systems: The Case of the Iowa Farm Bureau Federation*, unpublished Ph.D. dissertation, Washington University, St. Louis, Missouri, 1964, pp. 150–170.

17. Harlan Hahn, *Urban-Rural Conflict: The Politics of Chance* (Beverly Hills, Calif.: Sage, 1971), pp. 33–69.

18. *Ibid.*, p. 67

19. James C. Larew, *A Party Reborn: The Democrats of Iowa 1950–1974* (Iowa City, Iowa: Iowa State Historical Society, 1980).

20. James L. Gibson, Cornelius P. Cotter, John F. Bibby, and Robert J. Huckshorn, "Wither the Local Parties? A Cross-Sectional and Longitudinal Analysis of the Strength of Party Organizations," paper presented at the Annual Meeting of the Western Political Science Association, San Diego, California, March 25–27, 1982

21. Samuel C. Patterson and G.R. Boynton, "Legislative Recruitment in a Civic Culture," *Social Science Quarterly*, 50 (September 1969):243–263.

22. See John R. Schmidhauser, "Iowa's Campaign for a Constitutional Convention in 1960," *Eagleton Institute Cases in Practical Politics*, ed. Paul Tillett (New Brunswick, N.J.; Rutgers University, 1963). Also, see Charles Wiggins, "The Post-World War II Legislative Reapportionment Battle in Iowa Politics," in *Patterns and Perspectives in Iowa History*, ed. Dorothy Schwieder (Ames, Iowa: Iowa State University Press, 1973), pp. 403–430. And, see Wiggins, "Interest Group Involvement and Success Within a State Legislative System," in *Public Opinion and Public Policy: A Reader in Political Linkage*, ed. Norman Luttbeg, 3rd ed. (Itasca, Ill.: F.F. Peacock, 1981), pp. 226–239; and Wiggins and William F. Browne, "Interest Groups and Public Policy Within a State Legislative Setting," *Polity*, 14 (Spring 1982): 549–558.

23. On the organization of the Iowa legislature and the development of partisanship in it, see Charles Wiggins, "Party Politics in the Iowa Legislature," *Midwest Journal of Political Science*, 11 (February 1967):86–97; and *The Legislative Process in Iowa* (Ames, Iowa: Iowa State University Press, 1972).

24. Quoted in Wall, *Iowa: A History*, pp. xvi–xvii.

5
Michigan
PETER KOBRAK

In some ways the 1982 state Republican convention dinner was typical. The popular state Republican party chairman, Mel Larsen, smoothly served as master of ceremonies, ticking off the names of the distinguished guests at the head table: former Governor George Romney and his politically active wife; gubernatorial aspirant, Richard Headlee; Senate candidate Phil Ruppe; and the variety of dignitaries who graced the convention with their presence or "made it all possible."

However, the man who epitomized the Michigan Republican party for 14 years was not there, and somehow his absence too was appropriate. The convention was addressed by David Stockman, stalking horse for the Republican President with whom Governor William Milliken had remained on correct, but never cordial, terms, since their political values and priorities differed so markedly. The convention was held in the Grand Plaza that symbolized the money and power of two radically conservative businessmen, Board Chairman Jay VanAndel and President Richard DeVos of the Amway Corporation. Their differences with the governor were never far below the surface. The convention belonged to the conservative wing of the party whose three 1982 primary candidates had combined 70 percent of the vote, thereby driving candidate Lieutenant Governor James Brickley out of his favored position as heir apparent of the moderate Milliken regime. It was, in short, the end of the Milliken era.

POLITICAL CULTURE: THE "GOOD COMMUNITY"

Michigan politics is a vehicle through which virtually every major group at one time or another attempts to gain the resources necessary to cope with the state's rapidly changing economic and social environment. The highly cyclical and volatile nature of Michigan's economy is associated in modern times with the automobile industry. The state, however, experienced earlier

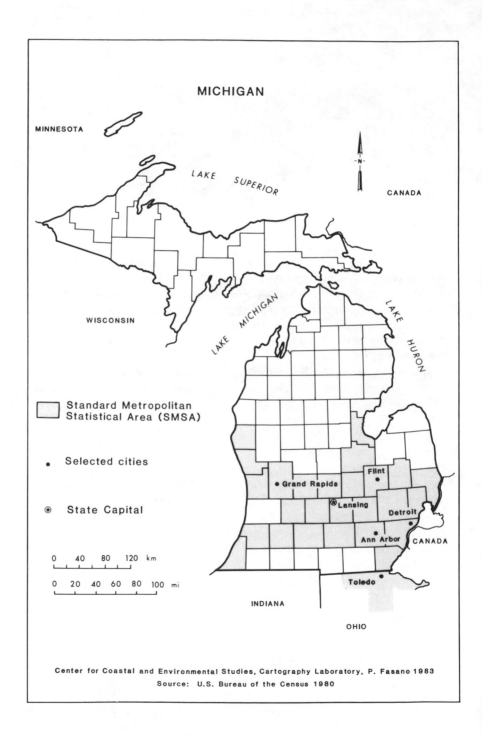

MICHIGAN

MINNESOTA

LAKE SUPERIOR

CANADA

WISCONSIN

LAKE MICHIGAN

LAKE HURON

Standard Metropolitan
Statistical Area (SMSA)

• Selected cities

⊛ State Capital

0   40   80   120 km

0   20 40 60 80 100 mi

• Grand Rapids

Flint

⊛ Lansing

Detroit

Ann Arbor

CANADA

Toledo

INDIANA

OHIO

Center for Coastal and Environmental Studies, Cartography Laboratory, P. Fasano 1983
Source: U.S. Bureau of the Census 1980

cycles of prosperity and decay that laid the groundwork for a "boom-and-bust" mentality that runs through the state's political culture.

Michigan's lumber industry cut a swath through large parts of the state in the mid 1800s. When in much of northern Michigan the assumption that the abandoned timber land would support agriculture proved largely false, the result was the elimination of the railroad lines built to serve those economic interests and the communities that had sprung up around them. Prior to that time, the fortunes of state entrepreneurs had risen and fallen with the fur trade, land speculation, farming, and most dramatically, mining in the Upper Peninsula. Here, mines were built, and later abandoned when more accessible and modern mines elsewhere led these substantial investments to be discontinued or postponed indefinitely. Even within the field of transportation, Michigan possessed a thriving wagon and carriage industry that, by the 1890s, included approximately 125 firms.[1] These horse-drawn vehicle manufacturers were replaced by a whole gamut of small automobile companies that in turn were consigned to oblivion as Ford, General Motors, and Chrysler eventually squeezed or bought them out.

One might expect that such experience with relentless cycles of industrial prosperity and decay would have left the state shellshocked and socialist in self-defense. Instead, the state developed a confidence and faith in economic growth, as the burgeoning earnings of the rapidly expanding corporate winners greatly overshadowed the economic hardship of the losers. Such faith in unlimited economic growth and technology became a substitute for economic planning and a surrogate for concern about the future.

These trends were reflected in the state's political culture, as it was three progressive, successful men from business families who transferred their growth orientation from the world of business to the world of politics. Democratic Governor G. Mennen "Soapy" Williams, an heir to the Mennen soap fortune, Republican Governor George Romney, a savior of the American Motors Company from a boom-and-bust fate, and Republican William Milliken, an executive in the family's Traverse City department store, revitalized the moribund political parties and reconstructed state government.

The commitment to progressivism was an easy one to make. Expanding resources eliminated the need to make painful choices between heavy taxation and extensive services or set stringent priorities as to which services should be expanded. Economic growth thus took progressive Republicans and Democrats alike off the hook; they could have their comparatively reasonable taxes and excellent services too. Expansive politics was a natural outgrowth of extensive economic growth.

Michiganians could also continue to manifest a belief in individualism even while big business, the automobile companies, the United Automobile Workers (UAW), and big government itself were creating an increasingly interdependent, and to some extent more vulnerable, state economy. In Daniel Elazar's terminology, the state has a moralistic political culture in which government functions as a commonwealth seeking to achieve the "good community" through positive action.[2] Increasing interdependence, though, remained relatively invisible. The automobile companies made decisions that maximized short-term profits at the expense of sufficient research and development, productivity improvements, and decisions to strengthen the capacity of the firm to react sensitively to changing market demands. Such choices camouflaged and postponed the day when challenges to the industry would place in jeopardy Michigan's sanguine political culture. As late as 1979, General Motors recorded one of its most successful sales years.

While state services expanded significantly under the leadership of moderates in both political parties, the citizenry never committed itself to the kind of tax base that could support big government on a solid footing. Despite significant efforts during and after the 1963 constitutional convention, proposals for a graduated state income tax were soundly defeated. When economic danger signals did arise in the late 1970s, well before the executive or legislative leadership in either party wanted to confront the taxation question, a substantial block of voters from both parties supported placing a stringent tax limitation referendum on the ballot in two different elections. Only concerted efforts by a coalition of politicians and interest groups on the second such occasion in 1978 prevented the adoption of taxation stipulations that would have sharply reduced the size and scope of state government.

Thus, there existed, behind this seemingly liberal view towards politics, a significant number of voters who assented to big government only when the economic largesse of the automobile industry would permit such policies at no particular cost to them. Voters viewed the state's culture more ambig-uously when confronted with the question of precisely what they themselves were prepared to fund. At that time, Michigan's citizenry revealed itself to be more conservative on economic issues than on cultural or social issues.

Michigan citizens are rarely effusive in extolling the virtues of their state, but they have been interested over the years in their history, pleased with their considerable travel throughout the state, and quietly satisfied with their comparatively high quality of life. While they no longer identify as much with the goals or future of the automobile industry, their fascination with cars and their history remains high. Thus, Flint, as an integral part of its economic development plans, intended to open AutoWorld in 1984—"Our own Disneyland about wheels," as the mayor liked to call it.

A more tangible and visible symbol of state pride may be found in the shower of affection poured on the University of Michigan's football team and its long-time coach, Bo Schembechler. In 1981, when the coach turned down a more lucrative offer from outside the state to remain with the Wolverines, the sigh of relief was almost audible throughout the state. Citizens also take pride in the educational facilities at the "Harvard of the Midwest." They manifest satisfaction as well with the rest of their extensive public education system, which includes: Wayne State, a wide-ranging "urban university" in Detroit; Michigan State University, with its world famous agricultural school; four regional universities that in 1981 had a combined enrollment of 67,000 students; the four-year colleges; and the still growing junior-college network.

Michigan is so far-flung geographically, however, and so heterogeneous in its ethnic composition that, as Neal Peirce and John Keefe point out, the state appears to lack a common personality.[3] Ever since the War of 1812, the state needed and used immigrants to work the huge mines in the north, build the railroads, and populate the lumber camps.[4] Hundreds of thousands of Germans, Canadians, English, Irish, and Dutch constituted that population wave; later in the nineteenth century, they were followed by Cornishmen and Scandinavians. The impact of these migrations could be seen at the 1850 Constitutional Convention where out of the 100 delegates, only one was a native of Michigan.[5] By the early twentieth century, the state was taking on something of the character of a mini-United Nations as Eastern Europeans, Italians, and Greeks moved into the industrial opportunities that arose in southeastern Michigan. Arabic-speaking peoples in the late 1970s were the most recent migrants, and they were more numerous in Detroit than in any other U.S. city.[6] By the 1970s, however, Michigan recorded a significant change in its migration pattern, as, for the first time in its history, the state experienced a net loss of 247,000 by outmigration between 1970 and 1978.

It was interstate migration between 1940 and 1970, that placed greater strain on statewide identification than Michigan had hitherto experienced. After World War I, Detroit was already a city with a population of one million, but with only 50,000 blacks. Then, during World War II, southern blacks and subsequently, southern whites were attracted to the prosperous southeastern Michigan industrial area. By 1973, blacks outnumbered whites in Detroit, and in 1982, 47 percent of Flint's population was black.

This large concentration of black and southern white emigrants, compressed into the southeastern Michigan area, with the now well-established previous immigrant wave, led to an undercurrent of tension. Two of the worst race riots in America's history occurred here. In 1943, 34 persons were killed, and in 1967, as the nation watched on television, 43 persons died. Neighborhoods near General Motor's international head-quarters and other Detroit landmarks burned. The ethnic and racial cleavages in Detroit were such that, when the city's first black mayor, Coleman Young, in 1975 completed his initial year in office, it was deemed a success by many, simply because the city had not "exploded."

Ironically, the potential for disaster of this situation so shook respon-sible politicians in both parties that it served to temper the normal outstate-downstate rivalry found historically in Michigan. State legislators from a number of outstate areas, and particularly the Detroit suburbs, had to watch out that they were not accused of being "too soft on Detroit." Awareness grew that, in some fashion, the state would be compelled to help the city. However, reluctantly, Michigan was one of those states in the forefront in adopting policies to aid large cities in establishing a more broadly-based tax program and assuming a greater responsibility for social program costs and transportation policy.[7]

While Michigan is often associated in the minds of outsiders with Detroit, the state's demographic makeup is changing significantly. According to the 1980 census, the greater Detroit metropolitan area accounts for over four million of Michigan's nine million citizens. This proportion represents a drop from 50 to 47 percent of the state's population from the 1970 census. That figure, however, understates the shifting balance within the state. The six county metropolitan area includes the balance of Wayne County and, more significantly, counties and suburbs removed spiritually and in some cases physically from the central city. The figure also misses such dynamics as the growth of the more removed but bordering counties of Lapeer, Livingston, and Macomb, and the extensive population drain in metropolitan Detroit. The actual city of Detroit reached a high of 1.8 million residents in 1950, had about 1.2 million in 1980, and, according to the projections, will have less than 1 million residents by the year 2000.[8]

The state also includes several other regions, and Michiganians often identify more closely with these comparatively homogeneous areas and their own communities within them. The Upper Peninsula thus possesses virgin timberland side by side with large areas developed by a rapacious mining industry. The area is characterized by waterfalls and mountains that beckon backpackers and campers, an economy that remains a perennial candidate for economic development, and a hardy frontier spirit among its residents. The northern region of the Lower Peninsula includes: much of the timberland poleaxed by the lumber industry; a tri-city area noted for its huge Dow Chemical complex and accompanying environmental controversies; and fruit farms and other agriculture that are second only to the main crop of tourists. Southwestern Michigan includes the state's most diversified economy, its second largest city, Grand Rapids, and much of the best farm land in the state.

Michigan citizens are not particularly supportive of their state government and politics, but normally they are reasonably tolerant of its shortcomings. Moreover, they do not appear to harbor deep distrust of the parties, actors, and institutions involved in decision making. Perhaps one reason that they view the state with equanimity is that they are generally not concerned with state affairs.[9] Furthermore, despite the relatively good coverage of state affairs in the *Detroit Free Press*, the *Detroit News*, and on Detroit TV stations, and with the absence of adequate media coverage elsewhere in the state, Detroit citizens manifest little more interest in such activities than their outstate counterparts.

Most state residents are reasonably satisfied that the people running state government are, at the very least, not crooks. Roughly half of those surveyed believed that not many Michigan officials are dishonest. An interesting exception is the 37 percent who identify themselves as Democrats and believe that there are quite a lot of crooks in state government.

Furthermore, when one compares Detroit and outstate residents, 35 percent of Detroit residents emerge as more skeptical of honesty in government.*

It is waste and inefficiency, rather than dishonesty, that seem to erode the support of Michigan citizens for their government. Democrats as well as Republicans doubt the ability of the state to control its budget and limit its expenditures. Fifty-nine percent of outstate residents and 72 percent of Detroiters expressed the view that people in state government waste a lot of money. Furthermore, while it is supposed to be Republicans who are most concerned with this issue, more Democrats than Republicans emphasized this concern.

Even before Michigan's economic woes intensified in the early 1980s, Michiganians were somewhat dubious of their leadership, particularly as symbolized in the state legislature. They were also split on the extent to which state bureaucrats and politicians could be trusted. In general, they manifested more enthusiasm for incumbent politicians whom they knew and liked than for the political system of which they were a part.

Given the highly competitive nature of Michigan politics and the issue orientation of the state's parties and many of its voters, it is surprising that Michiganians are more attracted to the candidate rather than the party. Ticket-splitting is increasingly common, and when voters find appealing incumbents, they stick with them regardless of party affiliation. Governor Soapy Williams, for example, was in office for 12 years before retiring; Governor George Romney cut short his term in office to run for president and eventually become secretary of the U.S. Department of Housing and Urban Development; and Governor William Milliken retired after a record 14 years in office.[10] In the U.S. Senate as well, voters reelected Democrats Philip Hart and Donald Riegle, and repudiated Republican Robert Griffin in his third try for office only after he had the temerity to show little enthusiasm for running yet again. The selection of these personalities is also done, in part, with that elusive, intangible idea of "quality" in mind.

A double whammy in the form of a tax revolt and economic decline in the late 1970s and early 1980s, it is generally agreed, reduced the trust of Michigan citizens in their regime. Initially, it was a tax revolt by a large, intense minority of Michigan residents that sapped this confidence in a bitter 1978 battle over tax reduction. While the established parties succeeded in preventing the passage of a crippling tax proposal, the voters were so fed up with the political process by the time of the general election that they defeated every nonproperty tax proposal on the ballot as well. They even voted down a noncontroversial proposal to restrict by law the civil immunity of legislators, and another to remove the lieutenant governor as presiding officer of the senate. The vote reflected the conservative mood in the country generally, and it is doubtful if many voters understood these proposals buried

---

*Since many Democrats in Detroit are receiving or dispensing one or more state services, familiarity either with Michigan agencies, or with Coleman Young's Democratic machine, or both, has apparently bred contempt.

at the bottom of the ballot, a long one, even by Michigan standards. Both proposals were supported by a popular governor and had no significant opposition. Such was the mood that voters were now saying no to their leaders, no matter what the issue.

Michigan residents, by the 1980s, were also feeling the impact of the changing economy. A poll conducted by the *Detroit News* shortly before the 1980 general election found that relief from economic hard times had become the electorate's first priority and that people were only marginally optimistic about the likelihood of economic improvement.[11] Confronted with a fiscal crisis, and fearing a harsher measure if they did not act, the governor and Democratic legislative leadership jointly put forth a ballot proposal that was supported by party, local government, labor, and business leaders. It would have simultaneously reduced property taxes, increased the sales tax, and allegedly provided sufficient funds to enable the state to balance its budget as required under the state constitution. The measure went down in a stunning 563,050 to 1,447,318 defeat. The vote left the governor little choice but to admit that distrust of leadership was a factor in the outcome. It also prompted the speaker of the house, Bobby Crim, to observe that such distrust threatened the success of efforts to revitalize the economy.

While Michigan residents may not entirely trust their government and its leaders, that does not stop them from seeking help from Lansing, the state capital, if and when the circumstances seem to require it. Individual supplicants, busloads of grass-roots groups from literally anywhere in the state, and lobbyist articulation of group demands are all frequent occurrences. Whether it is in the chips or close to bankruptcy, state government is expected to produce on demand. It is commonplace for politicians, regardless of their political stripe, to be caught in a squeeze between irate taxpayers on the one hand and demanding groups of all kinds on the other.

As of 1980, Michigan was spending approximately $1000 per state resident, and 41 percent of its general fund budget was returned to local governments. Education, social services, public and mental health, and transportation—the services that most directly affect the citizenry—accounted for 79 percent of the total state budget.[12] Indeed, part of Michigan's economic difficulty in the early 1980s stemmed from this very generosity. The state found itself locked into entitlement programs whose tentacles, when one combines state and federal monies, extended in some cases from one of every eight to one of every ten citizens throughout the state.

Michigan voters expect their politicians to exhibit enthusiasm for the job and work hard. They like their candidates to be "nice people," but they also look for a certain toughness.[13] They thus were attracted to William Milliken, a man noted for his civility, concern for people and their problems, and charm. Yet they went along with one of his initial acts as governor, the ouster of the conservative speaker of the house, who was a vigorous opponent of his party's moderate wing. Voters approved when George

Romney, widely respected for his integrity and intelligence, overhauled a moribund Republican party. Some years earlier, they acquiesced when Governor Soapy Williams, known for his cheerful demeanor, his polka-dotted bow tie, and his concern for the poor, dispatched an equally moribund Democratic party faction to permanent political oblivion and replaced it with his labor and liberal allies.

Politics is also expected to be honest, fair, and free of corruption. The occasional state legislator who is caught in an illegal act is thus quietly but firmly edged out. Political campaigns tend to be hardhitting, but relatively clean. Emphasis, however, is not always placed on the high quality of debate. Newspaper analyses and discussions among politicans often sound more like assessments of prize fighters than evaluations of competing party platforms. The view that Michigan parties come close to the type of ideologically cohesive political parties found in European countries is not supported by the evidence.[14]

Other than taxes, the issue that cuts across the politics of moderation continues to be race. Historically, Michigan has provided economic opportunity in the automobile industry for blacks, and its constitution in 1963 was the first in the country to specify in detail the nature and duties of its civil-rights commission. Moderate Democratic and Republican party activists alike were in the forefront of the effort to assist blacks. Governor Soapy Williams encouraged a drive to use the state's power to grant broker licenses as a lever to end discriminatory practices in real estate transactions.[15] Governors Williams, Romney, and Milliken all made visible and concerted efforts to reach out to Michigan's black population, and during their tenure, the number of black executive, legislative, and judicial officials grew appreciably. The Republican party moved more slowly in this direction, but by 1970 both political parties had black vice-chairmen.[16] In 1978, when he ran for reelection, Governor Milliken's support for programs benefiting Detroit and its low-income black population enabled him to achieve the unprecedented feat in modern times, even for a moderate Republican, of winning a plurality of Wayne County's gubernatorial vote. When he retired in 1983, three black department heads, from among the 19 departments of the executive branch, retired with him.

This liberal attitude of the moderate party elite stands in some contrast to the more ambiguous views of the Michigan electorate. Less enthusiastic attitudes towards blacks than towards whites reflect recurring circumstances that place in question Michigan's progressive reputation. Hard-fought school desegregation battles have been waged in Detroit and several outstate urban areas. School desegregation tensions partly explain the success that George Wallace enjoyed, when in the 1972 Democratic primary, he won 51 percent of the vote in a campaign heavily tinged with racial appeals.[17] Two of Michigan's smaller cities, located in the same county in southwestern Michigan, are separated merely by a river. One, Benton Harbor, is predominantly black, while the other, St. Joseph, is almost exclusively white. In such decaying urban centers as Detroit, Pontiac, and Flint, blacks continue to be located in downtown "target areas" where, in the now all too familiar story, public transportation atrophies and economic growth shifts to outlying areas. By the 1980s, shrinking resources appeared to leave Democratic and moderate Republican party leaders more sympathetic to black needs and demands than the Michigan electorate as a whole. It remained to be seen whether an emerging new generation of UAW leadership, led by Owen Bieber, would continue the enlightened policies of its founder, Walter Reuther, and its elder stateman, Douglas Fraser, or depart to join the bulk of its membership that had long since migrated to the suburbs.

POLITICAL STYLE: CIVILITY AND PRAGMATISM

In reflecting on Michigan politics, former Governor Williams argues that the state has developed what he is pleased to call "programmatic, participative politics." This kind of politics is "idealistic, but practical."[18] The parties have retained some of this programmatic flavor, but the state's politics has gradually evolved into a strange admixture of relatively important political parties and individualistic candidates seeking to mount a strong personal appeal to an increasingly independent electorate. Because of Michigan's moralistic political culture, candidates seem to emerge from a somewhat similar mold, and are expected to possess a political style that is not set down in systematic fashion, but may be seen through media analyses, candidate and party strategies, and voter expectations.

Given the state's history of programmatic parties, ethnic, racial, and religious tensions, labor and business antagonism, and an upstate-downstate rivalry, the potential is certainly there for the state to tear itself apart politically. It may be the very presence of these tendencies that has led to a political ethos in both parties that places great emphasis on personal and group moderation. Candidates are carefully assessed in newspaper editorials and analyses on the extent to which they exhibit the necessary "responsibility," "gentility," "prudence," and "restraint." In choosing to endorse James Blanchard as its candidate for governor, the *Free Press* expressed disappointment at his fuzzy stands on some key issues, but opted for a "unifier rather than a polarizer," a man who understands the need for compromise, and who is willing to be a "listener and a learner" in relation to a wide range of groups.[19] In comparing former Governors Soapy Williams and Milliken, veteran journalist Judd Arnett, in a similar vein, pointed to "compassion, lack of intolerance, faith in humanity, and willingness to deviate from ancient customs" as characteristics that the two men shared.[20] Former Governor Romney also shared these traits. On one occasion during his 1963 campaign, he showed up uninvited for a civil-rights demonstration against housing discrimination in fashionable Grosse Pointe, an all-white suburb of Detroit. After he gave a speech in which he declared that the "elimination of injustice and discrimination is the most critical and urgent problem" in the nation, the demonstrators gave him a standing ovation.[21] Michiganians value such acts of political commitment. In evaluating the Milliken era, friend and foe alike paid tribute to the integrity with which the governor approached issues over the years as he worked with members of both political parties.

Effectiveness in projecting a sense of responsibility, character, purpose, and of being on top of the job is more important than a long-time party affiliation. When Romney initially ran for governor, he played down his Republican affiliation. His opponent in a subsequent gubernatorial campaign, Zolton Ferency, was unable to make much political headway with his frequent quip that "I called Romney a Republican and was immediately accused of conducting a smear campaign."[22] Journalist Robert Sherrill was surprised to find that, in Grand Rapids by the 1970s, some key actors became politically involved not through long-time partisan convictions and affiliations, but through personal recruitment by respected statewide candidates. Democratic district chairman Robert Kleiner was not a Democrat until the mid-1950s, when Phil Hart, then lieutenant governor, "persuaded me that's where I wanted to be." A decade later, Kleiner's cousin, William Seidman, was recruited by George Romney to take on the Republican label, and run for state auditor general.[23] When Senator Donald Riegle changed political parties, he took much of his personal network of business supporters with him, and simply added additional labor strength to the unions that were already supporting him.

Michiganians expect their candidates to project this personal style not only through party activities and the media, but also through individual contact with the myriad groups active throughout the state. When Soapy Williams resurrected the Democratic party in the 1950s, he did so partly by traveling widely in the state and demonstrating this highly successful political style to these groups. He spoke from the heart when he later observed that "the dedication to church, lodge, farm organization, business club, union, conservation club, veterans organization, charity, or other group by countless Michigan citizens must be seen and experienced to be fully grasped."[24] Williams astutely combined his travels with a wide variety of communication techniques, including television appearances and a weekly newspaper column. He displayed the kind of approach that Michiganians like to hear when he warned that, "once you get too far ahead of the people you become ineffective and your legislative and administrative programs then tend to lag."[25]

Michiganians may want their candidates to project a certain political style and ability to relate to them, but they do not want their political leaders to be just like them. The four Republican primary candidates for the U.S. Senate race in 1982 and Senator Riegle himself were all associated with some combination of the University of Michigan or Ivy League schools and successful professional or business careers.

These candidates tend to be amateurs either in the sense that they had little prior political experience in running for elective office—as in the case of Williams, Romney, and Headlee—or because they developed their political position at least partially through independence from their political party. Sometimes they chose to remain aloof. When Governor Frank Murphy won the Michigan governorship in 1936 on the strength of his personal campaign, the Depression, and Franklin Roosevelt's coattails, he was not an experienced leader in the weakened state party, and he did not subsequently try to control and strengthen party machinery.[26] Former Senator Phil Hart also showed little enthusiasm for party institution building. In both cases the result was to reduce party effectiveness, since candidates able to project the appropriate style are party assets in a state where party identification is often relatively weak.

While sometimes new to politics, these candidates were not amateurs in the sense of being mere dabblers or dilettantes or lacking in competence. In 1948, Governor G. Mennen Williams linked up with UAW labor leader Walter Reuther and Ann Arbor businessman Neil Stabler, and together they exhibited what author Theodore White subsequently termed a "high-minded yet hard-knuckled" approach, as they built an effective citizen-politics organization.[27] They supplanted the traditional, unsuccessful, patronage-oriented Democratic party with a programmatic coalition of liberals and labor unions, seeking greater social change, power, and legitimacy through the medium of state government. Another amateur, George Romney, set the stage for similar change in the Republican party, as he overshadowed the conservative clique of General Motors and Ford executives who, since 1940, had largely held control of the party reins.[28] It was ironic that Romney, himself a product of the programmatic leadership provided by the auto companies to the Republican party, should have laid the groundwork for such a different party. In the 1962 campaign, he lashed out both at the domination of the Democratic party by labor and the domination of the Republican party by business.[29] The result was to open control of the party to the moderate wing, and it was the then state Senator William Milliken and others in the legislature who seized this opportunity; Milliken fundamentally changed the character of the Republican party when he later became governor.[30]

The result of these machinations was to create two centrist parties increasingly interested in reaching out to voters throughout the state, competing successfully in a highly uncertain political environment—and winning. To achieve this end, neither party could afford to be identified in the voters' mind exclusively with labor or business. Events in the early 1960s served to underscore this danger. During the two-year tenure of Democratic Governor John Swainson, the liberal and labor party factions drifted apart until by 1962, they were supporting different candidates for the position of Democratic state chairman. In a sharp power struggle, labor prevailed.[31] However, in doing so, the party and labor left themselves open to the accusation that the two were synonymous. The moderate Michigan citizenry demonstrated its distaste for such cooption when gubernatorial candidate Romney then skillfully exploited this vulnerability:

> For some considerable period of time, it has been my conviction that any government bearing the brand of any single clique or class, and thus deriving its strength primarily from one faction or special-interest group, is doomed to eventual failure . . . such actions and policies, designed for the benefit of the dominating group, must—of sheer necessity—bring harm and hardship to those members of the community who live and have their being outside the border of the privileged circle.[32]

By winning the 1962 primary and general election, Romney succeeded in dispatching the legitimacy of an exclusive big business tie to the Republican party and the exclusive big labor tie to the Democratic party. The victory hardly terminated these party-interest group relationships, but it did cement in Michigan's political culture the good government expectation that candidates and parties must demonstrate a broader aspiration of the public interest. Victory and ideology were incompatible, and Michigan politics would be better served by a generous dose of moderation and pragmatism.

The absence of clear issue stances does not mean that issue orientation does not play a role in Michigan's political culture. The 1982 gubernatorial election, for example, evolved into a contest over where various candidates could be placed on a liberal-conservative continuum. As a conservative entering the lists against moderate Lieutenant Governor James Brickley in the Republican primary, Richard Headlee paid the requisite homage to the center. Classifying himself as a "progressive conservative," Headlee assigned himself a rating of eight on a ten-point liberal to conservative scale, and positioned Brickley as a four. He also attacked the UAW and Democrats for jointly creating an inhospitable business environment. In that respect, however, he proved less eloquent than his mentor, George Romney, who 20 years earlier had attacked the AFL-CIO head, charging that, "the inherent character of the Gus Scholle Democratic party structure is politically corrupt, morally wrong, economically unsound, and socially indefensible."[33]

The election could be won if it were turned into a referendum over the UAW and Detroit, as had occurred in times past. Republican candidate for lieutenant governor, Thomas Brennan, yearned to tilt with his rival, Martha Griffiths; not to clash over issues so much as to dissolve a perception that he and Headlee were extremists.[34] As so often is the case in Michigan, the battle was more over philosophic image than programmatic vision. Rather than taking a programmatic position for the voters, the candidates sought to position themselves near the voter. The quest for a moderate political style congenial to the majority of Michigan's voters became a struggle over strategy rather than substance. The *Free Press* bemoaned Blanchard's success during the primary in "hunkering down over the Democratic party and refusing to define himself in any way that is potentially divisive." The editorial then correctly predicted that Blanchard, in the general election, would preempt the middle, hold his party's left wing, and isolate Headlee on the right. He need not propose expensive, controversial social programs, but could simply invite the perception that he would be less of a threat to public institutions if times were good, and "wrap Reaganomics around Mr. Headlee's neck" if times remained bad.[35]

If Blanchard was fuzzy on the issues, he was remarkably explicit on his strategy. During a number of newspaper interviews, he sounded more like a football coach giving a chalk talk than a candidate seeking to win the hearts and votes of the people. For Blanchard, the Democratic candidate for lieutenant governor, Martha Griffiths, would be a "key to winning independent and moderate Republican votes." She had represented a congressional district that "probably would have gone Republican if not for her," and "she helps the business profile."[36] No attempt was made to place a veneer of program over the goal of winning. "We're going after independent-minded Republicans and other Independents. This is a state that prefers moderates so long as they're competent."[37] Declaring that Headlee is "a guy who's willing to give fetuses rights in the U.S. Constitution that he's not willing to give women," Blanchard explained that he had to bring these social issues into the open to avoid a last minute "Pearl Harbor" by Right-to-Life and Moral Majority groups. He noted, "that way the abortion issue will come out as a wash and, on the ERA issue, I end up a winner."[38]

The 1982 election marked something of a departure for Michigan's moralistic political culture. Its three gubernatorial giants had all previously assumed the expected stance of competing to win office in such a political climate, as Elazar has put it, for a greater opportunity to implement policies and programs.[39] Milliken, for example, had campaigned for such unpopular causes as adequate aid for the city of Detroit and open housing, and Williams, while he might not have wanted to move too far ahead of the people, had stood for higher taxes and better services for the poor. Blanchard and Headlee, by contrast, stood for election.

The altered tone and style of this particular election, however, must be seen more as a product of a new politics that had gradually been attaining greater strength in both political parties than as a comment on the character of the two gubernatorial candidates. The increasing presence and influence of computer-trained professionals, sophisticated pollsters, and communications consultants, mixing and matching their census and survey data, could be traced back to the 1960s. Then, Democratic gubernatorial candidate Zolton Ferency had already observed that the most important decision to be made in a campaign was the choice of an advertising agency. In 1970, Carolyn Stieber wrote that candidates were being "sold to the public by repetition and eye appeal, much like any other commercial item."[40] Speeches tended to be "canned," and they were increasingly limited to short spots on television rather than long addresses on major issues delivered at party rallies.

By 1982, when George Romney staged a three-day blitz on behalf of Richard Headlee during the Republican primary, he made his successful impact solely through a series of interviews attended seemingly by more TV cameras than people. Juxtaposition of issue symbols had now supplanted programmatic party platforms. One effect of these machinations has been a reduced emphasis on political risk taking and problem solving in the state's electoral competition. Political innovation now lies not in competing policy proposals, but rather, in the electoral strategies themselves.

POLITICAL INTERACTION: BIPARTISAN COMPROMISE

Given the presence in Michigan of the archetypes of American big labor and big business, perhaps it was inevitable that its politics and government would be big and complex too. By the end of the Milliken era, a tug of war existed between a resuscitated legislative branch and a somewhat bloated executive. However, executive officials and key legislators managed a reasonable degree of administratiave centralization and concentration of power, if for no other reason than to serve the big interest groups demanding services and favorable regulatory policies. The structure of Michigan politics and government can be seen in the nature and scope of its political participation, the organization of its numerous groups, and the distribution of its governmental power.

Michigan citizens participate in government within their state directly at several levels; and indirectly through interest groups that sometimes develop close relationships with parties on an ad hoc basis. Michigan townships are among the strongest in the nation, and the state's 83 counties became more professionalized during the 1970s as their functions expanded in nature and scope. The autonomy of these jurisdictions is jealously guarded in Lansing by their well-financed lobbying organizations, the Michigan Township Association and Michigan Association of Counties.

The statewide level of participation on the electorate's part generally is above the national average, but not dramatically so. In 1980, 60 percent of the state's voting age population cast their ballots in the presidential election. Voters in Michigan are required to register, and this figure constituted a record high of 70 percent of the state's registered voters. It appears that strong voter interest in three tax proposals also on the ballot led Michigan to buck the lower turnout trend experienced elsewhere in the nation.

Not surprisingly, voter turnout drops off when participation is limited to state elections. Michigan turnout trends are difficult to track in recent years because of rulings by the state supreme court and the secretary of state that liberalized registration procedures. Probably more useful are the average turnout figures for registered voters in the three presidential elections and the three gubernatorial races during the 1970s. Voter turnout for the presidential races averaged 72 percent while the statewide races during this period attracted an average of 61 percent of Michigan's registered voters. In recent years roughly 83 percent of the state's eligible voters have usually been registered.

Michigan primaries have attracted a considerably smaller proportion of the electorate, a circumstance that results as much from party design as from individual choice. In 1972, the state passed its second presidential primary law. It had previously used the presidential primary four times beginning in 1916, but repealed the statute authorizing it in 1931.

The new statute facilitated a wide open presidential primary, since Michigan has no party registration. The party is able to assert some control, since the primary is an indirect one in which voters are setting the apportionment of the delegates rather than selecting the delegates themselves. The actual selection of delegates is done in congressional district caucuses for district delegates and by the state central committees for at-large delegates. Nevertheless, when Independents and Republicans crossed over to assist in providing George Wallace with 51 percent of the Democratic vote, party regulars were embarrassed, and felt that he would never have achieved such a result if the party had performed its rightful nominating function. The Republicans came close to a similar experience in 1976 when favorite son Gerald Ford was challenged by Ronald Reagan.

In addition to the philosophical question of who should perform the nominating function, there was also the more immediate political question of who should control the decision. The choice between the direct primary and the traditional state convention setting for selecting delegates was an important one. As Richard McAnaw points out, a direct preferential primary, as envisioned by the reform commission, would have established a presidential politics outside the ordinary institutions of the Democratic party. When Michigan adopted a presidential primary in 1972, labor, black, and other interest-group Democrats were careful to avoid the adoption of procedures that would have compelled them to compete openly in public politics with the zealous supporters of each presidential candidate. They, therefore, successfully fought to obtain an indirect preference primary with the retention of the convention for the actual selection of delegates.[41]

In 1980, the Democratic party shunned the open presidential primary altogether in favor of closed caucuses in which only party members could vote. The state's major Democratic candidates acceded to the state party's request that they not appear on the primary ballot. The result was not only to avoid the "beauty contest" condemned by some party leaders, but also to limit voter participation. While 595,176 Michiganians cast ballots in the Republican presidential primary, as few as 78,424 voted in the Democratic primary.

The state's parties have experienced the political irony that, as partisan identification has ebbed, competition at the statewide level and in a number of local areas has increased. Part of this increased competition is the result of voter independence. Such ticket-splitting can be seen in the 1980 election, regarded by at least some Michigan party pros as a "Republican mini-landslide." Reagan won 53.5 percent of the presidential vote, as Republicans turned out in disproportionate numbers throughout the state, and Republicans continued to attract impressive numbers of voters at the county level. Democrats, however, retained control of the state senate and house. Democrats also attracted 57.5 percent of the total congressional vote, and won three of the eight board of education and university trustee races.

Overall, political parties are perceived as playing a relatively constructive role in the political system. The majority of partisan voters and independents alike feel that parties help, to some degree, in making the government pay attention to what people think. Less than one-quarter of both partisans and independents, on the other hand, think that parties are not much help.

Michigan citizens also manifest a relatively high degree of confidence in both parties. When asked whether they thought that the Democratic and Republican parties "are concerned about people like you," only 15 percent lacked confidence in both parties. Moreover, in keeping with the relative civility of Michigan politics, those identifying with one political party harbor relatively moderate feelings about the other party. Eighty-five percent of those responding to a survey felt that at least one, and sometimes both, of the parties "believe in the importance of helping the other," while only 8 percent felt that neither party was "open to new people."

The moderate views of partisans and independents alike stem largely from the pragmatic posture that seems to characterize Michigan voters. The great majority of Republicans, Democrats, and Independents manifest medium or strongly positive feelings toward both liberals and conservatives, and classify themselves as moderate or middle-of-the-road in their issue orientation. In one survey, only 14 percent of the Democrats expressed negative views of conservatives, while 13 percent of the Republicans made such remarks about liberals. In rating themselves, 26 percent of the total sample classified themselves somewhere within a conservative range while 26 percent placed themselves within the liberal range. The parties, though, do retain something of a liberal and conservative connotation in the electorate's mind; 43 percent of those sampled perceived the Michigan Democratic party as liberal while 44 percent considered the Michigan Republican party conservative.

Michigan citizens also participate in the political process through generous use of the statewide referendum. Since passage of the 1963 constitution, they have always had at least one referendum on the ballot during even-numbered election years. In 1978, they voted on a record high of ten referenda, and in 1982, they were faced with another long ballot that included six proposals. The 1982 referenda dealt with such issues as a freeze on nuclear disarmament, a proposal to bar due-on-sale clauses in mortgage loans, two proposals relating to public-utility regulation, and a proposed constitutional amendment establishing minimum staffing levels for the highly regarded department of state police. Public-service unions, other interest groups, and ad hoc citizen groups played a prominent role in garnering signatures in support or opposition for these proposals as well as for those presented in previous years.

Michigan's political parties have evolved during this century from a one-party to a competitive two-party system. Each of the parties has moved through several philosophical permutations that partly explains the factionalism that characterizes both of them. A detailed account of Michigan party factionalism shows that the Republican party began as an economically-oriented alliance that later gave way to patronage-seeking opportunists before it developed into a modern party.[42] If one traces the Republican party back to its inception in 1854, however, it is clear that even the nature of that economic orientation has changed markedly. Bruce Catton writes of the odd assortment of abolitionists, free soldiers, anti-slavery Democrats, and conscience Whigs who had drifted into populism from one cause or another and who together formed the Michigan version of the GOP.[43]

Governor George Romney, for his part in revitalizing the party, was credited with being a moderate on the basis of his liberal record in civil rights and his opposition to the John Birch Society and other forms of extremism. The governor, though, claims to have been and to have remained a fiscal conservative.[44] That contention seems borne out by his strong support in the 1982 primary for conservative Republican gubernatorial candidate Richard Headlee. He contended in more than one press conference that the moderate Republican candidate, then Lieutenant Governor James Brickley, was implicated in the current political leadership's "shortsighted and deceptive budget policies," while Michigan needed a governor who would "make the tough decisions to cut state costs." A number of other economic conservatives also appeared to be repudiating the moderate wing's economic policies by their actions in 1982. The Headlee defeat insured that in the 1980s these two factions would continue to be the primary actors competing for party supremacy.

Political factions have also fueled Michigan Democratic party successes and contributed to its failures. It was a conscious coalition of liberal businessmen, academics, and labor that enabled the Democratic party to rise from the ashes. By the 1960s ethnic and minority groups were also achieving greater party prominence. Blacks, in particular, were playing an increasingly significant role in party affairs, both through their involvement in the UAW and as a growing party faction with a Detroit power base. This growing power came as no surprise in that by 1980 blacks constituted 13 percent of Michigan's population. By this time, blacks were concentrated not only in Detroit, but also in Flint, the state's third largest city, where they represented 46 percent of the population, and in several other medium-sized places.

Intraparty factionalism can often generate as much emotion as inter-party competition in Michigan. While programmatic party differences may have become fuzzier—as both parties court Michigan's many centrist voters—the self-interest of the party factions and their interest-group allies has remained at least as clear as ever. A case in point is the conflict that arose late in 1980 between Mayor Coleman Young and Morley Winograd, former Democratic state chairman.

Winograd accused Detroit area Democrats of not actively working for the Democratic gubernatorial candidate, William Fitzgerald. That charge is not denied. Indeed, Young, by making clear to his machine and to Detroit voters his respect for Milliken, facilitated the rare occurrence of a Republican gubernatorial candidate winning Wayne County.

Young was unrepentant as he explained his belief in such "coalitions of self-interest." For some time, the mayor had depended heavily on Governor Milliken's assistance in moving Detroit-related bills through a recalcitrant state legislature. He also continued to work closely with GOP-leaning wealthy businessmen in Detroit both individually and through business groups. The conflict took on some religious and racial overtones, as Young contended that the split was based on "differences of philosophy between some Jews and some blacks," and accused Winograd and Sam Fishman, a UAW official active in the party, of opposing affirmative action that would increase black influence in the party. Fishman denounced this approach as a "hustle," and said that blacks accused anyone who opposed their demands of "racism" and "then try to play on the guilt we're supposed to have."[45]

While such exchanges added pizzazz, the conflict reflected the type of tough infighting involving political stakes and party and group alignment that so often occurs in this well-organized state. Young wanted control over the fourth Democratic seat on the state reapportionment commission charged with redrawing the state legislative district boundaries. The object was to reduce the potentially negative impact of such redistricting on Detroit, due to its declining population. Winograd, essentially a skilled party technician, had hoped, it is rumored, to offer the position not to a Detroit black, as was the tradition, but rather, to someone with a Polish surname from Michigan's "thumb area." Such a move would thereby widen the party's ethnic and geographical appeal. Eventually the position went to a Detroit black, who was closely affiliated with the UAW.

A number of party pros were frank in saying that they did not trust Young, and feared that he might make a deal with the Republicans that would enable them to break the four-to-four party balance on the commission. The Republicans would then gain upstate, and the blacks would benefit in Detroit. Attempting to mediate the dispute was Douglas Fraser, then President of the UAW. He said nothing about loyalty to the Democratic party and its ideals, but rather stressed that Young was "conciliatory" and only seemed adamant because hard-liners were pushing him. All in all, Fraser sounded like a man whose union had a long-term and substantial investment—this time not in the Chrysler Corporation, but rather, in the Democratic party. Young returned to the party fold when the apportionment battle ended, in time to support the liberal Democratic gubernatorial candidate, and oppose Richard Headlee who had made little effort to hide his lack of enthusiasm for Detroit.

Party competition has become more widespread throughout the state.

Formerly, the city of Detroit was a virtually indestructable Democratic stronghold, often sufficiently large for the party to gain the heavy pluralities necessary to offset Republican strength in outstate areas. However, as Detroit has shrunk in size and political clout, counties in other areas have changed sufficiently to keep the Democratic party competitive on a statewide basis. Counties in the northern region of the Lower Peninsula have revealed increasing Democratic strength in recent years, apparently because of retired UAW workers, who moved there in the 1970s, carrying their original party convictions with them. The Republicans, though, have made gains among those younger UAW workers who have gravitated into the more affluent Detroit suburbs. Democratic party strength is found not only in traditional bastions such as the Upper Peninsula and Flint, but also in such medium-sized cities as Kalamazoo, Battle Creek, Jackson, Midland, and Saginaw. The Republican party has maintained its hold in the rural counties and made inroads in the traditional Democratic vote in the southeastern Michigan tri-counties of Wayne, Macomb, and Oakland.

Michigan politics is essentially programmatic in nature. The party factions and interest-group allegiances vary too greatly to merit a discussion of party ideologies per se. Nonetheless, the parties do differ in orientation, and such are the divergences and contradictions among politicians and voters alike that the parties must be seen as possessing less elegant but identifiable belief systems. So close are the parties in their competition for power, however, that the party pros see little party stability emerging from such programmatic differences. Voters shift not between parties but from each party to voting independently with little hesitation. The resulting ticket-splitting belies the myth of strong party identification in Michigan, and leaves party strategists more concerned with issue salience, candidate appeal, and turnout strategies than with straining towards ideological consistency.

Money too moves with alacrity between parties, as many donors prefer a particular candidate or simply a winner to a winning philosophy. In 1974, when Democrat Richard VanderVeen decided to run for then Vice President Ford's old congressional seat in Grand Rapids, he was able to attract the chairman of a major firm and a group of prominent businessmen who raised the previously unheard of sum of $100,000 for a Democratic campaigner in that area. When Ford heard what had happened, he is reputed to have come before them, and shrieked, "You men don't know what you're doing. You don't know which side your bread is buttered on."[46]

Under these circumstances, each party's candidates have a shot at the other's fat cats. The 1982 Republican senatorial candidate, Philip Ruppe, was embarrassed to learn, when he telephoned Henry Ford II that not only was Ford committed to the Democratic incumbent, Donald Riegle, but he was giving a fundraiser at $1000 per person at the exclusive Detroit Club for the senator. Riegle's fundraising contacts in 1982 extended through a wide range of business and professional political action committees as well as labor PACs. Ruppe was hardly without resources. According to one columnist, he was led to understand that "a vast network of wealthy

Republicans and well-heeled GOP political committees (stood) poised to contribute when and if Ruppe . . . can demonstrate that he might be able to win."[47]

While escalating campaign expenditures continue its impact on the U.S. Senate races, Michigan, in 1976, adopted a public campaign act that places a limitation on gubernatorial expenses of $1 million for any primary or general election. For the general election, each candidate representing a major party receives $750,000 in public funds, and then may spend on additional $250,000 in private donations. To receive public funds for a primary election, the candidate must raise $50,000 in approved donations to meet the threshold requirement. Once this threshold is met, the candidate is eligible to receive two dollars for each one dollar he or she receives in approved donations. The maximum amount of public funds allowed for a primary candidate is thus $660,000. A limit on private contributions has been set at $1700 for individuals, $17,000 for independent committees, and $25,000 for the candidates and members of their families. In an analysis of Michigan's initial experience with the law, McAnaw found that "the reform opened up access to meaningful participation in the political process . . . (to those) . . . who might otherwise have been ignored." McAnaw also concluded that the law is, at least in the Michigan experience, favoring incumbents by limiting the opportunity for insurgents to outspend them and gain name recognition.[48]

In theory, both parties are grass-roots organizations in which precinct delegates elected to county or district conventions, elect, in turn, delegates to the state convention. While such democratic procedures might be expected to yield a cross-section of representatives who would then participate in the candidate selection, in practice, such is not the case. Delegates to the state conventions are generally either distinctly better-off personally than the voters or are representatives of well-to-do interest groups. The Republicans held their 1982 state convention in the most expensive hotel in Grand Rapids, while the Democrats held theirs in the most expensive hotel in Flint.

Competitive, policy-oriented parties, particularly when they each control a branch of government, can certainly create deadlock and instability. Michigan faced such a situation in 1959 when Democratic Governor Soapy Williams tried to push through a Republican-controlled legislature a corporate-profits tax to balance his then record budget. The Republicans balked, and instead proposed a sales tax. Neither side would give in, and Williams allowed the controversy to drag on to the point where there were several "payless paydays" in order to embarrass, and thereby bring pressure on the legislature. The tactic backfired. The governor and legislature alike were held up to ridicule, Michigan bond prices sagged, and industrial development efforts were dealt a black eye. The controversy resulted in a joke that year about a drink called "Michigan on the rocks."[49]

The incident was somewhat overblown in the sense that at that time no one doubted that Michigan could easily raise its tax base. Indeed, Governor Romney proved this a few years later by putting through a tax reform package that was three times the size of the Williams budget. There is no question that the governor is blamed when such a fiasco occurs.[50] That may explain why Governor Milliken, faced with a divided legislature himself, placed such great emphasis on "bipartisan cooperation" during his regime. While commentary has focused on Milliken's skillful use of this approach to solving and salving party competition, the governor was simply making an art form out of a bipartisan tradition that could be traced back to the early 1960s in Michigan politics. When the Democrats captured the legislature in 1964, they consciously and successfully followed such a bipartisan strategy—a fact that was hardly lost on Milliken who was then lieutenant governor.[51] President Gerald Ford may well have drawn on this tradition in the skill that he exhibited in forging a bipartisan alliance to heal the wounds of the Watergate scandal.

Milliken found it necessary to bridge the gap between the executive and legislative branches on such critical issues as raising sufficient revenue for Detroit, enacting welfare, health, and other social legislation, and developing acceptable tax and economic development strategies. Recognizing the statewide danger in Detroit's plight,* Milliken forged an alliance with Mayor Coleman Young, that partially explained Young's success in Detroit and Milliken's success with the Democratic legislature. By fusing together Democratic party strength and moderate Republican legislators, Milliken isolated Republican conservatives from the outstate areas. The financially generous nature of the governor's social legislation is also partly explained by the nature of this coalition. This alliance, constructed on the basis of generosity to the state's urban areas and lower-income citizens in good times, proved less successful in grappling with the new challenges of economic decline and budgetary reduction in the 1980s.

Both Michigan legislative parties are well organized in comparison to most other state legislative bodies, and function through party caucuses. The nature and number of offices reflect the degree of legislative party organization. In addition to the speaker of the house and majority and minority floor leaders, there are a speaker pro tempore and associate speaker pro tempore, assistant floor leaders, party whips, and caucus chairs and vice-chairs.

Legislative party leadership in the late 1960s and 1970s was strengthened by several structural staff changes that broke the virtual monopoly of information enjoyed by the executive branch. Among the new legislative provisions that grew out of the 1963 constitution was a requirement for the

---

*Detroit's financial problems predated the Milliken era. When, in 1968, Mayor Jerome Cavanaugh attempted to improve the city's fiscal situation by asking the state legislature to hike the city's income tax to 2 percent for residents and 1 percent for nonresidents, the legislature rejected the tax for nonresidents, and thereby increased the city's eventual fiscal vulnerability.[52]

establishment of a bipartisan legislative council to provide bill drafting, research, and other legislative services.[53] Within both houses, the Democratic and Republican caucuses also have established office staff that are under the direct supervision of the legislative party leadership. These staffs provide research, write speeches, handle constituent services, and work with the media. While these staffs do become engaged in political activities, particularly during election periods, there is an expectation that much of their normal activity should relate to legislative support.

House and senate fiscal agency staffs also were established through state statute, and these nonpartisan professionals assumed increasing importance in the early 1980s, as they examined the economic assumptions behind the overly optimistic revenue projections in the executive budget.[54] These assumptions are prepared by the division of management and budget for the governor, along with the controversial fiscal mechanisms through which the Milliken administration chose to meet its constitutional requirement to submit a balanced budget. These legislative and executive staffs, sometimes directly and sometimes through their legislative and executive bosses, sparred frequently in the media. Except for the executive's advantage in actually preparing the budget figures and gaining a vital familiarity that comes from such detailed preparation, the battle was waged on relatively equal terms, and reflected the delicate balance in Michigan between the executive and legislative branches.

The governor is not without his resources either, although, in typical "good government" Michigan fashion, these formal and informal powers are constrained in numerous ways. Through the "state of the state" and "budget" messages and other such visible opportunities for leadership, the governor can set much of the policy agenda. The governor's legislative veto is rarely overridden. As the state's chief executive, the governor also presides over a Michigan bureaucracy that has doubled in size since 1961 to approximately 60,000 persons. The governor's own staff includes between 40 and 50 positions. Depending on budgetary exigencies, the appointment power allows for a total of approximately 1700 positions including nonelective single department heads, provisional appointments, and the numerous boards and commissions that populate Michigan government.[55] However, the appointive power extends by constitutional fiat, only to the director and five additional nonclassified employees even for the largest department, and the state civil-service department has proved most adept at defending its turf.

The political party composition of the legislature since the 1963 constitution has generally favored the Democrats. They enjoyed supremacy in the house for most of the Milliken era, and also took control of the senate in 1972. Leadership was often able to impose its will through the caucus, but party factionalism periodically asserted itself here too. The conservative Democrats sometimes would team up with Republicans to support changes in controversial workers' compensation legislation and other business initiatives, and moderate Republicans would often join liberal Democrats on social legislation. Caucus sessions in both parties were often stormy, as the Democratic leadership struggled to hammer out compromises acceptable to its own fluid and heterogeneous elements, as well as to the Republican party.

Bipartisanship between Michigan political parties, however, has its limits. In 1980, both state legislative and congressional reapportionment were thrown into the state courts, and in one case into a federal court, as tough party pros haggled to a standstill. Reapportionment also threatened to play a role in throwing the delicate party balance-of-power out of whack, and opened up, entirely anew, the question of who would rule in the state legislature and which branch, if any, would dominate in the state's politics. An incumbent-oriented congressional reapportionment plan seemed likely to perpetuate a Democratic majority in the 18-member delegation through the 1980s. Whether it would remain at 12-6, as it stood in 1983, however, was open to question. It was in the state legislature where reapportionment heightened party competition. Analysts in both political parties expected that, as a result of maintaining even the tenuous edge of 20-to-18 in the state senate in the 1982 election, the Democrats in the mid-eighties might well succeed, through further reapportionment and the advantage of incumbency, in maintaining control. Democratic supremacy in the house looked even more likely, given the the lead of 63 to 47 seats compiled in 1982.

Whatever the legislative balance in the years ahead, there is no question that one other group of actors will continue to play a key role in Michigan decision making. Interest groups, and the lobbyists who frequently represent them, not only attempt to influence legislators, agencies, and, less frequently the governor, but also often initiate legislation, and are sometimes physically present during virtually all phases of policy formulation.

Michigan's dominant economic interests remain entrenched on the Lansing scene. The best organized interest group, as its enemies and allies alike attest, is the labor movement. It is reputed to be the most powerful labor movement of any state. As of 1980, there were 1,255,000 union members or 1 out of every 17 union members in the U.S. That number includes 500,000 in the UAW and 270,000 in the state AFL-CIO.[56] While the AFL-CIO and Teamsters are certainly not bashful about protecting their interests in Lansing, it is the UAW that established the most potent influence by combining its financial and lobbying clout with a close grass-roots affiliation with the Democratic party. In a number of Detroit metropolitan areas, the UAW staffs many of the precincts with its own people, and thus provides a channel of political participation for unionists at several party levels.

Labor maintains a powerful voice not only in economic concerns of direct benefit to this constituency, but also in other social policies where the UAW in particular persists in maintaining its liberal tradition. In 1982, Michigan's two labor powers—the UAW and state AFL-CIO—merged again after a decade of division. According to UAW Vice-President Donald Ephlin, the merger is intended to streamline the often duplicative lobbying and fundraising activities of the two groups, and enable the unions to present a stronger, united front in dealing with the private sector.[57] Michigan's industrial decline has left these proud but struggling unions anxious to maximize their political strength in the state capitol.

A nice question is how much longer UAW workers, who are increasingly middle class in their orientation and removed from the social liberalism of Walter Reuther, will persist in performing the mundane tasks necessary for a political machine to win. Nevertheless, in 1982, the UAW for the first time endorsed a candidate at the primary level, and proved able to deliver campaign funds and a substantial vote in southeastern Michigan for Governor Blanchard at a time when he was relatively unknown.

Those corporate giants based in southeastern Michigan have also shown a predilection to flex their economic muscle in state politics, more so than their counterparts located elsewhere around the state. Sometimes such powerful symbols of Michigan as General Motors and Ford have chosen to exercise their influence directly to protect their firms' balance sheets. Often, however, they have worked through corporate or more broadly based coalitions designed to maintain the economic viability of Detroit as a whole. Thus, southeastern Michigan businessmen, professionals, and labor leaders dominated the governor's Michigan Economic Action Council, charged with examining the state's economic situation in 1975 and recommending legislative and executive action. In 1981, some of these same labor and management leaders actively lobbied the state legislature in support of a Detroit resident and nonresident income tax designed to stave off another fiscal crisis. When Governor Blanchard took office in 1983, some of these same business and labor "power brokers" had already joined in the 70-member Economic Alliance for Michigan, and were ready to provide suggestions on how the state might be guided out of its misery.

While labor-management relations remain tense on the plant level, big business and big labor have long since banded together in a variety of Michigan public-private partnerships perceived as one pathway to economic survival. Indeed, the "Chrysler bailout" was simply a logical extension of this philosophy. Public-private coalitions also exist within Detroit to deal directly with the city's problems, and the common means of exercising power is through these coalitions rather than through a corporate, labor, or professional elite. The public sector has adapted to this *modus vivendi*; Michigan and city of Detroit funds often are channelled through one or another of these groups. Unlike Henry Ford II, Doug Fraser, and other southeastern Michigan business and labor leaders of earlier eras, the upcoming leadership generation, that populates these coalitions, functions not on a personal, but rather on an institutional basis. Little known, within as well as outside of Michigan, these leaders occupy key positions as a result of their organizational position and role; they derive their power solely from the institution with which they are associated. The coalitions function as extensions of organizational power bases, rather than as mediums through which prominent personalities exercise individual initiative.

While the dominant economic groups are most visible in Lansing when they choose to move, Michigan interest-group activity now comes in many shapes and sizes. Agencies and the state legislature alike will sometimes wait for these various groups to reach agreement on proposed legislation, and if they do not do so, will simply postpone action until they do.[58] Subgovernment arrangements found at the federal level are also common in Michigan. These networks usually involve agency divisions, legislative committees, and interest groups or their lobbyists, who are expected to "broker" agreement within the subgovernment or build the necessary coalition.

It is the presence and unusual power of lobbyists as such that somewhat distinguishes Michigan's political culture from that found in many other state governments. The major lobbyists are personalities in their own right whose names and activities are known not only to the lobbied but also to actors throughout Lansing. The media chronicle their movements, and the most prominent of these individuals are not bashful to express their views, publicly or privately. A number of former legislators and staffers are lobbyists, and a network of contacts and good information are clearly part of the game. The more powerful lobbyists are not only closely affiliated with wealthy businesses, trade associations, and professional organizations, but also with the growing number of political action committees that are moving into state politics. Actual bribery of legislators is rare, but in a competitive state with expensive political campaigns, money is influence.

Interest group and lobby interaction with the state legislature is widely perceived, at least in Lansing, as an integral, unavoidable, and sometimes healthy part of the state's body politic. The greater range of participation by professional, citizen, and provider-of-service groups, along with the traditional economic interests, is seen at least by some legislators as promoting a more equitable decision-making process. House Speaker Emeritus Bill Ryan, for example, has argued informally that lobbyist can be played off against lobbyist in group conflict that yields more information than was previously available to the legislature. Through such machinations, each interest group is more likely to receive what is defensible, and the final product bears a closer resemblance to the public interest. To some extent, then, individual interest groups have become less powerful than was formerly the case because of the countervailing power that now invariably surfaces in Lansing.

Given the horror stories of interest-group activity earlier in the century, it seems likely that partial neutralization of those groups with financial muscle has occurred. Nevertheless, interest groups and their lobbyists are far from created equal. Lobbyists are expected to participate in virtually all stages of the legislative process, and so it is the large, more expensive lobbying firms that possess the manpower and knowledge needed simply to reach all of the key actors when it is important to contact them. So much happens informally in this interaction process, involving state legislators and lobbyists, that it is imperative to touch all of the requisite bases before deliberations in smoke-filled rooms begin. The lobbyist must have the necessary information early in the game and be able to reach the right "buddies" once negotiations are underway. Sometimes lobbyists are less involved in the legislative process or in purveying information of sufficient quality than one might expect but the more critical the issue, the less likely will such a vacuum materialize.

The media are also active between as well as during elections. Like the lobbyists, the media tend to focus on the main political executives, the legislators, and the governor's office. Economically, they argue that it is simply not feasible for either the print or the broadcast media to extend their coverage further unless a highly visible story captures the public's attention. The two Detroit newspapers, the *Detroit Free Press* and the *Detroit News*, cover the state capital more thoroughly than their outstate competitors, and since these newspapers possess a statewide audience, it is widely believed that their views are read with interest by the governor and the legislators. The Detroit media also undertake a certain amount of investigative reporting that has attracted the interest of a small attentive public, party elites, and legislators.

The early 1980s did not represent the first time in its modern history that Michigan had grappled with economic hard times. In the 1930s, it suffered the most serious of the cyclical declines that pockmarked its history, and in 1959 it confronted a breakdown in its political economy that led to "payless paydays." The most recent decline, however, was different, because it stemmed from structural as well as cyclical problems in its auto industry. No one doubted that it would sell more cars later in the decade, but no one predicted that Michigan would ever regain the market share that the state had held in its heyday. The change was perhaps best underscored when several Japanese companies, in 1982, guaranteed $500 million in Michigan notes, and thereby enabled the state, with its battered credit rating, to borrow funds to cover a sagging cash flow. This turn of events led one wag to suggest that the state's economic development slogan, "Say yes to Michigan," should now be altered to read "Say yen to Michigan."

Until 1983, the state legislature and governor had remained true to Michigan's political culture, and had treated this decline as yet another "boom-and-bust" cycle that would be followed by yet another boom. The state, like its auto industry, had persisted in doing little advance planning, but the traditional assumption of unbounded resources that underlay its political economy was coming unhinged. Michigan would have to learn new ways and get its fiscal house in order. The state would draw on its political culture, and downsize its budget in the most humane way possible. It would maintain its civility, and, as it became clear that there was no alternative, draw on its resiliency and substantial human capital to move to a more careful planning for the future. Periodically, inelegant state legislative behavior and black humor would continue to punctuate basically responsible politics. Parties, even while planning more systematically, would continue to be merely flavored with ideology, as they remained pragmatic to the core. The resulting destiny would prove less dazzling than the past, but would retain the state's many midwestern virtues.

NOTES

1. Willis Dunbar and George May, *Michigan: A History of the Wolverine State* (Grand Rapids: William Eerdmans, 1980), p. 469.
2. Daniel Elazar, *American Federalism: A View from the States* 2nd ed. (New York: Crowell, 1972), p.100.
3. Neal Peirce and John Keefe, *The Great Lakes States of America* (New York: Norton, 1980), p. 201.
4. Bruce Catton, *Michigan: A Bicentennial History* (New York: Norton, 1976), p. 155.
5. Dunbar and May, *Michigan: A History of the Wolverine State*, p. 336.
6. *Worldmark Encyclopedia of the States* (New York: Harper & Row, 1981), p. 276.
7. Charles Press and Ken VerBurg, *State and Community Governments in the Federal System* (New York: Wiley, 1979), p. 249.
8. Kurt Gorwitz, "Michigan's Current and Projected Population Trends." (Discussion paper by Public Sector Consultants, Inc., 1 September 1982), p. 2.
9. The writer would like to thank Mr. Mel Larson, chairperson, Michigan State Republican Party, and Ms. Mary Lukens of the Market Opinion Research Corporation for graciously making available the data from a 1975 survey on which this section is largely based. Needless to say, the interpretations of that data are entirely my own.
10. Larry Sabato, in his study of American governors rated all three of these Michigan governors as outstanding and they were in the statehouse for 23 of the 25 years he examined. See his *Goodbye to Good-Time Charlie* (Lexington, Mass.: Heath, 1978), p. 52.
11. Michael Traugott, "Voters Prefer Risk with Reagan," *Detroit News*, 28 October 1980.
12. League of Women Voters, *The State We're In* (Lansing: LWV of Michigan, 1979), pp. 69–70.
13. For a discussion of Romney and Milliken in this regard, see, for example, Anthony Ripley, "A New Governor Finds Civility Pays," *Detroit Free Press*, 2 February 1969; and Dan Angel, *William Milliken: A Touch of Steel* (Warren, Mich.: Public Affairs Press, 1970).
14. Norman C. Thomas argues that Michigan parties, at least when he wrote in 1961, possessed the type of "party responsibility" model supported by the American Political Science Association in its 1950 report, *Toward a More Responsible Two-Party System*. See his "Politics in Michigan: The Curse of Party Responsibility," *Paper of the Michigan Academy of Science, Arts, and Letters* 47 (1962):311–24.
15. For an interesting discussion of the "Rule 9" controversy concerning an administrative rule to halt racial discriminatory real estate practices in the exclusive Michigan suburb of Grosse Pointe, see Norman C. Thomas, *Rule 9: Politics, Administration, and Civil Rights* (New York: Random House, 1966).
16. Carolyn Stieber, *The Politics of Change in Michigan* (East Lansing: Michigan State University Press, 1970), pp. 39–49.
17. Peirce and Keefe, *The Great Lakes States of America*, p. 182.
18. G. Mennen Williams, *A Governor's Notes* (Ann Arbor: Institute of Public Administration, University of Michigan, 1961), p. 56.
19. *Detroit Free Press*, 19 September 1982.
20. Judd Arnett, "Remember Soapy, Bill?" *Detroit Free Press*, 12 September, 1982.
21. Clark Mollenhoff, *George Romney: Mormon In Politics* (New York: Meredith, 1968), p. 203.
22. Stieber, *The Politics of Change in Michigan*, p. 72.
23. Robert Sherrill, "What Grand Rapids did for Jerry Ford—and vice versa," *New York Times Magazine*, 20 October 1974.

24. Williams, *A Governor's Notes*, p. 5.

25. Malcolm Jewell, "The Governor as Legislative Leader," in *The American Governor in Behavioral Perspective*, eds. Thad Beyle and J. Oliver Williams (New York: Harper & Row, 1972), p. 132.

26. Jewell, "The Governor as Legislative Leader," p. 129.

27. Theodore H. White, *The Making of the President 1960* (New York: Atheneum, 1961), pp. 137–38.

28. John Fenton, *Midwest Politics* (New York: Holt, Rinehart and Winston, 1966), pp. 12–24.

29. Mollenhoff, *George Romney: Mormon in Politics*, p. 172.

30. Dan Angel describes in considerable detail this interesting political battle for control of the Republican party in *William Milliken: A Touch of Steel*.

31. Fenton, *Midwest Politics*, p. 23.

32. Mollenhoff, *George Romney: Mormon in Politics*, p. 172.

33. *Ibid*, p. 179.

34. "Political Debate Roars On," *Detroit Free Press*, 20 September 1982.

35. "Blanchard and Headlee face two different campaign challenges," *Detroit Free Press*, 12 August 1982.

36. "State Democrats buoyant at convention," *Kalamazoo Gazette*, 28 August 1982.

37. Pete Plastrik, "Milliken administration hit by voters in both parties' primaries," *Kalamazoo Gazette*, 11 August 1982.

38. Hugh McDiarmid, "Blanchard hints at faith as a factor," *Detroit Free Press*, 23 September 1982.

39. Daniel Elazar, *American Federalism: A View from the States*, pp. 84–127.

40. Stieber, *The Politics of Change in Michigan*, pp. 99–100.

41. Richard McAnaw, "Michigan's Presidential Primary," *Michigan Academician* 12 (Summer 1979):5–6.

42. Stephen and Vera Sarasohn, *Political Party Patterns in Michigan* (Detroit: Wayne State University Press, 1957), p. 68.

43. Catton, *Michigan: A Bicentennial History*, p. 176.

44. Author's interview with Governor George Romney, 29 September 1982.

45. Adam Clymer, "Growing Disputes Split Black and Jewish Democrats," *New York Times*, 29 March 1981.

46. Sherrill, "What Grand Rapids did for Jerry Ford—and vice versa," p. 88.

47. Hugh McDiarmid, "Riegle rolls in dough—to Ruppe's chagrin," *Detroit Free Press*, 22 September 1982.

48. Richard McAnaw, "The Public Funding of Campaigns: The 1978 Michigan Experience," *Michigan Academician*, 14 (Spring 1982):403–14.

49. A more dire account of this episode's implications may be found in Fred Greenstein, *The American Party System and the American People* 2nd ed. (Englewood Cliffs, N.J.: Prentice-Hall, 1970), pp. 82–3, and in Malcolm Jewell, "The Governor as Legislative Leader," p. 140. These critiques, however, seem to underestimate a party system's capacity for adapting to the threat of such deadlock effectively.

50. Sabato, *Goodbye to Good-Time Charlie*, p. 70.

51. Stieber, *The Politics of Change in Michigan*, p. 89.

52. William Serrin, "How One Big City Defeated Its Mayor," *New York Times Magazine*, 28 October 1968, p. 138.

53. Albert Sturm and Margaret Whitaker, *Implementing a New Constitution: The Michigan Experience* (Ann Arbor: Institute of Public Administration, University of Michigan, 1968), p. 93.

54. The writer would like to thank Mr. Thomas S. Husband, former clerk of the house, for his assistance in making information on Michigan's legislative staffing arrangements available.

55. Robert Morris, *The Electoral Gubernatorial Transition: Michigan's First in Twenty Years*, project paper submitted in Western Michigan University's MPA program, 1982.

56. Peirce and Keefe, *The Great Lakes States of America*, pp. 178–84.

57. Pete Plastrik, "Merger of state's two big labor powers nears completion," *Kalamazoo Gazette*, 31 August 1982.

58. See, for example, Press and VerBurg, *State and Community Governments in the Federal System*, pp. 270–71.

6

Texas

ANTHONY CHAMPAGNE and RICK COLLIS

There is, according to the lyrics of a popular song, a Texas state of mind. It is a politically conservative state of mind, one that is infused with individualism to the point of social Darwinism. It is a state of mind that worships money and growth to a degree that would warm the cockles of the hearts of the 19th century's most notorious barons.

Texas cannot be understood without recognition of the enormity of the state. It is, as Neil Peirce has noted, a "megastate."[1] Texas is the fourth largest state in population and the second largest in area, encompassing over 267,000 square miles. There are counties in Texas with areas greater than some states; one county has a larger area than Connecticut. Texas is the nation's largest oil and gas producer and the first-ranked state in oil refining and petrochemicals. It has more farms and farm acreage than any other state. It is a leading financial and insurance state. Texas is also a leading port state with 13 principal ports. Houston's port usually ranks second or third in the nation in annual volume of tonnage.

Though it often invokes images of the frontier, Texas has long been an urban state. It has 25 Standard Metropolitan Statistical Areas (SMSAs), which is more than any other state. By 1979, 80 percent of all Texans lived in one of the SMSAs. The state is a tri-ethnic composite of Anglos, Mexican-Americans, and blacks. The black population, which is roughly 12 percent of the state, is concentrated in, but not limited to, east Texas, which was the cotton-producing, Old South part of the state. Along with other Texans, blacks have abandoned agriculture and moved to the cities. Mexican-Americans constitute roughly 20 percent of the state's population and are concentrated in the 60 counties that are clustered along the Mexican border. In 1980, Texas was second only to California in the number of Spanish-surnamed residents.[2] An unknown number of illegal aliens from Mexico also live and work in Texas. Their life styles vary; many return to Mexico after working briefly in the States, but others remain and raise families in Texas. The natural reluctance of the illegal aliens to make themselves known to the

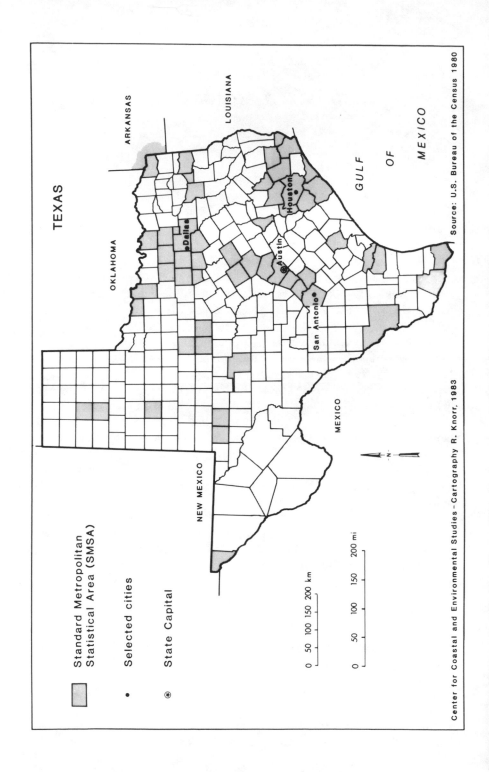

census takers means that Texas actually has more than three million Spanish-surnamed residents.

Anglos account for roughly 70 percent of the state's population. The Anglo population falls primarily into two groups: native Texans and transplanted northerners. It is largely among the transplanted northerners that the Republican party has found a base. Though transplanted northerners have in the past been well-educated and skilled, the current recession has brought a new migration of Democratic blue-collar workers. For these new migrants, the welcome mat is not always out.[3]

Texas has enormous resources and opportunities to accumulate private wealth. It has one of the nation's lowest unemployment rates and, until recently, has undergone an economic boom that lasted for roughly two decades. In spite of the state's prosperity, however, many of its residents have not participated in the state's economic growth. Though many of its residents are in poverty, the role of state government is limited to economic development objectives. Welfare programs and the regulation of business are frowned upon. Additionally, a tradition of discrimination against blacks and Mexican-Americans, two groups at the lower end of the economic ladder, still exists.

POLITICAL CULTURE: UNLIMITED PRIDE AND LIMITED GOVERNMENT

Texans take great pride in their state. Their children are weaned on stories about the heroes of the Alamo and the leadership of Sam Houston, though the stories are often selective. The brave exploits of Crockett and Bowie are stressed, rather than their roguish past. Houston's brilliant generalship and his character is emphasized, rather than his adamant opposition to secession. When a Texas politician was quoted as saying that the Alamo had so many heroes because it had no back door, he was forced to apologize.

Texans are of course stereotyped as braggarts about their state, which always seems to be the biggest and best—Texans know that if all the ice melted in Alaska, Texas would be the largest state. *Texas Monthly*, one of the state's most popular magazines, has actually published articles calling for Texas to divide into five states[4] and even suggested that Texas secede from the Union. It has been pointed out that if Texas were indeed the Republic of Texas, it would rank as the 33rd nation in size and 45th in population. Texas would also rank ninth in the non-Communist world in gross national product and third in gross national product per capita. One could go further and point out that Texas would rank as the fifth nation in the world in petroleum production, the thirteenth in cattle, the fifth in cotton, and the fourteenth in beer production.[5]

In spite of a degree of state chauvinism that must be the greatest in the nation, such state pride and support do not extend to government.

Government is viewed as a necessary evil that must be kept small and unable to interfere with the free-enterprise system. Texas' ten billion dollar a year state government is far from small, but it is relatively free of interference with private enterprise. Politicians, whether they are professionals or businessmen in politics, are also regarded as necessary evils. Successful ones have learned that they must promise to cut the size of government and trim waste, even if there is little waste to trim.

Daniel Elazar has suggested that the political culture of Texas is strongly individualistic and traditionalistic.[6] The traditionalistic culture is found in Texas' economic and social conservatism, its dominance by a loose one-party system, its personality-based politics, low voter participation levels, and a long-term racist tradition. The individualistic culture of Texas is found in the strong support of private enterprise, the opposition to big government, and faith in individual initiative. Individualistic culture is also illustrated by the tendency of Texans to view politics negatively and to expect corruption in government.[7]

The interaction of individualistic and traditionalistic cultures has produced a strong elitist strain in Texas politics. Traditionalism emphasizes an elite based upon the connections of friendship and family. Individualism emphasizes a commercial elite. In Texas, the combination of these subcultures creates a government with limited purposes run by elites who are an interlocking network of successful businessmen. Within the Texas administrative system, for example, the governor appoints the heads of large numbers of boards and commissions, most of whom are persons prominent in oil, banking, and insurance and who hold properly conservative attitudes.[8]

Individualistic values mask the utility of Texas government for Texas conservatives. Conservative political leadership is strong and dominates the Texas political system. While these conservatives praise the merits of free enterprise, growth, hard work, and a strong economy, the leadership ensures that the role of state government will be custodial and noninnovative. V.O. Key noted those dominant political values in 1949 when he wrote that Texas political values were created by:

> [T]he personal insecurity of men suddenly made rich who are fearful lest they lose their wealth. In 40 years a new rich class has arisen from the exploitation of natural resources in a gold rush atmosphere. . . . Imbued with faith in individual self-reliance and unschooled in social responsibilities of wealth, many of these men have been more sensitive than a Pennsylvania manufacturer to the policies of the Roosevelt and Truman Administrations.[9]

The modern Texas view of government is probably best articulated by Eddie Chiles, a wealthy businessman who, most appropriately, made his fortune in the oil business. From time to time, Chiles saturates the media with advertisements attacking liberals, big government, the welfare state, and deficit spending. For Chiles, free enterprise without the restraint of governmental regulation is the key to a prosperous America. The extent of Chiles' free-enterprise thinking becomes clear once one notes that Fort Worth Congressman and Democratic Majority Leader Jim Wright is for Chiles an ultra-liberal.

Chiles reflects the prevailing political ideology when he says that "Capitalism allowed me to start out with nothing and start my own company and get rich." His fear is that young people will not have that opportunity of starting out poor and getting rich. To fight that threat, Chiles has worked "to keep this nation from becoming a socialistic nation." His solution to this perceived danger is to "get the government out of business, and we must get property back into the free-enterprise system. Wealth comes from people, wealth does not come from the federal government. It's the free-enterprise system that will put people back to work—if they're willing to go back to work. I want the government to do four things. Guard our shores and guard them well, balance the budget, deliver the mail on time, then leave me alone."[10] It should be added, however, that Texans want their politicians to be pragmatic social Darwinists. That is, ideology cannot be so rigid that a politician becomes incapable of functioning in Washington or Austin. Senator Lloyd Bentsen's huge victory over Republican opponent Jim Collins can be seen as a victory for pragmatic conservatism over ideologically rigid and ineffective conservatism.

The social Darwinist strain in Texas politics now overshadows the rural Texas populist tradition that was reflected by Sam Rayburn and Ralph Yarborough. The Populists gained much of their strength from the small farmers of rural Texas. It was the Populists who fought the "interests" in behalf of the "common man." Populists traditionally supported railroad regulation, utility regulation, rural electrification, social security, and the expansion of veterans' benefits. Populists in Texas were strongest at the turn of the century when small farmers were caught in the stranglehold of high rail rates for farm products, and during the Depression when people turned to government for aid.

From time to time, a dyed-in-the-wool populist can still win office in Texas. Jim Hightower, for example, was colorful enough and his opposition was incompetent enough for him to win a minor statewide office on a populist platform. Even moderate Democrats such as Jim Mattox and conservative Democrats such as Mark White find a favorable response from voters when they use populist pro-regulation rhetoric, especially, regarding the state's utilities. Utilities in Texas, it seems, have become the equivalent of railroads in Texas during the 1890s. That is, they are so unpopular due to their high rates, that even conservative politicians are willing to talk regulation of that industry. Nevertheless, to speak of a return of populists to power in Texas goes too far. The governor's office, the office of the lieutenant governor, the speakership of the house, and the legislature remain safely in conservative hands.

Among contemporary Texans the dominant view of the role of state government is that it should do as little as possible, though with somewhat obtuse reasoning it is argued that Texas government should do more than the federal government. Appeals to "states rights" still receive applause from Texas political audiences.

Texas has a sales tax, but no corporate or personal income tax. Its great advantage is its oil and gas production. Texas owns much mineral-rich land and oil and gas production taxes alone produce roughly two billion dollars yearly in tax revenues.[11] The large oil and gas tax revenues are created by large production volume rather than a high tax rate. Natural resources severence tax rates are low. Texans have come to expect regular budget surpluses.

Texas' state and local government tax revenues are 8.4 percent of personal income, the third lowest percentage in the nation. State and local expenditures in Texas as a percentage of personal income are also the nation's third lowest.[12] Although Texas has an excellent (albeit decaying) highway system, public transportation is a travesty. Texas in general ranks low in the delivery of social services. It is 34th in the nation in per pupil educational expenditures and 13th in the nation in teachers' salaries.[13] Though one Texan in seven is in poverty and one-fifth of all Texas children are in poverty, Texas ranks 49th among the states in the size of welfare payments received by individuals.[14] Only part of the calculated need of AFDC recipients is provided them,[15] and the state's welfare eligibility standards are generally higher than other states. It does not provide state general assistance for poor people not covered by federal programs nor does it participate in assistance programs for unemployed parents. University of Texas Professor David Austin has noted that Texas has a "history of voting for highways and not for people."[16] Former state senator "Babe" Schwartz, one of the state's leading liberal politicians, recalled: "There never was in my 25 years in the Legislature an original human social idea advanced by a Texas governor or Texas agency that I knew anything about, and I think it is unlikely that there will."[17] There are limits, however, to the anti-welfare bias in Texas politics. Texans recently overwhelmingly approved a constitutional amendment that will allow the state legislature to increase payments to children receiving AFDC—the first increase since 1969.

The combination of traditional and individualistic cultures led the chairman of the state's welfare agency, Hilmar G. Moore, to suggest that welfare recipients have mandatory sterilizations or abortions to prevent unaffordable childbirths. Moore also suggested that welfare recipients, including children, be required to work to receive government aid. He recalls that he had a full-time job at the age of 13 and he feels children on welfare could also learn to work, although he concedes that "no legislature is going to pass that."[18]

People at the lower rungs of the economic ladder have traditionally had little influence with state government. Lately, however, the minority vote has begun to be influential in state races. In 1982, blacks and Hispanics were actively courted by both gubernatorial candidates. Nevertheless, the state is a right-to-work state and only 11 percent of the nonagricultural labor force is unionized. Forty-seven states have higher proportions of union members. Blacks, Mexican-Americans, and poor whites are poorly organized; although minority political power is increasing. While they have some voice in the politics of Dallas, Fort Worth, Houston, and San Antonio, there is no statewide or even regional minority leader who can unite minorities and poor people into a political force. The long heralded alliance of blacks and Mexican-Americans in the state has simply not occurred—nor is it likely to occur given the religious, cultural, and ideological differences that exist between the two groups. Many Texas Republicans believe that Mexican-American political values are such that the Democratic hold on the Hispanic vote can be broken by an attractive Republican candidate who directs an appeal for their vote.

While social Darwinism is the prevailing economic ideology, law and order is the dominant theme for civil liberties questions. Crime must be the fault of the criminal. Without a theory of societal responsibility, a philosophy of "lock 'em up and throw away the key" has left the heavily minority, maximum-security facility at Huntsville drastically overcrowded. Overcrowding is so great that many prisoners are now housed in army tents. Those convicted of crimes in Texas serve prison sentences that are among the longest in the nation. The state prison at Huntsville is roughly the equivalent of a viper pit.[19] Inmates from Dallas, Houston, and San Antonio are taught such job skills as rodeo riding, license-plate making, and cotton picking. Yet, Huntsville prison life is more pleasant than life in many of the local jails in the state, some of which come close to being medieval dungeons.[20]

The solutions to crime are not the liberal panaceas of better and more jobs, housing, or education. Nor is it believed that prison improvements would reduce crime within prisons and outside the walls once inmates are released. Instead, the solution to crime lies in efforts to imprison more people, which is done by creating more judgeships, by passing a law allowing wiretapping in certain kinds of drug cases, and by allowing admission of oral confessions in some cases.

POLITICAL STYLE: MONEY MATTERS MOST

In the old days one won major offices in Texas by being a character. "Pappy" O'Daniel would tour the state with a hillbilly band, "The Lightcrust Doughboys," and after daughter Molly sang a patriotic song, O'Daniel would speak. His platform was the Ten Commandments and the Golden Rule. O'Daniel was not a fool, though he did cultivate the image of a buffoon; instead, he was a shrewd manipulator of the electorate and the media. He knew that in a one-party state where numerous candidates were seeking an office and where each candidate had to build a personal following to get that office, a candidate had to be a character to get the attention of the voters. As voters in Texas have become better educated and more urban, clowning is no longer sufficient for victory.

However, the traditionalistic-individualistic culture continues to sustain a very personal political style where party is of little significance. The personality of the candidate still provides a foundation for electoral activity. It was personality politics that played a major role in the defeat of Governor Bill Clements in 1982. Clements' personal style was one of insufferable arrogance. It was quite easy for the Democratic opposition to label Clements as "mean," so much so that "meanness" became a major factor in Clements' demise. Once in office, politicians may appear crudely self-serving, as corruption is expected in politics and leads to no political reaction unless it becomes extreme. In such cases, the too-greedy can expect political reprisals.

Statewide political leaders in Texas are white, male, Protestant, and without a clear ethnic identification. A few of these leaders can speak some Spanish, but English is the dominant language of politics. There are blacks and Hispanics who hold city and county offices. There are even blacks and Hispanics in the Texas legislature and the Texas congressional delegation. None, however, hold statewide elective office though there are numerous offices with a statewide constituency.

Today, Texas politics is the politics of business and the politics of wealth. The business groups in Texas are so well entrenched as political powers in state politics that the business-political alliance is commonly known as the "Establishment." While anti-Establishment politicians do exist in Texas, there has been no major politically successful anti-Establishment figure since Ralph Yarborough was defeated in the 1970 Democratic senatorial primary by Lloyd Bentsen, and even Yarborough was careful to support Texas' powerful oil and gas interests.

The pro-business state government will not give business everything it wants. For example, in the last legislative session a savings and loan association backed bill, that would have made it difficult for the high interest-paying money market funds to do business in Texas, was overwhelmingly defeated. Additionally, sunshine laws and public meetings laws exist that aid in preventing much backroom wheeling and dealing. Still, business groups generally get their way. As long as business groups are not too blatant in lining up at the public trough, they are likely to achieve their goals. Huge increases in utility rates, readily granted by the appointed members of the state's Public Utilities Commission, were seen as too blatantly pro-utility by voters. The alliance between the Public Utilities Commission and the utilities became a major issue with which Jim Mattox, a moderate Democrat, and Mark White, a conservative Democrat with a moderate's vocabulary, gained the attorney general's office and the governorship. One business interest pitted against another business interest is usually the closest thing in Texas to real political competition.

Business works its will for many reasons, one of which is that the sheer size of the state requires huge expenditures for campaigns. Former-Governor Bill Clements spent over seven million dollars in his successful 1978 bid for the governorship and he spent over thirteen million dollars in his unsuccessful race for reelection.[21] Though most of the big money went to incumbent Bill Clements, Mark White was able to successfully challenge Clements with the "meanness" issue, the utility issue, a strong and united Democratic ticket with an especially strong draw, Senator Lloyd Bentsen, at the top of the ticket, and, it should not be overlooked, the fairly hefty sum of nearly eight million dollars in his own campaign fund. Such sums are not likely to be raised by those who support the interests of lower-economic groups.

In addition, state representatives' districts and state senate districts in Texas are enormous in population and often in area. A state senator's district, for example, is not much smaller than a U.S. congressman's district. These districts are large enough that successful candidates need donations from business groups, groups that are not in the habit of supporting ideological enemies. State legislators are also likely to reflect a pro-business mentality. Since the salaries of legislators are only $600 a month and require displacement from jobs that can be hundreds of miles from Austin, legislators often have to be able to afford the diversion of public service. Those persons are likely to be lawyers whose businesses actually benefit from service in the legislature or persons who are well off. Neither group tends to reflect the values of the downtrodden, especially when the downtrodden tend to be politically apathetic and unorganized.

Contemporary Texans like their leading politicians to be rich, or so one would think by examining the bank accounts of the state's leading political figures. Frequently, state politicians are multi-millionaires. In the 1982 U.S. Senate race in Texas, for example, Democratic Senator Lloyd Bentsen, who is one of the wealthiest men in the Senate, faced Republican challenger Jim Collins, who is one of the wealthiest men in the House. In Texas a poor boy can hold a major state office, but suspicions are likely to be raised about the integrity of such a person. For example, Ben Barnes was, until several years ago, the rising star in Texas politics. He was the youngest speaker of the house in Texas history and was the youngest lieutenant governor as well. In ability, personality, and political horse sense he was described as being the state's next Lyndon Johnson. Yet, doubts persisted about Barnes' character because he survived in public office with a salary of only $4800 a year. Voters took the opportunity to express their doubts about Barnes by voting him out of the office.[22] On the other hand, a lieutenant governor such as Bill Hobby was viewed as too rich to be corrupted. Governor Mark White is an exception to the rule since he has little personal wealth and so far has escaped attacks upon his integrity.

Great wealth is also useful in Texas because of the enormous funds now needed for statewide races. Candidates for such offices as the governorship often find it necessary to borrow from themselves to fund their campaigns. If they win office, they can easily repay themselves by holding fundraisers to collect from contributors who have had a post-election recognition of the merits of the officeholder. Former Governor Clements was able to pay roughly two million dollars in campaign debts with a one night fundraising dinner in Dallas. If a candidate loses the election, however, he must be able to absorb the financial losses. Jim Collins, for example, spent more than one million dollars of his own funds in his unsuccessful race against Senator Lloyd Bentsen. Collins absorbed his loss and made no plans to recoup any of the money. He noted, "It's just like a dry hole in oil. If you're elected, you can do like Bill Clements (after the 1978 Texas gubernatorial election) and raise six million dollars. When you lose, you've got a dry hole."[23]

Wealth also puts the aspiring candidates into the social circles of the powerful in Texas and so they gain the political advantages that accrue from association with the Establishment. This is not to say that poor boys cannot be successful in Texas politics. The Establishment is open to poor politicians who reflect their views. For example, it welcomed Ben Barnes and Mark White into its circles. However, the barriers to high office for those without great wealth do exist and those barriers are great.

The two greatest twentieth century Texas politicians were poor boys—Lyndon Johnson and Sam Rayburn. Rayburn and, to a lesser extent, Johnson, reflected that Texas populist tradition that urged governmental assistance to the "common man." Johnson, the model for most Texas politicians, accumulated great wealth as well as power during his career in government and politics. Rayburn, on the other hand, cared little for money and made no effort to accumulate any. When Johnson died his estate was valued in the millions. Upon Rayburn's death his entire estate consisted of a small farm, a small ranch purchased during the Depression for a few thousand dollars, and several thousand dollars in a checking account.[24] Given the natural interest of most people in money and the money-oriented culture in Texas politics, it is not difficult to understand why most poor boys choose Johnson's combination of officeholding and money making over Rayburn's style of officeholding.

Actually one can easily and legally accumulate money by holding office in Texas. Campaign funds, for example, can legally be converted for personal use. A leader in the state legislature, such as the speaker, can easily have several hundred thousand dollars in campaign funds deposited in his officeholder account, money that can be used for any purpose. Even a lowly state representative can hold a fundraiser as an incumbent and be assured of enough donations from business lobbies to send a child to college.[25]

Lawyers in the legislature who are friendly toward the business lobby often find that legal business comes their way as a result of their office. Indeed, of all occupations the lawyer's is handmade for profiting from legislative service. Officeholders can also use their positions to profit from a variety of business opportunities that are likely to come their way. As influentials in their communities and in state government, they move in the right social circles and are afforded opportunities to buy bank stocks, receive directorships in small companies, and to have investment opportunities in promising oil and gas ventures.

Other than blatant bribery or outlandish behavior (such as that of one representative who is alleged to have had himself shot to gain voter sympathy), an officeholder can usually lead a comfortable and an indict-mentfree existence. A good player on the Establishment team can even expect some very nice perks for his service. When the legislature is in session, lobbies run free buffets and a lobbyist is almost always around to pick up a restaurant or bar tab. There is such a thing as a free lunch when one is in the Texas legislature. Additionally, lobbies such as the Texas Chemical Council provide pleasant diversions for legislators. The council provides legislators with trips to Mexico for dove hunting. The trips are complete with free travel, food, liquor, lodging, and even shotgun shells and "bird boys" who pick up the legislators' fallen prey.[26] For the more talented allies of the business lobbies, a position as a lobbyist awaits those who retire from office or who are somehow defeated in a bid for reelection.

In one sense the political system in Texas is very open. Candidates with money need not serve a political apprenticeship; they can seek and win high office without serving time laboring in the political vineyards for a party or other political organization. Political parties in Texas mean so little anyway that most candidates prefer creating their own political organizations and thus having a personally tailored vehicle for their political ambitions. Former Governor Clements, for example, could flood the 1978 Republican primary with money and overwhelm his opponent, Ray Hutchinson, who was chairman of the Republican party in Texas and who had widespread contacts in the state and a long list of credits for work in Republican causes. Clements was a political unknown in the state, with service only as a deputy secretary of defense to his political credit, but Clements was rich.

The governor's race is becoming such a high-stakes game that even millionaires worry over their lack of funds. State Senator Peyton McKnight, an oil and gas millionaire, recently withdrew from a gubernatorial race. He had loaned his campaign a million dollars and then was faced with loaning it another million. McKnight feared that he would soon loan his entire fortune to the campaign. Since he had suffered from heart disease, McKnight became fearful that he would die after spending everything he had on the race. Rather than risk his fortune, McKnight chose to withdraw from the race in favor of railroad commissioner Buddy Temple, whose family fortune is so immense that the loss of a few million would do little harm.[27]

Playing politician in Texas is a game for the big money and with all such games there are rumors of corruption. Memories of the Sharpstown scandal persist and give meaning to such speculation. In 1971 Preston Smith was governor and shared state political leadership with Lieutenant Governor Ben Barnes and House Speaker Gus Mutscher. Frank Sharp was an extremely wealthy businessman, a type with ready access to Texas politicians. Sharp wanted to remove his bank, the Sharpstown State Bank, from federal regulation. He tried to do this by getting the Texas legislature to pass legislation that would create a state deposit insurance program. The bills removed participating banks from the jurisdiction of the Federal Deposit Insurance Corporation and the inquiring federal examiners who would question twenty million dollars in loans to Sharp and his associates. Sharp arranged for large loans to influential politicians so that they could buy stock in National Bankers Life, a Sharp company. The price of the stock was then manipulated so that the politicians sold their stock at a profit and repaid the loans.[28]

Public outcry followed the disclosure of this comfortable financial arrangement, and mild reforms were instituted. Currently another kickback probe is being conducted by federal prosecutors. Soon the investigation may shake the state to the extent of the Sharpstown scandal. This probe of county commissioners receiving kickbacks on road and bridge supplies has already resulted in 20 convictions or guilty pleas in 8 east Texas counties. Federal prosecutors are not pushing the investigation across the state. Interestingly, since news of the federal investigation surfaced in 1980, prices paid for road and bridge supplies in some counties have dropped as much as 20 percent even though inflation has been roughly 12 percent.

One study of 51 counties showed the cost of road and bridge supplies declining in 23 of them since the federal investigations came to light. The dramatic price declines are often attributed to a post-investigation morality on the part of supply salesmen and county commissioners.

For decades, however, such corruption was accepted. In one county the kickback practices had existed for more than half a century. In another, kickbacks were so common that a commissioner told a salesman, "Boy, if you want to do business in this county, you come in with your pockets full or you don't come in at all."[29]

As long as it doesn't get out of hand, little concern is generated by politicians trying to make a few dollars. There was barely a ripple of excitement when it was disclosed that former Speaker Billy Clayton had tried to obtain mineral leases from a state agency, the Lower Colorado River Authority. Though authority Chairman Harry Shapiro said that he felt the speaker's efforts had been improper, Speaker Clayton apparently offered a satisfactory explanation. It was, claimed Clayton, "just a straight-up business deal" that raised no ethical questions since "it would just be like leasing a lot from the city."[30]

Considerably more excitement was generated by the bribery trial of Speaker Clayton. After Clayton was found not guilty, he did lend his support for ethics legislation, the most important aspect of it being a requirement that campaign expenditures for personal use be reported. The most glaring weakness of the legislation, however, is that campaign donations can still be converted for personal use. In 1979, for example, Senator Tati Santiesteban used $16,000 in campaign funds to make mortgage payments and put two daughters through college. Santiesteban explained, "I have a very expensive Anglo wife and I enjoy the good life. I drive a nice car. I like cocktails and I like good wine and I certainly am not wealthy."[31] In 1981 Senator Ike Harris used nearly $74,000 in campaign money to play the real estate and municipal bond markets and to provide college money for his daughter.[32] Texans can, however, draw satisfaction from the statement of Senator Dee Travis who when questioned about his campaign fund stockpile responded, "No one has to pay me to work for business. I do it for free."[33]

POLITICAL INTERACTION: THE ESTABLISHMENT

One of the most notable characteristics of Texas politics is that its citizens do not vote. Texas in 1980 was 47th in the nation in voter turnout for the presidential election. This lack of presidential voting was not a fluke. In the five presidential elections from 1960 through 1976, only 41 to 48 percent of the Texas voting-age population cast ballots while 54 to 63 percent of the national voting-age population voted.[34] Texas also ranked 47th in turnout for the 1978 elections. The state's voting rates in congressional races from 1960 through 1976 bear out this pattern of nonparticipation. From 21 to 44 percent of Texas' voting-age population cast votes for the U.S. House, but nationally 36 to 59 percent of the voting-age population voted.[35] When voter turnout is higher than the norm, as in the 1982 election, Republicans are likely to be the victims. High turnout means a Democratic turnout, especially a minority turnout. The anti-Clements vote by minorities in Dallas was so great and so unexpected that polling places ran out of ballots, and in some minority precincts, stayed out of ballots for hours.

In off-year local races very small numbers of people can affect elections. For example, in the 1982 mayor's race in Fort Worth, only about 10 percent of the registered voters turned out at the polls.[36] The main cause of political nonparticipation is probably the lack of indigenous groups that maintain grass-roots contact with voters. There is little union organization in Texas, for example. Even political parties in the state tend to be labels under which contesting politicians construct personal organizations rather than grass-roots structures that maintain lasting contact with voters.

This emphasis on personal organization means that if one wishes to get involved in politics, one contacts a candidate and works for that candidate. The supporter becomes attached to a personality rather than a party and the supporter's fortunes rise and fall with the career of an individual candidate rather than with the success or failure of a party.

Until recently the Democratic party was virtually unchallenged in Texas. Politicians who were serious about becoming officeholders had to have a Democratic affiliation. With that affiliation, they could build personal organizations and form alliances with groups and other politicians within the state to gain and keep power. The Democratic party held every variety of political ideology from the extreme right to the most dedicated New Dealer.

When V.O. Key wrote about Texas in 1949, he found a one party state with a liberal-conservative split.[37] It is increasingly hard to find liberals in Texas politics. The word liberal has become an insult that is used to attack political opponents. In Texas only 16 percent of the people identify themselves as "liberals," while 40 percent consider themselves "conservatives."[38] In 1978, when Republican Bill Clements ran against Democrat John Hill, Clements viciously attacked Hill's character and forever smeared it by not only publicly calling Hill a "liberal," but also by calling him a "lawyer."

Today politics in Texas consists of a small liberal wing in the Democratic party, a small moderate wing of national Democrats such as Congressman Jim Wright and Martin Frost, and a very large and dominant conservative wing. The Republican party can best be described as having a conservative wing and a more conservative wing. Victory is gained by trying to convince the electorate that a candidate is more conservative than his opponent. Thus, when Republican Congressman Jim Collins sought the U.S. Senate seat held by Democrat Lloyd Bentsen, he tried to label Bentsen a liberal. Given Bentsen's political orientation, Collins had his work cut out for him. Senator Bentsen, according to one estimate, supported President Reagan 70 percent of the time. Collins supported Reagan 70 percent of the time.[39] In 1970, Bentsen won the Democratic primary over Ralph Yarborough by labeling Yarborough a liberal and convincing the public that he was the appropriate conservative alternative to Yarborough.

Without question the most striking political development in Texas is the growth of the Republican party. Texas had a tradition going back to 1952 of voting Republican in presidential elections and Democratic in state and local elections. Now Republicans are a mounting threat for these offices. Republicans hold a Senate seat, several congressional seats and a growing contingent in the state legislature. Republican strength is in urban centers, especially the suburbs of Dallas and Houston. In spite of the party's growth, however, to be victorious in statewide elections still depends upon disorder in the Democratic party. Republican U.S. Senator John Tower has remained in office because of the support of conservative Democrats and also because in Tower's early years in office, liberal Democrats refused to support the Democratic opposition to Tower, Waggoner Carr, who they distrusted and viewed as too conservative.[40] Bill Clements, the first Republican governor of Texas since Reconstruction, was elected because of support from conservative Democrats who felt his opponent was too liberal.[41] Democrats united behind Mark White in the 1982 gubernatorial race and thus defeated Bill Clements whose party needed disaffected Democratic voters for victory.

While there are Democratic politicians who are very partisan, the dominant conservative wing of the party tends to find ideology more salient than party. Except for the "yellow dog" Democrats who retain memories of the Civil War, or the Depression, or who just naturally hate Republicans and would vote for a yellow dog before supporting a Republican, there is a surprising degree of cooperation between the two parties.

The shifting nature of alliances in Texas politics is such that during the recent congressional reapportionment, many black Democrats and conservative white Democrats in the legislature joined with Republicans to support a Republican congressional redistricting plan. Since the 1980 elections, numerous Democratic judges in Dallas County have even changed their party affiliation so that they will be able to run for reelection as Republicans in a county that is increasingly Republican. There is some tension between those Republicans with long-time loyalty and work for party and those Republicans who switched from the Democratic party when it was politically expedient. However, the Republican party continues to welcome these crossovers and allows them to benefit from the Republican label.

Statewide candidates for office might obtain the endorsement of interest groups such as farm organizations or teachers' groups. They will not fight for the endorsement of labor; they will be more inclined to fight against it. What is most important, however, is the support of business groups. There one gets the money necessary to put together a personal organization, travel the vast distances of the state, buy time on the state's numerous radio and television stations, buy advertising in its many newspapers, and rent billboard space along scores of highways.

Television is increasingly recognized as an essential component of a statewide campaign. In a state as large as Texas with no political infrastructures, this is the only way a candidate can contact large numbers of voters. All major gubernatorial candidates in 1982 devoted the lion's share of their campaign budgets to television commercials. One candidate, Democrat Buddy Temple, spent 90 percent of his hefty campaign budget on television commercials. According to Democratic candidate Mark White's campaign manager, "You've got to be on television to be a serious candidate." A slick, expensive television campaign is not enough to win office in Texas, but it is considered a necessary foundation for victory.[42]

There is no newspaper so influential in Texas that its support is seen as essential for victory. The major papers, such as the Dallas *News*, Dallas *Times-Herald*, Houston *Post*, Houston *Chronicle*, and *Fort Worth Star Telegram*, can be counted on to support one of the candidates of the business establishment. Yet, the papers in no way control the politics of the state. The only consistently liberal paper in Texas is the Austin based *Texas Observer*, a bimonthly paper usually bordering on bankruptcy. While it is not a paper with policymaking influence, for Texas politicians it functions as a major irritant by regularly printing stories on political corruption and the cozy relationships between politicians and the business community.

The avenue chosen by candidates to reach voters will vary from candidate to candidate, but above all the politician must create his own mechanism for reaching voters since no institutional structure exists. With the support of the business establishment, a candidate will have enough money to try to saturate the media with commercials, spot ads, slogans, and jingles. Along with media saturation, a candidate must make his presence felt throughout the state. The candidate will have to speak at one Chamber of Commerce, Rotary Club, or Lion's International luncheon after another. This rubber-chicken circuit will include stops in as many of the state's 254 counties as possible.

Along with "pressing flesh," it will be necessary for the candidate to try to construct personal organizations in almost all the counties. These organizations will be built by hiring campaign help in the county, calling in chits for past favors, asking old friends for help, or, in desperation, calling on unknown supporters to try to win the county over. Some candidates, such as former Governor Clements, placed the greatest stress on media saturation, but former Governor Preston Smith was very successful with his remarkably well-organized local personal organizations.[43] Reagan Brown, former Agriculture Commissioner of Texas, who was elected statewide, has shown that bad jokes, rambling speeches, and hundreds of civic club dinners can also be a political formula for statewide officeholders.[44] In 1982, however, Brown also showed that racial slurs, even accidental ones, and a colorful and witty opponent can lead to defeat—and even when the opponent, Jim "Whole Hog" Hightower, could honestly fit under a liberal label. Clearly, campaigns require large treasuries and great media expenditures, but beyond that the recipe for victory varies from candidate to candidate.

Politics in Texas is dominated by three persons: the governor, lieutenant governor, and the speaker of the house. Each office is independent and each has its own power base, though all three offices feel the financial influence of the business lobby.

The governor is the most visible state official. For that reason, voters consider the governor to be the leader of state government and they look to him for determination of the political agenda. While the office has some powers attached to it, most notably vast appointive powers over numerous boards and agencies, the governor's powers are limited. Powers are shared with a large number of other elected officials. Even in reference to the governor's appointive powers, it usually takes four to six years before the governor can be certain that his appointees will control a state board or agency. Nor does the governor have any role to play in the selection of legislative leaders.

Perhaps most restrictive of the governor's power is legislative control over the state's budget.[45] The governor has veto power, including a line-item veto, and can call special sessions of the biennial legislature, but it is the speaker and the lieutenant governor who control the legislature. Prior to the Sharpstown scandal that control was exercised in arbitrary fashion. Opponents of legislation supported by the leadership would simply be excluded from the process. For example, they would be denied copies of bills until it was too late to research or even read them. Opponents would not be told where or when committee hearings would be held, even if the opponents were members of the committees. The leadership had the power to kill any legislation and the leadership would oppose legislation sponsored by those who would not go along.

The outcry over the Sharpstown scandal did lead to some legislative reforms. The leadership no longer behaves in as arbitrary a fashion and there is greater opportunity for the opposition to evaluate proposed legislation. Instances of the opposton being frozen out of the process are now rare, but the leadership still controls the legislature. It has the power to appoint the membership of committees. The leadership also maintains control through several procedural techniques. In the house, for example, the speaker routinely delays legislation needed by representatives until after the speaker's legislation is considered. In the senate the lieutenant governor controls the legislative agenda with the two-thirds rule. The rule requires that legislation may not be considered out of order unless two-thirds of the senate agree. Since routine bills fill the agenda, a major bill may never be considered unless it is given priority by a two-thirds vote. However, the lieutenant governor's appointive powers guarantee him at least one-third plus one votes in the senate and therefore veto power over any legislation that he opposes.

There are limits on the power of the leadership, as is illustrated by the "killer bee" episode prior to the 1980 presidential election. Lieutenant Governor Bill Hobby wanted the senate to pass a bill that would place the presidential primary on a day separate from the party primaries for other races. A separate-day presidential primary would permit conservative Democrats to vote with Republicans for the president and then return weeks later and vote in the Democratic primary for candidates in congressional, legislative, and other races. Without a separate-day primary, conservative Democrats would vote in the Republican primary and moderates, liberals, and minorities would grab a bigger share of Democratic nominations for other offices. It was also thought that the separate-day presidential primary would aid John Connally, since conservative Texas Democrats would favor Connally over Reagan. A spring Texas primary would give Connally a well-timed, major-state victory. However, much to Lieutenant Governor Hobby's chagrin, the two-thirds vote needed in the senate to bring up a proposal out of order worked against him. Ordinarily, the rule greatly aided Hobby since it meant that he could kill any bill by corralling 11 of the 31 senators. This time, however, Hobby wanted to pass a bill rather than kill it. More than one-third of the senators opposed the bill, and therefore Hobby tried to change the ground rules. Resorting to an obscure parliamentary device that had not been used since 1961, Hobby tried to bring up the bill without two-thirds support. The opposing legislators could do nothing to fight Hobby's move except to run from the senate and hide. Without two-thirds of the senate present, there was no quorum and there could be no vote on the bill. Hobby had to content himself with ordering the arrest of the absent senators, known as the "killer bees," and orchestrating an attack on their behavior by the remaining senators, known as the "worker bees." Hobby eventually had to compromise with the "killer bees" and give up his separate-day primary bill.[46]

The power of the lieutenant governor and the speaker forces the governor to share his influence over the legislative process with these two officials. In addition, there are numerous other elected statewide officers who produce enough independent baronies to make effective unified state government unlikely. In the early 1970s there were unsuccessful efforts to pass a new state constitution that would have eliminated this fragmentation of power. These independent elected officers include the attorney general, the land commissioner, railroad commissioners, the agriculture commissioner, the comptroller, and the state treasurer. Tension is built into the process since state officeholders tend to vie with each other for other statewide offices. In 1982, the land commissioner, a railroad commissioner, and the attorney general sought the governorship—and conflicts between Attorney General Mark White and Governor Clements were especially sharp. Former Speaker Billy Clayton recently announced his retirement from politics, but until that announcement it was widely believed that he coveted the land commissioner's job. Clayton's decision not to run for land commissioner opened up the opportunity for liberal Democrat Garry Mauro to win the powerful and little known office.

Perhaps the most visible of these offices is the attorney general's. He controls a vast legal apparatus, since he is the officer in charge of the state's litigation. Many of the other statewide offices sound obscure and meaningless, but most are not without some authority. The state treasurer is influential by virtue of his control over where state funds will be deposited. The comptroller enforces the collection of sales taxes, a highly discretionary power. The comptroller also must certify that revenues will be available to cover state expenditures. This power allows the comptroller to get much of what he wishes from the legislature since a hostile comptroller could force a tax increase or a major budget cut by estimating that revenues will be substantially below expenditures. The land commissioner controls state land and state oil and gas leases. The land area under his control is larger than the state of Maine. The railroad commissioners may run the nation's most powerful regulatory agency, one that controls oil and gas production in Texas. Among other things, it establishes spacing regulations for wells, regulates drilling such as the policing of slant-hole drilling, and sets production restrictions on all oil and gas wells within the state.[47]

The plethora of elective offices has led to some questionable voter choices. Jesse James, for example, served for years as state treasurer. The voters knew little about his ethically questionable activities or the issues with which the treasurer's office dealt, but Jesse James was a good name for such an office. In a similar fashion, Warren G. Harding held the office until his indictment provided the opportunity for Ann Richards to seek and win that post on a promise to reform questionable financial practices. One of the greatest election embarrassments occurred in 1976 when Don Yarbrough was elected to the Texas Supreme Court. Voters apparently confused the name with Don Yarborough's, a three time gubernatorial candidate, or with Ralph Yarborough's, the veteran liberal U.S. senator. Yarbrough won office in spite of a large number of questionable dealings that eventually led to his resignation and criminal conviction. Not even the write-in candidacy of Judge Sam Houston, however, could stop the election of Yarbrough.[48]

Texas government is replete with wealthy men who have used their wealth to promote the winning candidate's interests and their own position. In 1981, for example, the Governor Clements Committee raised about three million dollars. Ten percent of that money came from a handful of persons who served on powerful, though mostly unpaid, boards, commissions, task forces, and advisory committees. It is not that political appointments are for sale. The governor made over 1000 appointments and only about 10 percent of these were major contributors in 1981. However, it is typical in Texas politics for wealthy contributors to receive major appointments and to have special access to the governor. It is a practice that critics claim results in government by the rich. As Texas AFL-CIO President Harry Hubbard has stated, "To a great degree, the effect of these appointments pits class against class, those who have it against those who don't."[49]

These positions in the bureaucracy are important political forums for wealthy contributors. For example, the parks and wildlife department recently offered oil and gas leases on several state parks, recreation areas, and wildlife management areas. The state insisted that these leases were offered with appropriate environmental safeguards. However, Perry Bass, the wealthy oilman and Clements' campaign contributor, is chairman of the department. He is in a strong position to oppose suggestions that costly directional drilling be used to protect environmental interests.[50]

These rich businessmen have their own theory of the public good and are inclined to pursue that notion much as they pursued profits for their corporations—single-mindedly and often with little regard for established procedures. An excellent illustration of this business-like style of government was the hiring of Texas A & M coach Jackie Sherrill. A & M has been the butt of more derogatory jokes than most of the nation's ethnic groups, but it is a rich university with a board of regents intent on building the school's reputation. "Bum" Bright is the chairman of the board of regents. He is an extraordinarily wealthy man who made a fortune in oil and another in trucking. Bright is one of Governor Clements' closest friends and was the finance chairman for the Clements' reelection campaign. To Bright's way of thinking, if A & M was to be a great school, it needed a great coach. That meant hiring Jackie Sherrill, even though it would cost more in university funds than the university president made. However, the $95,000 base salary was only the beginning. Sherrill got a five-year rollover contract, meaning a five-year contract that is renewed at the end of every year. The contract also provided for $130,000 yearly through radio and television programs, board memberships, and endorsements. Another $150,000 home subsidy was provided as were two cars, $200,000 worth of insurance, and a country club membership. The deal was, of course, consumated without faculty input and was directly contrary to statements made to the previous athletic director by the university president. "Bum" Bright bought his idea of what made an excellent university—the highest paid college football coach in the world.[51]

Governance by campaign contributors is not limited to the chief executive's office. Warren Harding as state treasurer had great control over where the state deposits its money. His list of political contributors was a "Who's Who of Texas Bankers," some of whom felt there might be a positive correlation between contributions to the Harding campaign and receipt of state deposits.[52] The bankers are dependent upon the treasurer and the treasurer is dependent upon the bankers. While there is nothing illegal about such a tie, the practice suggests governance in behalf of a narrow elite's interests. Indeed, it is argued that Texas loses at least twenty million dollars in interest annually because of this practice of spreading its money among 1400 banks at a rate below the prevailing market interest rates.[53]

The Texas railroad commission also maintains a cozy relationship with the interests it is supposed to regulate. Commissioner Mack Wallace has a $43,500 officeholder account that pays for incidental political expenses. More than 80 percent of Wallace's money came from oil, gas, and trucking interests, all of which are under the regulatory authority of the commission. Another commissioner, Jim Nugent, held a fundraiser recently where the president of Texas Mid-Continent Oil and Gas and the president of Empire Drilling Company helped pick up the tab. Commissioner Buddy Temple, who comes from a family with enormous wealth made primarily in land and timber, was able in 1980 to defeat an incumbent railroad commissioner whose campaign was well funded by the oil and gas industry. When Temple took office he found that the same people who funded his opponent now readily shelled out money to pay Temple's campaign debts.[54] The industries regulated by the railroad commission received their greatest fright in years in 1980 when Jim Hightower maverick, intellectual, consumerist, populist, ran for the railroad commission. Hightower is one of the few charismatic personalities now in Texas politics. In a campaign where he was outspent by more than two-to-one, he was beaten by an industry-backed opponent by only 45,000 votes.[55]

The 1982 election saw more extremely large campaign contributions than ever before. Campaign chests were so heavily financed by wealthy and generous donors that there has been some demand for campaign reforms. The record contributions were made by rancher-oilman Clinton Manges who contributed over a million dollars. Most of this money went to liberal and moderate Democratic candidates. Manges has been the subject of investigations and has had legal problems. Questions about Manges' problems plus the enormity of his contributions has led to the current controversy over campaign funding.[56] Cynics might add that Manges' clear preference for non-Establishment candidates has fueled this new concern.

Even Texas judges have a strong tie to financial contributors. Judges are elected in Texas, and Common Cause has suggested that many lawyers consider contributions to judicial races as investments. Jim Marston of Common Cause has said: "Lawyers consider it an investment, frankly, and I know the oil industry does, too. It's always easier to raise money from lawyers for judges than for other candidates." Several Texas supreme court justices refuse donations offered in nonelection years. Justice Joe Greenhill even returned $17,000 in donations when he found that he would be unopposed. However, dependency on campaign donations from interest groups is the norm even for the Texas Supreme Court.[57]

Governor William Clements calls William Wayne Justice "goofy." There are many, however, who consider Wayne Justice to be the real governor of Texas. Justice has been federal district judge in the eastern district of Texas that is headquartered in oil-rich, conservative Tyler. Justice is not a product of that environment, but is instead from Athens, Texas, an oil-poor rurally based community that was once a hotbed of the kind of agrarian populism that produced the likes of such politicians as Sam Rayburn and Ralph Yarborough. In fact, Justice's political mentor was Senator Ralph Yarborough who had Justice made U.S. attorney and then a federal district judge. From that position Justice reigns as the most powerful remnant of the liberal-populist Texas tradition. In that position, Justice has done much to promote liberal-populist policies in Texas, a task that has been impossible through the electoral process given the overwhelming Establishment dominance of elected offices.

The state of Texas, however, remains firmly in the hands of the low services-low taxes oriented Establishment. Disadvantaged groups and individuals have little chance of influencing public policy through the political process. As a result, the disadvantaged frequently turn to the federal courts to assert their interests and William Wayne Justice is by far the most liberal and most activist federal judge in Texas.

Justice has ruled: that Texas' juvenile corrections system is unconstitutional; that Texas' adult prison system is unconstitutional; that Texas could not deny a free public education to the children of illegal aliens; and that Texas must provide a bilingual education to Mexican-American children. Justice has also been very active in trying to ensure the integration of public schools. He has tried to remove some of the more oppressive symbols of Texas public education such as hair length regulations and the use of Confederate symbols at integrated public schools. In the environmental area, Justice has tried to ban clear-cutting, a timber harvesting technique that involves cutting all timber in the path of the lumbermen's saws. He has also enjoined construction of a major water reservoir due to the inadequacy of the reservoir's environmental impact statement. In addition, Justice played a major role in the state's recent reapportionment controversy where he prevented the Democratic Texas legislature from drawing district lines that would have made it impossible to elect some liberal Democratic congressmen. In taking such liberal-activist positions, Justice has become the most effective voice in Texas politics on behalf of the interests of minorities and the poor.[58]

Every Texas school child knows that Texas was once an independent nation. States-rights thinking has a long hold on Texas and many Texans still believe that union was a grave error. This Lone Star State sentiment is reflected in relations with the outside world. The national government is commonly used as a whipping boy by state politicians. Texas is also frequently at odds with energy consuming states, the result of a natural incompatibility of interests between energy consuming and energy providing areas. Moreover, while some claim that the ties between Texas and Mexico have improved, that relationship remains fundamentally weak because of discrimination against Hispanics in Texas. Problems also exist with several neighboring western states over the use of surface water. The water problem will reach crisis proportions in Texas by the year 2000. Finally, in spite of its attractive climate, its economic prosperity, and its unlimited growth philosophy, the scarcity of water may turn what is left of the Lone Star State's boom to bust.

NOTES

1. Neil Peirce, *The Megastates of America: People, Politics, and Power in the Ten Great States* (New York: Norton, 1972).

2. Eugene W. Jones, Joe E. Ericson, Lyle C. Brown, and Robert S. Trotter, Jr., *Practicing Texas Politics* (Boston: Houghton Mifflin, 1980), pp. 4–12.

3. Dennis Holder, "The Michigan Migration," *Westward Magazine*, 20 September 1981, pp. 6–7, 13–19, 30–32.

4. See Griffin Smith, Jr., "Divide and Conquer," in *Texas Monthly's Political Reader*, ed. Rod Parker (Austin: Texas Monthly Press, 1978), pp. 206–209.

5. See "A Place in the Sun," in *Texas Monthly's Political Reader*, ed. Rod Parker (Austin: Texas Monthly Press, 1978), 210–211.

6. Daniel Elazar, *American Federalism: A View from the States* (New York: Crowell, 1966), pp. 93–114.

7. Jones, et al., *Practicing Texas Politics*, pp. 22–23.

8. Beryl E. Pettus and Randall W. Bland, *Texas Government Today* (Homewood, Ill.: Dorsey, 1976), pp. 16–20.

9. V.O. Key, Jr., *Southern Politics* (New York: Vintage, 1949), p. 255.

10. "'Mad Eddie' Chiles Wows 'Em at Ut-A," *Texas Observer*, 26 March 1982, pp. 18, 20.

11. Patti Kilday, "State Bonanza: Oil, gas taxes exceed $2 billion," *Times Herald*, Dallas, 4 November 1981, p. D3.

12. Bert Holmes, "Budget numbers game," *Times Herald*, Dallas, 6 April 1982, p. A14.

13. "President Speaks," *Texas Teacher*, April 1982, p. 2.

14. Patti Kilday and Saralee Tiede, "For Texas: a philosophical change," *Times Herald*, Dallas, 28 January 1982, p. 1, 13.

15. See *Jefferson v. Hackney*, 406 U.S. 535 (1972).

16. Kilday and Tiede, "For Texas: a philosophical change," p. 13.

17. *Ibid.* p. 13.

18. "Sterilization suggested for recipients of welfare," *Post*, Houston, 28 February 1980, p. C7.

19. See *Ruiz v. Estelle*, 503 F Supp. 1306 (1980).

20. For an example of Texas jail conditions see, *Taylor v. Sterrett*, 344 F. Suppl. 411 (1972).

21. Texas Democratic Party Chairman Bob Slagle has said, "For a major state office now you're talking about being able to raise and expend $5 million to have a reasonable chance to be elected. If you're running against someone like Bill Clements, that may just be the lowest marginal amount you can spend to have a chance at all." Virginia Ellis, "War Chests: Campaign

funds grow as age of big-money politics dawns in Texas," *Times Herald*, Dallas, 3 July 1981. p. B3.

22. Jimmy Banks, *Money, Marbles, and Chalk* (Austin: Texas Publishing, 1971), pp. 213–228.

23. Richard Fly, "Collins to swallow campaign loss," *Times Herald*, Dallas, 19 November 1982, pp. 1, 6.

24. Robert A. Caro, "The Years of Lyndon Johnson: Lyndon and Mister Sam," *The Atlantic Monthly*, November 1981, p. 41–63.

25. Steve Kenny, "The Last of the Old Time Legislatures," *D Magazine*, May 1981, pp. 104–107, 160–165.

26. Virginia Ellis, "Legislators hunt doves and chemical lobby pays," *Times Herald*, Dallas, 27 September 1981, p. C3.

27. Saralee Tiede, "McKnight: No regrets in ending campaign," *Times Herald*, Dallas, 5 April 1982, p. C3.

28. The best treatments of the Sharpstown scandal are Charles Deaton, *The Year They Threw the Rascals Out* (Austin: Shoal Creek, 1973); and Sam Kinch, Jr. and Ben Proctor, *Texas Under a Cloud* (Austin: Jenkins, 1973).

29. Charlotte Anne Lucas and Richard S. Dunham, "Texas County road costs fall after U.S. probe," *Times Herald*, Dallas, 14 February 1982, pp. 1, A20.

30. "A Tale of Two Speakers," *Texas Observer*, Dallas, 29 January 1982, p. 3.

31. "Using campaign funds," *The Times Herald*, Dallas, 20 January 1982, p. A16.

32. *Ibid.*, p. A16.

33. "Truth in Purchasing Award," *Texas Monthly*, July 1981, p. 104.

34. Janice C. May, Stuart A. MacCorkle, and Dick Smith, *Texas Government* (New York: McGraw Hill, 1980), p. 54.

35. *Ibid.*, p. 54.

36. "Ft. Worth Mayor's Election," *Morning News*, Dallas, 17 January 1982. p. A34.

37. Key, *Southern Politics*, pp. 254–276.

38. Richard S. Dunham, "Liberal-Baiting," *Times Herald*, Dallas, 12 September 1982, pp. B1, B4.

39. "Riding with Reagan," *Texas Observer*, January 29, 1982, p. 19.

40. However, Allan Shivers, one of the state's most influential political figures, attributes Carr's failure to an effective Tower organization. Banks, *Money, Marbles, and Chalk*, p. 128.

41. See, Kent L. Tedin and Richard W. Murray, "Dynamics of Candidate Choice in a State Election," *Journal of Politics*, 43 (May 1981):435–455.

42. Saralee Tiede, "Politics on the air," *Times Herald*, Dallas, 14 March 1982, pp. 1, 13.

43. Jerry Conn has examined the remarkable personal organization that was constructed by Preston Smith. See, Jerry Douglas Conn, *Preston Smith: The Making of a Texas Governor* (Austin: Jenkins, 1972).

44. Skip Hollandsworth, "Reagan Brown," *Westward Magazine,* 6 December 1981, pp. 6–20.

45. Pettus and Bland, *Texas Government Today*, pp. 153–173, 322–336.

46. Robert Heard, *The Miracle of the Killer Bees: 12 Senators Who Changed Texas Politics* (Austin: Honey Hill, 1981).

47. A superb treatment of the Texas Railroad Commission is David F. Prindle, *Petroleum Politics and the Texas Railroad Commission* (Austin: University of Texas Press, 1981).

48. Paul Holder, "That's Yarbrough-Spelled With One 'O': A Study of Judicial Misbehavior in Texas," in *Practicing Texas Politics*, ed. Jones, et al., pp. 447–453.

49. Saralee Tiede, "Contributions enhance appointment success," *Times Herald*, Dallas, 6 February 1982, p. A24.

50. "State Secrets," *Texas Monthly*, March 1982, p. 240.

51. Dan Balz, "We Believe In You, Coach," *Texas Monthly*, March 1982, pp. 160–166.

52. Patti Kilday, "Many bankers invest in Harding's campaign," *Times Herald*, Dallas, 6 February 1982, p. A24.

53. Saralee Tiede, "Texas passing up at least $20 million annually," *Times Herald*, Dallas, 12 February 1982, p. B3.

54. Virginia Ellis, "Funding the System," *Times Herald*, Dallas, 6 February 1982, p. 22.

55. Rod Davis, "Jim 'Whole Hog' Hightower," *Westward Magazine*, 2 February 1982, pp. 14–25.

56. Virginia Ellis, "Political contributions flow like water in '82," *Times Herald*, Dallas, 29 May 1982, pp. A1–22.

57. Ellis, "Funding the System," p. 22.

58. Most of the discussion of Judge Justice is from Paul Burka, "The Real Governor of Texas," in *Texas Monthly's Political Reader*, ed. Rod Parker (Austin: Texas Monthly Press, 1978), pp. 217–225.

7
Florida
DOUGLAS ST. ANGELO

Florida's politics are mainly marked by change and instability. The shifting kaleidoscope of Florida's society and politics, sifted through prisms of growth, can cause even those with longtime Florida roots to feel that they, like the greater part of the population from somewhere else, are merely transients held in place. A recent British prime minister proclaimed that two weeks is a long time in politics. In Florida two days can sometimes constitute a political era.

POLITICAL CULTURE: SO FEW FLORIDIANS

Manning J. Dauer has called Florida "The Different State," attributing the difference to its population growth.[1] Rapid growth profoundly influences Florida's politics. The census counted 2.8 million Floridians in 1950 and just under 10 million in 1980. Florida gained four additional congressmen in 1983; having gained three in the preceeding decade. Even Floridians have a difficult time conceptualizing such growth. The addition of three million persons to 1980's census count means that—allowing for deaths and out-migration—well over half of Florida's current population was not here ten years ago. Think what it would mean to any state to gain, in only ten years, the equivalent of the total 1970 population in these cities: Atlanta, El Paso, Louisville, Oakland, Pittsburgh, Rochester (New York), St. Paul, and Tuscon. Over two of each of three Floridians were born somewhere else and that figure is nine of ten in some of the metropolitan areas. Even in the state legislature, out-of-staters predominate. Half the states in the nation are represented as birthplaces of members with about one-half of the representatives and two-thirds of the senators born outside of Florida. Northeastern states dominate the birth list, followed by midwestern and other southeastern states.

A recent study, utilizing hundreds of variables to characterize and

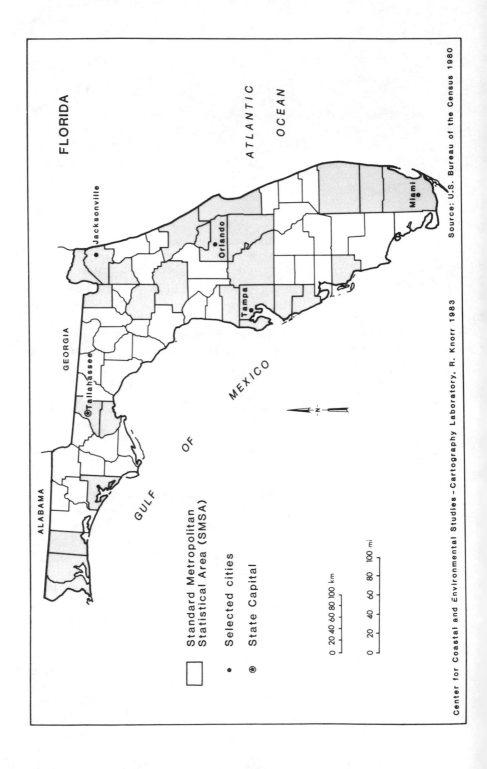

Source: U.S. Bureau of the Census 1980

Center for Coastal and Environmental Studies – Cartography Laboratory, R. Knorr 1983

cluster the states, ranked Florida with a set of states that included Texas, Missouri, Maryland, and Virginia.[2] Like other states, the position of Florida varied widely on individual characteristics. Florida's economy still shows a low level of reliance upon industrialization, but this sector is growing. Much of the state income depends upon growth services such as retail sales, insurance, finance, and construction. Tourism, with over thirty million visitors a year, is a major income activity. Export-import activity is showing up as increasingly more important and the official figures do not include the illegal drug traffic. Agricultural-forestry harvesting and processing are also a major economic factor in the state.

It should also be noted that social security payments are the single most important source of personal income in Florida. Florida, however, has not always been a magnet to older people. In 1900 the percentage of the state population over 64-years old was 2.6 percent, clearly less than the nation's 4 percent. It was not until the 1950 census that Florida surpassed the national average in senior citizens and the difference was a bare 8.6 percent to 8.1 percent. Air-conditioning, pension programs, and colonization were clearly permitting the Sunbelt to exert its growing attraction. Currently, the senior population—at almost 18 percent—makes up one of four of Florida's voters. During the decade ending in 1970, the over-64-year-old population continued to increase faster than the remainder of the population. If these trends continue into the future, in 40 years the seniors may account for a majority of the state's voters.

The proportion of seniors now in Florida is almost 60 percent above the national average, and is well above the second-ranking state, Arkansas, at 13 percent. Florida's seniors also have the nation's highest degree of spatial concentration. For example, four of Florida's urban counties had more than 100,000 seniors each. These were the three southeastern counties (Dade, with Miami; Broward, with Fort Lauderdale; and Palm Beach, with West Palm Beach) and the central Gulf coast county of Pinellas, with St. Petersburg as its largest city. Over one-third of Pinellas County's citizens are 65 or older; in some years the county has more deaths than live births. Beyond these counties, the aging rates are high in all south and central counties except a few of the inland, low-population, agricultural counties. Senior growth is even lapping away at some of these and is also pushing north and becoming noticeable at the edges of the panhandle. The older citizens no longer fit (and they never did) the rich caricature. Florida's seniors rank in the upper one-third of income inequality among all states, indicating a widely dispersed pattern of incomes. This population group is also ranked rather high among the states in illness and disability. It is also higher in multifamily residency status.

The point of these demographic facts is that there can be no enduring political culture under these circumstances and that any discerned elements of culture that can be said to exist are subject to rapid modification. In fact, so many Floridians come from somewhere else that it is somewhat misleading to speak of their identification with the state. Florida is a state of diversity with few, if any, common elements that pull citizens together. Its geography denies it the advantage of a dominant state newspaper or common television contact. Unlike some states, no single media source blankets Florida. The state possesses several major media markets; each market has a dominant morning daily and several still have a second evening paper. The St. Petersburg *Times* and, increasingly, the Miami *Herald* have national reputations for their coverage and journalistic quality, but neither are influential with citizens outside of their main advertising markets. Television is also localized. The widespread advent of cable transmission has not yet done anything to extend the regional limits of existing state television stations. Public radio and television both have a statewide network and do produce daily-weekday programs focusing on the Florida legislature during sessions; however, the coverage is bland and the audiences are small.

In addition, no single state institution, such as the state university in some of the midwestern states, acts as a unifying force. The older state universities, Florida State University and the University of Florida, were not co-educational until after World War II and Florida A&M University drew allegiance only from blacks. All three now have strong athletic programs, as does the private University of Miami. But none of these institutions enjoy the kind of statewide stature most Floridians might identify with. Things change too fast. In the course of the past two decades seven more state universities sprang up and the largest post-secondary education institution in the state— with over 50,000 students—is the community college in Dade County.

Florida has two professional football teams. Miami has the Dolphins and Tampa has the Bucs, but neither galvanizes the state. Their support is regional and even within their regions they must compete with old affections for the teams where many fans used to live.

Cities in Florida are largely a collection of subcommunities and tend not to have major centers. Residents are diverse and come from all over the nation. Its retirees tend to colonize on the basis of acquaintances from "back home." Most Floridians have only a dim understanding of what the geography of the state, beyond their own environs, is like. Disney World may be the only place that most of them could locate. This all may be another way of saying that—except for politicians, journalists, and traveling professionals—there is little reality to being a Floridian.

Given the ephemeral quality of Florida's political culture, it is difficult to generalize about levels of support and expectations of state government. Public opinion information gathered by the policy science program at Florida State University since 1978 does give some clues.[3] Two important trends emerge. First, Floridians are not well-informed about their state government, and second, in comparative terms, Floridians are fairly well satisfied with their government and its leaders. More than eight of ten Floridians gave the state a high rating, but more than half of these were "fairly satisfied" rather than satisfied. The governor has consistently secured higher approval ratings than Presidents Carter and Reagan; the state legislature outpaces the congress. Comparisons to surveys in other states also indicate that Floridians rank their governor and legislature higher than do citizens in the 20 other states having state polls. These approval figures, of course, are low everywhere as shown by the fact that while the Florida legislature leads in approval, those ratings were still below 50 percent. Furthermore, it is interesting to speculate on the possibility of an inter-connection between the higher ratings given to Florida and the high level of misinformation that its citizens have about Florida politics. It must also be noted that contemporary, sophisticated techniques—widely used in Florida campaigns—contribute little to voter enlightenment.

Floridians are not very confident about the honesty of state officials. In a 1979 survey almost one-third replied that quite a few state officials were a "little crooked" compared to 25 percent who stated that hardly any state officials were a "little crooked." Still they felt that Florida officials were more honest than their national counterparts. Corruption is a brooding, omnipresent cloud over Florida politics. Every year produces several major corruption stories. Florida is clearly not as clean as the work-ethic states of the upper midwest, but it is not subject to the continuing revelations of dishonesty occurring in some of the urban mid-Atlantic states either. Corruption is there, but it is not overriding. Citizens seem to perceive the situation pretty well, but the attentive public is more cynical than the general public on this issue.

Floridians want good service from government. Even in counterpoint to decreased taxes, they consistently express support for increased public spending for the elderly, education, health care, the environment, and transportation (public transportation being favored over roads). Recently, concern about crime and refugees gained importance, particularly in southeastern Florida.

There was fair recognition among those surveyed that Florida is a low-tax state. Almost 50 percent knew taxes were lower in Florida, many thought they were about the same, but one in five thought they were higher. Ambiguity was present on tax cuts. Nearly half favored a Florida Proposition 13, but most opposed a constitutional limit on state spending and convincing majorities did not want service reductions in order to secure tax cuts. Overall it appears that Floridians, while not liberals,* give survey responses that are less conservative than existing public policy, since state policies are more often characterized as moderate to conservative on these concerns.

Other elements of this difference in citizen performance and state policy are apparent. Floridians, as evidenced in surveys, oppose population growth and promotion of economic development, but the governor and the legislature give development a high priority. On the matter of support for the elderly, citizens of all age groups—the senior group only more so—are

---

*About 41 percent of Floridians designate themselves conservative, an equal number consider themselves moderate, while 17 percent choose a liberal designation.

strongly positive. Yet three Republican congressmen from areas with very high age levels score zero on the National Senior Citizens Council voting scale.[4] It remains to be seen whether these differences point to a more liberal Florida or if they are merely a product of low voter information that permits elected officials a wide degree of personal choice.

POLITICAL STYLE: PORKCHOPPERS AND ENTREPRENEURS

In *Southern Politics*, V.O. Key noted that the dominant Democratic party in Florida did not organize the state's politics and that there were no enduring factions.[5] Finding no evidence of steadfast coalitions, he maintained that the dominant political pattern for candidates and elected officials was "every man for himself" depending on a system of substate regional support that he labeled a pattern of "friends and neighbors." Hindsight suggests that Key's perceptions remain accurate. His writing did, however, come a year or two early for him to fully appreciate one psuedo-institution that did much to shape the state's recent politics and influence the dominant political style. The urban press labeled this group the "porkchoppers."

For over ten years the porkchoppers established a political culture of north-south regionalism. They constituted a relatively small group of rural north Florida legislators, members of both houses, and a few urban "traitors." The porkchopper power was awesome and depended on two bases. The first was seniority, gained by representing small stable counties that consistently returned these legislators to Tallahassee. With continuity of service these porkchopper legislators gained considerable knowledge and influence in the legislature.

The second element of their power was a badly malapportioned legislature, that before the 1963 to 1967 period, had totally ignored the massive shift of the state population to southern Florida. Prior to the long series of federal court ordered reapportionment actions, Florida was notorious, even among many other badly apportioned states, for the extent of its voting inequality. Hence little Jefferson County with 3500 people—the majority of them blacks who were prohibited from voting or were certainly not encouraged to vote—had nearly the same representation in the legislature as those counties approaching, and in one case exceeding, one million people. While reapportionment in the 1960s noticeably increased urban power, the senate is still under continuing porkchopper influence. The endurance of this phenomenon rests upon the divided party representation in the urban areas and the skill of a long-standing leader, Dempsey Barron. It is sustained by a hard-ball approach to politics, the skillful use of patronage, and the fears of members regarding the loss of access.

The old porkchoppers were noted for their fiscal and social conservatism, concentration of state spending in the rural north, friendliness with the state's large commercial and financial interests, and continuation of the old

Florida tradition of treating state government as the private property of elected officials. Lobbying for friendly interests was duck soup in those days. Favors for the few invariably secured the desired action. Porkchopper style was confident and haughty. Committee proxies were permitted and held by the chairmen. One committee chairman was asked by a reporter, as the two of them walked down a capitol corridor, when his committee was going to act on a reform bill. The chairman replied that the bill was in his coat pocket; he indicated that he had taken the vote while they were walking, and he announced that the bill had failed.

Reapportionment has made important differences. State money, political power, and institutions have flowed south and to urban areas. Prisons, mental institutions, universities, community colleges, highways, and such have sprung up in those areas. Funding formulae have been adjusted to be more favorable to those interests. Policy making has not become liberal, but it is more moderate. A new constitution was adopted strengthening the powers of the governor, although the Florida governorship still remains weaker than most. State administration was reorganized and the legislature was more professionally staffed. The rural interests continued the tradition of using political power to favor their districts, but the growth of urban power was sudden and demonstrates the instability of elements in Florida's political culture.

Up to the 1970s, when meaningful reapportionment occurred, a standard role model did prevail for most of Florida's political leaders. The dominant model was that of the small town merchant-banker mixed with a softening touch of down-home and good-ole-boy crackerism. The style could be misleading. Under that gentle southern geniality lay a strong dose of audacity. That audacity was utilized to get what one wanted for oneself and one's district. In the interest of securing turkeys—a current name for dipping into the pork barrel—decisions on roads, institutions, contracts, jobs, and such were openly political. The appetite for turkeys is still there, but the style lingers among only a few old-time north Florida senators. Diversity of style is the current mode of Florida political leadership. This diversity can be demonstrated by focusing upon two current prominent and contrasting Florida Democratic politicians.

Governor Robert Graham and Senator Dempsey Barron provide the contrast. Both have law degrees, Barron from a state university and Graham from Harvard. Both have money, Graham's originally stemming from his father's huge dairy operation and Barron's largely accumulated since he gained political power. Barron hails from the heartland of North Florida, Graham from south Florida's mighty Dade County (the first Florida governor to come from the state's most populous county). Both served for years in the state senate, where Barron has steadily held power, and continues to do so, and Graham never did. Graham, small of frame, is an urban sophisticate. Barron is tough, direct, and decisive while Graham equivocates and, according to many informed persons, has a reputation for sloppy administration. Barron had an early reputation as a conservative,

Graham as a liberal; in fact, both are pragmatists. The press and TV, until recently, adored Bob Graham. Barron has long been the scourge of big media.

One important difference between these two men is in their goals. Barron appears to be right where he wants to be; Graham wants to be president of the United States. To that end, Graham courted the eastern press, made overtures to the Council of Foreign Relations and the Trilateral Commission. He courted and supported Carter sufficiently to be selected to give the keynote speech at the 1980 convention and then blew his opportunity by being cool in a hot setting. Barron continues to extend his political clout within the state.

While the Barron-Graham contrast clearly demonstrates the diversity of Florida leadership styles, it may overstate the case. Reference to Florida's six most recent governors should provide balance, as these comparisons show that political leadership here has been marked by similarities as well as diversity. Included in these comparisons are LeRoy Collins (1957–61), Farris Bryant (1961–65), Haydon Burns (1965–67), Claude Kirk (1967–71), Reubin Askew (1971–79), and Robert Graham who was first elected in 1978 and who was reelected in 1982. The turnover rate is not as high as this list indicates, because the state had a one-term limit until 1967; both Burns and Kirk were denied second terms by the voters.

Legal training was one thing making for similarity, five of the six having earned law degrees. Burns was the only exception. Two-thirds of these governors possessed legislative experience. Burns had been a metropolitan mayor. Kirk, alone, held no previous political position. Two scholars, Colburn and Sher, rated most of Florida's governors as ineffective administrators and all of them as ineffective in their legislative relations.[6] These authors also saw most of the state's chief executives as pro-business with conservative tendencies on economic issues. There have been, then, some trends toward similarity among these governors, but on each item there was always one or more exceptions.

Colburn and Sher also noted some marked differences among these governors. On racial and social issues, half were rated as conservative, while the rest were ranked as moderate. Only half were given high marks on political honesty. Three of the six were seen as charismatic, while the others were considered reserved. I would classify the images portrayed by three—Collins, Bryant and Askew—as in the tradition of southern gentility. Burns and Kirk projected an image of entrepreneurial promoters. Graham has a made-to-measure media image.

The style of Florida legislators can best be described as brash. One prominent and respected lobbyist, with experience in many states, has privately said that the Florida legislature holds the southeastern states' export license for ego. Two background characteristics may account for this high level of legislative confidence. Florida legislators are young and they have been in their current chamber for only a short period of time. At the outset of the 1981 session, the average age of house members was 38 and only three members were over 60. The 1983–84 speaker designate and his expected seven closest associates averaged 37 years. The average age of senators was 47 with only two members over 60. All of this in a state that leads in senior citizenship! Turnover is high in both houses. Sixty-three percent of the senators had served two or less years in the senate, while only two members had served three or more complete four-year terms. Dempsey Barron was the senate "dean," having served four and one-half terms. The average house member had served only 1.8 two-year terms and only four had served as many as four terms. This combination of youth and high turnover limits legislative memory and contributes to the state's political instability.

Brashness, youth, and short tenure have not provided Florida with a gullible or misinformed legislature. Recent leadership has largely been intelligent and decisive, and it has made good use of able staff. Overall, the legislative process in Florida is characterized by a high degree of profes-sionalism and legislative losses in the policy process are rarely incurred as a result of incompetence or political stupidity.

The thrust of this discussion suggests that Florida's political style, like almost all matters pertaining to the state, is malleable and transitory. Even during a period of a little more than 25 years, no element of political style remains constant as nothing is enduring or long-remembered in Florida politics. Two of the last three U.S. Senate incumbents, one from each party, lost their reelection bids. A popular speaker of the house of representatives, who had enjoyed much favorable media attention, took a job with the Carter administration. Returning to Florida to run for election to the U.S. Senate, he found that the polls showed that only 7 percent of the population knew who he was.

POLITICAL INTERACTION: DISPERSED POWER

Florida largely remains a one-party Democratic state. Republicans are, however, making gains and those gains seem tied to population migration. Since 1952 Republican presidential candidates have dominated the elec-tions, losing only in 1964 and 1976. Republican legislative strength grew more slowly, reaching an apex of 36 percent of the seats during Claude Kirk's term as governor. Kirk, the only Republican governor of the century, was a one-termer. Republicans have been strongly contesting statewide elections since that time. Paula Hawkins won a seat on the public service commission before those posts became appointive. Edward Gurney became a one-term U.S. senator in the law and order campaign year of 1968 and Paula Hawkins gained the U.S. Senate seat in the Reagan sweep of 1980. From the Kirk era to 1980, Republican strength in the legislature suffered a slight decline. Small gains were made in 1980 (to about one-third of the two houses), but GOP strength still lagged behind that of the Kirk years.

Traditional Republican voting power has been a central and south

Florida phenomenon. Its county distribution has been horseshoe shaped. It begins in Broward County (above Dade), sweeps up the east coast and swings through the Orlando area, omits Tampa, includes St. Petersburg, and completes the other side of the horseshoe by going south along the west coast. Aberations occur. Goldwater lost some retirement counties, such as Pinellas, in 1964 and Johnson lost almost all of the traditional Democratic rural north Florida to the racial backlash of that year. The far northwest military counties went to Ford and Reagan in their campaigns against Carter. In 1980 Dade County went to Reagan; this was attributed to the Republican swing, the Cuban vote, and reactions to Latino immigration. The GOP also picked up three state house seats in the strongly Democratic Miami area in the 1980 election.

The two-party pattern of the 1960s was a steady growth of Republican voting. That trend was offset in the 1970s by a Democratic restoration. The 1980 election suggests a swing back to the GOP. The continuity of the new Republican trend, in Florida as elsewhere, will depend upon the perception of President Reagan's performance in office.

Underlying these trends is a certain volatility in voter identification, particularly among Republicans. Seven surveys—covering November 1978 through April 1981—found that at the beginning of the period, 23 percent of Floridians identified with the Republican party. This figure rose to 25 percent three months later, fell off to 20 percent in the next six months and then gained over the next three surveys to reach 31 percent by April 1981. Democratic identification, during the same period, was more stable; it hovered at 44 to 45 percent in the first five surveys, dropped to 38 percent in the four months between October 1980 and the following February, but then gained 2 percent—reaching 40 percent—in the next two months. A national survey does not show that kind of Republican volatility in the rest of the country.[7]

The 33 percent range of fluctuation in Republican identification, in just over two years, reemphasizes the instability of Florida politics. From 1981 to 1982 Republican identification again declined and Democratic identification gained in both Florida and the nation. Summarizing party identification in Florida, it appears that—depending on the month—Florida Democrats hold somewhere between an 11 to 25 percent advantage over the state's Republicans. Sometimes Florida is a safe Democratic state, and sometimes it is marginal; election results support this contention.

Party organizations are now, and have always been, too weak to deserve much notice. With a one-party tradition, the Democrats did not need party organization and did not develop one. The Democrats do now have a small paid state staff; the Republicans have a somewhat larger one. Reflecting their minority status, Republicans are more active in recruiting and supporting candidates. Both state party organizations maintain a strictly neutral official position in their primaries. The important function of selecting party candidates is beyond the power of the party organizations in Florida and

organizations get a portion of the filing fee from all candidates entering their primaries.

Beyond partisan coalitions, there are other discernable groups that should be considered. Given Florida's large senior population, one should first note that group's policy success—or, more aptly, its lack of success in state politics. Lobbying by senior groups on their own behalf is usually successful only on symbolic issues that do not cost money. A small program to support families that keep older persons in their homes—rather than sending them to institutions—is an exception to the rule; even that program has been supported by a low dollar level. Senior lobbying organizations depend upon volunteer lobbyists. Even one organization with over a million members in Florida depends upon volunteer lobbying by retired persons. Support comes to these efforts from bureaucrats, when permitted, and from other social-issue lobbyists. The overall effort, however, is feeble.[8] Obviously, if the senior citizens voted cohesively on age-related issues, they would be a considerable political power. That cohesion is not yet there. In view of the lack of cohesion and the weak lobbying, the state's lawmakers know that they can get by with only symbolic attention to their senior constituents.

There are four other sometimes identifiable voting blocs in Florida. Blacks constitute 15 percent of the population and can be influential in some of the more populous urban areas along with a few small rural counties where they are about 50 percent of the total population. However, the state's black voters are so widely dispersed that they have less power than their numbers suggest they should have at the state level. A black was elected statewide to the supreme court against weak opposition after having been appointed to the post by Governor Askew. In 1981 blacks had no state senators and only 5 house members out of 120 (4.2 percent). Black forces in state politics can sometimes keep things from happening. Preventing the merger of a formerly all-black state university with a nearby formerly all white one is a case in point. But they cannot seem to make things happen.

The situation for Hispanics is reversed. They are gaining power in a few concentrated areas in Dade County. These areas are highly populated and could swing some legislative races and be important in statewide races. Almost 33 percent of Dade County is now Hispanic, but only 25 percent of the Latinos were registered to vote in 1981. Hispanics that year did elect their first legislator, a Republican, in a low-turnout special election. Dade is the state's most populous county. The leverage provided by those two forces, blacks and Hispanics, is potent.

The third force is the "born again" native white southern vote. The influence of this group on social issues has been significant in a number of Florida elections. Their power has not been demonstrated since 1972. With the departure of their more moderate fellow "born again" symbol, Jimmy Carter, and the emergence of a more strident Moral Majority, they may again develop as an important political voting bloc.

A fourth group can be termed the military bloc. Florida is fourth among all states in military spending. The western panhandle counties from Pensacola to Panama City are saturated with miltary facilities and voting in that area often reflects a strong military orientation. These counties strongly supported Ford in 1976 and Reagan in 1980. Congressional elections in that district also turn upon military and related local-economic issues.

Florida comes uniquely close to possessing a plural executive. Six cabinet-level officials are elected statewide and, barring any very major scandal, they stay in office as long as they want, while the governor is limited to two terms. The cabinet has fairly extensive policymaking authority. It meets biweekly on Tuesdays with the governor presiding. Each member has an office of cabinet affairs headed by an aide. The aides, and their assistants, meet prior to the Tuesday meetings in what is called the "mini cabinet." Most of the executive business is ironed out in these sessions; hence much of the Tuesday business is a formality.

The cabinet actually meets as a group of commissions, with differing memberships—much like subcommittees, but the process flows so evenly that a casual observer could be unaware of the shift from one commission or board to the next. The cabinet still selects key administrators for and directs the activity of some agencies. It also enjoys authority over many legislative delegated decisions and rule-making procedures. In a sense, the cabinet is a third house of the legislature.

Cabinet power was greatly reduced by the constitutional revision of 1968. That revision was the by-product of legislative reapportionment and the new urban political power that had not looked favorably upon the cabinet system. It was a testimony to cabinet power that the institution was not then destroyed and the members made appointive rather than elected. Indeed, the change gave the cabinet constitutional status, where formerly it had been statutory.

Prior to constitutional revision, the governor was subject to a single four-year term limit. That arrangement clearly made Florida governors the weakest in the nation. Under the new constitution gubernatorial authority was increased. The governor now directly controls the budget-formulating process and some big departments, subject to confirmation of their nominated secretaries by two-thirds of the senate. The big departments shifted to the governor are; health and rehabilitative services, transportation, commerce, labor, and community affairs. These shifts strengthened gubernatorial power. The compromise still left the cabinet with its own agencies: legal affairs, agriculture, education, banking and finance, department of state, and insurance (and treasury). Some important agencies are jointly controlled: law enforcement, highway safety and motor vehicles (including the state patrol), natural resources (a real money tree), revenue, clemency, and parole and probation. In these areas, as with budget proposals, four of six cabinet members can control outcomes. So the governor's power is greater than it had been, but still weaker than most. In a nation where it is customary to distribute political power across the landscape, Florida almost scatters it randomly over its sandy soil.

The state legislature, in contrast to the governor and the executive branch, is quite powerful and has gained power in recent years. By some estimates it is one of the most effective legislatures in the nation. Over the past 12 years new legislative strength has come by way of constitutional amendment and statutory action. Among these are provisions for a short organizing session two weeks after the general election. This permits change of leadership six months prior to the annual session. Due to a pledging system among Democratic members, the biennial choice of the house speaker and senate president are usually foregone matters at this session. The leadership is, hence, in position to name committee assignments and subcommittee assignments, as well as their chairs at this early session.

The legislature has also moved from biennial to annual sessions with biennial budgeting. The legislature may call special sessions, a power formerly assigned to the governor alone. The auditing department has been moved from executive to legislative control. Perhaps most important, the legislature has moved from minimal committee and member staffing to strong and massive staffing. The weak spot in legislative strength is a tradition limiting the speaker and the president to a single two-year term. In practice this is mitigated by the influence of outgoing presiding officers in the choice of their successors and a powerful leader can upset that tradition. This happened recently.

Perhaps, in the understanding of Florida politics, nothing is more important than the schism between the state house and senate. This schism has spanned more than a decade. While it is true that the house is more liberal than the senate, the schism's roots are more associated with power, personality, and advocacy for pet projects. Through this period Senator Dempsey Barron has controlled the senate, first as its president, later by skillful political action that permitted him to be pivotal in designation of subsequent presidents. In the spring of 1981, Barron was hospitalized. In his absence, his hand-picked president, W.D. Childers, attempted to create an independent power base. The overt issue was a sales tax increase. Childers announced his support for the increase, knowing that Barron opposed it. Barron, upon his return, forged a new power base in the senate from among about half of the Democratic senators and almost all of the Republicans. Reapportionment efforts in 1980 and 1981 became an uncompromisable issue that the courts had to settle, as Barron and the house leadership went to war over the effort of Barron to protect his coalition through the reapportionment process.

In this area of bicameral schism, the house leadership has come and gone, but the animosity has endured from one set of house leaders to the next. Both Askew and Graham, as governors during this era, tended to align with the house. Barron's hostility to both has been open and vociferous.

The results of this bicameral warfare has made conference committees the major battleground and, on major issues, the real legislature. Bicameralism has lost allure in this era. A respected group of former legislators mounted a petition drive to place a constitutional amendment on the ballot providing for a single-house legislature. The petition drive succeeded and was certified by the secretary of state, only to have the amendment's wording struck down by the supreme court as too broad and vague. Hence, the amendment never got to the voters, but the concept is still alive and has support.

No meaningful assessment of Florida's interactions can ignore lobbying and interest group activities. Diversity or not, entrepreneurism dominates state policy. This is demonstrated by the prominence of business occupational backgrounds among elected officials. Real estate and construction interests outpaced all other professions, even law, in the self reports from the 1980–1982 state senators and representatives.[9] In all, 63 percent of the legislators declared a business interest. With lawyers included, that figure rises to 82 percent. Florida's diversity has not overshadowed the influence of commerce; lobbying in Florida reinforces this point.

Lobbying in Florida is something of a growth activity. Lobbying registration began in 1955. Since then the only rule changes have been in the direction of lower registration requirements. Even so, registrations reached 1000 in 1972 and were just shy of 4000 in 1982. Nearly 1400 organizations were listed as having lobbyist representation in 1982. Commercial interests accounted for 57 percent of the organizations represented and covered 433 individual corporations and firms as well as 303 trade and professional groups. State and local governmental lobbyists are also required to register and these lobbyists listed 259 separate units. Twenty-five private labor groups were registered and 81 employee unions, mostly from local school districts, were represented. There were also 58 public interest group registrations, including church and women's issues organizations. In addition, 14 environmental groups appeared, along with 14 senior citizen groups, of which half were retired teachers organizations. Four groups represented animals, 25 spoke for gambling interests, and 9 groups represented military or veterans organizations.

Lobbying activities have caused a boom in hotel and restaurant construction activity in the capital city of Tallahassee. Lobbyist sponsored parties occur almost nightly during the legislative session with as many as four gatherings on some evenings. One newly developed mall-like street has blossomed with lunchtime eateries that are frequently used for lobbying entertainment. An expensive private "Governor's Club" has been organized on the same street with bars, dining rooms, and a "library." It depends heavily upon lobbyist members. Policymakers in Florida can make it through a legislative session without buying food or drink, including breakfast.

More and more political campaigns depend upon interest-group funding. Almost 400 political-action committees and the more permanent committees of continuing existence pump money into campaigns. One moderately influential senator, in 1981, raised $50,000 at one $15-dollar-a-plate event; most of this came in large donations from interest groups. Seven years earlier, in his first campaign, that senator raised and spent only $25,000 with very moderate interest-group money. "Legislative dinners," sponsored by either political party's legislative leadership, can raise a quarter of a million dollars, virtually all of the money coming from interest groups. Business contributions dominate campaign giving, followed by the unions—especially the public-employee groups. As these lobbying activities have expanded, lobbying access and lobbying interaction have also expanded.

In addition to growing since the 1960s, lobbying has also become institutionalized. The fifty or so major lobbyists represent many clients. Offices with staffs of up to 40 persons are not uncommon. For the big-time lobbyist the rewards are significant. Fees per client often reach $50,000 or higher and contingency fees, paid upon passage of a specific policy, of $500,000 are a matter of record. A sense of professionalism is developing among these groups. Regular meetings of lobbyist groups are common, ad hoc meetings are pervasive. Coalitions of lobbyists grow from these encounters; some are fairly permanent, while others shift and change with the issues.

Business interests, as we have seen, dominate in numbers. They usually also dominate in influence. There are general umbrella interest groups active in the lobbying mix; these include the Chamber of Commerce and several groups representing small business, but towering over all of these is the Associated Industries of Florida whose extensive operation represents only the largest corporations with Florida interests. A wide variety of insurance, banking, and finance groups also have active lobbyists. Petroleum and phosphate interests are heavily represented.

Others mounting major lobbying efforts include the medical establishment, trial lawyers, utilities, and telephone interests. Agribusiness, realtors, and building-oriented groups are especially influential as is the tourist industry. Alcohol and gambling interests abound (Jai Alai, along with horse and dog racing are legal in Florida; casino operators have been attempting to gain this status). All of these are joined by a wide variety of other professional and business groups with Tallahassee operations. Many of the business interests are avidly pro-growth and, for such efforts, they are often joined by the large lobbying force in the governor's office and from state agencies such as commerce and transportation.

The lobbying power of Florida business is demonstrated by two admittedly extreme examples. The first of these stems from agribusiness influence surrounding the reorganization of the Florida Citrus Commission. The Florida Citrus Commission is so powerful that it hardly needs to lobby at all. Some years ago it won a massive statute that made the industry self-governing, self-taxing, and self-regulating by converting a state executive agency into a board appointed by the governor and confirmed by the senate. This board sits in central Florida and does what it wants, including bringing you the Florida orange juice tree and, formerly, Anita Bryant.

The other example centers on the tourist industry's effort to secure the Disney World facility. This effort entailed the giving away hunks of government to the Walt Disney Corporation to secure Disney World. Among other things, the legislature and the executive branch cooperated to turn the Disney holdings into a governmental subdistrict titled the Reedy Creek Improvement District. Sprawling over tens of thousands of acres in three counties and including two incorporated areas, the district is self-governing. Each landowner gets one vote for each acre. The corporation owns 95 percent of the acreage. The constitutionality of this arrangement has yet to be challenged.

The commercial interests do sometimes lose. Reubin Askew effectively campaigned his way to the governorship on the establishment of a corporate profit tax and it got passed. However, Florida taxes remain among the nation's lowest. Private business did not strongly oppose public-employee collective bargaining, a victory to a weak, but growing, union movement in a 12-year old revision to the constitution. That development has strengthened unionism in Florida. Noncompetitive truck and bus franchising was abolished in spite of heavy lobbying against deregulation by those interests. Even when business lobbyists are not fighting each other they do not always win in Florida, but they still win more often than not.

Some lobbying groups with resources too limited to engage in social lobbying and campaign contribution activity also have had policy successes. The environmental groups and Common Cause are notable among these. Others in similar circumstances, such as the lobbyists for the less privileged and senior citizens, have not done as well. About 25 of these groups have formed a loose coalition under the name of the Human Services Clearinghouse.

In addition to lobbying, Florida policy is sometimes reactive to the national media. The state dependency on tourism is a continuing concern that feeds this emphasis. When the director of tourism announces that tourism has dropped off, usually due to weather, economics, and bad publicity, it is a major state news item. Florida, which used to love media attention, has been getting bad press, such as the coverage given to the Cuban and Haitian migrations, the Miami police trials, and the illegal drug traffic. Britain's *Economist* loves to feature Florida. "Sixty Minutes" has done exposures on Florida farm workers, capital punishment, illegal drugs (three features), prisons, and police fundraising practices. Couple this with a governor and ex-governor hoping to be president and it is not difficult to understand why Florida is reactive to the national media. Florida's correctional system has long been despicable; it became a problem only when covered by the national media. In this sense, a portion of the state's policy agenda is shaped elsewhere. Increasing media focus on Florida is still another facet of the state's political change.

The change can be so rapid that the media attention sometimes seems schizoid. In 1981, *Time* magazine, in a cover story titled "Paradise Lost," dismissed the Miami area as lost to crime, race riots, and environmental decay. By late 1982, the *Economist* was saluting the Miami area as a boom-town able to capitalize on its 20 years of Latin immigration to create a base for economic prosperity, now hailing Florida as the trade and banking center for the American southern hemisphere and an emerging new concentration for high-tech industry.

Projections agree that Florida will continue to serve as a magnet for those fleeing south to the sun and north to stability. Those forces should keep Florida's politics in change and in the national eye.

NOTES

1. Manning J. Dauer, "Florida: The Different State," in *The Changing Politics of the South*, ed. William C. Havard, (Baton Rouge, La.: Louisiana University Press, 1972).

2. Douglas Dobson and David Carnes, *Public Policy Formation and Senior Citizens* (DeKalb, Ill.: Program for Applied Policy Research, Northern Illinois University, 1979).

3. Public Policy Program Surveys, Florida State University, Tallahassee Florida, 1978–1981.

4. Johnathan Peterson, "A Washington Game Without Rules," *Tallahassee Democrat*, 18 April 1982, pp. B1ff.

5. V.O. Key, Jr., *Southern Politics in State and Nation* (New York: Alfred A. Knopf, 1949).

6. David R. Colburn and Richard K. Sher, *Florida's Gubernatorial Politics in the Twentieth Century* (Tallahassee, Fla.: University Press of Florida, 1980).

7. Paul A. Beck, "Realignment Begins? The Republican Surge in Florida," paper presented at the Annual Meeting of the American Political Science Association. New York, September 4–6, 1981.

8. Douglas Dobson and Douglas St. Angelo, *Politics and Senior Citizens: Advocacy and Policy Formation in a Local Context* (DeKalb, Ill.: Program for Applied Policy Research, Northern Illinois University, 1981).

9. *Clerks Manual*, Tallahassee: The Florida House of Representatives, 1981.

8
Georgia
LAWRENCE R. HEPBURN

The political editor of the Atlanta *Constitution* claimed in January 1982 that "What voters want, for the most part, is as little state government as possible, and Busbee delivers with a vengeance on that score."[1] At the time, George Busbee was serving his eighth year as Georgia's governor. That was a feat unrivaled since 1865 when Governor Joseph E. Brown's term in office was abruptly ended by the arrival of Union troops.

During most of the intervening years, Georgians consistently got little government, but a lot of politics. The state had a national reputation for bad roads, weak schools, inadequate health care, and a notorious prison system. To the outsider, Georgia's politicians, from Tom Watson to Eugene Talmadge to Lester Maddox, were aggressive and noisy. Georgia's politics seemed to consist of demogoguery, clowning and confusion, and violence. It was never dull.

By 1974, Georgia politics seemed to have changed. Voters chose low-keyed George Busbee by a wide margin over flamboyant ex-Governor Lester Maddox. Within two years, political observers were claiming, "Busbee is the epitome of the consensus politics that Georgia has created."[2] Also, in 1976, Georgia legislators and the voters, seemingly happy with this new state of affairs, amended the state constitution to allow gubernatorial succession. The immediate beneficiary was reelected in 1978 with only token opposition from Republicans or Democrats.

Into the 1980s, Georgia politics was marked by almost unbroken tranquility. "Busbee," continued the Atlanta journalist, "groomed himself into one of the leading minimalists of our times. Except for some advancements in education and a campaign of luring foreign businesses into Georgia, the governor has not tended to intrude unnecessarily on our collective consciousness."[3] Whether he minimized or epitomized, Busbee's style reflected two salient features of Georgia's political culture: little government and consensus politics.

Little government has a long tradition in Georgia. In the 1870s, the

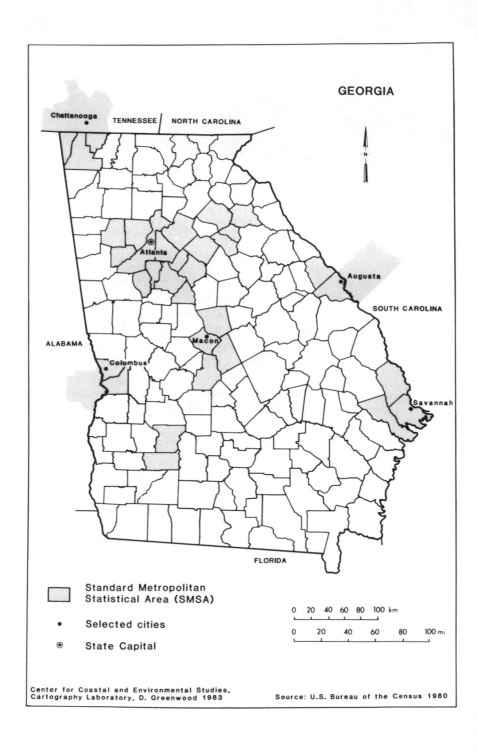

GEORGIA

Standard Metropolitan
Statistical Area (SMSA)

• Selected cities

⊛ State Capital

0 20 40 60 80 100 km

0   20   40   60   80   100 mi

Center for Coastal and Environmental Studies,
Cartography Laboratory, D. Greenwood 1983

Source: U.S. Bureau of the Census 1980

bourbon Democrats, who "redeemed" the state from the rule of radical Republicans, developed the "less is better" formula. It was designed not only to prevent recurrence of the financial excesses of reconstruction government, but also to provide northern investors an environment conducive to business expansion. The bourbons also believed in noninvolvement in social and economic matters and toward that end they wrote into the constitution of 1877 severe restrictions on public authority to raise and spend money. Much of that restriction remains in Georgia law, and "less is better" is still reflected in the campaigns of successful politicians and in their policies as officeholders.

Certain aspects of Georgia history contributed to the longevity of the bourbon formula for government. They were: 75 years of economic depression, a racially segregated society, and a largely rural population.

From the end of the Civil War to the start of World War II, Georgia was economically depressed. Its agriculture-based economy depended heavily on one crop, cotton. Sharecropping and a crop lien system of credit—both offsprings of post-Civil War economic chaos—meant almost perpetual poverty and debt for generations of white and black tenant farmers.

The existence of a biracial society also supported the bourbons who were able to use fear of black social equality to focus poorer whites' attention on "white supremacy." From the early 1900s to the 1960s, blacks were all but eliminated from political participation. White supremacy meant more in bourbon politics than merely disfranchising blacks. For almost a century it was the fixed consideration against which the original bourbons and their neobourbon successors made social and economic policy. For these reactionaries, maintenance of the racially segregated society was threatened by progressive measures such as compulsory education, the minimum wage, public housing, and old-age benefits. All implied social equality.

Georgia's rural-agrarian character also harmonized with little government. Until 1960, the population majority was rural. The people worked the land or in small country mills, rather isolated from the main currents of American life. Of the outside world, only the vagaries of the cotton market regularly impinged upon their lives.

Homogeneity and localism were characteristic of both black and white populations. People seldom moved far from the county in which they were born, although the boll weevil forced thousands to abandon their cotton fields in the 1920s. There were few concerns beyond the local community. Newcomers were rare before World War II. So untouched was Georgia by immigration in the late 19th and early 20th centuries, that a 1932 state publication boasted: "Georgia's people are 99½ percent American-born . . . Georgia's people speak no polyglot of languages. Their language is English, the mother tongue."[4]

Much of the reality that supported little government is long gone. The economy has boomed, society is desegregated, and the population is predominantly urban. Nevertheless, many of the attitudes and habits of the past remain to influence the working out of a second feature of Georgia's political culture obvious to most observers—consensus politics.

Consensus politics does not have a long tradition in Georgia. Its origins are in the social and economic upheavals of the decades following World War II. Industrial and commercial expansion brought the beginnings of prosperity. Cities and suburbs burgeoned. Concurrently, the biracial system of social relations began to crumble in the face of home-grown civil rights activity and the intervention of the federal government.

The wide assault on segregation generated violent political reactions that had the potential for undermining Georgia's new-found economic prosperity. In the late 1950s, white supremacist demogoguery and the massive resistance tactics of tactics of neobourbons in state government began losing the vital support of the business community (although white majority support held). In particular, Atlanta's commercial and financial leadership and moderate politicians, including Mayors William B. Hartsfield and Ivan Allen, Jr., took the lead in working out with leaders of the black community reasonable alternatives to confrontation and conflict. By the mid-1960s, Atlanta was billing itself "the city too busy to hate."

The main concern of Georgia's essentially conservative business leaders was neither white supremacy nor social equality, nor any other moral/ethical issue; it was economic well being. Gradually, more decisionmakers in business, government, education, religion, and civil rights organizations joined in finding ways to minimize conflict. The consensus-derived policies they worked out might not please everyone, but they were ones with which most groups could live. By the 1970s, consensus politics had become a dominant feature of Georgia's political culture.

POLITICAL CULTURE: GOOD BUT SMALL

The majority of Georgians strongly identify with the state. There is even a popular notion abroad that Georgia is somehow special. Low national rankings on school expenditures, welfare assistance, and other indices notwithstanding, Georgians are generally proud of what they have.

Jimmy Carter's election to the presidency in 1976 was a source of immense state pride, despite his relative unpopularity in the state when he left the governor's office two years before. Across Georgia, there was a lot of good-natured wisecracking about teaching Yankees how to think and act Georgian.

The University of Georgia is another source of pride for many Georgians (notable exceptions are Georgia Tech students). While football seems to draw in everyone, the university law school, from which generations of state leaders graduated, and the agricultural extension service, that touches practically every farmer in 159 counties, also generate fanatical loyalty.

The university, and other institutions of the university system, enjoy an almost sacrosanct status. Ever since Governor Eugene Talmadge's political interference in 1941 almost lost the state colleges their accreditation (and directly led to his loss of office in 1942), politicians have generally maintained a "hands-off" policy. Moreover, the colleges are better funded than the public schools.

Both the schools and colleges pay homage to the state with requirements in Georgia history and government. Practically every school child visits the state capitol, whose gold leaf dome has in the past 25 years been twice gilded through public subscription. Georgia's history, especially the state's role in the Revolutionary and Civil Wars, is well-honored through special days and annual pageants, state-operated historical sites, historical preservation programs, and countless markers, statues, and courthouse square monuments. In Georgia, it is difficult not to have some sense of state history and identify with it.

Georgians are also affected by superlatives. They like to think they have the best and are proud of their tallest hotel, oldest state university, busiest airport, most famous soft drink, best state park system, and so on and on.

Yet, to say there is an integrated state personality would be misleading. There is great diversity among Georgians, much of it not readily apparent to the casual observer.

A most apparent difference: there are black Georgians and white Georgians. Whites and blacks sometimes identify with the same institutions, but sometimes they do not. Racial identity, itself, sometimes makes for political differences, but not always. The existence of two large racial groups makes generalizing about "Georgians" risky.

Also, there are "traditional" or native Georgians whose ancestors settled the Georgia wilderness, fought in *the* war, and struggled through the Depression. Their rural way of life was characterized by individual enterprise, social conformity, and private paternalism.. The loyalties of traditional Georgians, black and white, lay with immediate family, kin, the church congregation, and a small community of neighbors. Their horizons were local; they looked after their own. Many native Georgians, who today live in the city or suburbs, have roots in the country and strong identifications with rural institutions.

Living next door to the native may be the newcomer, a recent immigrant from the Snow Belt, who does not identify with the traditional institutions of the state. The new Georgians, many with urban backgrounds, have imported ideas and culture traits, different perceptions of social problems and social relations, even different styles of political participation. Sometimes, the new elements blend well with the traditional; sometimes they bring conflict.

Where people live in Georgia makes some difference in their identification with its institutions. There are three geographic regions in the largest state east of the Mississippi River.

South Georgia, extending from the coast and Florida north to the center of the state, remains sparsely populated with few urban centers, notably Savannah and Albany. Agriculture and forestry are big business and most of south Georgia retains the traditional rural way of life, only superficially changed by the influx of newcomers and new business to the state. From county to county, black/white population ratios and levels of prosperity and poverty vary widely. However, identifications vary little from the local community and rural institutions. Socially and politically, white south Georgians are consistently the most conservative people of the state. For them, south Georgia, stable and unchanged, is the real Georgia.

Across the center of the state runs the "fall line," where rivers and streams fall from the red hills onto the flat sandy plain of south Georgia. From here, the Piedmont region extends north to the Appalachians. At the fall line Georgia's 19th century manufacturing centers—Augusta, Macon, and Columbus—were built. To them came the produce of the "black belt"— cotton lands of huge plantations and huge black populations. The Piedmont was the heart of the old "Empire State of the South" and it is today the heart of Georgia's new prosperity. The region, especially the sprawling 15-county Atlanta SMSA, is the focus of Sun Belt immigration. It boasts the fastest growing counties and the wealthiest suburbs. Here are Georgia's major industries and financial institutions, all the universities and most of the colleges. The population is most diverse—native, newcomer, urban, rural, black, white, Hispanic, Asian. In this region, there is less common identification with institutions and, measure by measure, less integration than elsewhere in Georgia.

In contrast, appalachian north Georgia has the most homogeneous population of the state. Mostly native Anglo-Saxon, some counties have no black population. Historically a region of small, not-too-prosperous farms, north Georgia has grown strong with textile manufacturing, poultry raising, and recreation developments. The last has injected change into the region's traditional rural-small town way of life; however, north Georgians' basic social conservatism and political independence remain in place. Their ancestors opposed secession and supported Republicans, Populists, and antibourbon Democrats. Today, they are more likely to identify with, and be protective of, their part of the state, and to care less about what goes on south of them.

Two geographical entities more significant than the three regions as loci of identification are Georgia's counties and the city of Atlanta.

Counties are important in Georgia and native Georgians strongly identify with their home county. There are 159 of them, the last created in 1924. Why so many? The popular story is that county seats were spread around so that no farmer was more than a half day's drive, by horse and buggy, from a country courthouse. A more prosaic explanation is that during Georgia's extended depression many towns aspired to be county seats because such status would create at least a dozen public jobs and extra business for local merchants. Local disputes, perhaps over poor representation in the legislature or between towns at opposite ends of a county, also led to the creation of new counties.

Until 1962, counties had a political role peculiar to Georgia, that heightened their importance and helped make them a focus of Georgians' loyalty. Under Georgia's unique "county unit" electoral system, each of the 159 counties had "unit votes" in statewide Democratic primaries that were analogous to the electoral votes cast by the states in presidential elections. The allocation of unit votes was based on representation in the lower house of the legislature. Since each county had at least one representative and as the legislature was grossly malapportioned, the unit system gave sparsely populated rural counties political clout far beyond that warranted by their size. The system was wiped out by an early one-person, one-vote ruling. However, for 50 years prior, Georgia politicians focused on winning counties, not popular votes. A legacy remains in the continued, albeit diminished, influence of courthouse politics on state government.

County politics often gets more attention than state politics. The elections of sheriffs, road commissioners, school boards and superintendents, judges, court clerks, tax commissioners, and even coroners are often hotly contested in the Democratic primary (and in the general election in a few counties where Republicans are found in sizeable numbers). As population growth now centers on unincorporated county areas, county politics should remain lively.

Just as many Georgians resent federal intrusion in state affairs, they resent state intrusion in county affairs. Until 1983, Georgia's constitution provided for local amendments by which counties were exempted from general provisions of the constitution. The General Assembly also passed "population acts,"* which had the effect of exempting counties from restrictions in general statutes.

Atlanta is a special entity. At one time, it was just the state's capital and largest city. Socially and politically it was fairly in tune with the rest of the state through the early 20th century. Its people did, however, exhibit somewhat more relaxed attitudes on liquor and segregation.

In the 1930s, Atlanta began developing a character that set it apart from the rest of Georgia. There had always been an air of "boosterism" about Atlanta, at least since the great cotton expositions of the 1880s and 1890s. In the 1920s, H.L. Mencken sneered that Georgia, meaning Atlanta, "exhibited the worst commercial bounderism of the Yankee."[5]

In the early 1930s, Atlanta's business and political leadership began "Forward Atlanta," an ambitious program to make the city the Southeast's major commercial, financial, and transportation center. Over the next 40 years, hundreds of headquarters and regional offices of corporations and federal agencies, and manufacturing and distribution facilities were located in and around the city.

Over those years, Atlanta grew away from the rest of the state. The population of the city proper became predominantly black. Its suburbs expanded exponentially with whites who fled the city or came from dying

---

*So-called because such an act applied only to counties of a specific population. This was a legislative device to get around the state constitution.

rural communities and from out-of-state. As Atlantans became more varied and cosmopolitan in their lifestyles than people elsewhere in the state, they found themselves increasingly alienated from other Georgians.

In the 1950s and 1960s, Atlanta, with its relatively liberal press, its moderate-progressive leadership, and its highly visible blacks, was viewed with distaste in much of traditional Georgia. Candidates for statewide office found the city a convenient target of racist demogoguery. As long as the number of counties won in the Democratic primary, not the popular vote, counted for election, the Atlanta area's burgeoning population counted for nought. Likewise, its representatives in the General Assembly had little influence on state legislation.

Through the 1960s, there were two Georgias: Atlanta, and the rest of the state. People were apt to identify with either Atlanta or Georgia. However, with the resolution of civil rights issues, the spread of economic prosperity throughout Georgia, and Atlanta's attainment of "major league" status in the nation, tensions between Atlanta and the rest of the state have greatly subsided.

In traditional rural Georgia, whatever needed to be done, the people generally did for themselves. Neither farmer cooperatives not labor unions grew big in Georgia. Nor did government loom big in the lives of rural people, at least not until the arrival of the New Deal. The common schools and farm-to-market roads—things Georgians could not provide for themselves—were about all they sought from government.

Today, traditional Georgians generally oppose government intervention in their lives. They expect to get little from government and expect to pay little for what they do get. They also prefer the status quo to trying something new.

Therefore, even though Georgians' ability to pay his risen sharply, they continue to resist expanding government services to the scope and level common in other states of similar wealth. Some public services long-established elsewhere in the United States, such as kindergartens, vocational schools, mental health clinics, and community recreation programs, are fairly recent (and not fully accepted) additions in Georgia.

The old bourbon prescription of noninterference in social matters and nonregulation of economic affairs partially explains the Georgia situation. Adding a new public service often requires a constitutional amendment. Until 1983, Georgia had the longest of the 50 state constitutions.* Between 1946 and 1982, over 150 general and 750 local amendments were ratified, but in the most recent elections voters have more frequently turned down amendments. To get around constitutional restrictions on financing, the General Assembly resorts to creating special authorities. Georgia building,

---

*A new streamlined constitution, approved in 1982, omits the cumbersome requirement for local amendments, but keeps tight restriction on raising and spending money.

hospital, housing, park, and port authorities raise and spend more money per capita than those of any other state except Washington and Nebraska.[6]

The heritage of depression, segregation, and rural individualism still influences attitudes toward government. The majority of Georgians expect to work out their economic problems in the marketplace and their social problems on their own.

Georgians expect their officials to be honest—at least as honest as they themselves. They assume public service may bring opportunities or advantages in private business, and to a certain extent conflicts of interest are tolerated. In the General Assembly the citizen-legislator is not expected to disadvantage himself for the sake of objectivity, and legislators have no qualms about voting on issues that affect their own business interests.

However, should an official use public employees and public equipment to pave his driveway or dig his stock pond, he invites swift condemnation in most communities. Since 1979 the voters have used the recall election to turn miscreants out of office. However, recall efforts have often been spurred by policy disputes, not alleged malfeasance. In 1982, the recall law was amended to make it more difficult to remove local officials.

With the demise of the county unit system, the old courthouse political machines did not completely pass from the scene. In some 15 to 20 counties there remains widely reputed chicanery wherein votes are bought, tax assessments manipulated, private roads graded, and drug dealers protected by local officials.

Compared to local government, Georgia's state government has been relatively free of corruption or scandal for 25 years. Legislators are often accused of being too influenced by business lobbyists; regulatory agency heads of being too cozy with people they are supposed to regulate. Now and then, an official is criticized for having a niece or son-in-law on the payroll. However, since the 1950s, no top official has been the subject of investigating committees or the target of media criticism for alleged corruption.

Georgia's newspapers and television stations give watchdog attention to state and local government and probably contribute to their good reputation. The *Journal* and the *Constitution* in Atlanta, the state's two largest newspapers, have in recent years focused in-depth on bid-letting practices, lobbying, expense accounts, judicial leniency, conflicts of interest, and discrimination in personnel matters. Georgia's long-time U.S. Senator Herman Talmadge discovered in 1980 the influence of "them lyin' Atlanta newspapers," as his father called them. Unbeatable in six previous races for the governor's office and the Senate, Talmadge lost his seat. The newspapers' relentless coverage of his financial dealings is given partial credit for his downfall.

Aside from being honest, or at least fair, and doing their part to keep government running smoothly, Georgia officials are not expected to do much more. Since politicians in the state seldom campaign for, or are elected to produce specific results, they are not supposed to be agents of change. They are not expected to be innovative in reorganizing government, or to take the initiative in finding new sources of revenue, or to propose more services. They are certainly not expected to look for social and economic problems to solve. They are not expected to try new things.*

Since 1940, among Georgia's governors the only full-blown reformer was Ellis Arnall, 1943–1947. Elected on a wave of popular resentment against Governor Eugene Talmadge's attacks on the University of Georgia, Arnall obtained the nation's first 18-year-old vote, abolition of the chain gang, elimination of the governor's pardon power, repeal of the poll tax, and a host of other progressive measures. Jimmy Carter, 1971–1975, obtained reforms in budgeting and government organization. While other governors, including Carl Sanders, 1963–1967, and George Busbee, 1975–1983, formulated moderately-progressive policies and legislation, none were reform-minded. If one governor was expected to produce specific results, it was probably Lester Maddox, 1967–1971. His supporters felt that somehow Maddox might roll back the measures of political and social equality blacks had achieved by the mid-1960s. Ironically, Maddox appointed more blacks to state government positions than any previous governor since reconstruction.

Expectations are rising as Georgia's population changes. Higher expectations are most often voiced at the local level and serve as new sources of political conflict.

Newcomers migrating from the Northeast and Midwest often expect the zoning, fire and police protection, garbage collection and mosquito-fogging services, summer school, and community education programs to which they were accustomed. The opposition of native Georgians to these innovations is as difficult for the newcomers to understand as it is for the natives to fathom why anyone would want, and want to pay for, such things. County after county, especially in rapidly growing once-rural now-suburban areas, has experienced bitterly fought contests over liquor, bond issues, government reorganization, and service expansion as county governments move from providing only ministerial functions to expanded municipal-type public services. Some counties are going through tense periods of transition as newcomers build political strength.

At the state level, too, a traditional status quo orientation is giving way to a more activist stance in economic, environmental, and social matters. The change is due in part to greater expectation voiced by the people (often through organized groups). Probably the increasingly professionalized character of the state civil service is partly responsible for the change. The state department of transportation, although still an important source of patronage, responds to popular concerns about mass transit, pollution, and green spaces. The state's office of consumer affairs aggressively pursues its legislative mandate to root out unfair and deceptive business practices. This

*However, Atlanta area politicians may be expected to take the initiative to bring about change rather than to maintain the status quo.

agency effectively demonstrated the results of government activisim when its investigations, extensively covered by the media, led to the closing of businesses that had been fleecing Florida-bound tourists travelling Interstate 75. Such media attention has made Georgians more aware of the possibilities of using government for their own ends.

Of course, there are many "good-ole-boys" still around, and the level of activism varies widely from one agency to another. In general, however, it is far higher than traditional Georgians have been used to. Little government is becoming slightly bigger government.

Consistent with their generally conservative political orientation, Georgians respect their government institutions and officials. Law and order they cherish, and the state patrol, the bureau of investigation, and local police are well-supported. They view as legitimate the enforcement activities of the departments of agriculture, natural resources, human resources, and other state agencies, as long as those activities have a long history or can be justified in dollars and cents. Georgians are pragmatic. When government activities—state or local—appear to be a departure from well-established norms, Georgians withhold their support.

Officeholders, especially at the state level, usually are well-respected by the public. However, the antics of a few legislators frequently bring ridicule down on the whole body. Georgians tend to be polite and they and the press are not likely to disparage the efforts of politicians or call them names. Among native Georgians, white and black, there is even deference—perhaps a hangover from the traditional paternalism of the past. Citizens may openly express the feeling that elected officials "probably know more about such things than I do." The deference of some groups, coupled with the apathy of others, means officeholders may go about their business with a minimum of public scrutiny. There is a good deal of trusting in the integrity of officials.

At the same time, governors have difficulty building support for policies that involve change, even when proposed changes are backed by the media and other influentials. Jimmy Carter discovered this during his struggle to reorganize the executive branch. Later, George Busbee took a long time to build support for statewide public kindergartens. In sum, conservatism means support for institutions, respect for holders of public office, but not necessarily backing for policies.

Moreover, there is an undercurrent of distrust of government power. The public can be counted upon to oppose vigorously any bill in the General Assembly that might give more power to officials. In recent years, their opposition has brought down bills that would have given legislators higher salaries, longer terms, more staff, and more office space. In addition, bills that would have provided for longer legislative sessions and made it easier to override the governor's veto were killed. Similarly, the one category of constitutional amendment that Georgians are likely to reject at the polls is that which appears to increase the power of government. The most significant recent departure from this rule was the voters' 1976 approval of the amendment to allow the governor two successive four-year terms.

Georgians' suspicion of power, and preference for the status quo, is also manifest in local politics. Since the 1930s, responsible state leaders have several times proposed consolidation of the 159 counties, 48 of which in 1980 still had populations of fewer than 10,000 people. Most of these counties had tax bases inadequate to support a minimum standard of service. All such proposals failed to get off the ground.* Likewise, attempts to consolidate city and county governments are likely doomed to failure. From 1969 to 1982 there were 12 city-county consolidation referenda in Georgia. Only one, merging the City of Columbus and Muscogee County, passed.

City-county consolidation failures illustrate some of the complexity of Georgia politics as well as the diversity of its people. Opposition to consolidation comes from whites living out in the country, who want neither urban services nor the higher taxes that go with them. Blacks living in the city often see in consolidation a dilution of their voting strength, so they oppose it. Consolidation proponents may be genuine "good government" reformers, who envision more effective use of tax dollars. They may also be members of the old white establishment who resent black political power in the city.

Traditionally, Georgians also oppose any infringements on their property rights. This opposition extends to building codes, leash laws, and noise ordinances. It wells up at the mention of zoning, that in some rural counties is viewed as a form of socialism. In 1982, a majority of counties still had no countywide zoning in unincorporated areas.

Some recent changes in Georgia are more attributable to the "carrot and stick" than to expressed needs of the people. In the 1970s, many communities began services, from public transportation and solid waste disposal to recreation and mental health, only because federal grants to do so were pushed on them. Even in metro Atlanta, the showpiece rapid-transit system was only narrowly approved by voters in the two largest counties, Fulton and Dekalb. Three other metro counties voted to stay out of the system. In transportation as in other matters, the private way is still the way to go for most Georgians.

POLITICAL STYLE: FRIENDS AND NEIGHBORS

Generally, Georgians prefer politicians who appear to be much like themselves. Therefore, the predominant political style reflects the rather conservative value orientation of most people: rugged individualism, but social conformity; material success, but moral restraint; informed intellect, but practical experience.

---

*However, in the 1960s, most counties joined multi-county units under area planning and development commissions (APDCs). These commissions acted as conduits for federal grant monies and also provided technical assistance to county governments in land-use planning, industrial development, and the management of services. With the drying-up of federal grants in the early 1980s, the APDCs have lost some member counties.

Being a little more successful than the voter may be useful in justifying "why I can handle the job better than my opponent," but a candidate must not appear too rich, or overly educated, or condescending. So, one dresses well, but not flashy; one is self-made, but a team player. The candidate has gone to college, but works with his hands (or at least used to). In short, the values and lifestyle of the successful politician must jibe squarely with those of most of the voters.

In 1970, candidate-for-governor Jimmy Carter did a good job of appearing "like us" to a wide majority of the voters. Carter, then a wealthy agri-businessman, projected an open-collared, work-a-day farmer image. His opponent, former Governor Carl Sanders, was dubbed "cuff-links Carl," the liberal-leaning, rich-boy candidate of the Atlanta establishment; a slick politician out of touch with real Georgians. Carter sympathized with middle- and lower-income whites who were concerned about school busing and racial quotas and said nice things about George Wallace and Lester Maddox. This "plain folks," somewhat populist approach paid off.[7]

The common-people approach is still important. Few politicians ever publicly admit to being politicians in Georgia. Even those who have held political office for two decades, and for whom it is their main source of income, refer to themselves as farmers, merchants, lawyers, bankers, and so forth, but never politicians. Like their neighbors, they mow their own lawns, drive ordinary cars, and teach Sunday school class.

Being conservative—in practically all meanings of the word—is very important. The campaign tactic illustrated above—of hanging the "liberal" label on an opponent in state and local races—is often attempted in Georgia. If the label sticks, the opponent is likely done for.*

In addition to espousing conservatism in fiscal and social policy, Georgia politicians also are conservative in behavior. They tend to be low-keyed, play their cards close to the vest, and take stands only on safe issues. Few are headline grabbers.

The business-managerial style of politics was well exemplified by George Busbee in his 1974 campaign for governor. Pitted against the flamboyant champion of the "little people" Lester Maddox, Busbee projected a cool, no-nonsense, hardworking middle-America image that many Georgians could identify with. His slogan was "elect a workhorse, not a showhorse." As governor, Busbee's quiet effectiveness, a far cry from Maddox's theatrics or even Jimmy Carter's confrontational style, made him extremely comfortable for most Georgians.

In 1982, Georgians opted for "more of the same" in choosing Busbee's successor, a businessman-legislator who stressed his expertise in fiscal matters, used the slogan "promises won't work, Joe Frank Harris will," and gave the traditional pledge, "no tax increase." Harris' primary opponent, a

*The significant exception to this rule is among urban black voters, and some white ones in Atlanta and Athens. There, one can be liberal and get elected.

normally conservative congressman, advocated mild progress in state services and was stuck with the dreaded "liberal big spender" label.

Throughout state government, and many local ones, too, "good-ole-boy" politicians are slowly fading from the scene, replaced by a rather homogeneous group, whose style is middle-level management. Of course, there is deviation. In rural areas the evangelical fervor of a Eugene Talmadge or Lester Maddox still has appeal. In the city of Atlanta, too, being aggressive, if not flamboyant, is admired.

Consistent with the generally conservative political orientation of Georgians, and their limited expectations of government, is "consensus politics"—the dominant style of the Georgia political process. Although this style is more consistently evident at the state than the local level, it is seen all over the state.*

Consensus politics, as it is played out in Georgia, focuses on maximizing the cooperation of disparate interest groups on economic issues. Farmers, teachers, financiers, developers, manufacturers, blacks, women, the retired, the handicapped—all are brought it. Consensus politics is played out in public, in press conferences, on the editorial pages, in the lobbies and on the floor of the General Assembly, in the offices of the governor and the mayor of Atlanta; and in private, in countless boardrooms and backrooms.

Property tax relief, teacher pay raises, road bonds, prison construction, public assistance, business regulation, retirement benefits—these are the kinds of issues that really matter. Arguments are always pragmatic—whether the state has the means to do something, whether or not it can afford not to do something. Whether or not the ends of some policy are worthy is, of course, sometimes debated. However, the most important end is finding something for everyone, so no one goes home mad. Achieving consensus requires all manner of compromises and involves alliances, coalitions, and maneuverings (often surprising) among interest groups.

Consensus politics is essentially nonideological. One may compromise position, but not principle. To minimize the kind of conflict that leaves bitterness, state leaders tend to avoid moral/ethical issues about which large segments of their constituents differ. Such issues intrude on, rather than contribute to, consensus politics. Thus, the General Assembly manages to sidestep or talk around issues such as teaching of creationism, abortion, collective bargaining, or making Martin Luther King, Jr.'s birthday a state holiday.

Georgia politicians do take stands on moral/ethical issues about which a consensus already exists, such as handgun control, prayer in the schools, and the death penalty. If a really controversial issue cannot be avoided, position-taking may be rationalized in the pragmatic manner. "I voted for Sunday

---

*Of course, the homogeneity of some rural counties obviates the need for consensus making. In them, the local establishment makes policy in the traditional closed-shop manner.

liquor sales in Atlanta because the city needs the income from conventions. However, I'm solidly against gambling on horse races."

The Georgia process style is also personalistic. The small town mode of operation is evident even in state government. Georgians like to do business on a first-name basis. Some counties only recently were forced to institute formal budgeting and record-keeping procedures. Bid-letting, written contracts, codified ordinances, and so forth are still novelties in many communities.

In the vast majority of city and county governments, officials are part-timers, not professionals. Social relations, established outside politics and government, are important to the political process. Georgians expect to pick up the phone or drop in on an official to get something done. They do not expect to go through layers of bureaucrats.

Georgia is still small enough so that county commissioners, legislators, judges and state agency heads know each other personally—not through any party structure, but through whatever social or work relationship brings them together. Sometimes derided as a "good-ole-boy" network, these personal contacts add an element of stability to an otherwise unstructured political process.

Of course, the process style is undergoing change. As state and local governments grow bigger and take on more specialized functions, often as mere agents of the federal government, they have become more professional and bureaucratic.

POLITICAL INTERACTION: BUILDING CONSENSUS

The popular picture of politics in traditional Georgia has thousands of rural folks jammed into a courthouse square, or newly mown pasture, to hear Eugene Talmadge "tell it like it is" from the back of a flat-bed truck. The summertime primaries of the Democratic party could generate a lot of excitement. Politics was entertaining and there was usually lots of free barbecue or fried fish, iced tea, and sweet pickles.

But, the crowds were misleading. The level of political participation was low and narrowly based. Of course, blacks could not vote then. Neither did most poor white tenant farmers or mill workers. Politics was the traditional preserve of the white farmers who owned their land, and therefore paid property taxes, or small town merchants, lawyers, and bankers. The courthouse gang—usually the sheriff, the judge, road commissioner, tax commissioner, plus a few others—would determine who would run in the Democratic primary for local offices and the legislature. Without two-party competition, there was little impetus to register and vote. Incumbents tended to stay in office a long time. The big exception was the governor's race.

More recently, registration has increased, but it still remains low by national comparison. In 1960, of the voting age population, only 57 percent of whites were registered, while only 29 percent of the blacks were. By 1976, the year Jimmy Carter ran for the presidency, 66 percent of white Georgians were registered and almost 75 percent of black Georgians were. However, even with a native son on the ballot, only 43 percent of the Georgia voting age population turned out to cast a presidential ballot. Over 54 percent did nationwide. In 1980, the Georgia vote was again 43 percent as Jimmy Carter lost the presidency. In 1982, registration varied greatly for both blacks and whites; from over 90 percent in some counties to under 30 percent in others.[8]

Not getting involved in "visible" public affairs is fairly characteristic of rural white Georgians (that privatistic trait again). A typical excuse: "If I was to register to vote, I'd get called for jury duty."*

In a few counties, registration and voting are still discouraged by local officials. According to the former Georgia secretary of state, about 140 to 145 counties do an honest, decent job of running elections. As for the others, "nobody from the outside—no court or anybody else—can do anything about it until the people in the county take a hold and make the change."[9]

Voting turnout is also kept down by continuing lack of opposition in the Democratic primary as well as general election. Incumbency carries a lot of weight in Georgia and unless the public really has something against an officeholder, he or she is not likely to be challenged.[10] This pattern holds for both state and local offices.

Despite a high percentage of unopposed candidates, Georgians still have many opportunities to make decisions. Most general elections call for at least one "yes" or "no" vote on local or general constitutional amendments. Special elections are often required for bond issues, liquor sales, government reorganization, recalls, and so forth. Added to the primary, which usually requires a run-off, these elections often mean half a dozen voting opportunities a year.

Although Georgia politics is no longer the exclusive province of middle-aged, white, Democratic males, its players are still a rather homogeneous group. This sameness is especially remarkable, if one remembers that Georgia is a state in which political parties play almost no role in recruitment; just about everyone can participate. Essentially, all one has to do to run for office is pick a primary (there is no registration by party) and pay a qualifying fee for the office one desires.

Recruitment, if there is any at all, is through a community's existing business-political leadership, sometimes called the "establishment" or the "power structure." Thus, membership in a church, business or law firm, country club, or community association is helpful. Organized labor is not a

---

*Because of nonparticipation by so many low-income blacks and whites in rural counties, the middle-class white farmer who always participates—because he sees direct relationships between voting, officeholders, policies, property taxes, and his own material well-being—may serve on several juries within the span of a few years.

big factor in Georgia, so union membership would not be a plus in most places.

Membership in the General Assembly provides a good example of homogeneity. In 1980, about 45 percent of the members were occupied in business and industry with another 11 percent in farming. Lawyers made up only 21 percent of the membership.

The largest religious denomination in the state is, by far, the Baptists. Baptists comprised about 42 percent of the legislative membership; Methodists accounted for 27 percent. Only 2 percent were Catholic; 1 percent is Jewish. Otherwise, the General Assembly was 95 percent male, 90 percent white, Democratic, and college-educated.[11]

Although women are not well represented in the legislature (only 17 out of 236 in 1982) and fill no top positions in the state executive branch, they do hold a variety of elective offices in local government, including county commissioners, mayors, judges, school superintendents, and school board members.

Until the 1960s, black Georgians had little direct role in politics and government. During Reconstruction, under Republican party patronage, blacks had voted, had been elected to office, and had helped write the constitution of 1868. With the end of Reconstruction, black participation waned, but did not disappear in the face of white intimidation. As long as there was viable opposition to the bourbons, black votes were courted. By the early 1900s, however, the Democratic party had used "white supremacy" to draw off Republican and Populist support. Various devices were instituted to disfranchise blacks, the most effective of which was the "white primary." White Democrats claimed their primary was a private affair, a party function, and they could exclude blacks if they chose (although after 1917 primaries were regulated by state law). While a few thousand blacks, mainly in Atlanta, continued to be registered to vote, exclusion from the primary of the state's one party meant they had no real political voice.

Not until 1946, two years after the white primary was ruled unconstitutional, would substantial numbers of blacks vote in the Democratic primary. That brought renewed efforts, including voter-list purges and a literacy test, to disfranchise blacks. Full black participation, including officeholding, had to wait until the 1960s.

Except in some rural counties, where racial intimidation still exists, officeholding is open to blacks. In the wake of increased voter registration following passage of the Voting Rights Act of 1965, black officeholding rose dramatically. From 1968 to 1979, the number of city and county black officials increased from 10 to 214. At the same time the number of black legislators increased from 11 to 23.[12]

In Atlanta, blacks became a major political force soon after World War II. They began by forming voting coalitions with middle-class whites in support of moderate white politicians against neobourbon reactionaries. By the early 1970s, blacks comprised the majority of voters in the city. With black and white support, Andrew Young was elected Georgia's first black congressman since Reconstruction and Maynard Jackson was elected Atlanta's first black mayor. The 1981 election of Young as mayor of the city revealed that black control of Atlanta politics was all but complete.

Except for Atlanta, and one rural county in the black belt, blacks dominate no local governments despite having several majorities, or near majorities, of registered voters. However, increased black participation has also had an effect on "white" politics. White candidates, who must now consider the interests of black voters, may have to take a more progressive stance than otherwise. Also, formerly alienated low-income, rural whites are participating more in many counties.

Georgia is not a strong party state. Also, it is not a two-party state. The bulk of Georgians are nominally Democrats. Since there is no registration by party, Republican strength can only be estimated by turnout in the primaries. A statewide Republican primary draws about one-tenth the number of voters as the Democratic primary. Republicans are found in measurable numbers in the suburbs of Atlanta, Savannah, Augusta, and a few other urban places, and scattered in the north Georgian mountains (where they have been since 1860).

Democratic dominance can be traced to Republican involvement in Reconstruction. After 1900, the Republican party, and the short-lived Populist party led by Tom Watson, provided no effective competition in the state. Meanwhile, in Washington, Georgia politicians had found that being Democrats gave them an inordinate measure of power in national politics during periods of Republican hegemony.

Within the Georgia Democratic party, factions have provided some semblance of party competition. The only really organized factions with any longevity were the Talmadge and anti-Talmadge factions, in the decades from 1936 to 1956. They battled over the governorship, the U.S. Senate and other offices and fought over issues ranging from participation in the New Deal (Eugene Talmadge opposed it) to support for Harry Truman in 1948 (Herman Talmadge opposed it). The anti-Talmadge faction split apart amid the "massive resistance" reaction following *Brown v. Board of Education* and disappeared with Herman Talmadge's 1956 election to the U.S. Senate. Since then, Democrats have publicly split into identified camps over big issues, such as Jimmy Carter's reorganization of state agencies; but none of these groupings survived the resolution of single issues.

As a result of one-party dominance, there is no organized opposition to keep state officers (all Democrats) accountable or to maintain public interest between elections. Being the only party for so long meant the Democrats had no need to create a strong party structure. Since most white Georgians were born Democrats, the party did not need to win converts or train recruits.

The Democratic party is officially organized in all 159 counties. However, county executive committee slots frequently are vacant. In general, the party apparatus functions substantively only in the larger counties, especially those around metro Atlanta where Republican strength is significant. To the present, Democratic dominance has rested more on informal ties among county and state officeholders than on formal party organization.

For many years, being a Democrat did not mean the same thing in Georgia as it did in Washington. From the 1930s through the 1960s, Georgia Democrats found themselves increasingly at odds with policies of the national party, especially civil rights policies. Until 1964, Georgia had always backed the Democratic candidate for the presidency. In that year, Barry Goldwater carried the state and Republican Howard "Bo" Callaway, a wealthy textile heir, was sent to Congress, the first of his party since Reconstruction. Amidst white backlash to the civil rights push of Lyndon Johnson's administration, the Republican party was reborn in Georgia. Two years later Callaway narrowly missed the governorship.

At the 1968 Democratic National Convention, "regular" Georgia Democrats lost half their seats to delegates led by Julian Bond, a black state legislator. Several top Democratic leaders walked out and joined the Republican party. By 1972, Republicans held two congressional seats and had made spectacular gains in the General Assembly; from 4 seats in 1962, they jumped to 37 seats ten years later. The future looked bright for the GOP in Georgia.

But, in 1982, Republicans were still a rarity in rural areas and often no votes were cast in county Republican primaries. The GOP was organized in urban and suburban counties, but not elsewhere. The party held one U.S. House seat and a U.S. Senate seat, but Republicans in the legislature had dwindled to 29. Not one state executive office was held by a Republican.

Outside suburban areas, Republicans have yet to establish a real base of support in Georgia. Black voters regularly see Republican candidates billing themselves as more conservative than conservative white Democrats on social issues. Rural white voters, some of them voicing the tradition of "never voting for a Republican," are not attracted by Georgia Republicans' country club image.

If not in name, at least in style, Georgia political candidates run as independents. Campaign ads regularly omit party identification and candidates stress their personal qualities and independent thinking on issues, not their party affiliation. Each candidate runs on his or her own, unaligned with any other candidacy. Reform slates, endorsed tickets, and such are not part of the Georgia scene. Candidates, however, do seek endorsements from interest groups.

To run for office, one only has to be a registered voter and pay a qualifying fee to election officials. No party membership is required or implied. Tradition and its dominant position make the Democratic label more attractive to most candidates. Candidates "from out of nowhere" frequently wind up as party nominees.

In the past, successful statewide candidacies depended on mass rallies and exhortation to whip up enthusiasm and on the courthouse gangs to deliver the county unit votes. In the early 1960s, with the demise of the county unit system, mass media became important to winning the popular vote of urban areas.

The 1980s saw the beginnings of grass-roots party organization, especially in metropolitan Atlanta, but not limited to that area. Slate making, vote canvassing, targeting, block parties, and the like are slowly entering the Georgia political vocabulary and influencing the traditional mode of politics.

Politics in Georgia is characterized more by the interaction of interest groups than by political parties. The parties, themselves, rarely make pronouncements on major issues and in the General Assembly voting is seldom along party lines. Interest groups, on the other hand, regularly make themselves heard and work publicly and privately to influence policymaking.

Georgia has its share of ephemeral consumer groups and grass-roots lobbies organized to influence resolution of single issues. Furthermore, there are plenty of Georgia-based and national associations concerned with social, humanitarian, or environmental matters that work year in and year out in the Georgia political arena. Often these special interests mobilize hundreds, or even thousands, of persons whose collective voice is heeded by Georgia policymakers. However, by far the most influential are business groups.

The influence of so-called "corporate lobbies" has long been a source of political controversy in Georgia, at least since the 1880s, when Tom Watson inveighed against the railroad and banking interests that manipulated the General Assembly to the detriment of Georgia farmers. Even Eugene Talmadge, more a bourbon than a Populist, castigated the big utilities in the 1930s.

In 1974, in his "State of the State" message, Governor Jimmy Carter told the General Assembly, "The influence of lobbyists is too great in our State Government. . . . Powerful and effective lobbyists have one of our ears. Our other ear must be constantly turned to our noninfluential con- stituents. . . . "[13] Carter went on to ask legislators to pay as much attention to consumers as producers, clients as practitioners, and borrowers as lenders.

The media frequently criticize the influence of business lobbies, especially in the General Assembly, once characterized as a legislature "run lock, stock, and barrel by big business."[14] The public's scrutiny is usually focused on corporate giants, such as Southern Bell, Georgia Power Company, Coca-Cola, Southern Railway, and the Citizens & Southern National Bank. However, generally recognized as especially influential are trade associations, such as the Georgia Business and Industry Association, the Georgia Farm Bureau Federation, and the Georgia Chamber of Commerce.

Georgia is not a strong union state and labor lobbies are not particularly influential. Nonetheless, the Georgia AFL-CIO has a generally good relationship with state leaders and its views are sought, on legislation affecting labor. The Georgia Association of Educators (GAE), with some 35,000 teacher-members, helps establish legislative priorities in public education. Gubernatorial candidates usually seek GAE's endorsement.

Aside from lobbies primarily concerned with economic issues, there are those whose focus is on moral issues, political issues, and environmental issues. In all, some 500 lobbies register at each session of the General Assembly.

Special interests' influence extends beyond the legislature. Executive branch agencies, both those with elected and appointive heads, often have strong ties with counterpart interest groups. These are not necessarily business groups. Such groups are helpful in the General Assembly by lobbying for agency requests (for appropriations or changes in the law) and at election time by channelling campaign contributions. Of course, agency officials can be expected to have concerns similar to those of interest groups.

In sum, the number of special interest groups actively engaged in influencing government policy has increased so much as to make it virtually impossible for any few giant entities to dominate Georgia politics. The Georgia Public Service Commission is a case in point. Once under the thumb of big utilities, this rate-making body now regularly considers consumer as well as corporate interests.

Given Georgia's traditional localism, little government, and development of consensus politics played with a huge cast of interest groups, political power in the state is naturally spread widely and thinly. The office of the governor carries importance and prestige in Georgia and its occupant wields considerable power. On a strong/weak ranking of U.S. governors, according to their formal powers, the Georgia chief executive runs in the middle of the pack. On paper, the governor looks weak because of an unusually large number of agency heads elected independently of the governor. In addition to the lieutenant governor, they include the secretary of state, attorney general, commissioner of insurance, commissioner of agriculture, commissioner of labor, and superintendent of schools. Each of these "constitutional officers," as they are collectively known, has his own constituency and no necessary ties or loyalty to the governor. In addition, they share appointive power with the governor.

With one exception, however, Georgia governors since 1931 have generally been strong governors, and were able to dominate state government by force of personality, political savy, and control of the state budget.

The Budget Act of 1931 made the governor ex-officio director of the budget with the authority not only to make up the budget proposal for all state agencies, but also to approve or deny spending requests. In addition, the governor had an item veto. Between 1931 and 1962, by many accounts, "the governor literally ran the state out of his hip pocket."[15]

An appropriations act passed by the General Assembly was more a recommendation than a law. The governor had a large discretionary fund and could even choose which programs in an agency would get funds. Moreover, until 1943, the governor might even strike names from the state payroll, which Eugene Talmadge frequently did.

With the Budget Act of 1962, the governor was required to comply with specifics of the appropriations act. But, that act normally contains only minor revisions in the budget proposal submitted by the governor each January. Actual shaping of the budget is done quietly behind the scenes, not during the legislative debate closely followed by the media. In the words of one political editor, "the governor always wants to assert his budget powers because he knows he'll lose them damn quick if he doesn't, and the legislative leaders want to prove they have the final word."[16]

By his own admission, Governor George Busbee spent the largest block of his time in office preparing and writing the annual budget.[17] The budget authority is the governor's one big source of power over independently elected constitutional officers.

In addition, several traditional powers of the office gave the governor great influence over the General Assembly. Until the mid-1960s he named the speaker of the house, speaker pro tem, the majority leader, and chairmen of major committees. Although he did not name the presiding officer of the senate, the lieutenant governor, he otherwise had similar influence in that chamber. Administration bills were almost always passed; so readily could bills he opposed be bottled up in committee that the governor rarely had to use the veto. During floor debate, there was even a direct telephone link between the governor's office in the capitol and the speaker's rostrum.

With the end of the county unit system, reapportionment and the breakdown of rural predominance, and the election of blacks and Republicans, the General Assembly began loosening itself from gubernatorial control. The biggest boost for legislative independence, however, was the election of outspoken segregationist Lester Maddox as governor.

The general election of 1966 produced no winner in the gubernatorial race. Conservative Republican Howard "Bo" Callaway gained a plurality, Democrat Maddox trailed by a few thousand votes, but over 50,000 write-in votes were cast for liberal ex-Governor Ellis Arnall. The Georgia Constitution provided for election by the General Assembly in case no candidate receives a popular vote majority. In January, 1967, the overwhelmingly Democratic legislature chose Maddox. In the meantime it had organized itself independently of the incoming governor, choosing its own house speaker and other officers. Without any governor-elect to direct them, legislators formulated their own legislative agenda. Maddox, who owed his election to the General Assembly, was not able thereafter to assert authority over it.

Since the Maddox years, Governors Carter and Busbee have reasserted gubernatorial authority, but not dominance. The governor appoints "administration floor leaders" who ride herd over administration bills in each house. As most legislators still belong to the party that the governor heads in the state, and as he controls the purse strings, the governor's backing or opposition on pet bills is usually crucial.

Another informal power of the governor is the tradition of appointing persons to nominally elective offices. Commonly, elected supreme court justices, court of appeals judges, and the constitutional heads of executive agencies resign in mid-term. This enables the governor to appoint an "incumbent" who then runs for election, often without opposition.

The most powerful state official, right behind the governor, is the speaker of the house. He names committee chairs, assigns bills to the committee, and may determine whether legislation comes up for a vote. The speaker's backing is usually needed for any controversial legislation; his opposition is usually fatal. The lieutenant governor is the speaker's counterpart in the Georgia senate. At one time, his power was comparable to the speaker's, but reformist Lieutenant Governor Zell Miller, when he took office in 1975, voluntarily relinquished several sources of power in order to make the body more democratic.

Although the collective membership of the General Assembly is often derided in the press, individual legislators generally enjoy the respect of their constituents. Much of their problem as a body is that they are handicapped in their competition with the governor for power. Georgia's is a part-time legislature, constitutionally limited to 40 meeting days a year. Staff resources are minimal, legislators' salaries are low, and until 1982, rank-and-file members did not even have office space at the capitol. Much of their reliance on lobbyists for information reflects these limitations.

Within the membership, power is diffused among numerous and not very cohesive groups. Coalitions develop and dissolve depending on the issues. Legislators may split urban/suburban/rural, big city/little city, north/south, liberal/conservative, black/white, and even Democratic/Republican. Pragmatism, not ideology, is the common motivator that helps explain temporary alliances, as between liberal black Democrats and conservative white Republicans against moderate white Democrats on the issue of reapportionment.

Although the courthouse gangs' control disappeared with the county unit system, county officials still have influence at the capitol. With district legislators, referred to as the "county delegation," county officials develop local legislation. Such legislation is passed as courtesy, without debate, in the General Assembly. Collectively, county commissioners have an effective lobby at the state capitol.

Georgia cities generally have some form of weak-mayor government. Even in Atlanta, where on paper the mayor appears stronger, he must share power with a usually independent-minded council. City politicians have not regularly had much influence in state politics. More than local officials, private institutions are generally acknowledged to be the focus of political power in most Georgia communities. In some places, a single large employer, such as a textile or paper mill, may dominate local government. More often, the "establishment" of business interests uses its combined resources and prestige to influence politics.

For much of the 20th century, Georgia suffered a rather negative national image. To many Americans, it seemed depressed, backward, and reactionary. Georgians themselves—at least white Georgians—often felt "put upon" by outsiders, especially the federal authority. Criticism in national media, perceived intrusion on "states rights" in the 1930s and 1940s, and real coercion on civil rights in the 1950s and 1960s, helped create widespread negativism toward the national government.

Beginning with the New Deal, however, the federal government provided the state with money for public services the likes of which Georgia neobourbon leaders would never consider. This other side of the federal relationship grew with World War II, which brought Georgia more than its share of military bases (second only to Texas), war industries, and civilian federal installations. In good measure, the federal establishment was responsible for the beginnings of Georgia's economic prosperity. The federal contribution to Georgia's well-being continues, as does federal monitoring of state compliance with civil rights measures. One effect of these dual aspects of the federal relationship is a commonly expressed attitude of ambivalence toward Washington: "We're gonna take the money (almost one-third of the state budget), but I wish they'd get off our backs."

Much of the federal largesse has been due in no small part to the special position Georgia and other southern politicians had in national affairs. Georgians' adherence to a one-party system and their preference for the status quo enabled their representatives in Washington to accumulate seniority in Congress, and influence in Democratic councils unrivaled by the politicians of most other states. Most notable was U.S. Senator Richard B. Russell, 1933–1971. Not only did his grasp of military affairs and political skill make him a Senate power, but also his patrician demeanor gave lie to the charge that all Georgia politicians were rabble-rousers. Russell's colleagues in the Senate, Walter F. George, 1922–1957, and Herman Talmadge, 1957–1981, and armed services counterpart in the U.S. House, Carl Vinson, 1914–1965, were also Washington heavyweights.

Georgia's growing prominence among the states, and continuing economic prosperity is today related more to geography than clout in Congress. The Snow Belt's loss in people and jobs has been Georgia's gain in material well-being and social equality. Even rural Georgia is becoming mainstream America.

Georgia politics is changing, too. In 1980, during the heat of campaigning, Herman Talmadge made an unfortunate remark about "carpetbaggers" and Mack Mattingly, a Republican from Indiana who had never held an elective office in the state, won Talmadge's seat in the U.S. Senate. That outcome spurred Republicans to an all-out (but ultimately unsuccessful) effort to win the governor's office in 1982. In turn, Georgia Democrats were roused to new levels of organizing, spending, and advertising, plus an uncharacteristic reaching out to practically all groups in the state. Two-party politics is still in Georgia's future, but it looms big enough to influence politics now.

NOTES

1. Frederick Allen, editorial, *Journal-Constitution*, Atlanta, 17 January 1982, p. B1.

2. Jack Bass and Walter DeVries, *The Transformation of Southern Politics* (New York: Basic Books, 1976), p. 149.

3. Allen, editorial, 17 January 1982.

4. *Georgia and Her Resources* (Atlanta: State Department of Agriculture, 1932), p. 12.

5. H.L. Mencken, *A Mencken Chrestomathy* (New York: Knopf, 1953), p. 187.

6. U.S. Bureau of the Census, *State Government Finances in 1981*, GF81-No. 3 (Washington, DC: Department of Commerce, 1982).

7. *Journal-Constitution*, Atlanta, 21 June 1970; *Macon Telegraph*, 24 August 1970; *The Journal*, Atlanta, 27 October 1970; *Constitution*, Atlanta, 26 August 1970.

8. Unpublished material provided by Elections Division, Office of the Secretary of State of Georgia.

9. Interview with the author, December 1978. Ben T. Fortson was Georgia secretary of state from 1946 until his death in 1979.

10. *Ibid.*

11. Compiled from information supplied by the members and printed by the Department of Archives and History, Office of the Secretary of State of Georgia.

12. U.S. Commission on Civil Rights, *The Voting Rights Act: Ten Years After* (1975), and *The Voting Rights Act: Unfulfilled Goals* (1981).

13. *Journal of the Senate of the State of Georgia, Regular Session*, 1974, pp. 42–43.

14. *Journal-Constitution*, Atlanta, 26 December 1976, p. A1.

15. Augustus B. Turnbull, III, "Politics in the Budgetary Process. The Case of Georgia," unpublished doctoral dissertation, University of Virginia, 1967, p. 73.

16. David Nordan, editorial, *Journal-Constitution*, Atlanta, 6 February 1977, p. 3.

17. Interview with author, October 1979.

9
Kentucky
MARC LANDY

On any Friday night the Interstates heading south from Michigan, Ohio, and Indiana are clogged with traffic. Kentuckians are going home. At the Kentucky border, the traffic flows out from these main arteries to highways and rural routes bringing the cars to destination points in all the far reaches of the commonwealth. On Sunday evening the process is repeated in reverse. The cars leave the little towns and farmsteads to begin the trek back north.

Economists teach us that the way to judge the value of an object is to observe what people are willing to pay to attain it. The gasoline and tolls involved in these pilgrimages, not to mention the lost sleep, show just how much these exiles cherish their birthplace. Kentucky, on the one hand, is poor—forty-sixth in the nation in per capita income—so jobs must be found elsewhere.[1] Kentucky, on the other hand, is where the kinfolks are; where grandpa is buried; and where the Wildcats play. It is the place to come back to. The place one never fully leaves. Understanding the distinctive character of Kentucky politics begins with appreciating the importance of this strong attachment to place and of the deep ties and sense of caring that it creates. However, local patriotism can foster defensiveness as well as pride. Kentucky's poverty, its rurality, and its low level of educational attainment might be expected to channel these local affections in the direction of the sort of bitter and narrow solidarity often found in urban slums and rural backwaters. While such sentiments are not absent from the Kentucky scene, they do not dominate it. Other elements of the Kentucky political landscape operate to direct the flow of energy that these powerful attachments release in a positive direction. Specific attributes of the state's central educational and cultural institutions, the distribution of formal governmental authority, the revenue structure, and the political parties combine with state patriotism to endow the political life of the commonwealth with verve, richness, and complexity. These elements mix with one another to create the particular

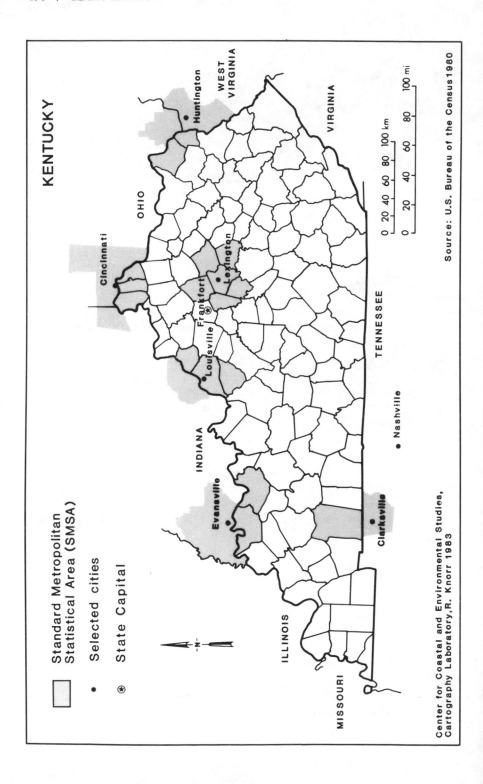

KENTUCKY

Standard Metropolitan
Statistical Area (SMSA)

• Selected cities

⊛ State Capital

Source: U.S. Bureau of the Census 1980

Center for Coastal and Environmental Studies,
Cartography Laboratory, R. Knorr 1983

citizen orientations, leadership styles, and patterns of interaction that form Kentucky's distinctive political blend.

POLITICAL CULTURE: PRIDE AND ALLEGIANCE

Kentucky possesses a few institutions whose influence extends state-wide and to which people accord a great deal of respect. The existence of these institutions serves to encourage Kentuckians to identify with the state as a whole and to integrate their local attachments with an attachment to the commonwealth.

One can best appreciate the contribution made by integrative institutions to the quality of state political life by comparing a place that has them, Kentucky, to one that does not, New Jersey. New Jersey is superior to Kentucky according to any socio-economic measure devisable, yet one has only to live for a brief stint in either place to sense the greater feeling of pride attached to Kentucky. New Jersey has no statewide media organ; its affairs are treated as an afterthought by the newspapers and TV stations based in New York and Philadelphia. Kentucky's statewide newspaper, the *Louisville Courier-Journal*, ranks among the best newspapers in America and earns its greatest distinction from its coverage of state affairs. Although it does not have a mass circulation outside of metropolitan Louisville, it is read avidly by virtually all politically engaged citizens from Pikeville to Paducah. When a hot piece of political gossip appears in the fourstar edition, the phone lines are soon blazing from one end of the state to the other. Not only does the *Courier* enable people to inform themselves about state affairs, but it conveys a sense of excitement that encourages them to view Kentucky political life as an enthralling, and amusing, enterprise.[2]

The University of Kentucky provides a focal point for state attention and pride to a far greater extent than does Rutgers, the State University of New Jersey. Rutgers must compete with other institutions of higher learning for the loyalties of New Jersey's young. Although most Kentucky high school graduates do not in fact go to U.K., there is no doubt in anyone's mind that it is the place to go. Such influence extends far beyond the student population. The agriculture school is the disseminator of technical expertise to the state's extensive, and politically influential, farm population. It serves as the control center for the USDA's agricultural extension service, whose agents make their presence felt in every county in Kentucky. U.K. also administers the state's community college system, thereby extending its daily influence into 13 cities scattered throughout the state. The education school dominates curriculum evaluation and research for the state's public schools. The medical school provides Kentucky with doctors, and the medical complex, nationally known for its excellence, is the only place that many Kentuckians will allow themselves to be taken if they are really sick.

As important as all these integrative aspects of the institution undoubtedly are, they pale in significance compared to the Wildcats. Basketball enjoys a popularity in Kentucky rivalled only by that to be found in Indiana and in the inner-city neighborhoods of the great metropolises. The University of Kentucky basketball team stands at the apex of a hierarchy of basketball fanaticism whose base rests in elementary school gymnasiums and backyard hoops throughout the state. Until quite recently, the Wildcats laid claim to the Southeast Conference title virtually as a matter of right. It reaches the hallowed "final four" NCAA basketball semifinals routinely and has won many national championships. On a Saturday afternoon during basketball season stores and roads are deserted as people sit by television sets and radios to watch or listen to the "Cats." Sports fanaticism is hardly unique to Kentucky, but elsewhere it does not normally play such a politically significant role. In Kentucky, the powerful emotions and loyalties that sports partisanship engender attach themselves to a state institution thereby strengthening the bonds linking citizen and commonwealth.

Although New Jersey has many lovely suburban and rural communities, there is no sense of a distinctive "good life" marking Princeton or South Orange as being different from their counterparts in New York or Connecticut. By contrast, Kentucky has the Bluegrass, which is both a place and a state of mind. When an east Kentucky coal operator strikes it rich, he leaves the coal dusty mountains for a farm in the Bluegrass. When a central Kentucky real estate developer finally finds the last tenant for his shopping center, his profits go to buy a horse farm in the Bluegrass. Literally, the Bluegrass is a set of counties emanating from the city of Lexington that contains particularly excellent terrain for raising horses. Metaphorically, it is a style of genteel rural living whose folkways revolve around the expensive hobby of horse racing. Keeneland is its Mecca; the Kentucky Derby, staged anomalously at seedy Churchill Downs in Louisville, its sacred rite. Few Kentuckians live in the literal Bluegrass; fewer still in the archetypical Bluegrass; yet its sheer existence gives them a sense of how life ought to be lived. This feeling, that the best life exists within the borders of their very own state, imparts to Kentuckians a sense of common identity, a feeling that Kentucky is its own republic, not just a strip of highway linking Nashville to Cincinatti.

The existence of these integrative institutions enhances Kentucky political life in yet another aspect, by fostering the creation of a cohesive political class. Most Kentuckians are not politically active; they do little more than vote. But among the minority of those more deeply involved in politics, an unusual air of collegiality exists. Despite intense rivalries and disagreements, a large percentage of the active and powerful citizens of Kentucky—be they Republican or Democrats, reactionaries or progressives—know and talk to one another. To some extent this is a result of the small town atmosphere of Frankfort, as well as the relatively small population of the state itself. There simply are not that many people that one needs to get to know. However, familiarity per se can breed contempt as well as build cohesion. Common attachment to, and participation in, the cherished institutions and activities emblematic of Kentucky mitigates the ill effects of intimacy and helps to forestall the development of the sort of partisan discord and abiding personal rancor that familiarity may breed.

Like politicians everywhere, the members of this class, whether they be allies or rivals, encounter each other at campaign rallies and legislative caucuses. Unlike other states where social and cultural life is more disparate, they also bump into each other continually at derby parties, U.K. alumni meetings, and other occasions that serve to remind them of just how much they really have in common. This does not lead them to forget their differences; yet the impact is discernable. The participants in this amorphous network return each other's phone calls; they act to dampen the maliciousness of the gossip that their own allies are spreading about the other. They do not necessarily disdain to engage in graft, but they do so according to a set of rules that they consider to be honorable. Although they cannot prevent the rise of bigots and scoundrels, they do their best to ostracize those who seek to foul the prevailing atmosphere of moderation.

These positive orientations towards Kentucky life and politics lead the public to accord a special degree of respect and deference to Kentucky's first citizen, the governor. Although Kentuckians are far too democratic to fawn upon him in monarchical fashion, the great dignity and celebrity in which he is held is more akin to that paid to a Venetian doge. As in that Italian city state, the reverence granted the leader reflects the love borne toward the republic itself.

Kentucky has produced several notable national politicians in modern times, including John Sherman Cooper, Alben Barkley, and Thruston Morton. Yet none of these estimable gentlemen enjoyed the same degree of prestige within the commonwealth as that commanded by governors like Bert Combs and Julian Carroll, whose names are hardly known beyond Kentucky's borders. When budding student politicians at the University of Kentucky doze in the library, it is the governor's chair alone that haunts their dreams. Visions of hosting the newly crowned University of Kentucky national basketball champions, and awarding the trophy to the winner of the Kentucky Derby sweeten their slumber.

The extraordinary repute in which the office is held is itself an important source of the governor's political power. When he gives a command or requests a favor people try to accede to him because they believe that it is right and proper to do so. They accord a special status to his requests and oppose him only when they feel their own vital interests have been threatened.

The political enterprises that governors embark upon are not always successful, especially if their objectives conflict with those of well-entrenched economic interests. Although a venture may be risky, the governor is capable of endowing it with a large stock of political capital and a long line of political credit.

The strong identification of Kentuckians with their state is complemented by strong expectations concerning the role of state government in their lives. These expectations are fed by accidents of geography and demography and by distinctive aspects of the state's fiscal structure.

Until the recent growth spurt experienced by metropolitan Lexington, Louisville remained the state's only big city. However, the atypical social character of Louisville prevented it from exerting the sort of influence on state affairs that a city of its size would normally exercise. The state of Kentucky is overwhelmingly Protestant, while Louisville is heavily Catholic. In many Kentucky counties the prohibition of alcohol remains in force; Louisville is the whiskey distilling capitol of the United States. Although conscious of being border staters, most Kentuckians consider themselves to be more southern than northern. Louisville is a distinctly midwestern city. Because Louisville is socially suspect it is politically ostracized. The mayor of Louisville cannot rival the governor of Kentucky for prestige and influence to the same degree that the mayor of Chicago rivals the governor of Illinois. Frankfort remains the sole important political arena in the state.

Furthermore, Kentucky's tax structure ensures the primacy of state over local government. The extreme poverty of Kentucky's local governments make county and local political organizations highly dependent upon the state. State tax revenues account for 73 percent of all state and local tax revenues. This figure is substantially above the national average of 55 percent and higher than that of any of the seven states that border Kentucky.[3]

The powerful effect of the state-local revenue mix on the development of a state-oriented political system is revealed by comparing Kentucky with its neighbor, Ohio. Ohio's localities receive more than half of all state and local tax revenues.[4] Since the mayors of that state's major cities have patronage sources of their own, they are reluctant to support the development of strong state political parties, the existence of which might threaten their prerogatives. Therefore, the character of Ohio politics remains highly fractionated. Several municipal arenas compete with the state for public attention.[5]

Kentucky's unusual revenue structure is also responsible for the great degree of concern for state politics shown by interest groups that in other states would focus most of their political attention at the municipal level. This is most evident with respect to the organized political activity of teachers. In states where salaries are determined primarily at the local level, teachers concentrate their political efforts upon school-board elections and local property-tax referenda. While these sorts of activities are not neglected in Kentucky, teachers find they must also devote themselves to electing a governor whom they consider to be education-oriented. The aggressive involvement of this very influential and active organized bloc and others like it serves to greatly enhance the prestige and importance of state politics.[6]

For much of the postwar period, the expectations of most Kentuckians regarding state government were framed in terms of a single objective, roads. Good government was defined as "more roads." The woeful condition of

Kentucky's transportation network was seen as the cause of the state's backward economy. Good roads were thought to provide not only more pleasant transportation, but also to serve as a necessary precondition for economic progress. During the decades of the 1950s and 1960s enormous progress was made in road improvement. Virtually every governor embarked upon some major road-building initiative. To this day a connection remains in the popular mind between particular roads and the chief executives who sponsored them. For example, the Mountain Parkway that provides a link between the isolated hill counties of east Kentucky and the Bluegrass is remembered to be the handiwork of Governor Bert Combs who was born and bred in Prestonsburg, the road's eastern terminus.

Roads were built and built quickly. Not only did they address the public's demand for improved transportation, but they also provided the administration with an opportunity to dole out enormous economic favors. Discretionary decisions were required with regard to every aspect of the construction process: the letting of design contracts, the choice of contractors, the leasing of equipment, the marketing of revenue bonds, and the hiring of maintenance crews.[7] Under any circumstances, such grand governmental largesse would elicit keen interest. In the tenth poorest state in the country it was conceived to be nothing short of the Comestock Lode.

Nor were these benefices solely aimed at individuals. The fate of entire communities came to depend upon whether they would be bypassed by the new roads or whether they would be favored with an exit. Since these favors were the governor's to give, the gubernatorial election, in reality the Democratic primary, came to be perceived as a critical event determining one's own future and that of one's community. Much of the immediacy and vitality of Kentucky politics stems from this perception that the outcome of the gubernatorial election really matters.

By the late 1960s the very success of Kentucky's road-building effort led to a decline in new activity. However, the political and economic function that this exercise had come to perform for individuals, firms, and communities was taken over by other forms of public works. For a community that had already succeeded in obtaining a parkway exit, an even higher mark of status could be won by prevailing upon the state to designate it as a site for a spanking new community college, built at state expense and maintained through funds allocated to the University of Kentucky.

This largesse was made possible in good measure by the increase in federal dollars for higher education which the state received during this period. It was also sustained after 1972 by the imposition of a coal severance tax that operated as a percentage of the price that the coal operators charge per ton of coal.[8] Kentucky is the nation's largest coal-producing state. In the wake of the 1973 Arab oil embargo the price of coal soared, swelling the coffers of the state treasury. The combined impact of increased federal aid and the coal severance tax was to improve the quality of state services at no perceived added cost to the average taxpayer.

In the 1980s, for the first time in memory, the dominant theme of state government has become one of austerity. Coal prices and production have stabilized, halting the acceleration of severance tax revenues. Federal aid has declined. Governor John Y. Brown has had to devote the bulk of his attention to reducing the state payroll and diminishing state services.[9] Perhaps these cutbacks will cause citizens to lower their expectations of state government. More likely it will serve to accentuate their sense of dependency and mobilize them to ever more strenuous political efforts to protect their share of a shrinking pie.

Regard for government and deference toward the governor coexist with deep suspicion of political ambition and political power. The state constitution prohibits the governor from serving more than one consecutive term. County sheriffs labor under the same restriction. The legislature convenes only once every two years and it must adjourn after only 60 working days.

Citizen suspicions are rooted in part in Kentucky's religious heritage. Kentucky was settled mainly by Protestant fundamentalists. The rural hamlets of the state are still dotted with small unadorned churches bearing the title Old Regular Baptist, Primitive Baptist, or Church of God. In recent times these churches have accompanied their congregants in migrating to Lexington and Louisville and other urban areas both within Kentucky and beyond its border.

Unlike more recent forms of fundamentalism, these churches emphasize the Old Testament themes of hope and redemption. Their religious vision should not be confused with the sort of fanatical puritanism that strives to rid men of all sin. Rather, they consider sin to be endemic to human nature. It cannot be rooted out in this world. Therefore, it is to be kept in check, exposure to it must be minimized.

The onerous restrictions placed upon governors and legislators result from the same set of religious precepts that cause most Kentucky counties to ban the sale of all alcoholic beverages. Men cannot be entirely prevented from wanting to drink liquor. Nor can politicians be totally freed from the impulse to engage in corruption. Therefore, even the most abstemious individuals and the most virtuous politicians require that rigid barriers be erected to help them resist the dictates of their baser nature.

POLITICAL STYLE: MOSTLY JUST FOLKS

In the course of the last several decades, the offices of governor, U.S. senator, and legislator have each developed their own distinctive political styles. The senatorial style was pioneered by Alben Barkley, majority leader of the U.S. Senate from 1937 until his inauguration as Vice-President in 1949. Barkley was the first Kentucky politician since Henry Clay to achieve national prominence. He provided the commonwealth with a symbol of pride at a time when the state's fortunes were waning. He virtually created the style of the border-state senator, which has since come to play such a dominant role in the U.S. Senate.[10] Its list of progenitors include Robert Kerr of Oklahoma, Lyndon Baines Johnson of Texas, and Robert Byrd of West Virginia. It has become the model for most of Barkley's successors including the two incumbent Kentucky senators, Wendell Ford and Walter D. Huddleston.

The border-state senatorial style reflects the hybrid culture of those states that lie between the North and South (or, in the case of Texas, between the South and West). This culture contains elements common to both its neighbors, as well as being free of those traits that each of the adjacent regions particularly abhors about the other. The border stater possesses the gentility and adherence to rural agrarian values that southerners find sorely lacking in their northern counterparts. On the other hand, the man of the border is free of the dogged inflexibility on issues of race and trade unionism that northerners often attribute to southerners. Because he so neatly straddles the political as well as the geographical boundaries between fractious regions, the border state senator is uniquely well situated to serve as an honest broker between them.[11]

Since the border stater's power derives from his ability to perform mediating functions, he adopts the style appropriate to those tasks. His role is to seek areas of agreement amidst the welter of conflict that often pervades the activities of the upper chamber. He tries to encourage his more parochial partisan allies to be more sympathetic to national trends and seeks to impress upon his more cosmopolitan associates the necessity of taking account of the particular, locally based, political imperatives under which some of their Democratic party colleagues must operate. Tact, cajolery, and a reputation for sticking by one's word are the tools he most often employs as he pursues the fine art of consensus building.

Kentucky governors adopt one of three styles that may be termed "insider," "outsider," and "freshface." The third category is really a hybrid of the first two; an insider in outsider's clothing.

The archetypical insider was the founder of the Administration Faction, Earl Clements. He was not given to rhetorical flourishes, but rather, sought to govern by means of astute rationing of patronage and the ruthless stripping away of power from his enemies. He prided himself on his ability to coerce the legislature into approving the budget that he submitted without changing a single digit, and within days of its submission.[12] For him, being chief executive was essentially an organizational and managerial task. He presided over a state administrative apparatus of which he was intensely proud.

Clements' approach to governing reflected his own intensely political background. In Kentucky parlance, "he went through the chairs," meaning that his rise to the state's preeminant office was preceded by a slow gradual climb up the ladder of lower offices at the county and state level. Prior to attaining the governorship he served as county sheriff, county clerk, and county judge of his native Union County. Then he was elected to the state senate where he rose to the position of majority floor leader. He also served a term in the U.S. Congress before entering the lists for the governorship in 1947.[13]

Other recent expositors of the "insider" style include: Wendell Ford, elected in 1971; Julian Carroll, elected in 1975; and the only post-war Republican governor, Louis Nunn, elected in 1967. Both Ford and Carroll were veteran state legislators who achieved leadership positions in the senate and house respectively. Each also served a term of apprenticeship as lieutenant governor. Nunn had been a county judge, and had further enhanced his organization credentials by managing two separate campaigns by Republican hopefuls for statewide office. Carroll and Ford had likewise played active and prominent organizational roles in previous Democratic gubernatorial campaigns.[14]

Although the great Kentucky outsiders, Happy Chandler and John Y. Brown, were not quite the political neophytes they claimed to be, they both rose to power by emphasizing their opposition to entrenched political organizations and by promising to represent the "ordinary guy" rather than "the interests." Brown, in particular, chose to emphasize his antipathy to "politics as usual" by promising to make use of his proven entrepreneurial skills to run the state as a business.

To compensate for their lack of organizational resources, both Chandler and Brown demonstrated a great flair for showmanship. Chandler was widely considered to be the best storyteller in Kentucky political history. He campaigned for office by tirelessly traversing the state, regaling and beguiling audiences, in every little crossroad and rural hamlet with his songs, jokes, and tales.[15]

Brown's skills have proven themselves to be more appropriate to the onset of the television age. He skillfully exploited the same marketing flair that he had used to develop his Kentucky Fried Chicken empire. Lacking Chandler's personal magnetism, he compensated for his somewhat bland manner by choosing to share the political spotlight with his wife, the TV celebrity, sportscaster, and former Miss America, Phyllis George. Through clever use of mass media and personal appearance, the team of John and Phyllis instilled a sense of glamor and exuberance into what had been, prior to their last minute entrance, an exceedingly lackluster gabernatorial campaign.[16]

Chandler and Brown governed as they had campaigned. Neither sought to impose the iron grip upon the legislature that Clements, and later Carroll, exerted. They appeared more interested in the ceremonial aspects of the job than in mastering the nuts and bolts of administration. Each sought to make use of his public relations talents to develop greater national awareness and appreciation of Kentucky. Both were more comfortable promoting the state than trying to manage its affairs.

As previously mentioned, the hybrid style arose from the desire of "insider" governors to perpetuate their influence by choosing their successors. Recognizing that the public lacks sympathy for insiders, they sought candidates who shared their commitment to organizational values but who were also able to project the "freshface" associated with the outsider. The outstanding examples of this mixed category are Bert Combs and Edward T. Breathitt. Neither possessed the flamboyant personality of a Chandler nor the celebrity quality of a Brown. However, both enjoyed outstanding personal reputations for honesty and probity. These credentials were invaluable political assets to the Administration Faction leadership that was being subjected to criticism from the *Louisville Courier-Journal* and other reformist organs of opinion for placing the patronage needs of the organization above a concern for good government. The press responded favorably to the candidacies of both Combs and Breathitt.[17] This ability to garner support among influential opinion molders, combined with the massive organizational resources of the Administration Faction, transformed these two political neophytes into formidable candidates.

Breathitt and Combs both adopted governing styles in keeping with their hybrid-leadership style. Their administrations were characterized by several efforts at policy reform, including adoption of a merit system for state employees, the passage of civil-rights legislation, and stringent efforts to control the environmental effects of strip mining for coal. At the same time great attention was paid to the political and economic needs of the Administration Faction. Patronage was dispensed to factional loyalists and factional opponents were purged from power whenever possible.

The defeat of the Administration Faction in 1967 was mainly attributable to the inability of Breathitt to choose a successor with a suitably "freshface" image. Although the faction's candidate, Henry Ward, was an able public administrator with a long record of public service, he suffered as a result of serving in the state's most politically sensitive post for a period of six years. It is the highway commissioner's responsibility to mete out the myriad forms of patronage associated with road building. Although Ward himself was never directly implicated in any illegal activity, even a person of his stature found it impossible to maintain his reputation entirely intact while becoming so heavily involved in the awarding of road-related contracts.[18]

The Kentucky legislature is likewise composed of varying political styles. It numbers among its members reformers of a liberal bent whose political orientations are more influenced by their sense of allegiance to national movements, most notably environmentalism, than to any special feature of the Kentucky landscape. In recent years, these issue-oriented representatives of the left have been counterbalanced by adherents of single-issue movement of the right, most notably supporters of The Right to Life.

Another segment of the legislature is composed of what can best be termed "gentry." These are men who come from among the leading families of small rural counties. They are often attorneys who are highly involved in local affairs. They serve in the legislature to fulfill the same sense of civic duty that motivates them to be involved in local conservation efforts, philanthropic endeavors, and other forms of community betterment.

An outstanding example of this sort of rural artistocrat is John Swinford, house majority leader in the 1974 session of the legislature. Swinford came from a Bluegrass county replete with elegant horse and cattle farms. Although he was careful to ensure that the interests of his constituents were carefully attended to during the session, in reality his prosperous constitutents made few such demands. Swinford devoted a disproportionate amount of his time to securing passage of amendments to the surface-mine control law, amendments designed to improve the quality of the land reclamation that would occur after mining was concluded. No surface mining occurred in his district. When asked why he was so concerned with this matter he replied that he had taken tours of surface-mining sites and he had become convinced that more stringent regulation was both necessary and practical. The good of the commonwealth was at stake; no further justification was required.[19]

The dominant style of the legislature is set neither by issue-oriented members nor by the rural gentry. Rather it is fashioned by those who function as emissaries of the local "courthouse gangs" that dominate politics at the county level. These representatives are united by their disinterest in broad policy issues and their preoccupation with local matters. In some cases, individual agendas are determined by the demands of dominant local economic interests. Some Louisville legislators serve as emissaries of particular labor union local; some coalfield representatives are there simply to "vote coal." In other instances, legislators adopt as their sole objective the acquisition of some particular form of state largesse for their constituents— be it a turnpike exit, a vocational school, or designation as a Class A rather than a Class B municipality. This bounty may or may not lie within the legislative domain. If it is rather a matter of gubernatorial discretion, the legislator will indicate his willingness to "trade" his vote to the governor on some matter of importance to the latter in exchange for the granting of this particular favor to the legislator's district.

Legislators comport themselves in a style commensurate with the small, but not inconsequential degree of power and prestige that they hold. Their passion for vote trading transforms the capitol into an oriental bazaar. In the various vestibules and corners of its ornate marble halls, legislators and lobbyists haggle with one another in whispered, conspiratorial tones. When not engaged in forming, or dissolving, these secret cabals, they are busy behaving like what they are—amiable, small-town, early-middle to middle-aged men, basking in the luxury of being away from home. They drink and smoke too much, engage in occasional dalliance, and cavort about like fraternity brothers enjoying their 50th reunion.

POLITICAL INTERACTION: GUBERNATORIAL PREEMINANCE

The political life of Kentucky is a process of interaction among and between Democrats and Republicans, administrative agencies and the two houses of the legislature, and the myriad firms, individuals, and associations seeking to influence public decision making to preserve and enhance their economic interests. Kentucky political and constitutional tradition put the governor in control of two of these political elements: the political party that nominated him and the agencies and departments comprising the executive branch. Gubernatorial command of these valuable political resources accounts for the distinctively dramatic quality with which Kentucky politics is endowed. The drama consists in the attempt of the governor to wield his authority as party leader and chief executive to combat the interest-group pressures and institutional impediments that undermine his ability to govern.

Party competition in Kentucky is lively but uneven. The Democrats dominate. Republicans have won only two gubernatorial elections since the 1930s and have never captured control of the legislature during this period. However, in contests for national office the pattern shifts. Kentucky tends to support winning presidential candidates regardless of their party affiliation. The state supported Nixon in 1972, Carter in 1976, and Reagan in 1980. Of the seven members of its delegation to the U.S. House of Representatives, four are Democrats. Currently both Kentucky U.S. senators are Democrats. However, during most of the 1950s and 1960s, Republicans controlled at least one Senate seat, and, for a period of time, both.[20]

Despite this success in national and senatorial elections, the Republican party is not really a statewide party. It is only able to elect local and state legislative candidates in a few specified regions of the state, most notably in the southeast-southcentral area and in Jefferson County, which encompasses the Louisville metropolitan area.

The southeast-southcentral region, comprising the Fifth Congressional District, consists of isolated counties, some of which are among the poorest in the state. The Republican allegiance is in many cases a holdover from Civil War times, since many of these counties sided with the Union. Unlike the region farther to the east, few of these counties contain significant deposits of coal. Therefore, they have not been subjected to the organizing efforts of the United Mineworkers, an activity that has shifted the partisan cast of politics in many coal counties in a Democratic direction.

The powerful Republican influence in Louisville reflects its midwestern orientation. The German-Americans in this river town behave more like their counterparts in Cincinatti and Evansville than they do like other Kentuckians. As Catholics who have retained the "gemutlich" traditions of their native land, they have little in common politically with the abstemious Protestant fundamentalists who are so influential in the Democratic party of the state.

Republican party factionalism has tended to mirror its geographical divisions. The task of maintaining party harmony depends essentially on preserving a rough equality of representation and perquisites between the two regions. During the long period between 1947 and 1967, when the party failed to elect anyone to statewide office, the dominant figures in the

Republican party were the two men who did manage to gain election to the U.S. Senate, John Sherman Cooper of southeastern Kentucky and Thruston Morton of Louisville.

The failure of the Republicans to win the governor's chair since 1967 is essentially the result of their inability to find a sufficiently popular issue to exploit that would enable them to convince the average Kentucky voter to overcome his Democratic bias. In 1967 the Republican candidate, Louie Nunn, emphasized his opposition to the civil-rights policies of the national Democratic administration and accused the state administration of being too soft in its reaction to campus demonstrations. In subsequent elections, the moderate stance adopted by Democratic candidates has deprived the Republicans of the opportunity to paint the opposition as being overly liberal. At present, the only significant office Republicans hold within the state is that of Jefferson County judge. No current statewide issue appears sufficiently volatile and controversial to so estrange the voters as to cause them to abandon the Democrats.

The most extraordinary aspect of the Kentucky Democratic party has not been its success in winning elections for statewide office (that is typical of the border states), but rather the stability and coherence of its factional alignments.

One faction of the Democratic party, nicknamed the Administration Faction, held the governorship and maintained effective control of the legislature for all but a single four-year period between 1947 and 1967.[21] Public support for this high level of political stability and coherence is not attributable to the patronage basis of politics. Most cities and states that share a similar materialistic political orientation, display a far more chaotic, multifactional mode of politics. Boston, for example, has never had anything that could be characterized as a political machine.[22] States like West Virginia and Tennessee, where the politics of roads are also central to the political life of the state, have not exhibited a similarly high level of factional coherence.[23] Public support for such a system in Kentucky is not solely a byproduct of the political orientations of its citizens; it is also attributed to skillful and creative political leadership.

The Administration Faction was the creation of Earl Clements who governed the state from 1947 to 1951. At the time of his election, state politics was extremely fragmented. His predecessor, Simeon Willis, had been the first Republican governor elected in 20 years. Clements, more than any previous Kentucky governor, shared the point of view of the national Democratic party. After taking office, he set about forging a political organization that, in important respects, mirrored the New Deal coalition that dominated the national party. Under his tutelage, the Administration Faction came to include local "courthouse gangs" from disparate parts of rural Kentucky, the Louisville political machine, organized labor, and a small group of highly educated and sophisticated Kentuckians who had served in Washington with FDR or Truman. Most prominent among this "braintrust" were Wilson Wyatt, a Louisvillian who had been Truman's housing administrator, and Edward F. Prichard Jr. of Bourbon County, who had been law clerk to Felix Frankfurter and an official in the treasury department.[24]

The cohesion of the Administration Faction was enhanced by its very disparateness. Its various members—unionists, Catholics from Louisville, New Deal intellectuals, and Baptist country folk—had so little in common that it was extremely difficult for any subset of them to try to secede and form the core element for a rival coalition. Each constituent element felt much more comfortable communicating with the faction's leadership than it did with any other member of the coalition. To the extent that horizontal ties were forged at all, they came to be based exclusively upon a sense of common factional identity.

Clements and his successors worked hard to cultivate this sense of common partisan identity. They reserved the spoils of victory for those who had demonstrated proven loyalty to the organization, and they intervened actively in legislative primaries to defeat those who had proven to be disloyal. These sorties were not always successful, but the occasional defeat itself served to inflict scars of battle that only served to accentuate feelings of fraternal affiliation.[25]

Since the demise of the Administration Faction, resulting from its defeat in 1967, no Kentucky governor has managed to have his chosen successor elected governor. Each new regime has brought with it a whole new cast of characters providing Kentucky politics and governance with an increasingly fluid and unpredictable character. Whether this change reflects a basic shift in the nature of public support, or simply a temporary paucity of skillful political leadership is impossible to say. However, a continued absence of leadership will, in and of itself, have important political consequences. The longer a stable and coherent factional organization capable of perpetuating itself in office remains absent from the scene, the harder it becomes to recreate one.

The degree to which a governor can control and direct the behavior of the agencies and departments of state government varies widely from state to state. The obstacles differ. In some states, like New Hampshire and Florida, important administrative agencies are controlled by multi-member commissions whose terms are not coterminous with the governor. They have no responsibility to report to him; he cannot fire them; and he can only replace those members, usually a minority, whose terms expire during his tenure in office. In other states, like Wisconsin and California, the governor has greater formal powers to hire and fire, but his executive power is limited by customs and traditions that have developed since the Progressive era. In these states, the public believes that state government should be nonpartisan and that merit should be the sole criteria governing the appointment of state officials. A governor seeking to impose his will upon those who are ostensibly his subordinates would find himself violating deeply cherished ethical norms.

The Kentucky governor faces no such formal or traditional barriers to rule. His ability to appoint department chiefs is restricted only with respect to education, agriculture, and law enforcement, the heads of which are elected. More importantly he operates in a political climate that supports the notion that he should be allowed to direct policy and control the behavior of his subordinates. His discretion is not unlimited. A merit system is in place. Nonetheless, the cultural support he enjoys enables him to exercise wide latitude in meting out rewards and punishments within the broad, and often ambiguous, constraints that the merit system imposes. He may lack the ability to fire a particular holdover from a previous administration, but both the letter of the civil service code and the traditions of Kentucky political life permit him to transfer that employee to more onerous duties in a new location hundreds of miles from the capitol.

The import of this tradition of gubernatorial preeminence extends beyond the mundane affairs of departmental decision making. If the governor's good will is a prerequisite to obtaining favorable administrative rulings, then the various firms, individuals, and interest groups whose well-being depends upon obtaining such outcomes will strive mightily to remain in his good graces. They can be coaxed, cajoled, and coerced into providing him with valuable political assets, financial support and other forms of campaign assistance for his political allies, and help in gaining support for his programs in the legislature. In Kentucky, the administrative, political, and policy-making aspects of the governorship meld into one.

The legislature labors under several institutional handicaps. The severest weakness results from its infrequent sessions. It meets for only 60 days every two years. Thus, while the governor and his administrative subordinates are always in Frankfort garnering the information and expertise that are the very stuff of political power, the legislature convenes episodically. By the time it has become sufficiently acclimated to even begin serious deliberations, the session is over.[26]

In recent years the legislature has enacted significant reforms aimed at strengthening itself institutionally. As a result of a constitutional amendment passed in 1977, an off-year mini-session, lasting ten days was held for the first time in 1983. The agenda included many of the housekeeping chores for the upcoming session including the adoption of procedural rules, electing the leadership, and appointing committees. A system of interim joint committees has been established. These committees meet regularly during the period between sessions in order to stay abreast of developments within their specific spheres of responsibility. The compensation of members has been increased, so that they can better afford to devote sufficient time to committee business. The staff of the legislative research commission has been augmented to improve the legislative branch's capacity to conduct its own policy research and analysis.[27]

These reforms, however, have not kept pace with the rapid expansion of state governmental responsibilities and the even more rapid increase in technical and fiscal complexity that that expansion has entailed. Members have no personal staffs; compensation for legislators remains so low that they can only devote part of their worklife to their legislative responsibilities; and, most importantly, they continue to spend only a small percentage of their time in the state capitol.

The General Assembly's comparative weakness does not provide the governor with a guarantee of victory in any particular policy struggle. The brevity and infrequency of sessions acts as a severe obstacle to positive action of any kind. In order to secure passage, a bill must be introduced, endorsed by committee, and passed in both the house and senate. Differences in the two versions must then be reconciled by a joint conference committee whose report must then be passed by both houses. Each stage—committee, floor consideration, and conference—offers opportunity for obstruction and delay. Unless the governor's lieutenants remain continually attentive, the session will end before all the legislative hurdles have been surmounted. Limits on the time and energy of his aides and legislative allies are therefore an important constraint upon the capacity of the governor to work his legislative will. Typically, this inertial bias limits his victories to those issues to which he has accorded the highest priority. Even in those instances, the dogged opposition of powerful private interest combined with carelessness or inattention on the part of his supporters, can cause the clock to run out before victory has been achieved.

Currently, the state of executive-legislative relations is in flux. Governor John Y. Brown chose not to exercise the close scrutiny and control of legislative affairs engaged in by his predecessors. This was essentially a matter of personal preference. His conception that government should run according to business principles implied that he should limit his own activities to executive management, narrowly defined, and leave the legislature to manage itself. Because the period of Brown's tenure coincided with times of severe economic recession, this extraordinary shift in gubernatorial strategy did not result in a very perceptible alteration in public policy. Since there was little money to spend, legislators could not put their unexpected freedom to much constructive use, and few new program initiatives emerged.

So far we have stressed the governor's political preeminence. His power is assailable neither by other elected executives, administrative appointees, nor by the legislature. The serious challenge to his dominion comes not from the public realm at all, but rather, from the sphere of the private economy.

In contrast to the primitive nature of administrative and legislative organization, the economy of the state is dominated by politically sophisticated economic institutions that intervene routinely in state political affairs to protect and enhance their interests. Among these forces are the tobacco industry, the leading banks of Lexington and Louisville, the thoroughbred horse racing industry, and the manufacturing concerns represented by the Associated Industries of Kentucky. Foremost among them are the firms and institutions involved in the commonwealth's leading industry, coal.

Kentucky is the nation's leading coal producer. It contains two major coal fields, one in the mountainous eastern part of the state and the other in the western region. Thousands are employed directly in the mining of coal, but this by no means exhausts the list of those with a direct stake in the success of the industry. Coal is extremely bulky. Transporting it from the mine mouth to the electric utilities and steel plants requires extensive use of truck and rail. When demand for coal is high, the narrow roads that traverse the coalfields crumble under the weight of caravans of coaltrucks. At the railheads, these heavy loads are transferred to coaltrains composed of seemingly endless numbers of specially designed coal hopper cars. When the market is depressed, the army of truck drivers, railway maintenance men, and mine construction workers join the miners on the unemployment lines.[28]

State public policy intervenes in many ways to affect the well-being of the industry. Regulation of surface mining determines how much money companies must spend on land reclamation. Safety regulation increases the cost of mine construction and maintenance. Maximum-weight limits restrict the amount of coal that can be loaded into a single truck. Workman's compensation laws determine how much the nation's most dangerous industry must contribute to the state's worker-protection program. These regulatory programs provide state government with sufficient enforcement authority to be able to shut down virtually any coal operation at any time. The industry therefore has a strong motive to insure that these programs are not implemented in a hostile manner. It is able to exert influence over the formulation and implementation of these regulatory policies by dint of the extensive political resources that it can command.

Kentucky election finance laws are not terribly effective. Therefore, it is possible for the industry to make enormous campaign contributions to gubernatorial candidates. All recent, successful gubernatorial aspirants have benefitted from large infusions of campaign assistance from one or another component element of the coal industry.[29] This sort of investment is especially productive when the elected governor functions as an "insider." Since he exerts tight control of both the officials in his administration and of the legislature, it is essential that he display sympathy for the concerns of the industry.

When an "outsider" becomes governor, the industry needs to supplement its influence with the executive with the maintenance of direct ties to members of the legislature. Since most legislators do not come from coalfield districts, the industry cannot depend on a natural affinity. In addition to campaign contributions, the industry develops goodwill by dispensing forms of patronage that it has at its disposal. A high percentage of the legislators earn their living as service-professionals—lawyers, bankers, and insurance brokers. The coal industry requires a vast amount of precisely the form of services that these legislators offer: insurance bonding, deed writing, bank deposit managing, and so forth. They can also reward these legislators indirectly by giving business to the equipment-leasing, engineering, and construction firms that these members either represent or are in some manner affiliated with. Therefore, remaining in good standing with the coal industry provides a virtual guarantee of prosperity for many legislators throughout the state.

In sheer money terms, the patronage resources available to the coal industry dwarf those available to the governor. In cases where policy conflicts develop between the industry and the state administration, narrow economic concerns would dictate that legislators take the industry's part. However, the history of such conflicts reveals that governors are often able to emerge victorious. This seemingly anomalous result can be understood only by recalling the distinctive nature of Kentucky political orientations, expectations, and leadership style.

Governor Breathitt was able to pass a stringent strip-mine control measure in the face of vociferous opposition from the coal industry by fully exploiting the political resources available to him. Several of the Administration Faction's staunchest legislative allies were intimately linked to the coal industry. Breathitt recognized how difficult it would be for them to vote for his bill, yet he desperately needed their support. In order to obtain it he exploited the fact that these legislators, and the courthouse organizations they represented, attached far more importance to their positions as emissaries of the state administration than to the actual cash value of coal-related patronage. They coveted their political role because of the power it gave them in determining the makeup of the political status hierarchy in their local domains. As "contact men," it was their privilege to decide who from their home counties could obtain a friendly audience in Frankfort and who could not. The deference and dignity that this privilege bestowed was worth far more than money.

Breathitt let it be known that a failure to support him on the strip-mine bill would result not merely in the loss of particular jobs or contracts, but in the loss of the privilege of serving as "contact man." "I simply said, 'I'll cut you off—you're either for us or against us'—I drew the line."[30] With only a scant number of defections, the pro-coal industry legislators voted for Breathitt's bill which passed by the narrowest of margins.[31] The success of the cut-off strategy depended upon the particular orientation toward political life adopted by the faction members. It worked because those members cared so deeply about state political life, because they valued their organizational membership so highly, and because they acknowledged the right of their leader to make such unpalatable demands upon them.

Breathitt's particular leadership style was an equally crucial component of the result. By definition, an "outsider" governor has no factional organization to command and so he has nothing to cut people away from. An "insider" governor would be most unlikely to risk the disintegration of his organization merely to accomplish a policy reform. It was Breathitt's hybrid style, his command of a powerful political organization coupled with his concern to maintain a reputation as a policy statesman, that provided him with both the motivation to carry out this policy reform and the resources to enable him to succeed.

This portrait of Kentucky politics presents a series of anomalies. First-rate institutions flourish in a climate of poverty and low educational attainment. One-party dominance, usually synonymous with chaotic and incoherent partisan activity, has accomodated itself to long periods of stable and coherent rule by a single party faction. Esteem for the governor and expectations of state government remain high despite the abiding mistrust of political power and ambition that its religious heritage imparts. Patronage-based political organizations provide the resources for high-minded reform. These anomalies cannot be analyzed out of existence. They are the complex reality of Kentucky state politics and provide a key for state level political analysis.

First of all, they reveal the profound influence of political culture and economic organization. No analysis of Kentucky that ignores Baptist fundamentalism, the strength of local attachments, or the political and economic importance of the coal industry could possibly do justice to political reality. On the other hand, these cultural and institutional factors cannot explain the existence of such magnificent state institutions as the *Courier-Journal*, the University of Kentucky, and the Administration Faction of the Democratic party. Other states with similar socio-economic and cultural profiles do not have them. They are best understood as the products of creative individuals who sought to build and to perpetuate something great. Their accomplishments were inspired by the deep ties to home and community that they shared with their fellow citizens. These accomplishments, in turn, served to expand the scope of those attachments. State as well as local loyalties were encompassed within the sphere of affection. The distinctive character of Kentucky politics owes as much to these individual expressions of creativity as it does to the cultural, institutional, and economic forces that operate there. In Kentucky, as elsewhere, the eye must focus upon discrete human actions as well as upon broad social patterns in order to bring political reality into focus.

NOTES

1. Bureau of Economic Analysis, *Survey of Current Business* (Washington, D.C.: U.S. Government Printing Office, 1983).

2. For a fine overall depiction of Kentucky political life and political culture see the chapter on Kentucky in Neal Peirce, *The Border South States* (New York: Norton, 1975). See also Marc Landy, *The Politics of Environmental Reform: Controlling Kentucky Strip Mining* (Baltimore: Johns Hopkins University Press, RFF Working Paper DD-2, 1976), pp. 44–52.

3. *Kentucky Tax Policy: Suggested Considerations,* Research Report (Frankfort, Kentucky: Legislative Research Commission, 1972), 69, p. 11.

4. *Ibid.*

5. John Fenton, *Midwest Politics* (New York: Holt, Rinehart and Winston, 1966), p. 141.

6. For a comparison of state versus local spending for education in each of the 50 states, see Robert H. Salisbury "State Politics and Education," in *Politics in the American States*, eds. Herbert Jacob and Kenneth N. Vines (Boston: Little, Brown, 1971), p. 417.

7. Malcolm E. Jewell and Everett W. Cunningham, *Kentucky Politics* (Lexington, Kentucky: University of Kentucky Press, 1968), pp. 43–44.

8. Landy, *The Politics of Environmental Reform*, p. 316.

9. For a fine portrait of the Brown Administration see the *Louisville Courier-Journal Magazine*, 13 December 1981, pp. 13–19, 54–57.

10. Alben Barkley, *That Reminds Me* (New York: Doubleday, 1954).

11. On the distinctiveness of border state political culture see Peirce, *The Border South States* and also John Fenton, *Politics in the Border States* (New Orleans: Houser, 1957).

12. Landy, *The Politics of Environmental Reform*, p. 68.

13. *Kentucky Historical Society Register* 46 (January 1948).

14. For more biographical informaion on Louie Nunn see Jewell and Cunningham, *Kentucky Politics*, pp. 113–116; on Wendell Ford see the *Louisville Courier-Journal*, 6 January 1972, A8; on Julian Carroll see the *Louisville Courier-Journal*, 6 November 1974.

15. For more detailed biographical information on Happy Chandler see Robert Riggs, "Happy Chandler Rides Again," *Saturday Evening Post*, 15 October 1955.

16. For a profile of John Y. Brown see the *Louisville Courier-Journal Magazine*, 13 December 1981.

17. Editorial endorsements of Combs and Breathitt appeared in the *Louisville Courier-Journal*, 13 October 1963, p. 4–2; 9 May 1971, A8.

18. Landy, *The Politics of Environmental Reform*, pp. 240–241.

19. Interview with John Swinford, conducted by the author, Cynthiana, Kentucky, 21 May 1974.

20. A summary of Kentucky election results appears in *America Votes* 14, eds. Richard Scammon and Alice V. McGillivray (Washington, D.C.: Elections Research Center, Congressional Quarterly, 1981), p. 165.

21. For a detailed account of the history of the Administration Faction see Landy, *The Politics of Environmental Reform*, pp. 43–98.

22. For an excellent depiction of the evolution of Boston politics see Dennis Hale, "James Michael Curley: Leadership and the Uses of Legend," in *Leadership in America: Consensus, Corruption and Charisma*, ed. Dennis Bathory (New York: Longman, 1978), pp. 131–146.

23. For a discussion of West Virginia politics see Fenton, *Politics in the Border States*; on Tennessee see V.O. Key, Jr., *Southern Politics* (New York: Knopf, 1949), pp. 58–81.

24. On the formation of the "braintrust" see Landy, *The Politics of Environmental Reform*, pp. 101–125.

25. During the 1947 campaign Clements gave a speech in which he referred to the pride that Democratic party politicians take in their scars of battle. See Landy, *ibid.*, p. 62.

26. For details concerning the Kentucky General Assembly see *1982 Kentucky General Assembly Directory* (Frankfort, Kentucky: Legislative Research Commission. January 1982).

27. *Ibid.* Also see *The Book of the States* 1980–1981 (Lexington, Kentucky: Council of State Governments, 1982), pp. 90, 92, 94.

28. For a profile of the Kentucky coal industry see Landy, *The Politics of Environmental Reform*, pp. 17–42.

29. *Louisville Courier-Journal*, 10 October 1971, p. E7; and 20 April 1975, p. A1.

30. Landy, *The Politics of Environmental Reform*, p. 142.

31. For a detailed chronicle of the passage of the strip-mine bill see Landy, *ibid.*, pp. 156–193.

10
New Jersey
MAUREEN MOAKLEY

New Jersey is something of a phantom state. As a physical place, a geographical location, its boundaries have long been established and its history and traditions stretch back to colonial times. The popular image of the state, however, is defined by an enduring and exaggerated stereotype. One thinks of the turnpike, of ugly industrial sprawl, of political corruption, and of New Jersey jokes. All stereotypes contain an element of truth and these images are real facts of life in the Garden State. The central reality behind these images is that they are the legacy of a highly individualistic political culture that resulted in a state politics that was all but invisible.

When Woody Allen quipped that, "A certain intelligence governs our universe except in certain parts of New Jersey," he hit on a fundamental truth about politics in the Garden State. If one takes intelligence to mean a rational, comprehensive force behind government, for many years there simply was none. State residents lacked a collective orientation and identified instead with their local communities. Political elites, whose fortunes were bound to powerful county organizations, viewed politics from a decidedly parochial perspective, and state government played only a minor role.

This reality is changing; New Jersey as a collective political entity has begun to emerge. However, the images are difficult to overcome because key aspects of political life are ingrained in the culture—in the parochial patterns of identification among citizens and elites.

POLITICAL CULTURE: NOBODY LOVES NEW JERSEY

The dominant fact in the political life in the Garden State is that New Jerseyans do not and never did identify with their state. While state chauvinism is generally less marked in the Northeast than elsewhere in the country, New Jersey is probably the extreme case. Many people from New

219

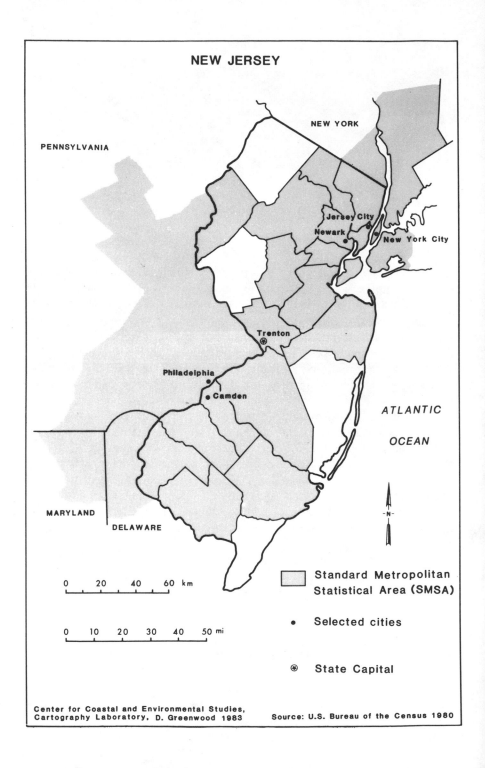

NEW JERSEY

NEW YORK

PENNSYLVANIA

Jersey City
Newark
New York City

Trenton

Philadelphia
Camden

ATLANTIC

OCEAN

MARYLAND

DELAWARE

-N-

0   20   40   60 km

0   10   20   30   40   50 mi

Standard Metropolitan
Statistical Area (SMSA)

• Selected cities

⊛ State Capital

Center for Coastal and Environmental Studies,
Cartography Laboratory, D. Greenwood 1983   Source: U.S. Bureau of the Census 1980

Jersey don't even like to say they're from New Jersey. Such lack of identification and low public consciousness has prevented anything that resembles an integrated statewide personality, and New Jersey as a state is considered to have the "largest inferiority complex in the Union."[1]

Public reaction to the interminable New Jersey jokes is symptomatic of the estrangement most New Jerseyans feel from their state. In other areas of the country, a public slur against one's place of residence invokes heated responses from citizen groups and elected officials and, in some cases, threats of legal action. In contrast, New Jersey put-downs have long been standard fare in northeastern humor. Indeed, it would seem that all aspiring stand-up comics along the eastern seaboard should have at least one brother-in-law from New Jersey. More recently, these quips have reached a new high or low—depending on one's perspective—in the attention given New Jersey humor in the national media. Johnny Carson's nightly monologue on the "Tonight" show frequently includes Garden State quips, and on "Saturday Night Live" Gilda Radner's Roseanne Rosannadanna periodically proclaims that living in New Jersey is so bad " . . . it makes me wanna' die."[2]

New Jerseyans take this all in stride, since in fundamental ways they themselves feel little connection with the state as a public entity. The political culture of the state is, in Elazar's terms, overwhelmingly individualistic. While there is little civic consciousness and often disdain for those things public, sources of satisfaction and any notions of the good society are essentially private. Politics is generally viewed as a necessary evil and most New Jerseyans take care to place some distance between themselves and the public order.

The negative images of the Garden State are belied by the fact that people like living here. A statewide poll on New Jersey images taken in 1980, asked a sample of residents to rate New Jersey as a place to live, and 68 percent answered "excellent" or "good." Moreover, when asked to compare life in New Jersey to other states, 71 percent of the sample thought living in the Garden State was "better" or "the same" as living in other states, while only 13 percent rated New Jersey as "worse" than other states.[3] However, such responses are based on perceptions of New Jersey as a physical place—on the natural environment.

The stereotype of a polluted industrial corridor notwithstanding, the Garden State has vast areas of farmland, stretches of beautiful ocean beach, mountains and lakes, as well as wooded suburban enclaves within commuting distance to New York or Philadelphia. When asked to rate two or three things they like most about New Jersey, most residents mentioned the natural environment, the overall quality of life, and the location convenient to New York or Philadelphia.[4] By way of contrast, New Jerseyans do not identify with most aspects of public life. In the same poll question, which was left completely open-ended, very few even mentioned any aspect of the public domain, such as education or other public services or any feature of government, as a source of satisfaction.

Where New Jerseyans do exhibit a high degree of chauvinism is at the local community level. New Jersey has always been a state of separate communities, and residents tend to view life from this perspective in a very positive light. All polling efforts indicate that New Jerseyans are consistently most satisfied with the character of their own local communities and the data suggest that residents engage in a pattern of selective perceptions on this score. Questions about the overall quality of government or public services generally elicit negative responses. Yet, these same questions focused at the local level prompt positive replies. In one poll, a large majority ranked problems of crime, pollution, and urban congestion as "serious" for New Jersey. Yet, these same respondents did not see these problems as "serious" in their own communities.[5] In another survey, people rated "the public schools" negatively, but then went on to give positive ratings to their own local public schools.[6] Such chauvinism, in the midst of the highly cosmopolitan megolopolis of the Northeast, takes on a kind of backwater parochialism that over the years has bred a marked indifference to the broader political environment.

Politically, this local ethic centers around the long-standing prerogatives of home rule. For citizens of the Garden State, this tradition has always been the dominant force behind public life and it would be difficult to overstate its importance in explaining the political, social, and economic development of the state. Recently, while discussing the seemingly intractable problems in overcoming insistence on local prerogatives in order to develop a comprehensive statewide program for dealing with the massive erosion of the state's shoreline and beaches, a former governor, Brendan Byrne, noted that while the issue of local control is a problem for all states, in New Jersey the concept of home rule is nothing short of religion.

This religion is as old as the state itself. The historical pattern of development in the Garden State was one of diverse and autonomous communities. To encourage settlement, communities of different ethnic and religious backgrounds were given a relatively free hand in managing their own internal affairs. Originally divided by the British into East and West Jersey, the orientation of the two Jerseys, in patterns of trade and communications, developed around the cities of Philadelphia and New York. Although this original cleavage was later transformed into an enduring north-south division, the primary orientation of New Jerseyans beyond their local communities is still focused on these two major cities. Along with home rule, the location of the state between these two major urban centers was a critical factor in the developing political culture of the state.

The pattern of historical development that encouraged localism was only intensified by waves of mostly poor and uneducated immigrants who came to New Jersey in large numbers especially after the Civil War. Streams of Dutch, British, Swedes, and Finns that settled in the state were followed by Irish, German, Russian Jews, Poles, Slavs, and Italians. More recently blacks and Hispanics have arrived in large numbers. New Jersey has always been more of a polygot than a melting pot in that many of these ethnic groups settle in the tight-knit communities that cling to their Old World origins and language. As a result, patterns of discrimination and tough ethnic infighting further promoted the parochial mentality that is the basis of individualistic politics.

While this type of politics reached its zenith in the form of political machines, for which New Jersey is justly renowned, parochialism in New Jersey goes beyond region or ethnic group or social class. A more contemporary variation has been dubbed the "Princeton mentality." Here, in one of the most affluent, well educated, and cosmopolitan areas of the state, constituents, in the words of one county politician, are intensely concerned about who gets elected to the local school board and who gets elected to the presidency—"The rest they forget."

While other states experience variations of the "Princeton mentality" as well as historical problems with localism and some form of sectionalism, the unique pattern of identification in New Jersey has had serious ramifications for the present. The orientations to one's community and beyond that to major metropolises outside the state have solidified the north-south cleavage and prevented the development of institutions and symbols of loyalty that, in other states, have encouraged a more modern statewide consciousness.

The north-south sectionalism that emerged after the Civil War still runs strong. The nature of this split has much to do with demographics; northern New Jersey is more industrialized, highly populated, and liberal, while the south is more rural and conservative. However, the influence of New York and Philadelphia reinforces these divisions. This is evident in language. People who grew up in south Jersey speak with a variant of a Philadelphia accent, while the speech of people raised in the northern part of the state resembles that of metropolitan New Yorkers. Feelings run particularly high in south Jersey where, especially after reapportionment reduced the political clout of southern legislators, people felt that this section of the state always got the short shrift. Recently, these tensions have abated somewhat as a home-building and industrial boom has transplanted many northerners downstate and brought increased prosperity to that area. However, the influence of New York and Philadelphia still deflects the orientations of New Jerseyans from their own state.

One reason for this has to do with media coverage and usage. Patterns of media coverage became established around New York and Philadelphia and with the growth of television (which has become the main source of news about government for most people), New Jersey lost out. The Garden State was, until most recently, one of two states in the Union that did not have its own VHF television station. Thus, coverage by commercial stations of New Jersey news events was limited to New York and Philadelphia networks. Although the FCC mandated that these out-of-state networks increase their coverage of New Jersey events, Garden State news inevitably has gotten minimal coverage—which further reinforces the existing orientations of residents away from their home state. Public television has produced a first-rate New Jersey nightly news show aired weekdays, but this broadcast cannot draw the audience that commercial networks command. Presently, however, one of New York's smaller commercial networks, WOR, is moving its home base to New Jersey as a condition for relicensing by the FCC.

In other states, identifications with professional or college sports teams promote a sense of pride and loyalty among residents. Until a short time ago, New Jersey had no major professional sports teams to call its own. Again, the loyalties of people were focused on major New York and Philadelphia teams; residents of northern New Jersey routinely followed New York teams while people in the south developed loyalties to Philadelphia clubs.

In the late 1960s, after a pitched battle over home rule involving local communities, the state established the Hackensack Meadowlands Development Commission, and began to reclaim 18,000 acres of swamp that had formerly been used as a dumping ground by industry and local communities. Part of the master plan called for construction of a sports complex that now includes a race track, a football stadium, and an indoor sports arena.

Residents of the Garden State now have their own teams to root for and they do so with considerable abandon. The New Jersey Nets basketball team presently draws much larger crowds than their counterparts, the Knicks, in New York. In 1976 the New York Giants' football team was successfully lured to a home base at the Meadowlands. Although present contract stipulations prevent the Giants from officially being called the New Jersey Giants, and the media still refer to them as a New York team, they have dropped the New York initials from their official logo and will probably come to be known as a Jersey team. In 1983 the New Jersey Generals, as part of the United States Football League, were established at the Meadowlands, and the New York Jets are scheduled to follow. The sports commission also lured the New York Cosmos soccer team and a Colorado hockey team, renamed the New Jersey Devils, to a home base here. These maneuvers prompted New York's former Governor Carey to remark that he's concerned everytime a New Jersey governor crosses the river into New York for fear of what he will take home with him.

Nonetheless, in terms of culture and entertainment, the influence of New York and Philadelphia have been overwhelming. New York, in particular, is a cultural center of such distinction that New Jersey's museums, performing groups such as opera, theater, ballet and symphony orchestras, as well as zoos and public parks, pale by comparison. When people in New Jersey say they are going to "the city," they mean they are going *out-of-state*. Approximately 12 percent of the labor force leaves the state daily for jobs elsewhere.[7] On Saturday night, 45 minute delays enroute to New York City are the norm and traffic jams at 2:00 a.m.—leaving the City for New Jersey—are not uncommon. Recent efforts at establishing performing-arts groups in New Jersey have been quite successful and such groups are probably comparable to performing companies in many other states. Still, the loyalties of a sizeable segment of the population, who would be most inclined to support the arts, remain focused elsewhere.

In some states, citizens' pride focuses on the state university. While Rutgers, the second oldest and largest institution of higher learning in the state, is nationally considered a state university of some renown, within the state, the university also has an image problem. A standing joke on campus was that the reputation of Rutgers got better the further away one got from New Jersey. These impressions, until recently, were probably deserved. As late as 1969, New Jersey had the dubious distinction of ranking 50th, nationwide in per capita spending for higher education.[8] During this time, one of New Jersey's largest exports was college students.

This is also changing. Funding has been increased by the legislature, enrollments have been expanded, and the university—ever mindful of its "image" problem—has channelled considerable funds into expanding sports facilities and programs, in an effort to gain broader recognition and support among state residents. Polls taken during the 1970s indicate that public approval of Rutgers shows a marked improvement. In 1978, 44 percent of state residents expressed "a lot of confidence" in the state university as compared with 33 percent in 1975.[9] Still, many New Jerseyans, particularly from more affluent communities, consider Rutgers a school of last resort; they prefer to spend substantial funds to send their children to less academically prestigious, but more socially acceptable, out-of-state colleges.

One of the less flattering images of New Jersey is the turnpike, but in many ways this 118-mile stretch of ugly toll road that cuts through the state, symbolizes a key aspect of expectations about government in New Jersey. The position of New Jersey, first along the transportation corridor between New York and Philadelphia, and then at the center of the major transportation network of the northeast, forestalled not only a collective sense of statewide identity and public consciousness, but also delayed a sense of responsibility on the part of state government.

During the early 19th century communities were developed and given broad local authority for the purpose of completing the rail route between New York and Philadelphia. By the end of the century, New Jersey became one of those states that was "owned" by the railroads. The state then became the end of the line for continental rail traffic. Spewing factories, refineries, and rail depots developed in a haphazard fashion around the state. During this time, tax revenues derived from railroads, banks, insurance companies, and toll fees virtually paid the bill to run the state.[10]

The construction of the turnpike in the 1950s added more economic development, more toll revenues, and more pollution and congestion, as well as creating the picture of New Jersey that most visitors come away with. The legacy of all this was a tradition of low taxation and low public expectations as to the role of state government in providing public services. It was not until 1962 that the state enacted a broad-based sales tax to support state spending and not until 1976 did the legislature, with prompting from the state supreme court, enact an income tax to sustain the growing needs of state government. So in a sense, until quite recently, the state was little more than a corridor or passageway and indeed traded on this fact.

While the role of state government has changed substantially over the past decade, negative perceptions remain. Polls taken over the past ten years indicate that ratings of the institutions of state government—the executive, the legislature, and the courts—have remained stable and pretty low. People remain indifferent and cynical about politics and government and these feelings tend to increase the further one gets from "home."

While we know that most Americans are generally more concerned with national and local news events,[11] residents of the Garden State appear even less inclined than other Americans to pay attention to state news. A joint state polling effort in Connecticut, Delaware, Kentucky, Massachusetts, New Hampshire, and New Jersey asked state residents about their interest in state politics. New Jersey was distinctive in two ways. It ranked last among these states in the number of residents who were "very" or "somewhat" interested, and first in the number of people who were only "a little" or "not at all" interested in state politics.[12]

Along with lack of interest, New Jerseyans display a noticeable lack of knowledge about state politics and officials in state government. Statewide polls conducted in 1980 found some curious patterns in the political knowledge of Garden State residents that clearly reflects the culture of the state. Although 87 percent of state residents could identify the governor, Brendan Byrne, who had been in office since 1973, only 33 percent of New Jerseyans could identify the then senior U.S. Senator Harrison Williams, who had been in office since 1958 and was, at the time of the survey, under national scrutiny for Abscam related activities. Moreover, only 25 percent of those polled could name Bill Bradley, a U.S. senator of some national celebrity. What was more telling, perhaps, was that in the same poll, the then governor of New York was much better known statewide than either of the state's U.S. senators. Fully 49 percent of all those polled could identify Hugh Carey, and among residents of the southern part of the state, 32 percent could identify Pennsylvania's Governor Richard Thornburg.[13]

In the 1981 gubernatorial election, national attention was paid to the fact that the winner, Republican Thomas Kean, won by the slightest margin— about 1800 votes—and the outcome, pending a recount, was up in the air for several weeks. While close races usually suggest high interest, a poll taken less than six weeks before the general election revealed that less than half of the residents of New Jersey even knew who was running for governor. At that time, more people could identify the mayor of New York, Edward Koch, than either of the gubernatorial candidates in their own state.[14]

New Jerseyans also appear to be a pretty cynical lot. In one survey, most state residents, 61 percent, viewed "politicians in general" in an unfavorable light—seeing them for the most part as incompetent and self-serving individuals who enter public office to serve their own interests.[15] When asked about politicians in New Jersey, however, 51 percent responded favorably. Curiously, when asked whether they thought politicians were more or less corrupt than people in other occupations, a full 71 percent figured there really was not much difference. Apparently, public cynicism among New Jerseyans is tinged with a healthy dose of realism and a chauvinism about their own.

Cynicism, indifference, and localism, however, do not translate into a kind of minimalist conservatism that often goes along with these attitudes in other states. People in New Jersey expect government to provide services. They always have. Particularly in the area of human services, the state has a long tradition of enacting progressive legislation. Even during the Gilded Age, when official corruption here as elsewhere in the country was in its heyday, the Garden State initiated a system of free public education, established welfare and correctional institutions, and created agencies to protect welfare and public health.[16]

Today, citizens not only expect these traditional activities, but also support a broad role for the government in the fields of health and child care, summer programs, senior-citizen aid, prison reform, and the like. With few exceptions and even during times of tight money, bond referendums have been supported by the state's voters. The political issue never was whether or not government should provide services, but rather, at what level of government these activities should be administered and, of course, who should pay.

Formerly, most public services, administered at the county and local levels, were funded through local property taxes. The resulting disparities and inadequacies in service were more the result of the fractionalized structure of politics than the minimalist orientation of citizens. In 1976, the New Jersey Supreme Court in *Robinson v. Cahill*, struck down New Jersey's system of financing public education through local property taxes. Reluctantly, the legislature, pushed to the wall when the courts closed the public schools, initiated a temporary statewide income tax that was due to expire in 1978. Since the late 1950s, chief executives had pushed for the adoption of such a tax, but found party leaders, and hence the legislature, intractable on this issue. Not only would such a structure of funding threaten the hegemony of local governments, but ultimately it was felt that, given the state's tradition of low taxes, New Jerseyans simply would not tolerate a statewide tax on income.

Thus, the gubernatorial election of 1977 became a virtual mandate on the issue of state income tax and, to the surprise of most everyone involved, New Jerseyans overwhelmingly supported it. Before the election, Brendan Byrne, the incumbent, was considered a virtual goner in that he had alienated most of the party bosses as well as most of the state's voters. His approval rating in the polls prior to the campaign was down to 21 percent. Moreover, he was campaigning on what was thought to be the most unpopular issue— the extension of the income tax as a permanent feature of fiscal policy. His Republican opponent, Raymond Bateman, a popular and well-connected state legislator, campaigned on a platform that included rescinding the income tax. As the campaign evolved, apparently voters came to realize that if public services were to be maintained on a satisfactory and equitable basis, they would have to pay up and accept a broader role for state government.

Moreover, at the time, the income tax was already in place; the alternative fiscal machinations proposed by the Republican opposition were untried (and, according to most press appraisals, unsound). Although early polls showed Bateman with a substantial lead, in the end, Byrne won handily.*

In other respects, political support in the Garden State remains akin to a two-track system. There is state and national government "out there" and then there is local government, with which people still seem more comfortable regardless of its faults. Depending on the character of the community, such support can take on a strong, almost tribal loyalty. Understanding New Jersey's reputation for tolerating corruption makes sense only within this context. Recent municipal elections provide a good example.

In May of 1982, nonpartisan municipal elections were held around the state. In Union City, William V. Musto, four-time incumbent mayor and member of the state legislature, won reelection. The previous day, Musto had been sentenced to seven years in prison on a charge of racketeering. On the same day in Newark, incumbent Mayor Kenneth Gibson ultimately won reelection. At that time, he and his strongest opponent, Earl Harris, were both under indictment on charges relating to a no-show job in city government. Subsequently, both Gibson and Harris were acquitted.

Out-of-state media, particularly the editorial pages of the *New York Times*, expressed a dotty outrage[17] that implied that political corruption was somehow unique to the Garden State. State papers, like Newark's *Star-Ledger* instead ruefully noted "the tolerant attitude of a sizeable segment of the electorate"[18]—alluding to the fact that what these elections reflected was the kind of intense solidarity that is characteristic of less affluent, ethnic communities of which there are many in New Jersey.

Union City is a lower-middle-class Italian community where Musto and his organization provided the kind of old style, machine help that tends to breed intense political loyalty. Moreover, not only was Musto one of them, but, as "dean" of the state senate, he was "somebody" in the state. Likewise, although blacks compromise over 10 percent of the state's population, they are relatively powerless in state politics. Newark is overwhelmingly black; Gibson is one of the few black politicians in the state with any political clout.

Local political support based on this kind of solidarity is quite common in New Jersey. Add to this the prerogatives of home rule, whereby contracts for public services are negotiated on an individual municipal basis, and the formula for political corruption becomes apparent. In New York City, for example, the contract for garbage collection that will service seven and one-half million residents is negotiated once; in New Jersey, garbage collection for the same number of people involves 567 individual contracts—presumably some of which will be subject to bribes and kickbacks.

---

*Byrne and the Democrats were undoubtedly aided by the timely mailing of property tax rebate checks that included an enclosure from the Governor. The checks arrived a few days before the general election.

And some are. The state's commission of investigation and attorney general's office are continually turning up instances of local political malfeasance. (Indeed, many in the state argue that the number of indictments in New Jersey is more a reflection of the overzealousness of these offices than any accurate indication of the extent of public corruption.) In July of 1982, the state commission of investigation recommended that the legislature delay the appropriation of $100,000,000 earmarked for local sewer projects, as hearings indicated that many local sewer and utility authorities were riddled by mismanagement and corruption.[19] While such occurrences are hardly typical of most localities in the state, there are a significant number of local communities in New Jersey where mismanagement and corruption are not unusual.

At the state level, however, things are different. New Jerseyans display neither sentimentality nor tolerance for corruption; any statewide public official connected with political malfeasance is not likely to survive. The case of Harrison Williams is instructive here. Although Williams had been a popular and respected senator in New Jersey for 24 years, upon his conviction in the Abscam case, his political support virtually disappeared. Most people were outraged at reports of his activities. In one poll taken shortly after the court trial, but prior to the Senate hearings, New Jerseyans were asked (in a question that allowed that the government may have acted illegally) whether they thought Williams should stay on or resign immediately. Only 20 percent of those surveyed thought Williams was fit to remain in office.[20]

In this sense, New Jerseyans expect honesty and efficiency from statewide officials and agencies—and for the most part, they get it. Political observers generally agree that although official corruption is still a problem at the local and county level, state government in New Jersey is relatively clean, particularly when compared to neighboring states like New York and Pennsylvania. Other observers are less sanguine about the ability of the state to resist official corruption in light of the gambling operations in Atlantic City that the state supervises. Thus far, however, the Casino Control Commission appears to be quite effective. A recent investigative series concluded that although the state incurred some failures at Atlantic City in terms of long-term planning and development, the "biggest success" has been in maintaining the integrity of the casino operation.[21]

POLITICAL STYLE: SMALL TOWN POLITICS

Political style reflects the culture and institutions of the Garden State. In terms of personnel style, one would want to note the diversity of individual actors as well as a basic shift from an old style machine orientation to a more professional, managerial ethic. Despite the change, the character of politics in the Garden State retains an interpersonal and face-to-face quality that sustains an informal and relatively closed political process. Politics in New Jersey is still small town.

First, diversity. Politicians in New Jersey reflect the heterogeneous character of the population. The garden variety WASP politician, who dominates politics in many other states, is in a minority here. Local candidates, state legislators, and congressmen are likely to reflect the ethnic and religious background of their constituencies. New Jersey has a substantial Catholic population (39 percent), and Catholics comprise a majority of the congressional delegation and dominate in the state legislature. Ethnic considerations are also important in local, county, and legislative politics. County party leaders are particularly sensitive to ethnic balancing in the slating of candidates; positions on freeholder boards, the county governing bodies, are often informally designated as "Jewish," "Polish," or "Italian" seats. In those legislative districts controlled by the party organizations, one's demographic background is a factor in party support for nomination to the legislature.

However, ethnic politics no longer appear important at the state level; except for the Irish, no other ethnic group ever solidified along party lines beyond the local level. At the turn of the century, the Irish vote, which was then solidly identified with urban Democratic machines, acquired sufficient political influence to take over a good deal of the state machinery at Trenton from the old guard Republicans.* While Irish surnames are still prominent among the political elite at the capitol in Trenton, this group, for the most part, has been absorbed into a broader culture and is no longer solidly Democratic.

Although Italians are now considered the the largest ethnic group in the state and are well-represented in elected offices, they never became a cohesive force in state politics. Their immigrant experience was different in that, initially, their partisan loyalties were divided. In the northern and urban parts of the state, these newcomers, like the Irish, were mostly poor and uneducated workers. Because they arrived a generation or two later, they were usually discriminated against by the Irish and were, in many cases, virtually locked out of the existing Democratic organizations. Hence, many urban Italians, who by virtue of their socio-economic status and religion would have normally identified with the Democratic party, became Republicans by default. Other Italians, who were farmers by trade, migrated to rural areas in south and west New Jersey where more discreet—but equally powerful Republican machines—persuaded these newcomers that it was in their interest to register Republican.†

---

*There are wonderful turn-of-the-century accounts of the reactions of aghast old guard Republican legislators, as the "rabble" of the Irish "barroom loungers" and "cheap sports" first arrived at the state capitol and periodically returned en masse when Democratic gubernatorial candidates were successful.[22]

† These organizations engaged in the kind of distribution of material benefits one commonly associates with urban organizations. Indeed, the proverbial "buckets of coal" were not unique to urban Democrats. During the early Depression a rationing system for coal and foodstuffs, by way of voucher, and based on assessed need, was established in rural areas. Vouchers were simply easier to get with more generous allotments for all "good" Republicans.

These cleavages appear to have held. In the 1981 gubernatorial election, an issue was made over the prospect that, after years of Irish domination, the office of the governor would finally be available to an Italian who had won the Democratic nomination. Although the candidate, James Florio, stressed his family's immigrant background and his own self-made success story, the "Italian" vote just never materialized. Instead, New Jerseyans elected Thomas Kean,the patrician Republican candidate whose ancestors included the first governor of the state.

While the ethnic image tends to dominate, New Jersey has a long and distinguished tradition of old guard, old money politicians who have always been active in state politics. Representative of a more traditional Republican constituency, this group, which eschews the more hardball approach to politics, often represents a type of loyal opposition to Democratic regimes in state politics. The political base of these Republicans centers in and around the exclusive estate land and horse country in the central part of the state. Governor Kean and ex-Congresswoman Millicent Fenwick are part of this tradition. Both enjoy inherited wealth and a distinguished social and political lineage, and both engage in politics with a distinctive touch of *noblesse oblige*. Well-spoken but low key, cultured but not chic,* they represent a cadre that has always been a presence in the statehouse and the Congress.

Of course, the rapid suburbanization of the state has affected a certain blending of styles. Politicians from New Jersey's many middle-class suburban communities look more like their counterparts in other states than any ethnic or social prototype. Political office, especially in these communities, is becoming highly competitive and, increasingly, hard work and hustle matter more than background characteristics.

Another notable feature of political style connected with this change would be a discernible shift in the perspectives of elites—particularly at the state level—away from a narrow machine ethos toward a more professional and statewide orientation.

While the vehicle of politics in New Jersey has always been the political parties, never in the state's recent history has there been anything that resembled a statewide party organization. Politics in the Garden State, until a very short time ago, had been conducted by partisan and shifting coalitions of strong county-based organizations. Hence, there was little in either the political culture or the structure of politics to encourage a statewide perspective or assimilation into a broader, policy-oriented political milieu. For most elected officials at the municipal, legislative, and county levels, it was expected that they would get what they could for their district or party (and maybe for themselves) and if things fell right, support broader policy initiatives. Moreover, the *quid pro quo* for such support was usually ample

---

*Shortly after being elected governor, Kean was named by a New York clothier to a national best-dressed list. This caused considerable amusement among his staff, who noted that the governor's style of dress ran more toward rumpled Ivy than New York chic.

amounts of pork, patronage, and favor trading. By current standards, ethics were fairly loose; deals and "honest graft" were the norm.

While such "old style" orientations still exist, things are changing statewide. There is a growing cadre of high-quality political elites whose orientations are decidedly statewide, whose political and policy preferences are geared toward a more modern notion of the public interest, and whose ethics exhibit a high degree of probity. This group includes present and past statewide officeholders and candidates, members of the congressional delegation, statewide bureaucrats primarily employed in and around executive departments, prestigious attorneys who take stints at public service, judges, a number of state legislators, and a few key lobbyists. This highly influential group is serious about the quality of state government in New Jersey, highly sensitive to the need to overcome the legacy of the past, and determined to bring some cohesion to the fractionalized character of politics.

Despite these shifts, politics retains a decidedly down-home cast. Political interactions—in a highly industrialized and urbanized state, with seven and a half million residents, in the center of a major megalopolis— reflect a curious small-town quality. Because the state is geographically small and the capital at Trenton is within commuting distance, most political functions are accessible; there is an informal network of associations that politicians stay plugged into. Members of the political elite know one another personally. Politics is primarily face-to-face and loyalty counts. One makes contacts, trades information and favors, and relies on established networks and friendships for political support.

The character of the mass media lends to the down-home style of New Jersey politicians. Public officials are not groomed by the media. Because of the fractured nature of the television market, statewide television campaigns are extremely expensive. Time purchased for the New York market reaches only half the state and has to be duplicated in the Philadelphia market for state coverage. Local candidates use television infrequently and even statewide candidates need not cultivate a commanding media image in order to be elected. Only in the most recent state elections have candidates shifted their focus to television. Moreover, once elected, public officials are seldom the object of extensive media scrutiny. Since commercial coverage of New Jersey politics is minimal, rarely do political elites have to face extended television coverage and explain the activities of their administrations. When they do, this lack of grooming shows. Few members of the political elite have developed a polished media presence.

Strong personal leadership is still what counts most in New Jersey politics and all the state's recent chief executives—who besides the two U.S. senators are the only individuals elected statewide—reflect this dominant trait. In his study of American governors from 1950 through 1975, Larry Sabato ranked the governors from all 50 states on the characteristics of "firmness," "ability," and "principle."[23] All New Jersey governors, except

Brendan Byrne (1974–1981), qualified by Sabato's criteria as "outstanding leaders." We would add Byrne to that list.*

These governors were all strong leaders who used a variety of personal skills within the structure of government to get things done. None were known for their commanding public presence. None were charismatic folk. Brendan Byrne is a good example. While Bryne was regarded by those in government as a knowledgeable, adroit, and forceful leader (when he cared about an issue), he was generally perceived as somewhat inept in front of large audiences and pretty bad on television. A New Hampshire legislator, on a visit to New Jersey, attended a political dinner at which Byrne gave the keynote address. After the speech, the legislator noted with amazement that in 1980, in a state like New Jersey, the chief executive could be so inarticulate and "downright hokey."

The present governor, Thomas Kean, came up through the ranks of the state legislature and has been in and around New Jersey politics for over 20 years. His political support in the gubernatorial race was based on established political networks rather than any broad, popular following. His political style is especially low-key. Kean comes across as warm and personable with small audiences, and like his predecessors, deals most effectively in small, informal groups. He is not a media man in any sense of the term. His television presence, although thoughtful and competent, is not particularly commanding. Moreover, in an effort to play down his patrician background, he sometimes affects a "regular guy" demeanor that lends a certain awkwardness to his image. When patrician Governor Nelson Rockefeller of New York donned a hard hat, it worked; when Kean models a new bullet proof vest for state troopers on a local nightly news show, he looks out of place.

An interpersonal and informal style of executive leadership seems to fit well with the character of the policy process. Although New Jersey ranks among the highest states in the nation in terms of population, urbanization, industrialization, and per-capita income, policy institutions are relatively underdeveloped.[24] Policymaking is still conducted in a closed, informal, and highly pragmatic way. Big government, on the order of New York, does not exist in New Jersey. Individuals, especially politically astute ones, still make a difference and bureaucratic layering and rigid formal channels rarely obstruct the course of political maneuverings. As Alan Rosenthal has noted, "What has counted in New Jersey are the ends, and the means are significant only insofar as they serve to achieve the ends. . . . Today things have tightened up considerably, but the processes still tend to be expeditious."[25]

---

*Byrne took office in 1974 and Sabato concluded his analysis in 1975. Although Byrne's performance at the beginning of his tenure was somewhat lackluster, his eight years in office were marked by significant achievements, and he will no doubt be remembered as an outstanding governor.

Policy formulation in New Jersey has always been relatively open-ended and decentralized.[26] Besides the executive agenda, initiatives from individual legislators, study commissions and standing committees, as well as proposals from interest groups and lobbyists, find their way to the legislature. Reports in newspapers such as the *Star-Ledger* and decisions of the judiciary also influence the policy agenda.[27] In such an open system, innovative initiatives have a way of surfacing and gaining the attention of the executive. New Jersey's history of enacting progressive social legislation is, in no small measure, related to the openness of the formulation process.

By way of contrast, the adoption process tends to be closed and centralized around the executive. Indeed, until the 1970s, the process could be described as quasi-feudal. Much of the more progressive legislation enacted in New Jersey in more modern times—like extensive programs to aid and protect the aged, high standards of automobile safety and emissions, environmental control legislation, and public financing of elections—was a result of this informal process. As a senior aide to Governor Byrne explained:

> Up until only a few years ago, if you wanted something done in New Jersey, you [the governor] called up a few leaders, sat down with them, made some deals and you got your policy. . . . The interesting thing was that seldom were these "few leaders" members of the state legislature. Usually they were a few notables and party bosses who so tightly controlled their legislative delegation—that if they agreed, you had your policy.

A story is told about Harry Lerner, the Democratic boss of Essex County, until the 1970s. When he instructed a state senator on a particular vote before the legislature, the senator complained that a vote as Lerner requested would be against the interests of the senator's constituency. Lerner then reminded him, "I am your constituency." The senator went along.

The process has changed considerably. Party bosses, who seldom were involved with the substance of policy, no longer streamline the process; policymaking is conducted within a much more professionalized setting, in which legislative leaders play a more active role. On any given initiative, the governor now has to reach out to a series of elites concerned, in order to get proposals enacted. In this sense, the mobilization and enactment process is more fragmented and decentralized and, from the governor's perspective, more difficult.

Overall, however, the process retains an informal character and remains dominated by the behind-the-scenes maneuvering of a relatively few legislative leaders and executive staff. When the governor and the legislature are controlled by the same party, the process is relatively smooth. The governor gets at least some of what he wants and the legislature gets at least some of what it wants. However, in those instances when partisan control is divided, the process is increasingly more difficult. That was the situation most recently when Republican Governor Thomas Kean faced a Democratic legislature. In part, increased partisanship among Democratic and Republican leadership has caused many issues, that normally would be informally resolved, to become political in nature. What has been happening lately may only be a ripple in an otherwise fluid system still characterized by give-and-take and trade-offs. In other states, when such stand-offs occur, a governor might be inclined to expand the scope of conflict and even take his cause to the voters. In New Jersey, Kean's success with his agenda would appear most likely to depend on his ability to maneuver quietly and informally with those key political actors that pretty much define the process.

POLITICAL INTERACTION: GREATER THAN THE SUM OF ITS PARTS

If the character of statewide politics is ultimately linked to the broader political culture, then New Jerseyans' interaction with state government indicates a growing, if somewhat unfocused, statewide awareness. Patterns of participation in the Garden State traditionally have been viewed as a reflection of low public consciousness and indifference—leaving the conduct of nominations and elections to county-based party organizations. Since the early 1970s, and especially since 1977, major changes have altered the political landscape. While participation by the rank and file has increased, the influence of New Jersey's powerful county organizations has declined.

The national decline in electoral participation appears to have reversed itself in New Jersey state elections. Traditionally, turnout in primary elections here was so low that party organizations virtually had their way in controlling access to elected office. Recently, however, more New Jerseyans appear to be getting into the act.

Primary turnout in gubernatorial and congressional races shows slight but steady increases.[28] Turnout in the gubernatorial primaries went from 23.9 in 1973 to 28 percent in 1977 to 29.4 percent in 1981. In congressional races, primary turnout rose from 16.4 percent in 1974 to 20 percent in 1978 to 23 percent in 1982. Primary turnout in the off-year legislative races of 1975 and 1979 remained around 13 percent, and increased slightly to 15 percent in 1983. Because of the off-year structure of New Jersey state elections, these races occur when no national, statewide, or congressional candidates are on the ballot.

The increased turnout in primaries in New Jersey has been especially important to Republicans. For a number of years, Republican primaries were dominated by a small portion of hard-core conservatives who were inclined to nominate conservative ideologues. These candidates would secure the Republican nomination, but then go on to get swamped in the general election. The increase in primary turnout has brought more moderate Republicans to the primary polls and placed more viable Republican candidates on the ballot.

In statewide general elections, the same pattern holds. The last three gubernatorial elections indicate an upward trend. The 1973 decline in turnout of 11 percent was slowed to a 1.4 percent decrease in 1977. By 1981, turnout increased by about two points as 44 percent of the eligible voters cast a ballot for governor. In the 1982 congressional races, turnout, which traditionally is lower than that of gubernatorial elections, increased again to 45 percent.

In presidential elections, however, turnout in New Jersey still reflects the national trend. Since 1960, it shows slight but steady decreases; while 71.4 percent of voting age citizens cast a ballot in 1960, only 55.8 percent voted in 1980. In each of these races, turnout in New Jersey remained just above the national average.

Another notable aspect of citizen participation is the response of New Jerseyans to the volunteer check-off on the state income tax return to publicly finance the gubernatorial primary and general election. Seventeen states, some of which are the most progressive in the nation, have initiated some form of public funding for these elections. Participation in the form of a check-off varies among these states, but the average rate among all other states is about 16 percent.[29] The rate of participation in New Jersey, however, is a surprising 39 percent. What that means is that in the past two elections, almost as many people who vote in state elections are willing to allocate money from their tax returns to fund these elections. While this response probably indicates that New Jerseyans are not particularly sanguine about the quality of the electoral process as tied to old-style party politics, it also suggests that they are willing to give the reform alternative a try.

If one had to consider the most significant change in New Jersey politics over the past decade, it would be the decline of county political organizations. Formerly state politics was pretty much defined by partisan coalitions of these organizations. Although the state has long been considered competitive at the statewide level, most counties were solidly one-sided in terms of partisan distribution; as late as 1977, only 5 of the state's 21 counties were ranked as competitive.[30] Democratic strongholds in Hudson, Mercer, Camden, and Middlesex were critical to Democratic statewide candidates, while Republicans looked for support to Morris, Somerset, Burlington, Cape May, and Hunterdon. Until the early 1970s, partisan groups of county chairs and a few key politicos would "pick" a gubernatorial candidate and enjoy direct access to the statehouse if their nominee won in the general election. If not, the "out" organizations—still completely autonomous—reigned over county and local politics and enjoyed indirect access to Trenton through their legislative delegation. Thus, until the tenure of Brendan Byrne, a few county-based elites usually dominated nominations to the statehouse and the Congress and virtually controlled access to the state legislature and the county freeholder boards.

The decline of county organizations came in the wake of shifting demographic patterns that upset established power bases along with the state supreme court rulings on reapportionment. The most critical of these was the 1972 ruling in *Scrimminger v. Sherwin*, which mandated that county boundaries need not be considered in drawing up state legislative districts. Thereafter, these organizations continually lost political ground and influence. The 1973 nomination of Brendan Byrne was the last to be engineered by a few party elites and, even in this one, the official influence of the county chairmen was minimal. After the election, when the Democratic county leaders arrived in Trenton with their empty "favor baskets," they found the game had changed. The party chairs no longer had a leg to stand on in terms of political influence and access to extensive executive patronage.

Once the chairmen lost power, the influence of organized parties steadily eroded. In 1977, Bryne was renominated without the support of most of the Democratic county leaders. The U.S. Senate primary contest of 1978 saw the regular organizational candidates in both parties lose their bids for the nomination to two outsiders who had only recently moved into the state. In the Republican contest, the U.S. Senate incumbent since 1955, Clifford Case, lost to a conservative newcomer, Jeffrey Bell. On the Democratic side, Bill Bradley, also a newcomer to New Jersey, swamped a number of organizational candidates. Moreover, several state legislators were successful in running off the organizational line—a most unusual feat in New Jersey politics.

This trend is exacerbated by the fact that ties to political parties are increasingly tenuous for a growing number of New Jerseyans. Over 40 percent of the electorate now consider themselves Independent—with the trend over the past five years showing a net loss of Democratic identifiers (from 36 to 31 percent) and a similar gain of those who consider themselves Republicans (from 18 to 22 percent). When pressed, many in this group of Independents will express leanings toward one of the parties, leaving the hard core of Independents closer to 13 percent.[31] Nonetheless, the partisan character of the state now includes a significant portion of "soft" identifiers, who rely more on short-term factors than on enduring partisan commitments at election time. Thus, statewide and presidential contests are highly competitive and unpredictable. In the last two presidential elections, although Democrats enjoyed the nominal edge, the state went for Ford in 1976 and Reagan in 1980.

Statewide contests are particularly volatile. Strong candidates with sizeable early leads are apt to experience dramatic declines and reversals, as a large uncommitted vote "breaks" a week or even days before the election. In 1977, gubernatorial incumbent Byrne, who was far behind in the polls, overtook his opponent in a last-minute surprise victory. The following gubernatorial contest saw the early 16-point lead of the strong and popular contender, James Florio, evaporate into a narrow loss to Republican Thomas Kean. Perhaps the most stunning upset was the U.S. Senate race in 1982.

Republican Millicent Fenwick was considered unbeatable, so much so that some likely Democratic contenders chose not to run. By election day, her 22-point lead had eroded and the seat was won by an unknown, but very wealthy, newcomer to politics, Democrat Frank Lautenberg.

Although party matters a great deal less among the rank and file, the climate of state politics remains highly partisan. Elites at all levels of government expect the political game to be played along party lines. The executive appointments of each administration are all made with an eye toward party affiliation, and executive patronage is an accepted fact of life. Whenever possible, state jobs will go to loyal partisans and their families. The Byrne Democratic administration even insisted on clearing all state summer jobs through the governor's office. His Republican successor continued the practice. In the summer of 1982, when teenage employment was at a national and statewide high—particularly in poor, urban areas— Governor Kean announced that all state summer jobs would be available first to loyal Republicans and their families. Few partisans raised any objections.

The 1981 congressional redistricting, drawn by a Democratic legislature, was a classic piece of partisan mischief. The Democrats attempted to convert an eight-to-seven congressional edge into a solid eleven-to-three plurality; New Jersey had lost one seat. The shape of one district—stretching from the northern urban waterfront down toward the center of the state at Princeton and back up toward the shore—should be used in introductory texts on American government as a classic example of a political gerrymander. Districts were specifically drawn to accommodate new Democratic challengers and a couple of Republican incumbents had to change their place of residence in order to run again. The plan initially paid off. While two of the Democrats more grandiose attempts at seats failed to win the approval of the voters, the delegation tallied a solid nine-to-five in favor of the Democrats.*

There is much less cohesion to statewide partisan politics now. The declining influence of the county chairs has created a structural vacuum at the top that has yet to be filled. The state committees, whose members are often regarded with disdain by old-line party regulars, have little authority. Nominations and elections for statewide and congressional office increasingly are becoming more candidate oriented and pollsters and professional campaign managers are assuming the role once played by party regulars. Whatever their faults, the county bosses and party elites lent considerable cohesion to electoral politics in New Jersey and, in the course of their political maneuvering, managed to provide the state with able executive leadership.

---

*In June 1983, however, the U.S. Supreme Court ruled against the plan and has mandated that the districts be redrawn for the next congressional election.

While interest groups exercise considerable influence, they do not completely dominate the political scene at Trenton. A comprehensive survey of interest-group strength in the state concluded that "New Jersey has a pressure-group system which can best be described as fairly strong."[32] While there are a few very powerful groups, most interests are organizationally fragmented and decentralized. Hence, while some interests can be very effective in lobbying for specific proposals, their collective influence, across broad areas of public policy, is generally limited. New Jersey, by and large, is not an interest-group state.

The most powerful lobby in the state is the New Jersey Educational Association (NEA), a well-organized and cohesive group that represents most of the state's public school teachers.[33] For years this association, which is considered one of the best organized teachers groups in the country, pretty much had its way on state education policy. Its influence, however, appears to have peaked insofar as public study commissions, school-board associations, and a rival teachers group (the New Jersey Federation of Teachers) are becoming increasingly involved in the politics of education. In addition, a state supreme court decision in 1978 severely restricted the negotiating prerogatives of public school teachers. The association, primarily through substantial campaign contributions, still enjoys a great deal of leverage in the legislature and is currently pushing a bill that will negate the 1978 court ruling that overturned many of the negotiating rights that the NEA felt it had already won from the legislature. However, given declines in school enrollments, aid to education, and Scholastic Aptitude Test scores among New Jersey students, public support for "teachers prerogatives" is likely to be guarded. Moreover, the rise of countervailing forces on questions of education policy and the election of a Republican governor who is bent on generally limiting the collective bargaining rights of teachers, suggest that this most powerful and professional group faces rough going in the future.

Business interests are traditionally viewed as being only moderately effective in New Jersey state politics.[34] This may be changing now. As in other northeastern states suffering from the Sun Belt boom, the growth and viability of industry increasingly is seen as critical to the health of the state's economy and employment opportunities for state residents. Corporate, real estate, and personal income tax policy are geared toward attracting new industry and well-paid executives to a home in New Jersey. Moreover, key corporate entities like Johnson and Johnson, Prudential Insurance, New Jersey Bell, and American Telephone and Telegraph have sponsored huge corporate investments in development and renewal projects around the state. While such investments were spurred by generous tax incentives, the corporate posture of these groups, for the most part, has been civic-minded and responsible. Insofar as their interest and the public interest coincide, these corporations enjoy considerable influence and prestige in Trenton. When and if these interests diverge, however, the corporate position is likely to be formidable. The business community as a whole, however, and particularly medium- and smaller-sized concerns, is still highly factionalized and thus not particularly powerful in state politics. Presently, the New Jersey Business and Industry Association is attempting to solidify this community and expand its influence in the state.

Even influential industries sometimes lose. The wholesale liquor lobby, which is controlled by a handful of family concerns that have dominated the industry since Prohibition, enjoys enormous influence in Trenton. While the liquor lobby was successful in beating back a recent proposal to impose a tax on alcoholic beverages, it lost on the issues of industry deregulation and the extension of the drinking age. Builders and developers have, through substantial PAC money, gained considerable leverage in the legislature. However, when pitted against state agencies and environmentalists on the issue of development in and around the Pinelands (an area earmarked as a land preserve in the southern part of the state), these interests were saddled with severely restrictive development and building codes.

Organized labor has been only moderately influential in New Jersey politics. Over the years, the power of the unions has been hampered by ideological as well as organizational factionalization within their ranks.[35] Moreover, since World War II, membership has declined so that the unions represent just over one-quarter of the total nonagricultural work force in the Garden State. In past years, the unions were perceived to be critical to the Democratic party in key local and statewide elections. They enjoyed favor during Democratic administrations and secured many of their "bread and butter" goals. More recently, the unions' vaunted power in producing votes, money, and campaign workers for Democratic candidates, appears to be waning. Their failure to establish long-term networks in state government has further diminished their political influence at the statehouse, particularly during Republican administrations.

The health services are well represented in state politics, but again, most interests are organized in separate and comparatively small units. Hence, their influence over broad policy issues is restricted. Dentists, as the largest contributors to political campaigns, are regarded as active and powerful and fairly successful on policy questions important to them. A nice example of their influence on nitty-gritty issues was during the 1979 gas shortage. When New Jersey went to an odd/even day rationing system, dentists were initially exempt; medical doctors were not. Physicians, as part of the large and prestigious Medical Society of New Jersey, enjoy influence, but have not been particularly active in lobbying efforts at the statehouse. However, as state government assumes a broader role in administering medical transfer payments, doctors are likely to flex political muscle about their concerns in Trenton.

Other groups exert influence in a more informal manner. The major banks, formally through lobbyists and informally through key officers, circulate with the political elite in Trenton and enjoy input on matters of importance to them. Pharmaceutical companies enjoy leverage, particularly at the local and county levels, and have successfully kept their interest in the fore in light of the state's efforts at toxic waste cleanup. The New Jersey Bar Association, while not active as a formal lobby, by virtue of the sheer numbers of attorneys involved in all aspects of politics, enjoys influence at every level of state government.

Civic associations have become more visible over the years.[36] Groups like the League of Women Voters, Common Cause, and environmental associations have developed research staff and professional leadership that have increased their influence on some policy issues. Particularly when aided by the state's major newspapers, which from time to time take up their causes, these groups have promoted a growing civic consciousness among a broader constituency in the state.

Overall, although there are many strong pressure systems and a few key interests that enjoy considerable influence, the diversity of the state's economy, the competitive nature of the political process, and the rise of countervailing organizations has prevented the ascendency of interest-group politics. While one could cite numerous examples of individual interests thwarting the policy agenda on specific proposals, there is no evidence of monolithic organizations that consistently either define or dominate the political process in New Jersey.

The print media play an important role in defining and influencing the policy agenda and exercise substantive influence on the political life of the state. In the absence of adequate television coverage, New Jerseyans are forced to rely on newspapers for information about state politics. While it was always thought that New York and Philadelphia newspapers held a sizeable readership in New Jersey, a recent poll found that only 18 percent of the population gets their news from out-of-state papers while about 75 percent of the state residents read a New Jersey daily.[37] Although the *Trenton Times* is read in and around the capitol, the *Star-Ledger* has the biggest circulation statewide and has become a political force to be reckoned with. The *Star-Ledger* does a first-rate job in covering statewide news, and also runs public policy and investigative series that often affect the state's policy agenda and influence levels of public support.

In contrast to politically powerful publications in other states, press coverage of politics in New Jersey is neither vindictive nor arrogant. Papers like the *Ledger* are fairly vigilant and obtrusive in investigating and exposing instances of public inefficiency and malfeasance, and stories in that paper have caused political embarrassment and prompted resignations in successive administrations. However, coverage is rarely personalized around individuals and news reporters accord, if not deference, at least a certain respect for the private lives of politicians. Personal peccadillos of public officials, which might be common knowledge among political folk and grist for the political-gossip mill, are not likely to appear in print.

For the governor, deference is the norm. While the press routinely takes issue with actions in and around each administration, personal coverage of the chief executive is limited and that which occurs tends toward folksy and complimentary. A minor brouhaha over Governor Kean's refusal to move into the newly refurbished executive mansion at Princeton received only summary attention in the press and indications of some misunderstandings between the governor's wife and the New Jersey Historical Society, which funded and supervised the restoration, were never pursued. A governor of New Jersey is not likely to be subject to the intense and often mean-spirited personal scrutiny that, say, Hugh Carey had to endure during his tenure as governor of New York.

In terms of governmental power in New Jersey, the executive dominates. The power of the governor rests on formal constitutional authority, a tradition of strong executive leadership, and the lack of any individual or collective rivals to his authority. Other political actors or groups may exert influence from time to time, but overall, the governor runs the political show.

Since the adoption of the new state constitution in 1947, New Jersey governors have enjoyed broad formal authority. In comparative state rankings, New Jersey governors come out on top with the most constitutional authority of all state executives.[38] As the only statewide elected official, the governor is endowed with extensive administrative authority and very broad powers of appointment. Hence, he sits at the top of a centralized and hierarchical executive. In addition, the provisions of the governor's veto include a conditional and item veto. These allow the chief executive considerable leverage in the legislature and most times New Jersey governors get what they want from the legislative branch and brook no infringement of their authority.

Formal power is only enhanced by a strong tradition of gubernatorial dominance. Regardless of the individual in office, it is expected that the governor will lead. As Rosenthal has noted, "Here the contemporary governor has dominated, and has dominated no matter what individuals bearing what party labels happened to have held office in the executive and legislative branches."[39]

While the system allows for give and take, on key issues the governor is expected to lead the way and assume responsibility for the direction of public policy. During the resolution of the 1983 budget, the Democratic senate and assembly came off the blocks fighting and did win some early concessions from the executive on several budget proposals. However, when the tax package came up for a vote, the Democratic legislature successfully (and somewhat to its own surprise) defeated the governor's revenue proposals and pressed, somewhat haltingly, for an escalation of the income tax instead. As the debate dragged on, it became apparent that the house and senate leadership had not expected to remain out in front. They assumed that somewhere along the line the governor would exercise forceful leadership, contain the debate, and assume responsibility for the final package. Kean, whose style of leadership is not geared to hardball tactics, was criticized afterward by Republicans and Democrats alike, for not taking control and leading the way. But a compromise tax package was enacted and a state budget was subsequently adopted.

Another component of gubernatorial dominance is the lack of any enduring opposition to the governor's authority. As we have noted, county leaders were once in a formidable position in that the governor usually had to rely on their influence in the legislature to enact key proposals; with their passing from the statehouse scene, power has become more fragmented and dispersed. Depending on the situation or the issue, different elites or various groups can wield substantial influence and obstruct aspects of the executive agenda. Still, there are no institutions, collectives, or individuals that pose any enduring counterpoint to executive authority in New Jersey.

Certainly the New Jersey legislature is not up to that task. Legislators in New Jersey were for so long instruments of local and county parties, that an anti-legislature tradition still runs strong in state politics. Over the past decade, the capacity of the legislature to actively participate in the policy process has improved considerably and the legislative branch has assumed a much more important role in state politics. However, for reasons that are probably tied to the legacy of the past, this institution, as a collective body, appears to lack the direction or commitment to accomplish anything near co-equal status with the executive.

Institutional supports have been expanded and improved. Working sessions have been extended and committees, which for many years existed in name only, have developed the capacity to divide labor, promote specialization, and facilitate a level of legislative expertise.[40] Staff has been increased and committee aides, fiscal analysts, leadership and caucus staff, and assistants to individual legislators are available to assist in the policy process. These changes have made a difference. Committees have assumed a much broader role in policy development and key legislative leaders are involved in every step of the process. On occasion, the legislature has even performed admirably, most notably on the development of several state income tax packages. On many difficult initiatives, however, the legislature is more inclined to pass the buck.

Periodically, the legislature indulges in passing questionable legislation to satisfy members' constituents with the implicit understanding that the governor will "take the heat" and veto their proposals. However, in the past governors have used considerable political muscle to assure that in those instances, there was no override of the gubernatorial veto. Again, Kean had problems with this system during his first year. In one instance, the legislature passed a constitutionally dubious bill mandating a moment of silence at the beginning of each day in all New Jersey public schools. Kean vetoed the bill, but in "good government" fashion encouraged members of the legislature to follow their individual consciences on this matter. The governor's veto was overridden, the state's attorney general refused to defend the legislature on behalf of the state, and the issue was placed before the courts.

Legislators in New Jersey are still part-time commuters who come to Trenton one or two days a week. Under such a system, long range commitment is hard to come by; members want to dispatch their business and go home. Moreover, leadership positions are usually rotated on a biennial basis, limiting leadership continuity. Although turnover among individual members has abated, many of the more policy-oriented members move up or out. While the legislature has become much more involved in the policy process recently, there is still a general reluctance to stake out a broader role for the institution.

Such reluctance is not shared by the courts. In New Jersey patterns of recruitment, court organization, and judicial administration all combine to make the state judicial system one of the most respected in the nation. In a state where other institutions of government, particularly the legislature, were relatively underdeveloped, a tradition of judicial activism evolved. Individual justices generally combine a strong sense of legal professionalism and an activist orientation that runs counter to the notion that the courts should refrain from setting or influencing the political agenda. One justice, commenting on the role courts played in a reapportionment case, expressed the prevailing orientation of the state's judiciary: "They should have known better. They should have known that no thicket was too political for us."[41]

And in they wade. Decisions rendered by the courts were the driving force behind the enactment of the statewide income tax, the breakup of the county parties' hold on the legislature, the development of the Meadowlands sports complex, and the establishment of state ownership over some local shoreline property. Also, by declaring the local property tax formula for funding education unconstitutional, and mandating "thorough and efficient" statewide standards for education, and also revoking exclusionary local zoning, the courts have severely curtailed the influence of home rule in New Jersey.

Government agencies also look to the courts to secure policy objectives. As one New Jersey official noted: "Many government officials find the legislative process so slow and painful that they come to rely on the courts. Sometimes you need an ally and you look around and all you see is the court. . . . Government officials are constantly being sued to do things they really want to do anyway."[42]

Over the past two decades, the judiciary has had a profound influence on the character of politics in New Jersey. While the federal courts initiated the breakup of organized crime's influence in the state, state courts laid the groundwork for curtailing corruption and influence peddling in the county court system. Both systems in the judiciary are especially zealous in maintaining high ethical standards. The state judiciary has also sustained the socially progressive policy tradition in New Jersey and, along the way, staked out a broader role for state government.

In terms of power, the situation at the top in New Jersey is soft and fluid. While the governor clearly dominates, depending on the issue, various elites or groups exercise substantial influence. In some cases, powerful forces like the courts, the legislature, or the press intervene; most times factionalized forces such as interest groups and local or county officials obstruct initiatives and whittle away at proposed change. On broad and difficult initiatives, like the development of mass transit, collective obstructions can be over-whelming. Most times, however, things get through.

Presently in New Jersey, there is much talk about a state renaissance. The potential of valuable waterfront property along the Hudson River, which for years was little more than an industrial dumping ground, is being realized and units of middle- and upper-middle class developments are sprouting up in place of the industrial eyesores that once lined the turnpike. Older cities, like Newark, Hoboken, Jersey City, and New Brunswick, are also undergoing extensive urban renewal and with the influx of Greenwich Village expatriots, some spots are becoming downright fashionable. The success of the Meadowlands project and the notoriety of the newly arrived professional sports teams have all contributed to the notion that the state of New Jersey is being reborn.

In a fundamental political sense, however, this misses the point. What these and other trends signify is the emergence of New Jersey as a state, the parameters of which are just taking shape. The restructuring of the tax system has mitigated the power of home rule, and public services and policy planning and development are being implemented in a more coordinated fashion at the state level. A growing number of politicians shun the parochial mentality that for so long dominated the style of politics and, ever so slowly, there is an increasing awareness among the citizens of New Jersey that they indeed are part of a broader culture that is the Garden State.

NOTES

1. New York Times Magazine, 14 September 1975, p. 103, as cited in Kenneth T. Palmer, *State Politics in the United States* (New York: St. Martins Press, 1977), p. 44.

2. These examples of New Jersey "humor" were originally cited in the Eagleton Poll news release on *New Jersey Images* 1980, Part I.

3. Eagleton Poll, *New Jersey Images*, Part I, 8 July 1980.

4. Eagleton Poll, *New Jersey Images*, Part II, 10 July 1977.

5. Eagleton Poll, *New Jersey Images*, Part III, 14 July 1977.

6. Eagleton Poll, *New Jersey Images*, Part IV, 17 July 1977.

7. New Jersey State Data Center, Department of Labor. (Summary Tape File 3A, Profile V), 1980.

8. Ira Sharkansky, *The Maligned States* (New York: McGraw Hill, 1972), p. 84.

9. Eagleton Poll, Press release #30-4, 7 March 1978.

10. Richard Lehne, "Revenue and Expenditure Policies" in *Politics in New Jersey*, eds. Richard Lehne and Alan Rosenthal (New Brunswick: Rutgers University Press, 1979), p. 236.

11. M. Kent Jennings and Harmon Zeigler, "The Salience of State Politics," *American Political Science Review*, 64 (June 1970):523–35.

12. Stephen Salmore and Janice Ballou, "Attention to State Politics: The Case of New

Jersey," paper delivered at the 1980 American Political Science Association convention, Washington, D.C., Sept, 1980.

13. Eagleton Poll, *New Jersey Images 1980*, Part VI, 24 July 1980.

14. Eagleton Poll, Press release #45-2, 2 October 1981.

15. Eagleton Poll, Press release #43-3, 27 February 1981.

16. Richard McCormick, "An Historical Overview," in *Politics in New Jersey*, p. 9.

17. *New York Times*, 24 May 1982, p. A18; one particularly obtuse editorial was Sydney H. Schanberg's "The Musto Experiment," *New York Times*, 25 May 1982, p. A23.

18. *Star-Ledger*, Newark, 13 May 1982, p. 16.

19. *New York Times*, 30 July 1982, p. 1.

20. Eagleton Poll, Press release #44-2, 22 May 1981.

21. Michael Pollock, "Winners and Losers," *New Jersey Reporter*, January 1983, p. 27.

22. See William E. Sackett, *Modern Battles of Trenton* (Trenton: J.L. Murphy, 1978).

23. Larry Sabato, *Goodbye to Good-Time Charlie* (Lexington, Mass.: Heath, 1978), pp. 52–53.

24. Richard Lehne, *The Quest for Justice* (New York: Longman, 1978), p. 67.

25. Alan Rosenthal, "The Governor, the Legislature, and State Policy Making," in *Politics in New Jersey*, p. 147.

26. *Ibid.*, p. 144.

27. *Ibid.*, pp. 142–143.

28. Turnout figures through 1978 are drawn from *Electoral Participation in New Jersey*, New Jersey Department of State, 1979 Report, pp. 2–4. Turnout estimates up through 1982 were obtained from the Office of the Secretary of State, Elections Division.

29. James Penning and Corwin Smidt, "Public Financing of State Parties and Candidates: The Views of State Legislatures," paper delivered at the Western Political Science Association meeting, Denver, Colorado. March 1981.

30. Maureen Moakley and Gerald Pomper, "Party Organization," in *Politics in New Jersey*, p. 9.

31. Summary data from Eagleton Polls 30, 37, 39 and 44 released in January 1978, September 1979, February 1980, and May 1981, respectively.

32. Philip H. Burch, "Interest Groups," in *Politics in New Jersey*, p. 111.

33. All information on New Jersey Educational Association was drawn from Paul Feldman, "Those who can, lobby." *New Jersey Reporter*, 12 April 1983, pp. 24–29.

34. Burch, "Interest Groups," p. 117.

35. *Ibid.*, p. 119.

36. *Ibid.*, p. 126.

37. Eagleton Poll, *New Jersey Images 1980*, Part V, 22 July 1980.

38. Rosenthal, "The Governor, the Legislature, and State Policy Making," p. 155.

39. *Ibid.*, p. 141.

40. *Ibid.*, pp. 156–157.

41. Lehne, *Quest for Justice*, p. 43.

42. *Ibid.*, p. 31.

11
New York
PAUL A. SMITH

Politics are important to the people of New York. Simple as it seems, this expresses the central characteristic of the state's political life. Although there are great variations in the types of political action that are practiced and approved in the state, there is a common recognition that these activities play a vital role in both the state and its local communities. Politics may be viewed with confidence or concern, but it is not discounted or ignored.

Near or far, few persons realize the diversity of New York.[1] There are the affluent "old line" suburbs of Westchester County; the massive "bedroom" communities of near Long Island; the small towns and fishing villages far out on Long Island; the dairy farms similar to those of Wisconsin in large middle areas; the mountains, lakes, and forests similar to New England in the north country; the industrial cities of Buffalo and Rochester on the Great Lakes; the wine country around the Finger Lakes; and the posh resorts of the Catskills—all in addition to the corporate, artistic, and commercial center of New York City.

Certainly New Yorkers tend to see other parts of their state as different, if not antagonistic. New York City, of course, has long been recognized as an ethnic melting pot (in which a nearby neighborhood could be another culture), but for its residents the traditional vision of the rest of the state populated by "hayseeds" continues to have considerable vitality. In fact, perceptions even of closeby places tend to reflect historical distinctions. New Yorkers living in Queens or the Bronx—two of the five counties or boroughs that comprise New York City—for example, often refer to Manhattan as "the City." Nevertheless, many of the various areas of the state are socially and culturally different from others, and these differences have political meaning.

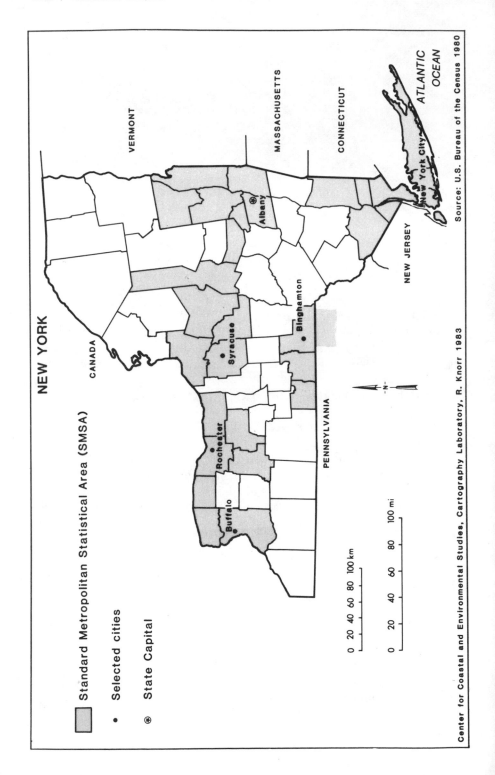

NEW YORK

Standard Metropolitan Statistical Area (SMSA)

• Selected cities

⊛ State Capital

Center for Coastal and Environmental Studies, Cartography Laboratory, R. Knorr 1983

Source: U.S. Bureau of the Census 1980

THE POLITICAL CULTURE: E PLURIBUS UNUM

With all its internal variations, it is debatable whether the state of New York has enough in common to qualify as a single political culture. There is, perhaps, more in common than is first apparent. Admittedly, unified feelings of identification with the state do not have an auspicious background. There is an enduring upstate–downstate division. The critical part of this sentiment is not a minor sectional jealousy, but an enduring identification of many with New York City rather than the state. George Washington Plunkitt, long ago noted that:

> This city is ruled entirely by the hayseed legislators at Albany. I've never known an upstate Republican who didn't want to run things here, and I've known many thousands. . . . [2]

Such identification is not likely to disappear, since it arises from long-existing differences in just about every walk of life—ethnic backgrounds, manners of speaking, political styles, economic activities, geography, and so on—between the City and much of the rest of the state. As we shall see, many of these differences have become blurred; yet, because they go back so far, they have taken on a life of their own in myths and traditions that are even more resistant to change than the differences themselves.* Thus, it is not uncommon for a City politician to accuse an upstate legislator of an anti-City bias when a simpler, more analytic, explanation would be superior.

Added to the presence of divisive factors is the absence of certain elements of common identification found in many other states. Perhaps chief among these is a long-established state university of distinction, especially one with major athletic teams, the exploits of which are a matter of concern throughout the state. New York has, by far, more colleges and universities than any other state, some very old and distinguished. None, however, captures the public's imagination in the manner of the major state universities of the Midwest and West. The State University of New York, a product of the state's belated post World War II effort to develop public education, is an enormous disjointed creature without historical traditions or a central campus. It does not draw statewide attention to the capital. As for the city of Albany, while clearly the center of state policy making, it is hardly in the same league as New York City as a center of art, commerce, sports, or communications.

Ironically, as the state has fallen on hard times, feelings of common identification have been strengthened. Although for years New York City

---

*A Gannett News poll taken early in the summer of 1982 found that three out of four New Yorkers agreed that a "serious conflict" existed between upstate and the City. Upstaters were particularly suspicious that the City not only was badly managed and wasteful, but also was getting too large a share of the state's federal aid. Upstate (and suburban) sensitivities were hardly mollified by Mayor Edward Koch's famous remarks in a *Playboy* magazine interview (February 1982), criticizing suburban ("sterile. It's nothing. It's wasting your life."), rural, and Albany ("small-town life at its worst") life.

seemed to teeter on the brink of financial disaster, it became commonplace that with some version of "creative financing" it would pull through.[3] A major reason for this was the vast reserves of wealth within the City.[4] By the early 1970s, however, its profound economic illness no longer could be masked or finessed,* and after a period of intense struggles and gyrations in 1975–76, extraordinary measures were taken.[5] These included: large federal loan guarantees; the active intervention of federal, state, business, and labor interests in the form, first of a state emergency financial control board, and later of the Metropolitan Assistance Corporation (Big MAC); increased state aid for the City; and sharp reductions in the City's workforce and services. The message was explicit: City politics could not be relied on to keep the City financially viable, and the state must assume much greater responsibilities for the City's welfare.[6]

Virtually at the same time, the extended practice of spending beyond means also caught up with the state. The departure of Governor Nelson Rockefeller (for the vice-presidency with President Gerald Ford), and the election of Democrat Hugh Carey in 1974, brought in a new set of state budget officials. It also brought New York face-to-face with the harsh reality that the Empire State was in the throes of a long-term economic decline that had been masked by Rockefeller's own creative financing—usually based on roll-overs and long-term borrowing. Moreover, the decline was much more serious upstate than in the City. Throughout the state the population was both getting smaller and growing older, and in numerous upstate communities, industry and commerce were stagnant.

Although many expected Carey, the first Democratic governor in a generation, to continue in the expansive tradition of Al Smith, Franklin Roosevelt, Herbert Lehman, and, of course, Rockefeller, he instead cut taxes and imposed cutbacks in state spending. To deal with losses of wealth and productive capacity—including population to the Sun Belt—mechanisms were invented to make the state more attractive to businessmen, vacationers, investors, and anybody else with resources. Some of these were in the form of softened regulations and larger aid packages for new industry, some were in the form of slogans. "I Love New York" and "The Big Apple" were at first taken lightly, but they were publicized so widely, and with such zeal and determination, particularly in song and dance television commercials, that by the end of the decade they had become part of the state's collective consciousness.

A significant aspect of the "I Love New York" advertisements has been their use of integrative symbolism. Attributes of the entire state have been systematically incorporated, so that the theater, music, art, and commercial

---

*A distinction must be made between the economic health of the City as a whole and the borough of Manhattan. At the very moment when the City was on the verge of bankruptcy, in Manhattan construction was beginning to boom, and the clothing, entertainment, broadcasting, and publishing industries continued to do very well. Today, even as the subways, street paving, and garbage collection are in extremely poor condition, other parts of the City are booming.

resources of the City, and the skiing, camping, wine tasting, manufacturing, and other highlights of the rest of the state have been brought together. In struggling to overcome its economic adversity, New York has developed the symbolism of common identification—and the feeling of being in the same boat.

This campaign was undertaken by state government, and its basis was not artificial. It has been a matter of interdependence—which almost incidentally has brought greater recognition to the state as well.* It is now evident that the City is heavily dependent on financial intervention by the state, and will remain so for the foreseeable future.[7] The City's huge bureaucracy—some two-hundred thousand employees (about one in twenty of the adult population)—remains a burden upon all the taxpayers.[8] Yet, at the depth of the financial crisis, pension funds of these public employees were used to purchase the City's very shaky bonds as part of the federal, state, and private salvage operation. Mutual interdependencies do not mean that City and upstate residents are happily unified. Both continue to harbor feelings of abuse at the hands of the other, aggravated by generally opposing party loyalties, not to mention the differences listed earlier. Thus, New Yorkers do have a common identification with their state, but it is beset by enduring sources of friction and distrust.

While mutual identifications are uneven within New York's political culture, political expectations have much more in common. Whether it involves the roles of village officials, state legislators, or congressmen, citizens of New York expect their elected officials to produce results. This can be hard going. Sometimes the problems to be solved are relatively intractable. The economic decline in New York is part of a broad regional trend, and at best requires actions that will take years to be felt. More commonly, expectations face the government with internal conflicts. Thus, the expectation that government will provide more services almost inevitably produces disagreements over "who gets what, when, and how."[9] As resources for public action have become more strained, such conflicts have become more threatening to officials—although, as we have already noted, the politics of scarcity have also led to a growing feeling of interdependence among New Yorkers.

Clear evidence that political problems are difficult may ease expectations, but it will not lower them much. New Yorkers expect their politicians to try, and try again. Whatever the origin of this cultural pattern, Sayre and Kaufman throw considerable light upon it in their classic study of New York

---

*Comparative size is not a major factor, but it may be indicative. For many years the City's budget was larger than the state's. The population of both have been dropping, but more so in the City; between 1970 and 1980, the state's population dropped by 4 percent, while the City's declined by over 10 percent. The City now has 7 million people, the suburban counties 3.8 million, and the rest of the state 6.7 million. However, while in 1950 the City cast almost one-half of the statewide vote, in 1980 it cast 31.6 percent, while the suburban counties cast 24.1 percent and the rest of the state 44 percent of the vote.

City government. The fluidity of City politics, they say, makes officials sensitive to any constituent demands (because tomorrow their votes might count), and encourages constituents to press their demands (because officials are willing to listen, and might be able to do something).

> So, when groups in the city cannot get what they want in the market place . . . they exercise the leverage upon city officials and employees afforded by the designed insecurity of these officials, and seek through political channels what they were unable to secure elsewhere.[10]

This pattern is not limited to the City. George Washington Plunkitt (after describing in detail how enthusiastically the City government should be used), tells how it was in Albany for upstaters:

> But just let a Republican farmer from Chemung or Wayne or Tioga turn up at the Capital. The Republican Legislature will make a rush for him and ask him what he wants and tell him if he doesn't see what he wants to ask for it. If he says his taxes are too high, they reply to him: "All right old man, don't let that worry you. How much do you want us to take off?"[11]

An integral part of these expectations that government will and should be an active force in social and economic life is diverse perceptions of how cleanly and efficiently it will act. Many downstate residents—not only those of old Tammany Hall Manhattan, but also of such places as Nassau County, where the politics of the Joseph Margiotta political machine holds sway—take it for granted that where there is politics and government, there is corruption. The only question is how much. While the citizens of upstate towns and villages agree that City politics are corrupt, they think themselves poorly served indeed if similar practices turn up in their communities. It is not that bribes and kickbacks are approved anywhere in the state. Rather, in some areas they are treated with resignation, while in others they are met with outrage.

Commonly in upstate communities, politicians are expected to govern for no personal gain other than a modest salary and the respect of their fellow citizens. Of course, what is expected of politics is what is perceived. In many of these small towns, issueless, stable one-party (Republican) politics mask a subtle corruption of its own.[12] Expecting that all politics are corrupt, but not perceiving much "politics" of that type locally, the citizens of these communities are free to think that local vigilance is keeping their officials honest while perceiving Albany and especially the City as hotbeds of waste, fraud, and corruption.* Ambrose Bierce's definition of politics as "the conduct of public affairs for private advantage" is considered apt but

---

*This picture of small-town upstate politics is changing. Television now provides direct, if limited, information about politics in Washington and on occasion, other parts of New York. Since 1970 there has been an increase in political competition and awareness of larger political issues in these local communities.

unacceptable. Meanwhile, down in Nassau County and the Bronx, politics is also perceived as normally opportunistic, if not outright crooked, but that perception is coupled with an attitude of inevitability; an expectation that once someone becomes deeply involved in politics, little can be done to prevent a certain amount of corruption.

Yet, whatever mixture of virtue and venality a New Yorker sees in political life, politics is expected to produce results, whether for the City or the small town.[13] This is particularly true for the politics of Albany. State government is expected to be actively involved in positive services. It also is expected to do negative things if left unattended. Both sets of expectations arise out of abundant historical experiences, and are built into constitutional powers of governmental action and norms of political leadership. Plunkitt saw that the "hayseeds" played a tough game in Albany, and complained that they constantly interfered with the governance of his own city. Roosevelt grasped the powers of the state to try out programs he would later develop for the nation.[14] He was followed by a succession of governors who did not hesitate to expand his initiatives. Through it all there has been the corruption—as fresh today with the conviction of Joe Margiotta, Republican chairman of Nassau County, as it was in the 1920s with the escapades of Mayor Jimmy Walker.[15]

What is more, the results of state action have been experienced in every local community. They have come in the form of state regulations and services, both extensive. To be sure, City politicians may be unique in feeling abused by the politicians in Albany, but they are not alone in understanding that state government is there to be used, and if it is not, it may be abused. New Yorkers expect very real things from state government—a mixture of carrots and sticks. They also expect their Albany representatives and local officials to get as many carrots and as few sticks as possible. The same pattern of expectations exists for the Congress and state in relation to the federal government. In varying degrees, politicians are not expected to be particularly noble or self-sacrificing (although these qualities are admired), but they are expected to look after their constituents and get the job done. Expectations of what government can deliver are lower today than a generation ago. Yet, for New Yorkers things are possible in politics: the promises persist and the expectations are resilient.

Expectations of the amount and quality of state action are linked to support for state authority. Of course, given the intensity of intrastate politics and the shortage of resources, this is not a placid stream of generalized approval. Few citizens do not feel some specific irritations about what the state is or is not doing, in part because the state has involved itself in so much. Yet, approximately three-fifths of the state budget is returned to localities in aid to schools and hospitals, welfare and medicaid payments, and public projects; state agencies provide numerous services ranging from licensing to environmental protection. New Yorkers know state government is there, negatively as a taxer and regulator, positively as a provider of money and services.

The authority represented by this large and mixed bag of functions is generally supported, warts and all. However, in the public mind there is no neat separation between the actions of the government and other components of the political process, namely elections, appointments, and party and pressure-group activities. Among these, especially, corruption is no stranger. Consequently, New Yorkers are not deferential toward authority. Their support for political institutions and offices is leavened by skepticism about the competence or honor of those manning them. Just as the norms of political conduct vary in different sections of the state, so does the degree of distrust. In parts of the City and Long Island, cynicism is the dominant feeling toward politics and politicians—even though there may be high expectations of their "productivity." In many upstate communities, there is considerable respect for local governments, although it is seldom free of the suspicion that their personnel will succumb to the blandishments of wealth, political advancement, or just opposing arguments.

All in all, the myth of authority is neither abstract nor very powerful among New Yorkers. Public officials are seen as human beings, as susceptible as anyone else to temptations and subjected to more than most. Especially in small upstate towns and cities, the exercise of authority is recognized as a legitimate function, and those having formal offices of government are accorded respect. Deference, however, is a rare commodity anywhere in the state, and is certainly not encouraged by a vigorous and rambunctious press that seems especially fond of puncturing political dignity and ostentation.[16] Whether covering the governor's marriage or the districting of the city council, the major newspapers of the state serve to expose corruption and challenge—if not trivialize—the mystique of "high places." As we shall see later, they also limit power.

Despite the rather strong tendency to observe the emperor's lack of clothes in New York, the clothes themselves are approved without question. The state's political system is firmly supported, and authority conceptualized as rules is generally attributed to the institutions of politics and government. Young New Yorkers consume the same mass media and read the same "civics" books as children in other states, so their "models" of authority are about the same. To be sure, the decline of political trust and support that took place in the nation as a whole during the 1960s and 1970s also affected New York, but not particularly so. Only in the City, where there is an overwhelming concern about crime, is there evidence of pessimism about government's ability to act.[17] In view of all the factors that could undermine confidence, trust, and support, political authority is active and surprisingly healthy in New York.

POLITICAL STYLE: AGGRESSIVENESS AND DEBATE

The patterns of political identification, expectations, and support are clearly reflected in the modal style of political leadership in New York. It is a style of assertiveness, even stridency, that grows out of the intense competitiveness and rich cultural diversity of the state. Much of this originated in the City, with its burgeoning mixture of ethnic backgrounds and social needs.[18] As immigrants crowded ashore in the nineteenth and early twentieth centuries, it was evident that in the rough democracy of the times, politics made a difference in how a part of the City would be treated, and in the tangible rewards for individual politicians. This is depicted vividly, if a bit benignly, by George Washington Plunkitt, and the use of politics as a vehicle for advancement is well established.[19]

At all times, however, City politics were neither well-ordered nor particularly clean. To get the payoffs, politicians needed to be alert to opportunities, energetic, organized, and smart. Great eloquence was not required, but as press and public scrutiny increased and public appeals for support became more important, the ability to speak well and hold one's own in debates before large groups of people became a definite advantage.[20]

Meanwhile, in most upstate communities social-cultural life was much less dynamic and political style more restrained. Local politicians were looked to for a sober demeanor and thoughtfulness rather than aggressive activity and loquaciousness. When these upstate representatives got to Albany, however, and confronted their downstate counterparts, stylistic adaptations took place. It is now recognized that in order to do well in Albany (or Washington, for that matter), a representative must know the issues, be able to articulate them, and have the wit to get good publicity and form winning alliances. Negligence and procrastination are usually culled out early. Television has made all—even local—politicians more visible, so that constituents are able to compare national, state, and local styles. The soft-spoken, slow-moving, taciturn political leader might at one time have been the model in certain local communities, but he is not in style today. Energy, articulateness, knowledgeability, and concern are now the standard, with City politicians being more aggressive and outspoken.

Other personal attributes of political leaders in New York show few commanding patterns. They are diverse. In the cases of age, sex, race, ethnicity, income, occupation, and so on, modal characteristics are hardly noteworthy. In leadership positions there are more men than women, more whites than blacks, more lawyers than any other occupation—all common patterns in American politics. Yet in New York the patterns themselves are uneven.

Take age, for example. Age does not appear to be distinctive in New York politics, as on all sides there is evidence of considerable diversity. The state's congressional delegation ranges in age from 28 to 67, and averages about 50.* The state legislature ranges from 24 to 70, with the assembly being a bit younger than the senate. In 1972, 86-year old Congressman Emanuel Celler, first elected in 1922, was defeated in the Democratic

---

*All data here are of mid-1982, before the 1982 elections, which did not make appreciable changes.

primary by 31-year old Elizabeth Holtzman in the 16th congressional district in the City. Similarly, 76-year old Senator Jacob Javits lost to a younger Alfonse D'Amato in 1980. Yet in 1981, the late Erastus Corning, born in 1909, and mayor of Albany since 1942, was reelected against vigorous younger opposition, while 31-year old Juanita Crabb was elected mayor of Binghamton after only two years of service on the city council. These representative cases show that both old and young can win office in New York, and in some cases hold office for a very long time.

As for the role of women, it is considerable, yet very much less than that of men. What is more, in legislative offices it is unimpressive when compared to national averages. Two of New York's 39 members of Congress are women, one a black woman. In the state legislature, 6 percent of the members are women, compared to about 12 percent nationally. A woman was lieutenant governor between 1974 and 1978, but lost when she challenged the incumbent governor, Carey, in the 1978 Democratic primary. Another young woman defeated the speaker of the assembly in the party primary of 1978,[21] and a woman is currently president of the New York City Council, one of the top elected offices of the City. Finally, Elizabeth Holtzman "came back" to defeat the Democratic organization's male candidate for Brooklyn district attorney in 1981.

Both upstate and downstate, women feel free to run for offices from bottom to top. Some of them win, but it is clear that being female is no guarantee of success. An interesting example of this, and of the effect of personal style, was Bella Abzug, who attempted to move from her seat in Congress to the U.S. Senate in 1976. An unusually dynamic, aggressive, even abrasive politician, Abzug lost very narrowly to Daniel Patrick Moynihan in the Democratic primary (coming in second in a field of four). A few months later she entered the City's mayoralty campaign of 1977, and was again defeated (the eventual winner was Edward Koch). Finally, in a special election to fill Koch's vacated congressional seat early in 1978, she was defeated once again, this time by Republican Bill Green. Abzug's case suggests not that a woman cannot win, but that a loud, abrasive style can only be pushed so far, even in the City.

A somewhat similar—but also different—situation exists for black and Hispanic participation in the state's political leadership. Black and Hispanic candidates can get elected in the state, but their victories are well below their proportions of the population. Two members of the state's congressional delegation are black and one is Hispanic, and blacks and Hispanics comprise about 7 and 3 percent, respectively, of the state legislature. All of these numbers are far smaller than the 14 percent black and 9 percent Hispanic proportions of New York's population.[22] Things are no better in the City, where most members of these minority groups reside.

The problem for these "newer" minority groups does not lie primarily in deep-seated racial prejudices. New Yorkers have been consistently more supportive of programs designed to aid minorities than the rest of the nation.[23] Rather, these groups are ill-prepared for the intense group competition in state—and especially City—politics. Nowhere has this been more dramatically illustrated than in the case of city council redistricting in 1981.

Two days before New York's September 10th primary, a three-judge federal panel ruled that the City was in violation of the 1965 Voting Rights Act in redrawing city council districts to reflect the 1980 census.* All City elections were enjoined, which as one would suppose produced a considerable hue and cry! The case was quite clear. The City's total population had declined by about 800,000 in 1980 while its minority population had risen by 320,000. The need to redistrict seemed patent—especially because there were only five blacks and three Hispanics to represent 45 percent of the City's population on the 43-member council.[24] However, the redistricting plan the council adopted (and the mayor signed) simply added two districts without making necessary changes to give the minorities a better chance of representation.**

As the convoluted facts emerged, and it was seen that black and Hispanic councilmen themselves had voted for the plan, it became evident that for all the members, "their dominant motive was the protection of their own seats."[25] Threatened with being redistricted out of their own seats, most of the minority members went along (and counted themselves fortunate). Obviously the black and Hispanic groups, out-voted and out-maneuvered before, had been out-maneuvered again—but this time in circumstances that caught the eye of the federal justice department. In any case, a delayed primary and general election were eventually held for all offices except the council. For the councilmen, however, the legal pulling and hauling created a legal morass (not uncommon in New York) so complex that at year's end they were allowed to continue sitting into 1982, even though their constitutional terms had run out![26] The council elections were finally held in November, 1982. With modified districts, the election yielded one more Democrat, but no general gains for blacks or Hispanics.

There is no doubt that a number of "inherent" personal attributes, such as those we have just discussed, are important in the recruitment of New York's political leadership. Tickets balanced with candidates of different ethnic and religious backgrounds are traditional in the state. This tradition continues, with the composition of tickets gradually changing to reflect new political numbers and initiatives of constituent groups. Blacks have now joined Jews, Italians, and Irish Catholics on these tickets, and Hispanics can

---

*Parts of the City—Brooklyn, the Bronx, and Manhattan—fell under the Voting Rights Act because they contained large numbers of blacks and Hispanics. Almost three quarters of the Bronx is now black or Hispanic, and fewer than half of their residents voted. This measure is routinely used to apply the act in southern states.

**The number of white councilmen representing predominantly black or Hispanic districts was revealing. For example, the Brooklyn district of the head of the Committee on Rules, Privileges, and Elections (dealing with redistricting) is now 85 percent black, while the councilman is white.

be expected to follow. As we shall see later, however, the new minorities are not yet politically active enough to be able to match the Jewish, Irish, and Italian faces in the public offices of the state. No matter what his or her family background, or occupation, or race, a candidate without personal initiative, quickness, and panache will have a hard time matching the competition.

This reemphasizes the arena of action—the process part of political style. The personal characteristics of assertiveness, knowledgeability, and so forth, when coupled with the intense competition among interests in the state, yield a political process marked by continual maneuverings, energetic discussions, and general activity. Much of this is visible, but by no means are state politicians committed to the principle of "open covenants openly arrived at." Backroom deals and quiet arrangements are well known in New York. In fact, as we have already observed, they are expected within the political culture—thus leading to keen attentiveness and quick accusations on the part of political opponents (which most politicians happen to have). These are heard by a press and public that are skeptical of all sides, yet intrigued by the controversy.

The result is a good deal of vigorous debate, often punctuated by charge and counter-charge, that tends toward a process that is more open than closed, despite some incentives to the contrary. Compared to earlier times, when political careers sometimes depended on ladders of advancement constructed by tightly controlled party organizations or local "establishments,"[27] the processes of recruitment into major offices, and of policy-making, is characterized by active and public competition. This, of course, is not true for every political office or policy decision in the state,* but it is the rule rather than the exception for most city, state, and national positions.

Coincident with this pattern of action is a strong tradition of reform in New York, both in the City (where reform has come, and often gone, for over a century) and the state as a whole.[28] There have been policy consequences stretching back to periods when the political process was less open than today. Over the years, New York pioneered in governmental programs designed to aid large disadvantaged segments of its population, and "earned the reputation of having the best and most innovative state and local government in the nation."[29]

Rather than explain these institutions and programs with the conventional wisdom that New York politicians are liberal in their policy preferences (which in some respects is true), it is more straightforward to link the policies to other elements of the political culture—to citizen expectations

*Many local offices, especially in Republican dominated, rural and small-town upstate areas, are essentially noncompetitive, with primary challenges not being part of local Republican usages and Democrats being so hopelessly outnumbered that candidates cannot be found. There is evidence, however, that Republican primaries are becoming much more common and partisan competition more extensive.

that government will act to deal with their needs, to the competitive style of politicians searching for popular support, and to processes of active and open competition. Such patterns of action, resulting in policies of intervention, may be seen as "liberal," but they also can be explained by their practical political outcomes.

Like the common knowledge that New York is Democratic, the assumption that it is overwhelmingly liberal runs into contradictions.[30] With all their willingness to argue, compete, and act, state policymakers refused to increase welfare payments between 1971 and 1980. During the 1980 presidential campaign New York voters were found to have opinions balanced toward the more conservative end of the scale although less so than the rest of the nation.[31] Harsh economic conditions now dominate the concerns of policymaking and the constituent messages politicians hear push them toward contraction rather than expansion of government. The gradually changing shape of the state's population from active disadvantaged to active advantaged pluralities is a fundamental factor in all of this.

In summary, with its great social-cultural diversity, New York's political style is surprisingly consistent, although certainly not smooth or uniform. The City or downstate style is decidedly aggressive, enterprising, and articulate (even loud). Upstate, the style is more soft-spoken, less "pushy," but equally calculating. Brought together in statewide competition for office and policy, downstate politicians lose some of their abrasive edge while their upstate colleagues become more articulate and enterprising. The result is a political process filled with competition, maneuvering for advantage, and active communication between leaders and followers. The development of television as a vehicle of communication has lessened the dependence of both on stable political organizations, and given politicians much more direct access to voters. Nevertheless, organizations and behind-the-scenes arrangements continue to be a vital part of the political process in New York. Organizing is still in style.

POLITICAL INTERACTION: THE SPUTTERING MACHINE

Political interactions are alive and well in New York and come in a multitude of forms. One set of these comprise party organizations, although the mother of the urban machine no longer can count on parties to dominate political activity and channel it in predictable ways. Other forms of participation have grown in importance and almost all of them are well-organized.

Voting continues to be by far the most common form of political activity by individual citizens, and despite the energy expended by the state's politicians, New York's citizens do not, overall, show impressive levels of participation in this activity. For many years New York's turnout in presidential elections hovered a little above the national average, but in the 1970s the state began falling behind.

In 1968, about 63 percent of registered voters cast a ballot in the presidential elections, as compared to near 61 percent in the nation as a whole. In 1972, turnout in New York was about 58 percent, while national turnout was just under 56 percent. By 1976, however, turnout in New York was down to 51 percent while national turnout was just over 54 percent. In 1980, turnout in New York dropped to 48 percent for a differential with national figures of close to 8 percent.

This decline in voting during the 1970s was not even across the state and reflects the changing composition of the electorate. New York's 4 percent loss of population between 1970 and 1980 involved significant internal differences. The greatest loss occurred in New York City where every element of the population declined except Hispanics. This group increased from 1.2 million in 1970 to 1.4 million in 1980.[32] The greatest loss occurred among middle-class whites. Blacks also left the City, but those that did were, like departing whites, mainly middle-class. As we have already seen, by 1980 the City's population had become 45 percent black and Hispanic—economically disadvantaged groups with very low voting turn-outs.* The decline was illustrated in the 1981 city elections in Albany and New York City.[33] The turnout was just over 43 percent in Albany and about 22 percent in the City. Essentially, during the 1970s, high-turnout whites were replaced by low-turnout minorities, depressing the overall participation in voting.

It is worth adding that there are a lot of elections in New York. In few communities will a year pass without several opportunities to vote, the number depending on the year and the occurrence of primaries. Other than the normal federal offices, balloting occurs for state gubernatorial, legislative, and judicial positions; county executives and legislators; city mayors and councilmen or town board members; and often school boards. These are distributed over all even- and odd-numbered years.

Other modes of political participation tend to be more demanding than voting, and while their extent is less than that for voting, they are nevertheless considerable and usually intensive in New York. Of course, only a small proportion of the eligible population runs for political office, but many more take part in the uncounted campaigns that are part of the numerous elections mentioned above. Then there is active work in regular interest groups, of which there are many, or in the creation of new "special" (and often single) interest groups. In the case of all of these political activities, there are sharp differences in degree of participation between various segments of the population. Jewish residents of Manhattan not only

*The low turnout of these groups was due, in part, to the lack of black and Hispanic candidates. For example, in the 1981 Democratic primary for the Manhattan borough presidency, blacks turned out in record numbers (almost 40 percent in one Harlem district) to support David Dinkins, a black, against incumbent Andrew Stein, who is Jewish. In a classic example of New York politics, after his narrow defeat Dinkins was courted by a number of politicians interested in running for state office—such as governor in 1982—and were impressed by Dinkins' ability to mobilize the black electorate.

have a high voting turnout, but also participate extensively in political clubs, special committees, and interest groups. A few miles away, blacks in the South Bronx rarely participate in public life at all. There is no evidence that anywhere in the state citizens feel intimidated not to run for public office, go to political meetings, or engage in other political activities; but on the whole, occupation, class, and race variations in participation appear to be identical to those found in the nation as a whole.

Political participation is encouraged and eased in New York by the ready availability of organized means. Just about every economic, ethnic, professional, religious, or even "public" interest alive in America is in some form organized in the state. Thus, interest groups are many and strong. Even in modest-size communities, it is not uncommon to have local "chapters" of state or national groups. The character of these organizations is generally consistent with elements of the political culture discussed earlier. As a rule, entry is easy, hierarchy is limited, and visibility is seen as a virtue. There is an enormous range of organizational forms, from the imposing structure of the Chamber of Commerce, on the one hand, to the ephemeral mobilization of local citizens striving to halt a state transportation project through their neighborhood, on the other. For most groups, sooner or later, state government is the target of attention, with interest groups in Albany being similar to those in Washington.

Throughout the state's economy, labor is organized; usually strongly organized. Some unions—such as the ladies garment workers, the longshoremen's association, and the transport workers—are well known. Whether their reputations precede them or not, unions are fully prepared to work for their ends through political means.

A noteworthy case of this is the public employees unions. Organized labor in New York long ago recognized the rich potential of state and local government workers, and these workers have been given detailed collective bargaining rights (and limits) by the state's Taylor Law. Police, firemen, sanitation and clerical workers, prison guards, hospital and university staff, local school teachers, and more, are organized in the state.

The strength of these unions arises from their presence in key public services, their occasional ability to act together, their large pension funds and union treasuries, and their impressive numbers. These political resources have been especially potent in the City, where governments have found it difficult to take action strongly opposed by the unions. The Taylor Law forbids strikes by public employees, but some unions strike anyway, and then in the final settlement, bargain to reduce the severe penalties the law specifies. With one adult in twenty on the public payroll, the City found it politically impossible to make major manpower (and budget) reductions for decades before the financial crisis of 1975. As we saw earlier, one consequence was that major budgetary authority was taken out of the hands of elected City officials and placed with the State Financial Control Board.

When they can work together, public employee unions exercise a great deal of political muscle. Their financial support alone can be critical if a campaign hopes to be competitive, and their combined votes can make or break a candidate. Since collective-bargaining issues usually involve the livelihood of families, the unions can activate not only their members, but also the relatives of their members, for a total variously estimated at between one-third and one-half of the actual voters, depending on the intensity of the issues and the size of the overall turnout. Because City politicians are well aware of this potential block of voters, their position on public-service issues is usually very carefully designed to express sympathy and avoid confrontation.

At the state level, public-employee unions have considerably less influence, as is evidenced by the restrictive Taylor Law itself. Although their total membership is formidable, they are crippled not only by the Taylor Law, but also by their diversity. So, their strength is heavily dependent on the wit and forcefulness of their leaders, who are generally well aware of their need to gain support from allied industrial unions. This, for example, is the usual strategy of the American Federation of Teachers and their associates in the American Federation of Labor. With the sharp downturn of the state's financial condition in the 1970s, state and local officials became much tougher at the bargaining table, almost always with considerable support from the "unorganized" public faced with rising taxes and service cutbacks. Not surprisingly, upstate legislators have little sympathy for the state "bailing out" a city whose officials are unwilling to reduce its inflated labor costs. Gradually and painfully the public-employee unions, including those in the City, have had to settle for less.

On the other hand, what can happen politically when the unions find a strong and common interest is illustrated by the gubernatorial elections of 1982. When, early in the year, New York City Mayor Edward Koch announced his intention to run for governor, most politicians and political commentators concluded that he would easily defeat Lieutenant Governor Mario Cuomo for the Democratic nomination, not to mention any Republican in the general election. After all, Koch had just been reelected mayor with the nominations of both the Democratic and Republican parties and 75 percent of the vote. However, Koch had managed to convince virtually all public-employee unions—and others as well—that he would be an even greater menace as governor than he already was as mayor. The unions mobilized intensively and provided almost all of the statewide grass-roots electoral organization of the Cuomo campaign. Cuomo's ensuing defeat of Koch in the Democratic primary is widely credited to union assistance, and undoubtedly has reestablished organized labor as a political force in the state.[34]

Business interests are at least equally well-organized, and are brought together in the powerful and well-led Business Council of New York, the strongest constituents of which are the statewide Chamber of Commerce and the Association of Industries. All of these organizations are continually present as far as state policymakers are concerned. They are staffed by professional lobbyists who stay in contact with their local members, handle the development of issues, and stay close to appropriate officials. In comparison to labor, they also are quite effective in overcoming the disparate interests of their local members. In any event, state policymakers approaching the annual legislative session can look forward to many lush parties and friendly personal contacts with these business groups.

Despite their great diversity and potential fragmentation, New York's business and labor organizations exhibit considerable centralization. This increases their ability to present relatively clear and united fronts to legislators and other officials in Albany. They also have made highly organized lobbying the norm in the state. It is very unusual to find an interest group—even those of modest resources—that does not have an explicit mechanism for reaching the state legislature (only the largest and most sophisticated attempt to influence the governor). Even if the group cannot afford a full-time lobbyist, it will make systematic efforts to intervene in the legislative process at appropriate points.

It is worth reemphasizing the great scope of interest organization, and its focus on state government in New York. Beyond the business and labor organizations already mentioned, there are religious groups, educational groups, taxpayer groups, public-interest groups, and so on. In circumstances that obviously are not favorable, there are also public-welfare groups, combining into the State Community Aid Association in Albany. Even local governments are organized, as are school boards, to monitor and bring pressure on state government. Especially in times of austerity, these interests are always in at least partial opposition to each other. Thus, very rarely can any major interest proceed without facing serious opposition to get what it wants from state policymakers. Wider in scope than political parties, and more continuously concerned with the substance of public policy, organized interest groups constitute channels of policy-oriented citizen activity in New York. They operate at every level of politics, targeting the units of government most relevant to their needs. In so doing, they serve to structure and limit power in the state.

New York is known as a strong party state, and in some respects it is. The formal policymaking units of government—legislatures and executives—are organized by party, and party organizations throughout the state struggle to control nominations for public office. Occasionally they succeed. Always they are understood to have a legitimate role. Parties as organizations are found throughout the state, are looked to as avenues to public office, and are relevant to public policymaking.

The image of Tammany Hall no longer captures the essential nature of party organizations in the state. It is true that, compared to many other states, numerous organized party units are alive from the state to election district (precinct) level. Political tradition is one reason for this—a tradition of intense party competition and of rewards to the faithful for their labors. Our old friend, George Washington Plunkitt, explained the form of some of these rewards in his classic phrase, "honest graft," and exemplified others by his position in the state legislature.[35] The City's Democratic machine, Tammany Hall, was able to compensate its membership by controlling entry into and exit out of government—especially City government, but state government as well. The key to this control was its ability to mobilize votes and limit internal competition through relatively centralized direction.[36]

The bases for centralized direction and the control of votes are now mostly gone. The City comprises five counties (boroughs) rather than Manhattan alone, and each borough has its own party organization, which is in turn fragmented by the Democratic clubs with their active, dues-paying members.[37] Moreover, the City is no longer composed of poor, uneducated voters, but ambitious immigrants from Europe, happy to trade their votes for tangible payoffs. The descendents of these immigrants, Catholic and Jewish and middle-class, remain Democrats, but they want to use the City government for their own purposes, not those of a party boss. True, almost half the City's population remains severely disadvantaged; however, their competition is not a patrician minority, but rather a vigorous, well-educated majority, who know the ropes and are firmly ensconced in a fragmented party. It is an unequal contest. The organizational structure that enabled the "tired and poor" to man the Tammany machine is missing for those who need it now.

Yet, there are still strong local party organizations in New York. Some are clubs in the City. Others are in suburban and upstate counties, such as the Republican machine of Nassau County led by Joseph Margiotta, who although indicted and convicted of using the spoils of office to sustain his organization, remains the county party leader.[38] Still others are in various older cities, the most notable being in Albany, which has the oldest urban machine in the nation. Until recently, it was led by Mayor Erastus Corning, who, until his death in 1983, was also Democratic party chairman of Albany county.

Moreover, the use of governmental resources to sustain party organizations is by no means finished in New York, although the coin is a bit different. Insurance contracts and legal fees are major sources of rewards. In numerous upstate counties the office of election commissioner (two per county, one for each party) is occupied by party chairmen, giving these leaders at least a modicum payoff. In addition, both state legislative and executive staff positions are often filled by local party operatives able to carry on their organizational work while being on the state payroll.

Nevertheless, these material rewards are fragmented and only enough to keep the major parties alive, and not enough to enable them to control nominations and elections. In most of the state, the major parties do not have the organizational resources to overcome three other forces in the party system: first, the deep-seated support for reform; second, the third parties; and third, the growing independence of political candidates.

A tradition of reform is part of New York's political culture—not dominant, but sufficiently embedded in historical precedents to be a continuing force. Plunkitt spoke of reformers as "only mornin' glories," lacking the knowledge, persistence, and common touch to hold Tammany down.[39] However, many political leaders of the state—Fiorello LaGuardia, Herbert Lehman, and Robert Wagner, for example—began and lived as reformers. The pattern endures. Mayor Edward Koch began his political career as a leader of the Village Independent Democrats, a reform club in the City that broke with Koch because of his recent conservatism and endorsed Mario Cuomo in the 1982 Democratic gubernatorial primary. No major politician of the state or City ignores the reform tradition. Moreover, the tradition has been institutionalized, first in the prolix state election law that specifies party structures and functions in detail, and second in the political clubs of the City.

Vigorous minor parties are another element of the state's political system. They span the ideological spectrum from the Socialist Workers party on the left to the Conservative party on the right. Some, like George Wallace's Courage party, appear only for a single election, but others— today the Conservative, Liberal, and Right-to-Life parties—have continuing organizations and are a major presence throughout the state. Over the years these third parties have developed sophisticated strategies that have weakened the nominating power of the Democrats and Republicans. A central aspect of these strategies is the use of candidate endorsements and cross-endorsements to confront the major parties with the threat that one of their defeated aspirants will appear on the general election ballot anyway—to siphon off enough votes to effect a victory for the other major party. This pressures the Democratic and Republican parties to adapt their nominations to the wishes of third parties.

There are many examples of this at every level of New York politics. One of the more recent and complex instances was the narrow defeat of Democrat Elizabeth Holtzman by Republican Alfonse D'Amato in the 1980 senatorial election. Republican Senator Jacob Javits, nominated by the Liberals, had been defeated by D'Amato, who was nominated by the Conservatives, in the Republican primary. In the general election, Javits won 11 percent of the vote, while Holtzman lost to D'Amato by less than 1 percent. Holtzman clearly would have won the Senate seat had Javits not been on the ballot. The Conservative nomination of D'Amato threatened the Republicans while the Liberal nomination of Javits threatened the Democrats, who were the victims of the Liberal effort to improve their ballot position vis-à-vis the Conservatives by using Javits to maximize the votes on their line.

The tendency of candidates to initiate and develop campaigns for their parties' nominations on their own follows the pattern seen in presidential nominating politics. In New York, this practice is affected by the resilience of local (county) party organizations and has taken on distinctive—even contradictory—features. The party symbols remain strong among Democrats and Republicans. While candidates for statewide (and local) nominations move aggressively to raise their own funds and build their own organizations, replete with pollsters, media advisers, and the rest, they also eagerly seek the endorsement and support of local party organizations. For their parts, both state and local party organizations have been responding vigorously—though with limited success—to third party efforts to capture their candidates with the cross-endorsements mentioned above.[40] At the same time, the depth of the problem can be seen in supposedly highly partisan New York City, where Mayor Edward Koch sought and obtained the unprecedented nominations of both the Republican and Democratic parties in the process of winning reelection in 1981. Although so-called "fusion" tickets have been well-known in the City since the election of Seth Low in 1901, always before they combined minor parties with only one of the major parties, usually the Republican. Under present circumstances, Koch's action obviously did not bolster the organizational reputation of either major party.[41]

It is fair to conclude that political parties as specialized organizations for political recruitment and policymaking remain strong in New York, but they are weaker than in the past and face major challenges from both minor parties and ambitious candidates. The parties are conscious of their weaknesses and are taking an increasingly dim view of candidates who seek third party endorsements. They continue to monopolize the machinery of government and, where possible, to use the resources of government to support themselves. In this respect, the last decade has seen the state legislature become an important arm of party organization. In each house, the majority party especially—but not only—makes a substantial effort to aid the elections of its members and to provide patronage to local party organizations. The amount of resources so distributed is modest, but it helps make statewide organizations a reality.

Party membership is, of course, concentrated in different regions of the state. In much of New York City the Republicans are essentially a minor party, while in countless small upstate communities many local offices are rarely contested by Democrats, although party competition has been steadily increasing in these areas. As of 1980, 53 percent of Democratic registration was in the City, while only 15 percent of Republican registration was there. Electoral strategists generally divide the state into three parts: the City, with about one-third of the vote; upstate with just under one-half; and the suburbs with one-quarter. Democratic candidates usually win overwhelmingly in the City, while Republicans tend to dominate upstate and lead, more narrowly, in the suburbs.* The two principal third parties also have interesting patterns of membership, with 49 percent of the Liberals and 30 percent of the Conservatives being registered in the City. The fact that the Conservatives are relatively stronger than the Republicans in the City has significance for the future of both.

The most obvious political organizations in New York are the formal agencies of government, which are vigorous, powerful, and separated. They also have solid constitutional bases, which means that persons seeking power

---

*The 1982 gubernatorial vote illustrates the party divisions within the state. Although Democratic-Liberal Cuomo won by just under four points (51 to 48 percent), he carried only seven of the state's 62 counties—the five boroughs of the City, Westchester, and Albany. Republican-Conservative Lehrman won, usually decisively, every upstate county except Albany.

and public recognition can find plenty of attractions within the legitimate framework of state government. Constitutional powers, while substantial, are not concentrated. Thus, while it may be said that New York is a "strong governor" state, the same may be said for the legislature and the courts. To complicate matters further, that special type of governmental organization known as the "public authority" is both numerous and assertive in the state. For their part, regular local governments, especially of cities and counties, are also alive and well as working organizations. As a general consequence of these strong yet diverse governmental organizations, the supposition that other centers of social power, especially business or labor, act as a sort of *imperium in imperio* cannot be sustained in the politics of New York.

The office of governor is strong, especially when its occupant acts to use the full powers—constitutional and otherwise—at his command, which is usually. Within the last half-century virtually all the leading governors— Roosevelt, Lehman, Dewey, Harriman, Rockefeller, and Carey—have used these powers. This has enabled them to combine their executive and administrative authority, their party leadership, and their press resources to influence policy far beyond the formal execution of the laws.

In addition to the "normal" use of patronage, the funding of local projects, and the approval of private bills, as a means to pressure legislators, the governor can restrict actual expenditures in order to frustrate legislative efforts to force unwanted budgetary changes upon him. Rockefeller was an outstanding, although probably not exceptional, example of how money can be used to support, or not support, party organizations and campaigns in order to control elected members of the governor's party (not to mention threatened members of the opposition party).

In recent years this gubernatorial power has been most telling in the manipulation of money. The executive budget division is used first to measure and estimate income, second to formulate a detailed budget, and third to exercise intensive control over expenditures. Not only does this provide the governor with an effective means for keeping track of the complex and far-flung operations of the state, but is also gives him great influence over the legislature and local governments that lack his resources of information and control.* Alexander Hamilton's conception of a powerful executive has tangible reality in New York.

---

*A fascinating addition to the governor's power over the budget emerged in the spring of 1982. One result of the 1975–76 fiscal crisis was a court decision that state borrowing could not proceed until the governor (and others) certified the state's budget as balanced. This was to protect Wall Street underwriters. Facing the strong possibility that many of his item vetoes would be overridden at the end of his struggle with the legislature over the size and composition of the budget, Governor Hugh Carey declared that he would not certify the budget as balanced if additional expenditures, desired by the legislature, were added. Since both the state and local communites were waiting for state funds they desperately needed to borrow, the senate decided not to attempt any overrides, thus handing the governor an apparent victory. It can be anticipated, however, that in the future, the legislature will adapt to this new gubernatorial device; one that obviously had been intended to increase the governor's responsibility, not his power.

While the governor clearly is more than a first among equals, he must operate within a structure of authority and overall resources that includes important limits on his power. Some of these are not obvious. An independently elected comptroller and attorney general can affect the state's expenditures and law enforcement, and embarrass the governor when they choose. Independent "public authorities," such as the Port Authority of New York and the Metropolitan Transportation Authority, have huge budgets and perform vital public functions. A number of these authorities were carefully designed by Robert Moses to be centers of action and power in their own right.[42] At the very least, they complicate a governor's overall programmatic control. In addition, the mayor of New York City, especially if strong-willed and skillful, has resources of votes—including those of state legislators from the City—and money that can only be overcome through bargaining. Moreover, other local governments, of both cities and counties, are also centers of power, particularly when they act together. These and the other interests mentioned earlier are quite prepared in New York to grasp the multiple opportunities open to them to make life difficult for an abrasive governor.

Then, there is the state legislature. Neither the 150-member assembly (currently Democratic) nor the 60-member senate (currently Republican) are automatically inclined to "go along" with the governor out of a sense of deference.[43] Elected for two-year terms, while the governor and other statewide officers have four-year terms, both assemblymen and senators are organized around very strong party leadership and over the past decade have increased the resources at their command.[44] Meeting every year far beyond the traditional January to April period of a generation ago, legislators receive substantial salaries and expense reimbursements. A significant minority of members treat the job as a full-time position. Relatively large staff resources enable members to have both Albany and district offices and make it possible for the leadership to commission a considerable amount of programmatic research. Thus, the legislature often can challenge the governor's facts and figures, as well as his efforts to influence legislative elections, since, as we have seen, legislative resources have been found to have electoral consequences.

The motivation to challenge is neither rare nor trivial. Because the state is heavily involved not only in its own programs but also in financing and regulating those of local governments, any budget has substantial local consequences. Local governments, and other interests, know very well that they can influence their state legislators more easily than the governor. The governor, therefore, frequently finds assemblymen and senators, including those of his own party, in vigorous opposition to his program initiatives. Such conflicts are intensified when various interests act in concert, and when legislative leaders aspire to become the governor, which is not uncommon. The result is that the legislature joins the other well-organized units of government in a system of intense competition, bargaining, and (usually) accommodation.

Taken together, the vigor and diversity of political organizations in New York reflect the basic characteristics of political interaction in the state. When contemplating politics, New Yorkers think first of organization. Usually some forms of organization are already available—indeed beckoning—as channels for action. If not, New Yorkers are quick to join with others to fill their needs. Consequently, new organizations are continually springing up, from neighborhood associations to statewide affiliations, to serve some political purpose. While we have already seen that New Yorkers are not particularly active in individual forms of political participation, such as voting, organizational activity for political ends is high.

As we have observed repeatedly, organized political interaction is linked closely to power in New York. Just as organization tends to concentrate power, organizational diversity and conflict tend to disperse it. Certainly, power is by no means distributed equally among the citizens of the state; yet, it also is not centralized in a small over-arching "elite." The power to govern is strong, but no unified combination always prevails among the numerous interests; no party machine invariably gets what it wants; no governmental official or agency "rules;" and no hidden agenda appears to suppress certain types of political controversies. It is rare to find a significant allocation of social benefits where one set of interests is not vigorously opposed by others. Although some interests are more successful than others, seldom does opposition fail entirely or permanently. Policy outcomes usually reflect considerable compromise, so while there are winners in New York, they do not take all.

A vital element in the play and distribution of power is the news media, particularly the press. The media are, indeed, a system of power in themselves. By shaping public images of political leaders, groups, and institutions, by reporting and questioning political performance, and by raising issues of public policy, the news media serve to restrain the exercise of power. Numbers, vigor, and internal competition enhance the media's effectiveness. New York City is, of course, the national television news center. Local television news broadcasts by affiliates of all the major networks cover state and local politics, and a weekly public television program, "Inside Albany," gives intensive coverage of state politics and is followed carefully by state politicians.

The newspapers of New York are relatively numerous, large, and in some cases distinguished. They are also reasonably well distributed, with every metropolitan area outside New York City having at least two major papers available. While the City has definitely not been immune from the privations affecting newspapers generally,* its daily papers remain imposing

---

*Since 1960, the City has lost four major papers: the *Mirror*, the *Journal American*, the *Herald Tribune*, and the *World Telegram and Sun*. As this is written, the *Daily News*, the world's largest paper, is struggling to reduce labor costs enough to survive, while the *New York Post* has been suffering heavy losses that its publisher, Rupert Murdoch, may at any time decide are too large to bear.

sources of political news. What is more, the healthy growth of the *Village Voice*, a weekly known for its in-depth coverage of City politics, offers little encouragement to those who hope to grasp policy and power without the scrutiny of an able, attentive, and ambitious press.

Initiative and competition clearly are the rule throughout the media, and New Yorkers can hear and see a lot about the public affairs of their state. Of course, they do not hear and see everything, since there is so much to cover in New York politics. Furthermore, all the state's newspapers are not paragons of journalistic excellence, and the media's search for "inside dope" may extend too far. Governor Carey observed that public life is not always a pleasure:

> There's no privacy left at all. The media have become more exotic as they've developed the capacity to track and trace every area of your life. They destroy you for no reason.[45]

A similar criticism from a different perspective has come from the press itself, as Michael J. O'Neill of the *Daily News* told other editors and reporters that the press "has become insensitive and arrogant, allowing its skepticism about public officials to turn into a hostility that has weakened government's ability to function."[46]

Although there is no doubt that the scrutiny of journalists serves to open up the process of politics and to restrain the manipulation of power, the precise scope and degree of the media's ability to influence the operations of government remains elusive. In 1954, for example, the *New York Times* carried a page-one series of articles on the City's poor trash collection, and sanitation pickups improved immediately. In 1980, the *Times* published an even more critical series but the streets remained as dirty as before.[47] Clearly, the news media are an integral part of New York's political system, but their effects depend very much on the particular circumstances. More accomplished politicians try hard to use the media, just as the media use them. In this complex interaction, the consequence is the diminution of concentrated power.

Within the nation the political position of the Empire State is no longer preeminent. Along with wealth, New York has also been losing population, and the losses are politically significant. As the result of the 1980 census, the state lost five congressional seats and electoral votes, more than any other state. New York leaders are not indifferent to these losses, and the political expectations and style of the state's internal politics are being newly focused on its relationship with other states and the nation.

Befitting its own politics, New York's relationship with the federal government is a series of contradictions. While Mayor Edward Koch defended his 1981 Republican nomination by claiming it would enable him to get more from the Republican president,* the fact is that even New York Republicans have received comparatively little from the Reagan administration.[48] The City is extremely sensitive to criticisms of its financial practices that are voiced in Washington. In the 1976 presidential campaign the Carter forces made federal aid to the City the central issue and distributed millions of fliers with the *Daily News* headline, "Ford to City: Drop Dead." The result was that Carter received a higher percentage of the City and suburban vote than any candidate since Lyndon Johnson in 1964.[49] Yet, while a supplicant, in important respects the City's place is secure. It remains the nation's cultural and financial capital, and the economic vigor of high-income Manhattan is undiminished.

Given its heavy investment in public programs of all sorts, the state is sharply affected by the amount and shape of federal expenditures. Insofar as economic health is concerned, when Washington sneezes, New York gets a cold. With their characteristic style, New York congressmen are taking leading roles in regional efforts to divert more federal resources from the Sun Belt to the Northeast and Midwest. Whether dealing with federal grants from Washington or acid rain from the West, New York is reaching out to work with other states. Yet in a subtle and significant way, the state's relationships with others has changed. In the past, New York led the nation in active government and innovative programs. It still leads today, but now with sophisticated programmatic research through which it analyzes the programs of other states before making decisions about its own. From prisons to the state university, agencies and interests approaching Albany for support are confronted by interstate comparisons that usually lead to a cutting back of aspirations.

The political culture of New York still calls for active, aggressive politics based on expectations that government can make a difference—a big difference. But over a long period of strained resources these expectations are likely to decline, leading to reduced rather than expanded government. While New Yorkers may be too proud to admit it, their state is now tending to follow interstate patterns rather than leading the band.

---

*In a classic example of the vagaries of New York politics, Koch, deciding to seek the Democratic nomination for governor in the spring of 1982, found himself caught between the White House and big city/Democratic partisans back home. Needing help from the Reagan administration (for his city) and Democratic party leaders (for his nomination), Koch essentially worked both sides of the street—and with some success. At one point in March, President Reagan commented that Mr. Koch had been a good mayor who would make a good governor—leaving Republican candidates in New York wondering who their national party leader would endorse next!

NOTES

1. Wallace S. Sayre and Herbert Kaufman, *Governing New York City: Politics in the Metropolis* (New York: Norton, 1965), pp. 25–30.

2. Plunkitt's remains the classic expression of the City standing against the state. William L. Riordon, *Plunkitt of Tammany Hall* (New York: Dutton, 1963), pp. 21–24.

3. Both the wealth and poverty of New York are explained by Ken Auletta, *The Streets Were Paved With Gold* (New York: Random House, 1979).

4. These are emphasized by Sayre and Kaufman, *Governing New York City*, pp. 20–23.

5. Roger Starr, "Making New York Smaller," *New York Times Magazine*, 14 November 1976, p. F32. Another view of what was happening during this entire period, and who was responsible, is in Jack Newfield and Paul DuBrul, *The Abuse of Power: The Permanent Government and the Fall of New York* (New York: Viking, 1977), esp. Ch. 2.

6. Auletta, *The Streets Were Paved With Gold*; and Andy Logan, "Around City Hall: Coalescing," *The New Yorker*, 3 November 1980, pp. 171–2.

7. E.J. Dionne Jr., "A Matter of Choices," *New York Times*, 9 January 1982, p. 28; and Clyde Haberman, "Koch, in Spending Plan for 1983, Forecasts Fewer Gains in Services," *New York Times*, 16 January 1982, p. 1.

8. An excellent analysis of City services is Charles Brecher and Raymond D. Horton, *Setting Municipal Priorities, 1982*, report prepared for the Third Annual Conference on New York City governmental programs, Arden House, Harriman, New York, 4–5 December 1981.

9. The classic phrase of Harold D. Lasswell, *Politics: Who Gets What, When, How* (New York: Whittlesey, 1936).

10. Sayre and Kaufman, *Governing New York City*, p. 59.

11. Riordon, *Plunkitt of Tammany Hall*, p. 22.

12. As illustrated in Arthur J. Vidich and Joseph Bensman, *Small Town in Mass Society* (Garden City, N.Y.: Doubleday Anchor, 1960), esp. Chs. 5–7.

13. *Ibid.* Speaking of Condor, New York, Vidich and Bensman make it clear that the citizens expected their government to do things, even if not for everyone equally.

14. His immediate predecessor, Alfred E. Smith, was even more impressive in reforming the machinery of state government during the latter 1920s. For a brief account, see Joseph Alsop, *FDR: A Centenary Remembrance* (New York: Viking, 1982), esp. pp. 99–104.

15. Although they are rarely surprised by corrupt practices in general, state level politicians are often embarrassed to find present or former political associates under indictment. They are then torn between the political costs of turning against the corrupt individuals or the costs of ignoring them. From Roosevelt's refusal to move against the City's corrupt Mayor James J. (Jimmy) Walker before the 1932 Democratic convention to the gingerly treatment accorded Joseph Margiotta by 1980–82 senatorial and gubernatorial candidates, the usual reaction is one of finesse rather than outrage. For example, Richard J. Meislin, "Margiotta Is Down but Not Out, Colleagues Say," *New York Times*, 10 December 1981, B6.

16. An example of what political officials can expect from the press is the treatment of Governor Hugh Carey's marriage to Evangeline Gouletas. No effort was spared to publicize the bride's romantic background, and the motivations and experiences of both bride and groom. A sober discussion is found in Richard J. Meislin, "The Careys of Albany," *New York Times Magazine*, 4 October 1981, pp. 25ff.

17. Richard J. Meislin, "Poll Finds a Mixture of Pride and Worry in City's Future," *New York Times*, 21 December 1981, p. 1.

18. Sayre and Kaufman, *Governing New York City*, pp. 18–20.

19. There are numerous historical studies, but see the excellent political analysis of Nathan Glazer and Daniel Patrick Moynihan, *Beyond the Melting Pot: The Negroes, Puerto Ricans, Jews, Italians, and Irish of New York*, 2nd ed. (Cambridge, Mass.: M.I.T. Press, 1970); and no summary is better than Arthur Mann's introduction to Riordon, *Plunkitt of Tammany Hall*, pp. vii–xxii.

20. These elements of style became more important with the weakening of machine politics, in which the organization could get out the vote despite the personalities of the party leadership or candidates. Arthur Mann points out that the early Tammany leaders had little formal education and sometimes harsh personalities. Riordon, *Plunkitt of Tammany Hall*, pp. ix and xix.

21. Helene Weinstein, who defeated Speaker Stanley Steingut in the Democratic primary, was later ruled ineligible to hold office because of residency requirements. Her father, Murray E. Weinstein, took her place and defeated Steingut, who persisted to run on the Liberal line, in the general election. Steingut had been in the Assembly since 1953.

22. Michael Barone and Grant Ujifusa, *The Almanac of American Politics 1982* (Washington, D.C.: Barone and Co., 1982), pp. 718–19; and Maurice Carroll "Influence and Numbers Swell New Wave in Hispanic Politics," *New York Times*, 24 January 1982, p. E7.

23. See also Jewel Bellush and Stephen M. David, *Race and Politics in New York City* (New York: Praeger, 1971), esp. Ch. 1.

24. Andy Logan, "Around City Hall: Remedy," *The New Yorker*, 28 September 1981, pp. 128–32.

25. *Ibid.*, p. 131.

26. Joseph P. Fried, "City Council is Allowed to Continue Legislating," *New York Times*, 2 December 1981, p. B3; and Joyce Purnick, "A Council Panel Offers New Plan on Redistricting," *New York Times*, 31 December 1981, p. B3.

27. The following contain good descriptions of what happened in the City during earlier periods: Justin N. Feldman, "How Tammany Holds Power," in *Civic Victories: The Story of an Unfinished Revolution*, ed. Richard S. Childs (New York: Harper, 1952), pp. 309–14; Edward J. Flynn *You're the Boss* (New York: Viking Press, 1947), esp. pp. 219–35; and William M. Ivins, *Machine Politics and Money in New York City* (New York: Harper, 1887). Vidich and Bensman in *Small Town in Mass Society*, esp. pp. 121–27, describe how a local establishment operated about 25 years ago.

28. For example, while *Plunkitt of Tammany Hall*, pp. 11–20, viewed reforms with concern, he saw reformers as "Mornin' Glories" that could never succeed themselves. Others at the same time viewed the same events as great triumphs. See Milo T. Bogard, ed., *The Redemption of New York* (New York: P.F. McBreen & Sons, 1902).

29. Barone and Ujifusa, *The Almanac of American Politics 1982*, p. 718.

30. *New York Times*, 21 October 1980, p. B9. This report of a major New York Times/CBS News Poll showed party identification in New York as less Democratic (44 percent) and Independent (20 percent), and more Republican (27 percent) than in the rest of the nation (which was 47 percent, 26 percent, and 24 percent, respectively.) Since 1948, Republican candidates have won five of the nine presidential elections in New York, the same as in the nation.

31. *Ibid.* The New York electorate was 23 percent liberal, 40 percent moderate, and 28 percent conservative, while the nation as a whole was 17 percent, 44 percent, and 32 percent, respectively. Clearly, on the opinion measures used, New Yorkers were relatively more liberal than many other Americans.

32. Hispanics in New York City come mainly from Puerto Rico. Their numbers grew rapidly during the 1960s and 1970s, but leveled off more recently. They now constitute one-fifth of the city's population. See Maurice Carroll, "Influence and Numbers Swell New Wave in Hispanic Politics," p. E7.

33. There were added factors that affected turnout in New York City. Since Mayor Edward Koch had no major opposition, turnout was probably discouraged. On the other hand, David Dinkins, a black running for Manhattan borough president, might have drawn more blacks to the polls. See Andy Logan, "Around City Hall: Getting Out the Vote," *The New Yorker*, 26 October 1981, pp. 161ff.

34. Joanne Wasserman, "Labor's Top Brass," *Empire State Report*, November 1981, p. 10ff.

35. Riordon, *Plunkitt of Tammany Hall*, pp. 3–6.

36. A brief, but insightful analysis of this Tammany organization is Daniel Patrick Moynihan, "When the Irish Ran New York," *The Reporter*, 8 June 1961, pp. 32–34.

37. Norman M. Adler and Blanche Davis Blank, *Political Clubs in New York* (New York: Praeger, 1975).

38. "Margiotta Gets Jail Term But Still Keeps Job," *New York Times*, 24 January 1982, p. E6. The Margiotta case went on for months and was extensively reported, He was convicted on five counts of extortion and one count of fraud.

39. Riordon, *Plunkitt of Tammany Hall*, pp. 17–20.

40. At this point the emphasis must be on the inability of the major parties to prevent third parties from manipulating their candidates. Frank Lynn, "For Many Candidates, Party Labels Are Flags of Convenience," *New York Times*, 8 November 1981, p. E7.

41. William H. Honan, "Mayor Goes the Fusion Tradition One Better," *New York Times*, 8 November 1981, p. E7. The mayor of Buffalo also ran as a candidate of both Democratic and Republican parties in 1981.

42. Robert A. Caro, *The Power Broker: Robert Moses and the Fall of New York* (New York: Random House Vintage, 1975), esp. Ch. 10 and much of Part IV.

43. Richard J. Meislin. "Swing of the Pendulum in Albany: The Legislature Goes Its Own Way," *New York Times*, 8 June 1981, p. A1.

44. Richard J. Meislin, "Party Chiefs in Albany: Powers Behind Voting," *New York Times*, 10 April 1981, p. B1.

45. Richard Reeves, "Along Tocqueville's Path—Part I," *The New Yorker*, 5 April 1982, pp. 62–65.

46. Jonathan Friendly, "Reporter's Notebook: Insiders on Journalism," *New York Times*, 8 May 1982, p. 8.

47. Richard Whitmire (writing for the Gannett News Service), "Newspapers Make, Break, Politicians," *The Saturday Press*, Binghamton, 9 January 1982, p. A3. On the other hand, the direct involvement of newspapers in discouraging or promoting candidates continues and could be seen clearly in the early phases of the 1982 gubernatorial campaign. Andy Logan, "Around City Hall: Yonder Peasant, Who Is He?" *The New Yorker*, 22 March 1982, p. 159.

48. Frank Lynn, "New York Republican Party Gets Few Top Reagan Posts," *New York Times*, 29 November 1981, p. A1.

49. Barone and Ujifusa, *The Almanac of American Politics*, pp. 722–23.

12
New Hampshire
RICHARD F. WINTERS

Over the last two decades, the state of New Hampshire has charted a distinctive social, economic, and political course. Along with Vermont, but unlike other states in the Northeast, New Hampshire has recorded sizable population gains, sharp increases in industrial and factory mobility, and rapidly growing employment. Surprisingly, however, the Granite State has made markedly different political choices in shaping these changes.

New Hampshire has followed a distinctly conservative political course. It has no state income or sales tax, and has lagged behind the other nearby states in adopting bottle-deposit bills, pollution controls and land-use plans.[1] It also ranks among the bottom 10 of the 50 states in spending support for secondary and higher education, welfare, prisons, justice administration and other key programs.[2] Its deeply rooted, conservative political ideology continued to manifest itself in the 1982 election when it was the only state in the nation to oust an incumbent Democratic Governor, Hugh Gallen, in favor of a conservative Republican challenger, John Sununu.[3]

In terms of social and economic characteristics, the state is a place of startling contrasts. Small-town New Hampshire is widely believed to be ethnically homogeneous and Yankee, yet the population includes a high proportion of residents of foreign stock within the state. Although one of the smaller states, it ranks as average in terms of personal wealth. While one of the least urbanized of the 50 states, it is also one of the most industrialized. Moreover, while New Hampshire is usually considered Republican and conservative, its voters have done an even-handed job of forecasting the presidential nominees of both parties.

These basic contrasts tend to be overlooked by outside observers. For example, the view presented every four years on the nation's TV screens of small-town rural natives greeting swarms of presidential primary aspirants, sandwiched between piled-high snow banks, is belied by the reality of the state's largest city, Manchester. Once considered to be an "industrial utopia," Manchester was to be the forerunner of the industrial city where

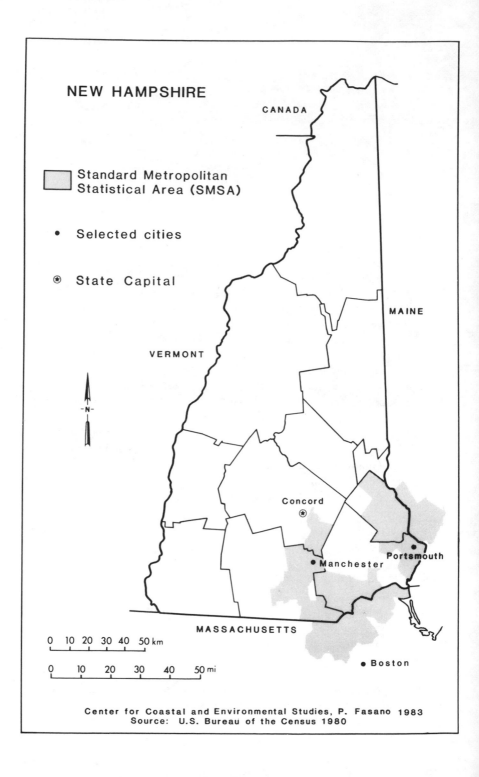

NEW HAMPSHIRE

Standard Metropolitan
Statistical Area (SMSA)

• Selected cities

⊛ State Capital

CANADA

MAINE

VERMONT

-N-

Concord
⊛

Portsmouth
• Manchester

MASSACHUSETTS

0 10 20 30 40 50 km

0   10   20   30   40   50 mi

• Boston

Center for Coastal and Environmental Studies, P. Fasano 1983
Source: U.S. Bureau of the Census 1980

workers would be united in common and voluntary bonds of the workplace: living nearby in factory-sponsored housing; attending factory-sponsored social gatherings; and participating in factory-supported sports and recreation leagues.[4] The industrial utopia never succeeded, but the early industrial revolution was a smashing success in this "Queen City" as attested to by the miles of extraordinary, multi-storied factory buildings that still line the Merrimack River.

POLITICAL CULTURE: CONSERVATISM TRIUMPHANT

In 1959, Duane Lockard best captured the political culture of New Hampshire by characterizing its state politics as "the triumph of political conservatism." Over recent decades, this triumph appears to be nearly conclusive. Conservatism in New Hampshire is rooted in an enduring localistic culture that values private, individual initiative, supports local community activity, but places severe restrictions on the scope of politics beyond the local level.

The most striking characteristic of the New Hampshire public is the strong local pride and loyalty of its citizens. The Granite State has few tangible symbols of statewide pride and loyalty: no imposing collegiate football teams; no marching bands and associated ceremony; and no great urban centers that provide an instant sense of recognition and identity. Instead, people are drawn to the enduring and intangible symbols that center around the personal values and life styles of historic New England.

People identify with the physical environment of the local setting. They take great pride in the mountains, forests, and lakes that contribute to the pristine beauty of the state. The characteristics of the environment also inspire associations with the values and symbols of the old Yankee ethic. The long snowy winters, for example, supposedly encourage the traditional Yankee virtues of self-reliance, thrift, and hard work. As part of this ethic, people value the notion that individuals should strive to be self-sufficient and communities should work out their own problems and provide for their own needs. Hence, they tend to be critical and wary of state politics and politicians. Such mistrust is not a contemptuous kind based on knowing cynicism, or a parochial kind based on the knowledge of past promises broken. It is rather a fundamental suspicion about the ability of politics, once removed from the grass roots of local communities, to express the best of common actions. While the same Yankee ethic has been broadened in Vermont to include a state-system orientation, in New Hampshire by and large, it remains narrowly focused at the town or municipal level.

The political cornerstones of these local loyalties are the town and school meetings. The continued vitality of these meetings should not be too surprising, as it is at this level that important public services are funded. While New Hampshire ranks last in state support for elementary and secondary education, it ranks first in local support for these school systems.[5]

Likewise, local tax collections, as a percentage of state and local taxes, are highest in New Hampshire as are local property taxes. Thus, town and city governments are the focal point of much of the effective political action in the state that touch the day-to-day lives of most people.

The ideological component of New Hampshire's localism is the dominance of political conservatism among political leaders as well as the rank and file. Several years ago, a survey asked voters to characterize their political philosophy.[6] Forty-six percent of the state's voters considered themselves to be "conservatives," while only 20 percent labelled themselves "liberals," and 26 percent claimed to be "moderates." The most striking finding was that conservatives were just about equally spread between the two major parties. Among the Democrats, 38 percent claimed to be "conservative" and only 29 percent considered themselves "liberal." Of all Republicans, 50 percent claimed to be "conservative" while 12 percent called themselves "liberal." Thus, self-designated conservatives numerically dominate both political parties.

Political conservatism has strong historical roots in both parties. Its strongest and deepest hold is in the traditional Republicanism of the state, a sentiment that reaches to the Civil War and the realignments of that era. New Hampshire was one of the early supporters of the Republican party in the 1850s, and this support has been continually affirmed since that time.

The conservatism of the Republican party is reinforced by the social, economic and cultural characteristics of its leaders and followers. Lockard described the party as being made up of "conservatives and not-so-conservatives."[7] The latter group had roots in the well-educated, professional classes, often drawing leadership from the legal profession, and with close ties to the business community throughout the state. This "not-so-conservative" wing of the party has produced some legendary figures: Concord educator and civic leader, Governor John Winant; businessman and manufacturer, Governor and U.S. Senator Charles Tobey; forest products and manufacturer, Governor and Presidential Assistant Sherman Adams; and others such as Norris Cotton, Hugh Gregg, and Lane Dwinell.

The backgrounds of the leadership of the "more conservative" wing of the party and its source of electoral support are not as clear and straightforward. Electoral support is distributed throughout the state: somewhat more in the north and east and less in the west and south; somewhat more in the smaller towns or cities; and somewhat more among Yankee and Protestant than ethnic and Catholic groups. However, one generalization about the current set of conservative Republican leaders is that many of them were born out of the state and moved into New Hampshire as adults.

Currently, the ideological conservatism of the state is focused, in large part, on the issue of taxation. New Hampshire is currently the only state in the Union with neither a broad-based retail sales tax nor a personal income tax levied on its citizenry. In New Hampshire this is the key issue. In many ways, a person's position either favoring or not favoring a broad-based state tax serves as a remarkably good proxy for his or her position on a wide number of other political issues.

There is considerable logic to the fundamental quality of the tax issue because lacking the revenue that broad-based taxes would generate, the state is unable to mount much of an effective and progressive set of programs that might be favored by the liberals in the state. Conservatives are hardly ignorant of the "lid" or "cap" that the lack of a broad-based revenue system imposes willy-nilly on the state. Indeed, they laud such a result and praise the private-sector initiatives that they claim flow from a system whereby personal income is not taxed by the state. Reaganomics was alive and well in New Hampshire long before Ronald Reagan became president.[8]

Observers have often noted that an important aspect of political conservatism in New Hampshire is its intensity. Neal Peirce once described it as a "snarling conservatism." This unusual degree of intensity has been developed and maintained, in part, by the presence of a unique factor in New Hampshire, the Manchester *Union-Leader* newspaper, long owned and dominated by its late, very conservative publisher, William Loeb. Politically, the *Union-Leader* is considered to be the most successful newspaper for its size in the country. The consensus among politicians is that it has profoundly shaped the politics of New Hampshire for three decades and shows only a few signs of abating since Loeb's death in 1981. New Hampshire is a small state, and with a circulation of about 65,000 daily the *Leader* is read by a significant portion of the state's population. It is the major daily in Manchester and is read across the state; the bright blue plastic delivery tubes attached to the rural mail boxes cover the state.

The keys to the paper's success are simple. First, it advocates a simple, practical, gritty conservatism of an uncomplicated politics. Opposition to new taxes, holding the line on increases in old taxes, opposition to growth in government, favoritism to the business community, and opposition to welfare and redistributive programs of any kind have marked the *Leader's* positions.

Additionally, the conservatism of the paper is pervasive. While one would expect this in editorials, it also appears in the news columns, letters to the editor, and in the editorial choices of the staff. These choices are represented in the stories that are printed about favored politicians, how the story is written (slavish praise) and whose press releases get published. It is also evident in the selection of either flattering or unflattering personal photographs of politicians.

The ideological cleavage promoted by the *Leader* over state taxes fits into a broader debate over expectations about the present and future functions of state government. Many citizens, leaders and followers alike, are wary of the activities of government. According to their logic, when government acts, private freedoms shrink. People often conceive of the relationship between public and private action as a sharp and negative trade-off. This is hardly an irrational or inexplicable view, as government does extract income from the private sector in order to fund public activities. But in New Hampshire the questioning of the marginal worth of any proposed government action is the general rule. Usually the presumption is that the loss of private action foregone by new public taxation or regulation will be greater than the benefits that might flow from the new or expanded government program.

The debate also reflects the changing social and economic situation in the state. The rapid growth of New Hampshire over the last couple of decades was no accident. Businessmen flocked to the state in order to take advantage of the low-tax environment; workers moved in to take the new jobs in the border towns or to commute to their old jobs in "Taxachusetts" from their tax havens in southern New Hampshire. The decision to move into the state is often straightforward and self-aggrandizing.

There are other twists to the story allied to perceptions of "tax shirking." Businessmen move to New Hampshire to enjoy low taxes while using the nearby publicly supported facilities in Massachusetts to ship their products out, or to fly from Boston's Logan Airport. State residents also drive along Massachusetts highways to attend publicly supported cultural amenities in nearby Boston. The New Hampshire merchant builds an establishment near the Massachusetts border to attract its residents to his store for the purchase of goods that are free from any sales tax.

State government has not ignored its opportunities. It has exploited its geographical location to provide services to residents of nearby states on a tax-free basis in New Hampshire. The most celebrated of these activities is the proliferation of state-run, discount liquor stores that ring the state's boundaries. These stores are immensely profitable. One store, for example, cleared enough in profit in the first three months of operation to cover the entire capital costs of its construction.[9]

Other conflicts with neighboring states center around tax policies that attempt to capitalize on the disparities in revenue policies. For example, for several years, while New Hampshire citizens enjoyed the absence of a personal-income tax, the state taxed the income of residents of nearby states who commuted to work in New Hampshire. New Hampshire is uniquely situated to exploit differences in state support for, and financing of, public goods and services. Furthermore, the prevailing public philosophy generally supports the rationale of instrumental policies for economic gain.

Certainly, not all citizens support this notion of government. A growing cadre of the state's residents question the viability of New Hampshire's version of the old Yankee ethic in more modern, complex times. Many disapprove of the inequalities and disparities in public services and many more are concerned about the rising level of local taxes and the long-term fiscal solvency of the state. Unlike other states, where political differences might be rooted in regional, ethnic, historical, or economic differences, divisions in New Hampshire are largely ideological and center on deep divisions about these basic political questions.

POLITICAL STYLE: AMATEUR AND HARDBALL

First of all, New Hampshire politics is open and permeable. There is little hierarchy in officeholding and less "ladder climbing" and having to "punch one's ticket" before achieving modest political success. Evidence for this is seen in the kinds of political backgrounds of the leading officeholders. Among governors, presidents of the senate, and speakers of the house, few have served long apprenticeships in order to reach political success.

The first-in-the-nation presidential primary has an impact here. Every four years large numbers of formerly inactive citizens are mobilized by the various presidential aspirants of both parties. Recruitment is generally outside the existing party organizations and appeals for workers are ideological and candidate-centered rather than partisan. A great number of young people and women are mobilized in this fashion. Indeed, the earlier New Hampshire organizing efforts of presidential aspirants seem to be made up almost exclusively of women and young people. These workers often continue their political activity in the New Hampshire house where typically one-third of the 400-member chamber are women and usually one-quarter are 35 years old or younger.

The importance of local politics and the large number of small and modest-sized towns also reinforce this political openness. Moreover, the key role of the town in New Hampshire politics often makes local selectmen and school board members a visible and credible set of public leaders, and ones who are readily accessible to citizens.

While openness connotes ease of entry into politics, exit must be considered as well. There is great dabbling in politics in New Hampshire. Activists seem to float into office for a term, decide not to continue, and simply drop out. Politics in New Hampshire is mainly sporadic, avocational, and amateur. Officeholding is largely a voluntaristic activity with little pay. State representatives and senators receive only $100 per year; leaders receive $50 more. In addition, they are allowed only a minimum amount for expenses and even have to pay their own phone bills. Most local board and council members receive no financial compensation. Moreover, political decentralization in the state increases the political burdens of local activity and responsibilities are often heavy and time-consuming.

Ease of entry and exit also comes about because there is little in the way of local or statewide party organizations to encourage the activist to continue in politics or establish a place in the political hierarchy. Both political parties are underfinanced and poorly organized. The state Democratic party committee has been in debt continuously since the mid-1970s and, at present, has no staff, relying instead on volunteer help at the state headquarters. There is little to supervise at the local level, as fewer than a dozen town and county committees are actively organized. Thus, in the towns and in the General Court, New Hampshire is an open and participant system—and the dominant style is decidedly amateur. Yet at the level of the highest state office that openness narrow dramatically. There are relatively few statewide offices, the governor being the only official elected statewide. There is no lieutenant governor and other executive offices in the state are all appointive positions.

An important consequence of this narrowness is the high sustained level of intraparty conflict over the nomination for governor. The gubernatorial party primaries, for example, have been contested in each election since 1970. During this period the Republicans held the governorship for four of the six bienniums and a serious challenge to the renomination of the incumbent was posed each time. Looking at the data for Republican gubernatorial elections in the past decade, the following conclusions can be drawn: the primaries draw a large number of candidates; there is substantial intraparty conflict that is usually based on ideological differences; incumbents are vulnerable to primary challenge; and incumbents challenged in the primaries are prone to general election defeat.

The Democrats have not escaped divisive conflict. New Hampshire's sizeable industrial establishment, with a large ethnic population, is concentrated in the old "mill towns" of Berlin, Manchester and Nashua. The state's immigrant population was originally drawn from Ireland, and then was followed by French-Canadians and Southern Europeans. The most recent migrants, from the other American states, make up the largest block of Democratic voters. For whatever reason—ethnic rivalries, latent political conservatism among the largely Roman Catholic groups, or the more instrumental conservatism already discussed—the Democratic party has never been able to mobilize the industrial working classes into an effective political force.

Sustained political conflict, focused to a large degree on ideology, manifests itself in an intriguing style of leadership behavior best described as "hardball politics." Lloyd Etheredge has described this style as "tough, ambitious, and shrewdly calculating."[10] In a sense, perhaps all successful American politicians must and do play "hardball." But it appears that this style is far more frequent in New Hampshire than elsewhere—at least at the statewide level and with regard to the offices of governor and U.S. senator.

The most manifest evidence of hardball-politics behavior appears in battles for the gubernatorial nomination of both parties. Many candidates of various ideological hues compete in the primary, and they seem incapable of resolving their conflicts either inside or outside the primary system. Party activity before the primary is especially divisive, and the coalition building that does appear after the primaries, seems to be forced on the losers as they face the even more unpleasant prospect of the victory of the other party's candidate. In part, this is an artifact of the singularity of the governor's office; singularity leading to keen competition. The evidence in New Hampshire is that even post-primary coalition building often fails.

The behavior of conservative Republican Meldrim Thomson, governor from 1972 to 1978, best typifies this hardball style. Over the course of more than a decade, Thomson was a perennial candidate for governor. In 1970, before serving his three two-year terms, he challenged the incumbent Republican governor, Walter Peterson. He lost the primary challenge by only a few thousand votes and then proceeded to take on the victorious incumbent as an American Independent party candidate in the general election. He fared poorly, gathering only half the number of votes he won in the primary, but he cut substantially into the margin of the winning incumbent Peterson. Thomson challenged Peterson in 1968 as well and also took on another conservative Republican, former-Governor Wesley Powell. In 1972, in Thomson's third Republican battle for the nomination, he defeated Peterson, but in turn was challenged by an independent, moderate Republican, Malcolm McLane, in the general election.

Personal, ideologically based, intraparty conflict, especially in the Republican party, seems to be far more prominent in New Hampshire than in other states. A systematic review of independent candidacies in all other states over the last decade shows no comparable cases of primary conflicts, failures at intraparty reconciliation and coalition-building, and instances of party bolting for an independent candicacy.[11]

POLITICAL INTERACTION: DEALING WITH TAXES

New Hampshire has a politically participant culture. Over the past 16 years, turnout in presidential elections, as a percentage of the voting population, has consistently been above national turnout levels. The gap or difference between state and national turnout levels in these elections, however, has narrowed substantially over these years. In 1964, turnout in New Hampshire was over 78 percent while national turnout was closer to 62 percent, for a difference of about 16 points in New Hampshire's favor. In 1968, turnout nationally was over 61 percent while that in New Hampshire it was just over 72 percent, a difference of about 11 points in the state's favor. In the 1972 and 1976 presidential elections, the gap narrowed further to about 9 points. In the 1980 election, turnout in the state was 58 percent while national turnout was 54 percent, a difference of just over 4 percentage points. Despite its diminution in recent years, the participant ethic continues and is evident in statewide elections as well. In gubernatorial contests since 1962, New Hampshire ranks in the top third of all states in the level of voter turnout.

A variety of studies have pointed out that voting participation figures are shaped by the socio-economic composition of the states' electorate, the competitiveness of their elections, and the laws and regulations that hinder or facilitate registration.[12] One study explored the effects of these factors on the 1960 presidential elections and discovered some interesting patterns for the New England states.[13] New Hampshire's socio-economic composition of better educated, older, Yankee voters with modest incomes, advantaged the state with a 4.2 percent higher turnout rate than the national average. While New Hampshire registration laws marginally depress turnout by 0.9 percent, the competitiveness of the 1960 election boosted turnout in these states. The striking finding is that these northern New England states had large, positive, unexplained residuals indicating far higher turnout than expected, given these three sets of standard factors. In fact, New Hampshire ranked third among the 50 states in turnout levels greater than that explained by conventional factors.

Surely the historically important role that local politics has played in the Granite State, with the town meeting as focal point, has engendered a strong participant culture. Only a small proportion of citizens usually turn out at these meetings; at most about 25 percent of the population attend and typically the average rate of participation is between 8 and 10 percent. But the very fact that this channel of direct democracy exists very likely makes the people of New Hampshire more sensitive to matters of political choice.

In addition, the operation of the tax system increases citizens' political sensitivity. As noted above, New Hampshire collects a larger portion of the combined state and local revenues at the local level than any other state. This revenue is collected largely in the form of the property tax, which, again, is the highest in the 50 states. The property tax is collected once a year in a highly visible fashion, and the directness of this taxation is one more probable cause of a politically sensitive and participant culture.

In terms of the partisanship of citizens, Republican party loyalties, while eroding, continue to dominate politics in the state. Most observers, since Duane Lockard in the 1950s,[14] have traditionally categorized New Hampshire as a strongly Republican state. A more general analysis, up through 1973, characterized it as a "two-party state," but just barely so. The state ranked eighth in the nation in degree of "Republicanness" of its electoral contests, separated only slightly from its neighbor Vermont, which was rated as the second most Republican of all states.[15]

More recently, however, a change in party balance has been occurring in New Hampshire. Party registration over the last twelve years shows some of this movement. In 1968 the Republican party registered about 42 percent of the voters, while the Democrats accounted for about 26 percent. The remaining one-third of the voters declared themselves to be Independents. Twelve years later, with a 38 percent increase in the number of registered voters, Republican registration had dropped slightly, to 40 percent, while Democratic registration had increased markedly to 32 percent and Independent affiliation declined to 27 percent. While all three official registration categories have grown in absolute size over the 12-year period, it is clear that recent changes have favored the Democrats.

A public opinion survey of the likely vote in New Hampshire, by and large, confirms this picture of the electorate and adds further detail. In a Cambridge Survey Research study, 43 percent of the likely voters in the state claimed to be Republican, while 33 percent labeled themselves Democrats and 25 percent claimed Independent status.[16] Regrettably there is no consistent-over-time polling data that might indicate some of the dynamics of the changing patterns of party identification. However, this survey confirmed that the "foreign stock" in New Hampshire is distributed unevenly between the parties. Voters who claimed "English" as the national background that most of their ancestors came from form the largest part of Republican identifiers (43 percent), while Democrats are French-Canadian (31 percent), English (29 percent), and Irish (12 percent). There is a fairly marked religious component as well. The religious affiliation of Republican identifiers is 62 percent Protestant, while 59 percent of the Democrats are Catholic.

The shift in party identification has resulted in changes in voting behavior as well. Democratic support in New Hampshire increased slowly but steadily over the past three decades. Thus, this formerly Republican stronghold has become more Democratic.[17] This should be expected, as the state has undergone tremendous social and economic immigration that has made it more like other states. Additionally, given that the state was so strongly Republican in the early years, it is not surprising that it would move in the Democratic direction. It is only one step further to predict the party balance in New Hampshire in the late 1980s.

The forecast is clearly that of an almost even competitiveness between the two parties. Projections of increased competition between the parties ordinarily implies shifts in the policy agenda. Ordinarily, the growing strength of the Democrats would suggest that the minority opposition, in this traditionally Republican state, could propose an alternative policy agenda—relating specifically to the tax question and the problems that it has generated—and be successful. But the dominance of conservatives, among the leadership and the rank and file of both parties, makes this scenario for the 1980s problematic at best.

The New Hampshire legislative chambers are a natural focus of outside interests, for reasons of absolute as well as comparative size. The house with its 400 members is nearly twice the size of the next largest state legislative chamber in the nation, and the senate with only 24 members is the fourth smallest among the state senates.

The structure of the house clearly reflects the localistic political culture as well as prevailing views on how representative government should be conducted. Politics in the General Court is decidedly amateur. Susan Fuhrman, in her analysis of education policymaking in New Hampshire, notes that the lower house "was intentionally designed to permit maximum local representation and maximum local control."[18] Given the size of the general population, it comes pretty close to direct democracy, where citizen-legislators can come and express the concerns of their individual committees. State business is not perceived as being very important; indeed, the general belief is that the agenda should be decided by ordinary men and women who are there to represent the interests of their local communities.

The size of the institution and its amateur orientation encourages an enormous volume of bills, most of which are either ill-conceived or poorly drafted. In such a situation, the role of committees becomes key. With so many members and so much legislation, committee chairmen are highly visible and important. In fact, these chairmen and a few party leaders are usually the only members that are known to the entire house. Recently, efforts to professionalize the legislature, by expanding resources and space for individual legislators, have been made but there is still little staff capacity and minimal assistance on matters of substantive policy.[19]

Ideological divisions characterize the state legislative chambers as well. During the 1975–76 session, a sample survey asked state legislators their positions on a wide variety of political subjects, including their reactions to various political leaders and their preferences for various kinds of spending increases or cuts and tax increases or cuts.[20] Consistently, a question on ideology ("Philosophically, do you consider yourself to be a conservative, moderate, or liberal, or somewhere between?") turned out to be a better predictor of legislator attitudes and preferences on budgetary and other issues than standard demographic or political variables including, most importantly, political party affiliation. Ideology cuts right across the partisan affiliation of the legislature; self-described conservatives are drawn almost equally from both parties (40 percent Republicans and 35 percent Democrats). Moreover, evaluations about the then-governor, Republican Meldrim Thompson, clearly indicated that ideological considerations outweighed party considerations by 10 to 1. Personal interviews with house and senate leaders and followers confirmed the pattern of party factionalization and ideological conflict. During this same session, the parties dramatically split on the final and most important amendments to the state budget. However, these most heavily sanctioned of all legislative votes were equally well explained by political philosophy as by party affiliation.

While conservatives make up the largest segment of the Republican party, which in turn has dominated the house over the last two decades, they have not yet been successful in dominating the legislative party in the house. Moderate Republicans such as the present speaker, John Tucker, and his predecessors, George Roberts and James O'Neill, and their followers have dominated the house leadership. This is not the case in the senate, where over the past several years a sizeable group of conservative Republicans allied with several conservative Democrats has maintained philosophical control. The leader of this coalition, Senator Robert Monier, was one of eight candidates for the 1982 Republican nomination for governor and the endorsee of former Governor Thomson.

The position of governor is the single statewide office in the Granite State, and this should confer upon it significant advantage. Nonetheless, an index of gubernatorial power ranked the state 41 out of 50 in terms of executive authority, and only in terms of budgetary powers did the New Hampshire governor rank among the more powerful of his peers throughout the nation.[21] Even this may be an exaggeration. While budgetary authority is a formal power of the governor, the broader politics of taxes and revenue shapes the outer bounds of that power. Additionally, it should be pointed out that part of the governor's budgetary power is shared by an executive council, a five-person elected council that also shares with the chief executive the power of political appointment. The power of appointment, moreover, is also influenced by the state legislature, which must approve appointments in at least several key cases.

The governor is elected for only a two-year term, and faces a "winner-take-all" direct primary held late in the electoral session. As noted above, this puts a premium on long campaigns and usually leads to divisive primary battles. The wounds of the long electoral season are often difficult to patch over before the general election. The party convention is held by law within one to three weeks after the primaries. Coming so rapidly on the heels of often divisive primaries, it often serves to ratify the winning candidate's victory rather than reconciling his opponents.

A final uncertainty hanging over the chief executive is the increasing electoral vulnerability of incumbents. Hugh Gallen's loss to conservative John Sununu in the 1982 general election suggests that New Hampshire continues to build a record in gubernatorial elections that may be unparalleled in modern American politics. Gallen is the third incumbent in a row, and fourth of five since 1960, to be defeated in a bid for reelection either in the primary or the general election. The tax issue in New Hampshire is the key, as it appears to account both for the incumbents' eventual losses and for the successes of the victors. That is to say, the effect of the tax issue is two-fold in the state. It affects winning elections; whoever takes the "pledge" or appears to be more faithful to an anti-tax stance is benefitted. It also limits the ability of incumbents to govern or to remain in office.

John Sununu won the election, as Hugh Gallen put it, on the basis of "that stupid pledge."[22] Gallen correctly surmised that Sununu's simple pledge to veto any broad-based tax presented a benign and, for the typical voter, a personally rewarding commitment that brought the party, philosophical, and issue faithful back into the Republican fold. Gallen's failure to "take the pledge" left him wide open to the double-barreled election attack by Sununu that claimed both an income and a sales tax would be adopted if Gallen were reelected. Such a campaign charge is difficult to refute. Gallen could only weakly counter that it was not true, but he refused to unconditionally pledge to veto a tax if one were enacted.

One election analysis claimed that the 1982 election was a "party" election,[23] in that it represented a statewide "reinstating" election where the established forces of party and philosophy asserted themselves. The analysis argued that in this election, a Republican and more conservative nominee won, as the "normal electoral forces" of Republicanism and conservatism turned out the Democratic incumbent. That representation of the election, however, begs the question somewhat, for Hugh Gallen was the only Democrat incumbent nationally to lose reelection. This suggests that the election was not simply a Sununu victory, but also an incumbent's loss, just as incumbents Wesley Powell in 1962, Walter Peterson in 1972, and Meldrim Thomson in 1978 lost reelection.

The absence of a broad-based tax in New Hampshire denies incumbents a political resource base sufficient to fuel programs that create successful gubernatorial "re-electoral coalitions" term after term. That is to say, the New Hampshire governor is incapable of winning a succession of terms because he lacks the wherewithal to demonstrate to groups in the state that government is actively involved in their political concerns. During his tenure in office, past electoral coalitions disintegrate and new ones are difficult to form. Thus, the tax issue has paradoxical qualities in New Hampshire politics. On the one hand, the crucial winning margins of the past three governors in their initial victories have been based on their opposition to new taxes. Yet, the absence of a broad-based tax system precludes the incumbent governor from creating ongoing electoral coalitions.

Gallen, like many of his predecessors, acted out the inevitable scenario. His 1976 candidacy was created and made believable by a tax issue. During his first years in office, no politician was more adamant in publicly posturing his opposition to new taxes. However, in 1982, as his coalition of support for reelection began to falter, he was caught in a profound dilemma. Reelection was contingent on producing proof positive of the worth of his candidacy. Worth of candidacy depended on a flow of benefits to key groups such as educators, state employees, contractors, and other support bases. But lacking the necessary tax base, there was no possible way such commitments could be fulfilled.

The tax issue is a powerful political instrument in gubernatorial politics. Gallen and many of his predecessors used it to forge winning efforts. The final lesson of the Gallen governorship and those before him, is that while the tax issue has the power to create victory, it also turns and manages to destroy the victor.

The powerful interest groups in New Hampshire politics have been the commercial, industrial, and business groups. Historically, these interests have varied from the railroads at the turn of the century, to gambling concerns in the post-war era,[24] to a modern economic mix that includes many recent corporate arrivals. Wheelbrator-Frye, Congoleum, AMCA International, Digital Equipment, and Anheuser-Busch, have recently located in the state, with the first three establishing their international headquarters here. The leadership of many of the old-line industrial firms, as well as many of the newer ones, has reinforced the influence of the moderate to conservative wing of the Republican party. Executives from these firms are often very active in "good government" political organizations, such as the Forum on New Hampshire's Future. Many volunteer their time in assisting the state in achieving efficiency and economy in operational activities, such as participating in the recent governor's commission on governmental efficiency or the funding of academic studies that attempt to establish political viewpoints.[25] Business groups allied together in the Business and Industry Association and other traditional groups such as the Chamber of Commerce are particularly concerned about the operation of the state revenue system. The fastest growing revenue source in New Hampshire is the business profits tax that businesses claim unfairly places the burden of financing state government on corporate shoulders while individual tax-payers are hardly touched.

Small businesses, especially small commercial interests, are important in the continuing tax battle. Their influence probably explains the difference between survey findings that indicate that the general public far prefers a sales tax to an income tax, if new revenue is required, while a sizeable majority of the state legislature, if forced to choose, favors an income tax. The direct losers, in the case of a new sales tax, would be the small business interests, and it appears that this sentiment has been brought home to state representatives. The current business profits tax, that is so widely disliked by large businesses, was set up to replace a stock-in-trade tax on business inventories, which was widely held to penalize small businesses.

Other active and influential business interests are those regulated by the state and by towns. Good examples of these are trucking, land development, and insurance companies. Also, these industries represent the three leading occupations of members of the state senate.

Over the past several decades various groups have mobilized to express their concern with the status of the New Hampshire revenue system. Typically, these are groups such as the Forum on New Hampshire's Future and the public-employee associations. The latter mobilize as they discover that their jobs and salaries are often the first target of new rounds of budget cutting in the state. Other interests with similar concerns are the towns and their municipal associations, school-board associations, and other educational groups affected by cuts in state aid to localities.

The federal government has not ignored New Hampshire. Federal district courts in the state have played an important role in shaping what the state must do in the coming years in terms of institutional additions, improvements and policy changes for prisons, state hospitals, and schools for the emotionally and mentally handicapped. The low level of state funding often puts the state in direct conflict with federal authorities and the continued difficulty in passing a broad-based revenue system just about precludes compliance.

The effect of the cap placed on state revenues by the continuing refusal to reform the tax system has also produced an inexorable devolution of power and program responsibility to the county and town levels. Two consequences flow from this pattern. First, there is a generally low aggregate funding for most programs, and, second, there is great variation and inequity across local jurisdictions in funding levels. Thus, the combined resources of state and local funds for public services leads to an effort that ranks only 38th among the states. While wealthy towns get wealthier, poorer towns do not get wealthy so fast. This leads to an increasing gap in spending between affluent, moderately affluent, and less-affluent towns. The problem becomes more intractable because wealth is attracted to wealth; middle- and upper-income residents are attracted to established towns with well-funded and highly regarded town services. The net effect of this trend is to lighten the tax burden among those towns that already have a greater ability to pay.[26] Poorer communities naturally have the opposite problem.

These problems cannot continue unabated. A resolution of the tax situation in New Hampshire will certainly come about as the inevitable political problems of decentralization are realized. Yet, the dominant cultural attributes of the state, that center around a highly developed sense of localism and the divisions and conflicts generated by the nature of ideological politics in New Hampshire, suggest rough going in the years ahead.

NOTES

1. This is the claim of a recent report of the Joint Economic Committee of the U.S. Congress, which claimed "New Hampshire was conspicuous in New England for its very low taxes and also for its substantial inmigration of resources." See "State and Local Economic Development Strategy: A 'Supply Side' Perspective", Staff study prepared for the Subcommittee on Monetary and Fiscal Policy, 26 October 1981.

2. The crucial quality of the taxing and spending issue is discussed in Richard Winters, "Political Choice and Expenditure Change in New Hampshire and Vermont," *Polity*, 12 (Summer 1980):598–621.

3. This is further documented in my "Damn Yankees and Others: New Hampshire's Electorate and What it Represents," a paper presented for a Conference on the New Hampshire Presidential Primary, Concord, New Hampshire, 1980.

4. For a spectacular historical and photographic account of the principles and practices of early industrial Manchester, see Tamara K. Hareven and R. Langenbach, *Amoskeag* (New York: Pantheon, 1978).

5. Data drawn from Table 2, "Revenue and Expenditures for Public Elementary and Secondary Education, 1977–1979" (Washington, D.C.: NCEC, January 1981), p. 12.

6. Data from an unpublished research report (Study #690) of the Cambridge Opinion Research Corporation, Cambridge, Massachusetts, 1976.

7. Duane Lockard, *New England State Politics* (Princeton: Princeton University Press, 1959), p. 50.

8. This is the implicit theme of Colin and Rosemary Campbell, "A Comparative Study of the Fiscal Systems of New Hampshire and Vermont: 1940–1974" (New Hampton, N.H.: Wheelabrator Foundation, 1976).

9. Discussion in the New Hampshire Senate Finance Committee, 1975, in the presence of the author.

10. Lloyd Etheredge, "Hardball Politics: A Model," *Political Psychology*, 1 (Spring 1979), p. 3.

11. Gubernatorial elections in the 50 states were examined for the last decade and significant independent candidacies were then traced back to the party primaries. The data is in *America Votes, 1980* (Washington, D.C.: Governmental Affairs Institute, 1981) and appropriate biennial volumes.

12. See Raymond Wolfinger and S. Rosenstone, *Who Votes* (New Haven: Yale University Press, 1980); and Jae On Kim et al., "Voting Turnout Among the American States: Systemic and Individual Components," *American Political Science Review*, 69 (March 1975):107–124.

13. Kim et al., *ibid.*, Table 4, p. 116.

14. Lockard, *New England State Politics*, chapter 3.

15. Austin Ranney, "Parties in State Politics," in *Politics in the American States*, eds., Herbert Jacob and Kenneth N. Vines, 3rd ed. (Boston: Little, Brown, 1976), pp. 51–92.

16. Cambridge Opinion Research report, (Study #690).

17. Data from Robert Craig and Richard Winters, "Party Politics in New Hampshire," in *New England Political Parties*, eds. Josephine Milburn and W. Doyle (Boston: Schenckman, 1982).

18. Susan Fuhrman, "New Hampshire" in *Shaping Education Policy in the States* eds. Susan Fuhrman and Alan Rosenthal (Washington, D.C.: Institute for Educational Leadership, 1981), p. 113.

19. *Ibid.*, p. 114.

20. Research conducted by the author. In a multiple regression equation of legislators' self-designated philosophy and their party affiliation, the philosophy variable significantly predicted evaluations of Thomson while the party variable was not significant. In terms of the budget vote, a multiple regression indicated that both party and philosophy variables were highly significant factors.

21. Joseph A. Schlesinger, "A Comparison of the Relative Positions of Governors," in *The American Governor in Behavioral Perspective* eds. Thad Beyle and J. Oliver Williams (New York: Harper and Row, 1972).

22. This statement was made in Gallen's concession speech broadcast on regional television throughout New England on WBZ-TV in Boston. It is also quoted in the *New Hampshire Times*, 8 November 1982, p. 5.

23. See the analysis by David Moore and Robert Craig in the *New Hampshire Times*, 8 November 1982, pp. 6–7. Moore and Craig did not use this well-known terminology of the classification of elections popularized by the Survey Research Center at the University of Michigan. However, their analysis is best summarized in those terms. For an introduction to the analysis of the Survey Research Center, see *Elections and the Political Order*, eds. Angus Campbell et al. (New York: Wiley, 1966).

24. See the discussion in Lockard, *New England State Politics*, pp. 48–51.

25. The Campbells' "Comparative Study . . . ," for example, was funded by a foundation organized by the Wheelabrator-Frye Corporation. Its chief executive officer, Michael Dingman, is the most active of the new crop of executives.

26. This is discussed more fully in Bruce Cooper, Majorie Robertson, and Richard Winters, "Tax-Based Educational Equity: A New Approach to School Finance Reform," an unpublished paper presented at the Annual Meeting of the American Educational Research Association, Boston, Massachusetts, 1980.

13
Vermont
FRANK SMALLWOOD

In his 1959 study, *New England State Politics*, Duane Lockard described Vermont as "a land of political paradox. It is conservative, but it has a liberal strain."[1] Almost a quarter of a century has passed since Lockard made this observation, yet Vermont still retains many of its paradoxical political qualities. Now, however, the tilt is toward the liberal, progressive side. Although Vermont has historically been regarded as a conservative, frugal, and strongly one-party Republican state, during the past two decades a marked shift in focus has occurred.

Vermont is now an innovative pioneer in the fields of environmental planning, pollution controls, land use planning, bottle deposit legislation, welfare rights programs, social rehabilitation, and community correctional programs. Moreover, the state has become heavily dependent on federal financial assistance, ranking first among the 50 states in the amount of federal aid dollars it receives in relation to the tax dollars it sends to Washington. It is a state with a substantial tax burden of its own, consisting of a state income tax (which is pegged at 26 percent of the federal income tax), plus a sales tax (which was raised to 4 percent in 1982). During this time, Vermont has become an increasingly competitive two-party state where voters in 1980 supported Republicans Ronald Reagan for president and Richard Snelling for governor, while returning Democrat Patrick Leahy to the U.S. Senate, and electing Bernard Sanders, an independent candidate and self-avowed socialist, as the mayor of Burlington, its only sizeable city.

The paradoxical nature of Vermont's shift from a conservative to a more progressive-liberal political stance can only be understood within the context of the state's underlying political culture and its personalized style of political interaction.

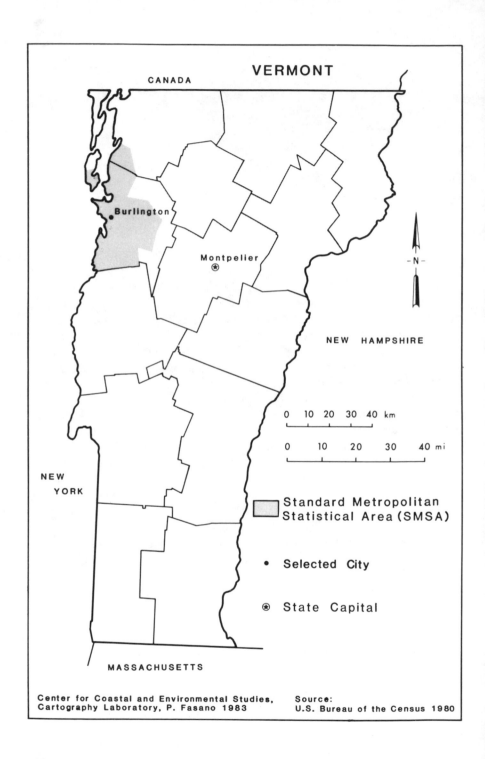

VERMONT

CANADA

Burlington

Montpelier

NEW HAMPSHIRE

NEW
YORK

0 10 20 30 40 km

0 10 20 30 40 mi

Standard Metropolitan
Statistical Area (SMSA)

• Selected City

⊛ State Capital

MASSACHUSETTS

Center for Coastal and Environmental Studies,   Source:
Cartography Laboratory, P. Fasano 1983   U.S. Bureau of the Census 1980

POLITICAL CULTURE: RADICAL CONSERVATISM

It is necessary to begin at the very beginning. Vermont originally developed a unique mix of progressive, almost radical, conservatism as a result of its historical evolution. This tradition first emerged during the period when Vermont was governed as an independent republic from 1777 until it was finally admitted to the newly formed federal Union as the fourteenth state in 1791.

The progressive political strain is seen in the 1777 Constitution of the Republic of Vermont the first in the nation to outlaw slavery, to abolish the requirement that voters must be property owners, and to provide for a uniform system of public school education. Yet, during its formative years to 1791, Vermont was also forced to develop a sense of more cautious conservatism in order to conduct the affairs of state of an autonomous independent republic—coining money, putting down internal insurrections, taking diplomatic initiatives, and fashioning a body of law through a functioning legislature.[2] The early legacy of political independence was strengthened by the fact that the state literally had to fight to preserve its political existence. After fending off land claims from both New Hampshire and New York, Vermont was finally able to gain congressional recognition as the nation's fourteenth state, but only after many delays and misunder-standings and only after the dispute with New York was finally adjusted in 1790 by the payment of $30,000.[3]

Once it had attained statehood, Vermont continued its tradition of political independence. Since it lacked an aristocracy of wealth, it was the most democratic—and in many ways the most radical and innovative—state in New England.[4] During the nineteenth century, Vermont was the first state to elect a U.S. congressman (Matthew Lyon) who was serving in jail for an alleged violation of the unpopular Alien and Sedition Acts (1800); give its electoral college votes to a third party presidential candidate, William Wirt, Anti-Mason (1832); and offer to provide Union troops in the Civil War (1861).[5]

Following a century-long period of political somnolence that lasted from 1860 to 1960, Vermont has once again emerged during the past two decades to demonstrate many of its earlier qualities of radical political innovation. This time, however, it has shifted its focus from its earlier skeptical defiance to a more comprehensive emphasis on social and environmental reforms. Since World War II, for example, Vermont has been the first state to elect a woman lieutenant governor (Consuelo N. Bailey in 1954); establish a Head Start program for disadvantaged children (in East Fairfield in 1965); and enact a comprehensive program of statewide environmental land-use legislation and a host of other environmental regulations during the 1970s.

The more recent shift to social and environmental initiatives highlights the nature of the political paradox that was noted by Lockard. Why has a traditionally Republican state embraced these more liberal, progressive programs? Why has a state that has long extolled the virtues of political independence and radical individualism been willing to accept the tenets of comprehensive, statewide social and environmental planning?

A number of explanations—grounded largely in recent state demographic changes and the emergence of a more competitive two-party political system—have been advanced in an effort to answer these questions.

In terms of demography, Vermont, along with New Hampshire, is one of a handful of states in the northeast that have experienced rapid population growth during the past three decades. Although it is still very small (ranking 48th among the 50 states), Vermont has seen its population grow from 377,000 to 511,000 between 1950 and 1980, an increase of over 33 percent. Yet, it is difficult to see how this population increase alone could account for Vermont's shifting political ideology because, in terms of ethnic and racial characteristics, the state remains very homogeneous. According to the 1980 census breakdowns, 99 percent—506,000 of 511,456 people—of Vermont's population is white, with only a scattering of blacks (1135), Asians (1355), Hispanics (3304), and others. Nor has the state become significantly more urbanized as a result of its new population growth. Again, according to the 1980 census, Vermont is the most highly rural of the 50 states, with over two-thirds of its population living in communities of 2500 or less.[6]

Vermont's current demographic homogeneity and rural character is a reflection of the state's historic economic development. Unlike New Hampshire and the southern New England states, Vermont was barely touched by the industrial revolution during the nineteenth century. Some light manufacturing emerged in communities like Springfield, which developed a high precision machine tool industry; but, by and large, Vermont never experienced the major type of industrial transition of the other New England and middle Atlantic states. As a result, it was not engulfed with any large influx of immigrants, with the exception of some French-Canadian population in the northern Burlington (Winooski–Franklin County) area, and small enclaves of Scots, Poles, Czechs, and southern European stonecutters in the granite quarries of Barre and other communities that developed extractive industries.

The bulk of Vermont's original settlers came from the other New England states and from New York. Eastern Vermont, along the Connecticut River valley, was settled by conservative farmers who migrated north from southern New England, especially Connecticut. Western Vermont, along the Lake Champlain valley, was populated by more radical land speculators such as Ethan and Ira Allen. Hence, the earliest distinctions in Vermont's political culture were grounded in a geographic and ideological split between its eastern conservatives and its western radicals, rather than in any deep divisions that grew out of economic, social, or ethnic heterogeneity.

Despite these geographical and ideological differences, all of Vermont's early settlers identified very closely with the state, partly because of its historic evolution as an independent republic and partly because of its physical beauty. By the middle of the nineteenth century, the new settlers were prospering as the result of the development of a profitable Merino sheep agricultural base. After the Civil War, however, the sheep industry began to diminish because of its inability to withstand the competition of western wool. The rural population declined as many farmers migrated westward. Eventually the agricultural base shifted to small-scale dairy farming. At this point, the state entered into a century long period of stagnation as its population grew from 314,000 to only 378,000 between 1850 and 1950.

The dairy, hill-farming lifestyle, which emerged during this era, reinforced many of the qualities that constituted Vermont's historic conservative political tradition, especially the qualities of independence, individualism, and self-reliance. Some elements of the more radical heritage remained, however, and Vermonters, who were violently anti-slavery in their views, turned to the Republican party in droves during the new party's earliest formative years. This more radical heritage was best personified during this period by Justin Smith Morrill, a prosperous merchant from Strafford, who helped organize the Republican party in Vermont and then went on to serve in the U.S. Congress (both House and Senate) for 44 years where he was best known for his sponsorship of the Morrill land-grant college act of 1862.

Following the Civil War, Vermont became a safe one-party Republican state, and the more radical political tradition personified by the Allen brothers, Matthew Lyon, and Justin Morrill began to disappear. The economic stagnation that resulted from the decline in farming ushered in the century-long period of political somnolence noted earlier. Under the growing power of the conservative Republican monopoly, the state's political ideology became much more insular and cautious. Increasingly, Vermont's political culture focused on a parochial tradition of localism. People identified with the state through their own small towns and communities. Reinforced by a town meeting form of government, the local community became the paramount concern of political life, and the major battles were fought over such issues as school consolidation at the town level.

Localism was reinforced in a state legislature that had been organized to provide for one representative in the lower house for each of Vermont's 246 towns and cities, regardless of their population size, an apportionment scheme that was to remain in effect until the *Baker v. Carr* decision in 1962. In terms of political expectations, people looked to the towns to provide the services that really mattered—roads, education, and even welfare (through local overseers-of-the-poor). Little in the way of positive political action was expected from the state. The dominant political norm was "the community axiom," a term coined by Frank Bryan to describe the basically parochial view that "man is happiest when he is in close contact with others (but not too many others) like himself in places whose boundaries are easily understood and where life styles are in plain view."[7]

Political leadership in Montpelier came to reflect this view of passive state government. The Redfield Proctor family dynasty, which grew up around the marble industry in the Rutland area after the Civil War, was basically characterized by a conservative ideology. It was not until the 1930s that the first evidence of a new political orientation finally began to appear within some elements of the dominant Republican party.

Two events occurred during this period that were destined to have a profound impact on the future course of Vermont state politics. The first, paradoxically sponsored by the conservative Republican leadership in 1931, was the adoption of a state income tax. The purpose was not to usher in a new era of activist state government. Instead, it was a very pragmatic decision. Vermont's government was going broke in the throes of the great Depression. It only seemed to be frugal common sense to provide some needed state revenues to keep the ship of state afloat even if nobody expected it to do much in the way of providing services. Thus, inadvertently, the 1931 income tax legislation provided the potential revenue base for a future outburst of more activist state government, should a new type of political leadership ever emerge that would advocate such an activist political philosophy.

The second event was the election of George Aiken to the Vermont house in 1930. Until Aiken's appearance in Vermont politics, "opposition to the Proctor candidates had been sporadic, weak, and usually disorganized."[8] Aiken, a quiet, unassuming horticulturist from Putney, represented a return to the more radical tradition that had characterized earlier Vermont political life. Assigned to the house conservation committee, he decided to take on the Republican leadership by opposing a bill to construct 80 dams on Vermont rivers. He hated the private power companies as much as he loved plants, and he won his fight against the bill. Two years later, he was elected speaker of the house, and in 1936, he was elected governor of the state. He turned out to be a startling departure from the prevalent caretaker model. An activist Republican governor, he liked to take on the "big boys" as he recalls now with a chuckle: "The power companies, the railroads, even the granite and marble industries. The 'old guard,' as we called them."[9] Aiken went on to serve in the U.S. Senate for over 30 years, but it was his stint as governor that marked the return of the more progressive tradition in Vermont politics.

Although the conservative faction in the Republican party fought to regain its control over state government, other moderate Republicans followed Aiken. In 1946, Ernest Gibson defeated Mortimer R. Proctor as the Republican nominee. During his two terms as governor, he got through a minimum salary law for teachers, a teachers' retirement fund, increased state aid for education, and he overcame sheriffs' objections to establish a state police department. A new pattern of more activist state government was clearly emerging. Even the more conservative Republicans, like Joseph B. Johnson who served as governor from 1955 to 1959, pushed for measures such as partial state funding for the University of Vermont, which, up to that time, had been a completely private educational institution.

At the same time that the new type of more moderate leadership was beginning to appear at the state level, Vermont was undergoing other important changes. During the 1950s and 1960, a number of high-technology industries, such as the IBM operation in Essex Junction outside Burlington, began to move into the state. A dramatic revolution in agriculture took place when many of the small dairy farmers were swept away by more efficient, large-scale operations. While the total productions of milk increased, the number of individual farms dropped from over 20,000 in 1950 to less than 5000 today. An expanding recreation industry was supplementing its traditional summer base through the development of large-scale, year-round ski area complexes. Finally, taking advantage of the new accessibility provided by the interstate highway system, Vermont began to trade on its natural beauty in order to attract a host of second-home urbanites and suburbanites, plus back-to-nature artisans, young people, and retirees, who wanted to become part of the "Beckoning Country."

It was this combination of factors that led to Vermont's postwar population growth. Even more significant than the absolute number of newcomers, however, was the shift in attitudes that many of them represented. To return to Frank Bryan's analysis, Vermont retained its champions of "the community axiom" of localized decentralization in the form of: the descendants of the old hill farmers who lived in mobile homes, drove pick-up trucks and manned the service sector operations of the state's economy; the small-town Yankee elite, of store owners and local business-men, who maintained a nostalgia for the simplicity of the good-old-days; and the newly arriving artisan population who harbored a "small but beautiful" arts and crafts mentality.

However, most of the newcomers, plus the emerging large-scale farmers, who were technocrats to the core (for example, "the rural technopolity"), advocated what Bryan calls, "a system axiom"—a more universal, cosmopolitan, centralized view of politics.[10] They paid lip service to the therapeutic values of the local communities, but they really viewed state government as the vehicle that could protect and preserve Vermont's natural beauty, and provide modern, efficient, streamlined programs to replace, and enhance, the more limited town services.

In short, the political climate in Vermont was beginning to change dramatically. The key question was how the political leadership groups within the state would respond to this change.

POLITICAL STYLE: PERSONALIZED AND AMATEUR

The two elements of political style that were most relevant to these shifts in Vermont's political culture were deeply rooted in the state's long-time reliance on a personalized amateur citizen's approach to public service and a long-standing admiration for independent political leaders who were willing to speak out forcefully on issues of public concern.

Vermont's citizen public-service orientation results from the fact that neither the material stakes, the scale, nor the social barriers in the state's political arena are very large. In terms of stakes, Vermont has always emphasized a part-time tradition of citizen involvement in politics at both the local and state levels. Small towns are governed by part-time boards of selectmen. The state legislature normally meets for three or four months each year, and nominal weekly salaries of $250, plus expenses, are only provided during the period when the legislature is actually in session. The state's highest elective officer, the governor, receives $44,900 a year, and there are only a handful of other full-time statewide elective offices, at considerably lower salaries. In addition, the state never developed any large-scale corporate economy, and has never attracted organized crime, so corruption is virtually absent from the political scene.

In terms of scale, much of the local political activity focuses on Vermont's numerous small towns and nine small cities. Even at the state level, the 150 members of the Vermont house represent an average of only 3400 constituents apiece, while the 30 state senators represent an average of 17,000 constituents, although some serve from multi-member districts with larger total populations. As a result, Vermonters have become accustomed to a very personalized style of politics—a sort of one-on-one approach where local officials, state legislators, and even the governor are approached in village stores and post offices to hear citizen complaints and to receive advice on pending public issues.

Social barriers to political involvement are virtually non-existent because of the absence of any deep ethnic or racial cleavages in the state. There is little emphasis on balanced tickets, or other criteria, that would tend to restrict access to political office. Under these circumstances, the state's basic political ethos places a high priority on political involvement as a civic duty, or as a form of gamesmanship that provides its own rewards in terms of tangible accomplishments or ego satisfaction to participate.

There is one very important economic constraint, however, that tends to limit the scope of political involvement in this type of system. This constraint makes it difficult, if not impossible, for lower-income groups to participate in state politics because they lack the time and money to become involved as amateur, part-time participants.

As a result, Vermont relies heavily on professional elites, such as real estate brokers, insurance salesmen, lawyers, and the like, whose schedules are flexible enough to permit them to engage in political activity at the state level. These groups are supplemented by older retirees and others who view politics as an avocation. Many of these people turn out to be very competent and committed politicians, but they tend to come from the middle or upper level of the income scale.

Vermont's political culture places extremely high values on such personal qualities as independence of mind and personal integrity in its political leaders. The mystique that stretches from Ethan Allen and his Green Mountain Boys to George Aiken's battles with the power companies has become an important part of the state's political culture. In his final reelection campaign for the U.S. Senate in 1968, Aiken took pride in reporting total expenses of $17.09, mostly for postage to thank people for circulating his nominating papers, "which I didn't ask them to do."[11] He ran unopposed and received 99.9 percent of the total votes cast.

Aiken was a unique political powerhouse, however, and present-day aspirants for political office have to spend moderate sums, although media and television costs are not exorbitantly high. If a candidate becomes too visible by spending very large amounts of money, a backfire can result. One of the unsuccessful 1980 U.S. Senate aspirants, James Mullin of Williston, appears to have lost support after he announced that he was putting together a one million dollar war chest for his campaign. This simply sounded like too much money to skeptical Vermonters who admire the personal qualities of honesty, integrity, and backbone in their political leaders. Vermont's current congressman, James Jeffords, gained support in the state during the summer of 1981 when he was the only Republican in the U.S. House who voted against President Reagan's income tax cut because he felt the overall tax package gave too many breaks to the oil companies. Most of the commentary that greeted Jeffords' announcement in the state's major newspapers was favorable on the grounds that he had "shown guts" in following the dictates of his conscience, and thus personified the historic Vermont tradition of political independence.

Hence, except for the financial problems that are faced by lower-income participants, the state political arena is relatively wide open in terms of access, and even the lower-income groups participate at the local levels. There was one additional historical constraint, however, that restricted access to state politics quite severely until more recent times. It was perfectly possible to succeed in Vermont's political system as long as one was a Republican. Vermont did not really begin to evolve into a more competitive two-party state until the 1950s.

POLITICAL INTERACTION: THE COMMUNITY WRIT LARGE

Although Vermont's Democratic party first began to show some signs of life in the 1930s, it was not able to sustain its momentum in the immediate post World War II years. In an analysis of inter-party competition among the fifty states, which covered the period from 1946 to 1963, Austin Ranney classified Vermont as the most strongly one-party Republican state in the nation.[12] The degree of two-party competition that has characterized Vermont's politics during the past two decades shows a marked contrast from this earlier pattern.

The initial support for the Democrats first appeared in the early 1950s. The major breakthrough took place in 1952 when a realignment occurred in Vermont. In the average town, Democrats increased their vote strength by approximately 14 percentage points and continued to maintain that level of voter support in subsequent elections.[13] In 1958, Vermonters shocked themselves by electing Democrat William Meyer to their sole U.S. House seat, but Meyer lasted for only two years. It was not until 1962, when Philip Hoff squeaked into office by just over 1000 votes to be elected as Vermont's first Democratic governor in over a century, that the full implications of the new realignment became apparent.

The degree of inter-party competition between the Republican and the Democratic parties has continued to increase since Hoff captured the governor's office for three successive two-year terms from 1963 to 1969. Hoff was succeeded by an elderly Republican, statesman-like governor Deane C. Davis, who served in the state house from 1969 to 1973 after winning with successive pluralities of 55 and 57 percent of the vote in the 1968 and 1970 elections. Davis was succeeded by a second Democratic governor, Thomas Salmon, who served from 1973 to 1977, after also capturing identical pluralities of 55 and 57 percent of the vote in the 1972 and 1974 elections. Salmon, in turn, was followed in 1977 by another Republican, Richard Snelling, who won the last four gubernatorial elections with between 53 and 63 percent of the vote. At the same time that the gubernatorial office was becoming more competitive, Democratic candidates were scoring some other notable successes. The most significant of these was Patrick Leahy's election to the U.S. Senate by a miniscule 1430 plurality in 1974, and his reelection to the Senate by a still very tight 3527 plurality in 1980.[14]

During the past two decades, Vermont has also witnessed the emergence of a third political grouping—the Liberty Union party—that has contested numerous state and national elections. In terms of its political ideology, the Liberty Union party represents the more radical (many would say socialist) tradition in Vermont politics, and it has relied heavily on the recent influx of the back-to-nature artisan left for its relatively modest support. Although Liberty Union candidates have not won any elections, the party pulled between 7 to 8 percent of the vote for such divergent offices as U.S. representative and Vermont state treasurer in the 1980 campaign. The most successful candidate to emerge from the party's ranks is Bernard Sanders, a former Liberty Union activist, who won an astonishing victory in 1981, while running as an independent candidate for mayor of Burlington, Vermont's largest city. Sanders managed to strengthen his position in the city's government during the 1983 election when he won a second term as Burlington's chief executive. However, it is still too early to tell whether these successes in Burlington indicate any long-range shift in the political allegiance of the Vermont electorate.

One byproduct of the increased scale of inter-party competition in Vermont during more recent years is a heightened public interest in political activity, a fact that is reflected in the relatively strong voter turnouts that have characterized the state's elections from 1960 through 1982.

The most dramatic indication of public participation in Vermont's political process is to be found in statewide electoral turnout during the past two decades. In the eighteen gubernatorial elections from 1946 to 1980, the average turnout has been 63.7 percent of the total registered voters, ranging from a low of 40 percent in 1946 to a high of 80 percent in 1960. As might be expected, voter participation has been highest during presidential election years. In the nine presidential elections from 1948 to 1980, the average turnout has been over 70 percent of the registered voters, ranging from a low of 64.3 percent in 1948 to a high of 81.2 percent in 1960. Although Vermont's participation in presidential elections reached its peak strength in the 1960s, it still remains well above the national average; it was nine percentage points higher in 1968, twelve points higher in 1972, fourteen points higher in 1976, and fifteen points higher in 1980.[15]

One explanation for this high degree of electoral participation is the more active party competition that has characterized Vermont's political life during the past two decades. In addition, in terms of voter efficacy, the factor of size or scale may play a role in strengthening political interest among Vermonters. Although the number of registered voters has almost doubled from 180,000 in 1946 to 312,000 in 1980, the state is still small enough for the electorate to feel that a vote can really count in determining the final outcome of a political contest. Moreover, the long-standing tradition of amateur public-service involvement that has characterized Vermont's political culture is still very strong. Finally, the state's general population is largely composed of small-town groupings that, traditionally on a national basis, experience higher than average voter turnout.

Although inter-party competition and electoral participation have both increased dramatically during the post-war period, Vermont's political life is not dominated by strong party or strong interest group organizations. Both Republican and Democrats have formal state and town organizations, but once candidates are elected to office, they often tend to follow a fairly independent course.

In part, this results from the fact that the financial requirements to run for public office are relatively modest in comparison to other larger states, and many candidates are not heavily dependent on major party financial support. While most statewide candidates receive party funds for their campaigns, other candidates receive little or no help at all. When I ran for the Vermont state senate in 1972, I did not receive any financial assistance from the party. During my term in the senate, there was only one occasion when I was asked to vote on a strict party line basis; within the limits of practical common sense, I was pretty free to vote as I chose on different legislative issues.[16]

A second factor that tends to weaken party discipline is Vermont's open primary system. Although the major parties have local organizations in towns and cities throughout the state, voters have the ability to influence party nominations by means of an open primary. Under the Vermont system, voters are free to choose either party's ballot during primary elections and moderate voters often tend to support popular candidates from different parties, depending on which party ballot they choose in the primaries.

The relatively loose style of Vermont politics is further reinforced by the absence of large and powerful interest-group organizations. There are a sizeable number of interest groups that participate in Vermont politics, and some of them, such as the Vermont State Employees Association or the Associated Industries of Vermont, do carry some weight. Most of these groups, however, are relatively small and fragmented. Union activity is very modest, and there is no such thing as big-labor or big-business that attempts to dominate the political process. In addition, the absence of strong ethnic and racial cleavages within the state tends to minimize this type of interest-group activity.

The open and independent nature of Vermont's political process is strongly supported by the press and media. The press is quite pluralistic since no single newspaper exercises a statewide monopoly comparable to that of the *Manchester Union Leader* in New Hampshire. Instead, the *Burlington Free Press* and the *Caledonian-Record* are the major dailies in the northern part of the state, while the *Rutland Daily Herald* plays a key role in the central area, and the *Bennington Banner* and the *Brattleboro Reformer* provide press coverage in the south.

Under the circumstances, Vermont's political process is characterized by a high degree of informal flexibility. The extent to which political power is exercised is largely dependent on the personal qualities of leadership of major public officials, particularly the governor. Although all of Vermont's governors have enjoyed certain institutional advantages, in the form of bureaucratic support and informational resources, the key ingredient that has shaped the course of Vermont's postwar politics is to be found in the leadership qualities that individual governors have brought to their office.

When Philip Hoff was elected in 1962, as Vermont's first Democratic governor in more than a century, he represented the perfect fit between the shift in values that was becoming apparent in the state's political culture and Vermont's long-standing admiration for independent, charismatic political leadership.

In his first 1962 campaign, Hoff actually ran against the entrenched old-line Democratic organization. He won a very narrow victory based on liberal and moderate Republican support, and then went on to reform the Democratic party in his own image. During his early years as governor, Hoff projected all of the qualities of personal political style that Vermonters respect the most. He appeared on the scene as a youthful, dynamic, articulate underdog who had an activist vision of state government. Although he captured only 50.1 percent of the vote in 1962, Hoff was reelected by remarkable margins of 65 percent in the 1964 gubernatorial election and 58 percent in the 1966 election.

In one of those rare accidents of political timing, all of the pieces started to fall into place at once. Vermont was beginning a period of population and economic growth, and the increasing revenues available from the old income tax law, which had been enacted way back in 1931, were available to finance an expanded role for state government. At the same time, many of the newcomers migrating into Vermont were looking to the state to play a more innovative role. The *Baker v. Carr* decision of 1962 led to a reapportionment of the legislature that reduced house membership from 246 to 150 and weakened the historic small town influence over the legislative process. In addition, the newly elected Democratic governor, Phil Hoff, surrounded himself with some of the more progressive legislators who had begun to run for public office, supplemented by a group of liberal administrative appointees. Vermont began to move into a much more activist era of state government.

The basic thrust of the policies advocated by Hoff, and his immediate successor, Republican Governor Deane C. Davis, was to shift governmental powers up from the local level, as the more cosmopolitan "system axiom" replaced the more parochial "community axiom."

Hoff, who served as governor from 1963 to 1969, set the process in motion when he stripped the towns of their historic overseer-of-the-poor welfare functions in favor of a series of centralized state welfare and human services reforms. In addition, he created a new state higher education system by gaining support to construct four new state college campuses. He also sponsored a comprehensive state student-aid financial assistance program. Moreover, the state adopted a new formula to help local communities finance school district costs.

Davis, who served as governor from 1969 to 1973, faced his most critical challenge very early in his first term when state revenues proved to be insufficient to finance Hoff's new human services and educational reforms. Instead of cutting back on these state programmatic initiatives, Davis persuaded the legislature to pass a new three cent sales tax to supplement the state income tax. He then went on to push through a series of comprehensive state environmental reforms, while also reorganizing state government into a series of large consolidated agencies.

There was much subsequent speculation as to why Deane Davis, an elderly Republican business executive, who had served as president of the National Life Insurance Company of Vermont, was willing to take these steps, especially since Davis had won the Republican nomination in 1968 against a more liberal Republican candidate, James Oakes, by campaigning against an activist role for state government. However, a combination of financial and environmental concerns influenced Davis to modify his views once he assumed office. The best evidence of this appeared in the form of an extremely successful television commercial he ran in his 1970 reelection campaign, which showed him using an old bucket to bail out a leaky rowboat. The symbolism was clear. Vermont was in precarious financial straits. Its bond rating was threatened because of potential deficits. Under the circumstances, a responsible conservative was once again forced to bail out the ship of state by providing new revenues in the form of a new sales tax just as the conservative leadership had previously bailed out the state with the original 1931 income tax legislation. By the same token, a responsible conservative was forced to take state action to protect Vermont's environment in order to preserve its old community heritage.

By the time Hoff and Davis left office, Vermont was so fully embarked on an activist course of state government that it was accepted as a *fait accompli* by both Democratic Governor Thomas Salmon (1973–77) and Republican Governor Richard Snelling (1977–85) with only slight modifications. Salmon, alarmed by the rapid purchase of Vermont land by outside investors, pushed the theme "Vermont's Not For Sale." Once again, however, he looked to the state to remedy the situation, and he successfully sponsored a new state capital gains tax that was designed to curb land speculation. Snelling, an extremely competent advocate of managerial efficiency, has devoted a major portion of his attention to negotiating long-range state hydro-power contracts with the Canadian province of Quebec in an effort to provide sufficient energy to meet Vermont's anticipated future needs. During the latter portion of his tenure, Snelling has turned increasingly to national concerns in his role as chairman of the National Governors' Association.

Hence, the shift in the state's political values that began to emerge in the late 1950s and early 1960s led to a completely new agenda for Vermont's state government as power moved upward from the local communities to the state. In addition, a second dramatic upward shift took place during this period. As the state assumed more responsibility for centralized human services and other programs, it increasingly looked to the federal government to help finance these programs. As a result, Vermont became locked into matching grants that have made the state heavily dependent upon the federal government for financial support. By 1980, Vermont ranked first among the fifty states in terms of the federal aid dollars it received in relationship to the tax dollars it sent to Washington.[17] In 1963, when Philip Hoff first assumed office, Vermont's state budget totaled just under $70 million with very little federal financial assistance. Almost two decades later, Governor Snelling proposed a fiscal year 1982 state budget of $642.8 million, with almost a third of this amount expected to come from federal funds.[18]

As a result of the federal budget cuts in Washington, the future course of Vermont's recent surge of state governmental activism is very cloudy at this juncture. As chairman of the National Governors' Association, Richard Snelling played a key role in initial attempts to negotiate an equitable formula with the White House regarding the potential transfer of federal and state programs under President Reagan's "New Federalism" proposal. The stakes in any such transfer are critically important for Vermont, which ranks first among the fifty states in the percentage of total state revenues that it receives from federal sources. While the average state obtained 21.3 percent of its revenue dollars from Washington in 1981, Vermont received the highest share of any state with 30.3 percent of its revenues coming from federal sources in 1981.[19]

In November 1982, Richard Snelling won an unprecedented fourth consecutive two-year term as governor following a tough challenge from Democratic Lieutenant Governor Madeleine Kunin. Although the recession of the 1980s did not hit Vermont as hard as the major industrial states, Vermont ran an unprecedented $30 million budget deficit in fiscal year 1983. In July 1983, Governor Snelling called a special legislative session and the legislature voted to raise the state income and cigarette tax while also enacting $7 million in budget cuts. It appears that Vermont's long-range financial problems are not fully resolved, however, and if this proves to be the case, a new politics of retrenchment will replace the recent expansionist trend in state government.

Whatever the future may bring, the fact remains that the recent upsurge in state governmental activism represents a remarkable turnabout in Vermont politics after a century-long period of passive state government. During the past two decades, Vermont—a state that had earlier rejected a federal government proposal to build an ambitious Green Mountain Parkway to stimulate its economy during the Great Depression, and was one of only two states (along with Maine) that had voted against Franklin D. Roosevelt's New Deal in 1936—had become, in the words of a *Rutland Herald* headline, "Uncle Sam's Ward."[20]

A complex mix of factors, including a more aggressive brand of gubernatorial leadership coupled with the development of expanding new federal and state revenue resources, contributed to the shift in Vermont's political priorities. The key catalyst, however, was a change in the public's underlying political values, especially those represented by the growing number of newcomers who migrated into the state during the post-war period. Although they still paid homage to their local communities as therapeutic manifestations of "grass-roots" town meeting democracy, many Vermonters increasingly turned toward state government as the vehicle to protect their environment, to rationalize their welfare system, and to equalize educational opportunities. Once this more cosmopolitan "system axiom" began to take hold, the majority of Vermonters shifted their allegiance from their local towns to the soft, rolling Green Mountain state itself as the central focus of their political concerns. The state became the "Beckoning Country," and "Vermont as a Way of Life" replaced the older, more parochial "community axiom" as the primary symbol of political loyalty. In essence, the state came to assume the role of the local community writ large.

NOTES

1. Duane Lockard, *New England State Politics* (Princeton: Princeton University Press, 1959), p. 8.

2. Frank M. Bryan, *Yankee Politics in Rural Vermont* (Hanover, N.H.: University Press of New England, 1974), p. 10.

3. *The New Columbia Encyclopedia* (New York: Columbia University Press, 4th Edition, 1975), p. 2880.

4. *Ibid.*, p. 2800. The early absence of an aristocracy of wealth resulted from the fact that Vermont lacked the natural resources susceptible to capital intensive exploitation, and was also geographically removed from the major commercial markets in the northeastern United States.

5. *Vermont Firsts in the Nation* (Montpelier, Vt.: Office of the Secretary of State, undated). For an interesting account of Matthew Lyon and other historic Vermont political figures see William Doyle, "The Vermont Political Tradition," *Rutland Sunday Herald*, Section 3, 10 January to 14 February 1982.

6. *United States Census 1980* (Washington: Department of Commerce, Bureau of the Census, 1981). Provisional state breakdowns on racial groups are summarized in "The New Population Mix," *New York Times*, 6 September, 1981, p. E5.

7. Bryan, *Yankee Politics in Rural Vermont*, p. 255.

8. Lockard, *New England State Politics*, p. 17.

9. Christopher Graff, "The Days of George Aiken," *Valley News*, Lebanon, NH, 6 January 1982, p. 12.

10. Bryan, *Yankee Politics in Rural Vermont*, pp. 255–67. Bryan's insightful observations on the shift from the "community axiom" to the "system axiom" provided the central conceptual focus for this analysis. For his observations on political leadership see his chapter on the New England governorship in Josephine F. Milburn and Victoria Schuck, eds., *New England Politics* (Cambridge, Mass.: Schenkman Publishing Company, 1981).

11. Gaff, "The Days of George Aiken", p. 23.

12. Austin Ranney, "Parties in State Politics," in *Politics in the American States*, eds. Herbert Jacob and Kenneth Vines (Boston: Little, Brown, 1965), Table 1, pp. 64–65.

13. Frank M. Bryan, *Politics in the Rural States* (Boulder, Colo.: Westview Press, 1981), pp. 125–31.

14. Voting data compiled from Richard M. Scammon and Alice V. McGillivray, eds., *American Votes* (Washington, D.C.: Congressional Quarterly Press, 1979); other data from *Vermont Legislative Directory: State Manual*, Secretary of State's Office; and *Vermont Almanac and Government Guide*.

15. *Ibid.*

16. Frank Smallwood, *Free and Independent*, 2nd ed. (Brattleboro, Vt.: Stephen Green, 1981).

17. UPI Release, "The Cost of Federal Dollars," *Rutland Daily Herald*, 1 June 1981, p. 12.

18. Stephen C. Terry, "Uncle Sam's Ward: Vermont," *Rutland Daily Herald*, 20 February 1981, p. 15.

19. "Who Gets What From Washington," *US News and World Report*, 6 December 1982, p. 13.

20. Stephen C. Terry, "Uncle Sam's Ward: Vermont," p. 15.

Index

About the Authors

CHARLES G. BELL, author of the chapter on *California*, is Professor of Political Science at California State University, Fullerton. He has taught and written about California government and politics for over 20 years. His most recent publication, a text co-authored with Charles M. Price, is *California Government Today: The Politics of Reform* (1980).

ANTHONY CHAMPAGNE, co-author of the chapter on *Texas*, is at the University of Texas at Dallas. He is an Associate Professor of Political Science and Political Economy, and his recent book on Sam Rayburn and his constituency is about to be published by Rutgers University Press.

RICK COLLIS, co-author of the chapter on *Texas*, is at the University of at Austin. He is a graduate student in political science, who has been active in Texas politics for a number of years.

LAWRENCE R. HEPBURN, author of the chapter on *Georgia*, is Educational Research Associate at the Carl Vinson Institute of Government at the University of Georgia. He has also written two textbooks—*State Government in Georgia* and *The Georgia History Book*—that are widely used in the state's secondary schools.

PETER KOBRAK, author of the chapter on *Michigan*, is Professor of Political Science at Western Michigan University where he is also Director of the Center for Public Administration Programs. He served previously as a staff member with the Committee on Education and Labor of the U.S. House and as a policy analyst in the U.S. Department of Labor. His research interests focus on employment and training policies and he has written widely in that field.

MARC LANDY, author of the chapter on *Kentucky*, is Associate Professor of Political Science at Boston College and Lecturer on Political Science at the Harvard School of Public Health. He is the author of *The Politics of Environmental Reform: Controlling Kentucky Surface Mining* (1976). He is currently co-editing a volume of the political essays of

Bertrand De Jouvenel and co-authoring a book on the Environmental Protection Agency in the Carter years.

MAUREEN MOAKLEY, co-editor and author of the chapter on *New Jersey*, is an instructor at Rutgers University and research assistant at the Eagleton Institute of Politics. She is just completing a dissertation on county party organizations in the state and has co-authored a monograph, *The Changing Politics of State Management* (1983), and chapters in *Politics in New Jersey* (rev. ed. 1979) and *American Politics and Public Policy* (1982). She is grateful to Henry Plotkin, Edith Saks and especially Alan Rosenthal for their comments on her chapter.

SAMUEL C. PATTERSON, author of the chapter on *Iowa*, is Professor of Political Science at the University of Iowa. His research on American state politics has included studies of state legislatures, state political party leaders, the political cultures of the states, and state elections. He is the author, co-author, editor, or co-editor of several books, including: *A More Perfect Union* (rev. ed. 1982), *Comparing Legislatures* (1979), *The Legislative Process in the United States* (3rd. ed. 1977), *Representatives and Represented* (1975), and *Comparative Legislative Behavior: Frontiers of Research* (1972). Professor Patterson wishes to thank Charles Wiggins of Texas A&M University and Russell Ross of the University of Iowa for helpful comments on an earlier version of his chapter.

ALAN ROSENTHAL, co-editor, is Professor of Political Science and Director of the Eagleton Institute of Politics at Rutgers University. He has worked with legislatures in about two-thirds of the states and has co-edited *Politics in New Jersey* (rev. ed. 1979), has co-authored *Legislative Education Leadership in the States* (1981), and has written *Legislative Life* (1981).

THOMAS H. SIMMONS, author of the chapter on *Colorado*, is presently employed by a regional planning agency. His prior publications include *Colorado Political Party Activists: Survey Results of the 1980 Democratic and Republican State Conventions* (1980), two directories of Colorado state legislators, and numerous contributions to the *Comparative State Politics Newsletter*. A Colorado native, he has been active in state politics for the past decade.

FRANK SMALLWOOD, author of the chapter on *Vermont*, is Orvil E. Dryfoos Professor of Government and Director of the Nelson A. Rockefeller Center for the Social Sciences at Dartmouth College. His book, *Free and Independent* (1976), describes his experience as a Vermont state senator. His most recent book is *The Other Candidates: Third Parties in Presidential Elections* (1983). Professor Smallwood is grateful to Frank M. Bryan of the University of Vermont and Jonathan N. Brownell of Dartmouth College for providing helpful comments on his chapter.

PAUL A. SMITH, author of the chapter on *New York*, is Professor of Political Science at the State University of New York at Binghamton. His research has focused on political behavior, party organization, environmental policies, and presidential campaigns. His most recent book is *Electing a President* (1982). The years he has spent observing and working in New York politics have sparked his interest in the forms and practices of the states as a political system.

DOUGLAS ST. ANGELO, author of the chapter on *Florida*, is Professor of Political Science at Florida State University, with which he has been affiliated for 20 years. At FSU he has been associated with the Institute for Social Research and has directed the Political Research Institute. He is a native of Indiana, did his graduate work in Illinois, and has taught previously in Minnesota. Professor St. Angelo is grateful to Manning J. Dauer of the University of Florida and to Daisy Flory and Elston E. Roady of Florida State University for their thoughtful comments on drafts of his chapter.

RICHARD F. WINTERS, author of the chapter on *New Hampshire*, is Associate Professor of Government at Dartmouth College, where he has taught for 14 years. He has published a number of articles on comparative state politics and on the politics of New Hampshire and Vermont and is currently working on an American state politics text.